DISINHERITING THE JEWS

DISINHERITING THE JEWS

Abraham in Early Christian Controversy

Jeffrey S. Siker

Westminster/John Knox Press
Louisville, Kentucky

© 1991 Jeffrey S. Siker

Scripture quotations from the Revised Standard Version of the Bible are copyrighted 1946, 1952, © 1971, 1973 by the Division of Christian Education of the National Council of the Churches of Christ in the U.S.A. and are used by permission.

Book design by Gene Harris

First edition

Published by Westminster/John Knox Press
Louisville, Kentucky

PRINTED IN THE UNITED STATES OF AMERICA

9 8 7 6 5 4 3 2 1

Library of Congress Cataloging-in-Publication Data

Siker, Jeffrey S.
  Disinheriting the Jews : Abraham in early Christian controversy /
Jeffrey S. Siker. — 1st ed.
      p.   cm.
  Includes bibliographical references and indexes.
  ISBN 0-664-25193-5

  1. Abraham (Biblical patriarch) in the New Testament. 2. Abraham
(Biblical patriarch) 3. Judaism (Christian theology)—History of doctrines—Primitive and early church, ca. 30–600. 4. Bible. N.T.—Criticism, interpretation, etc. 5. Theology—Early church, ca. 30–600.
6. Christianity and other religions—Judaism. 7. Judaism—Relations—
Christianity. 8. Christianity and antisemitism. I. Title.
BS580.A3S47 1991
222'.11092—dc20   72540   90-19893

For my parents

Dr. Ephraim S. Siker

Eileen Bohnel Siker

tekna tou Abraam

CONTENTS

Preface

This study has grown out of the convergence of two interests: (1) the history of biblical interpretation and (2) the development of the early relationship between Christianity and Judaism. I have sought to combine these interests by examining how early Christianity used and reshaped traditions about Abraham, a figure who was central to early Jewish identity as well. My hope is that by looking at early Christian use of Abraham, we will gain some new insights into both the development of early Christianity and the separation of early Christianity from early Judaism.

On a more personal level I am sure that my interest in early Christian use of Abraham has much to do with my own religious heritage. I was raised in a family where one parent comes from the Jewish tradition and the other comes from the Roman Catholic tradition. In addition I have always been intrigued by an uncle who is a rabbi and who barely escaped the Holocaust. I suppose it makes sense that, somewhat on my own, I grew up in the Presbyterian church (it was down the street), was later ordained and am still active as a Presbyterian minister, and now teach at a Roman Catholic university! I continue to be very much interested in Jewish/Christian relations. The present study has thus involved the sorting through of Jewish and Christian roots, as both lay claim, if in different ways, to father Abraham and so to God.

This book began life as my doctoral dissertation at Princeton Theological Seminary. It has been thoroughly revised in its present form. In particular, several excursuses have been omitted, many of the notes have been cut, and much of the

discussion with secondary literature, necessary for disserta-
tions, has been shortened. Readers interested in fuller docu-
mentation may consult my dissertation (available through
University Microfilms), "Disinheriting the Jews: The Use of
Abraham in Early Christian Controversy with Judaism from
Paul Through Justin Martyr" (Ph.D. diss., Princeton Theological Seminary, 1989).

I would like to thank several individuals who have contributed significantly to the writing of this book:

Professors Martin de Boer, Joel Marcus, Chris Beker, Kath-
leen McVey, James Charlesworth, Paul Meyer, and David Ad-
ams, all former teachers at Princeton Theological Seminary,
for their comments and suggestions

Professors Neil Elliott, Bart Ehrman, Jim Brownson, Gordon
Zerbe, and Beth Johnson, fellow sojourners from Princeton
days, for their friendship and engaging discussion of this
material

The editorial staff of Westminster/John Knox Press for their
interest, support, and expertise, especially Dr. Cynthia
Thompson, Dr. Jeff Hamilton, and Dr. John Gibbs (formerly of
Westminster/John Knox)

My colleagues in the Department of Theology at Loyola
Marymount University

Jodi Roy, my very able research assistant at Loyola Marymount University, for helping to compile the indexes, for
work in the library, and for her many hours at the keyboard,
all with good humor

Paul and Sally Sampley, loving mentors and friends.

I thank my parents for support of all kinds. They have been
gracious beyond measure. I dedicate this labor of love to them
as a partial expression of my gratitude.

Finally, I am particularly grateful to my wife and colleague,
Dr. Louke van Wensveen Siker, who has provided constant
encouragement and love and who, with our son Derek, has
helped me keep this project in perspective. They have had
the patience of Abraham!

Abbreviations

ANF	*The Ante-Nicene Fathers*. Edited by A. Roberts, J. Donaldson, et al. 10 vols. New York: Charles Scribner's Sons, 1885–1925.
Ant.	Josephus, *Jewish Antiquities*. Edited and translated by H. St. J. Thackeray and R. Marcus. Vols. 4–10. Loeb Classical Library. London: W. Heinemann, 1926–1965.
BJRL	*Bulletin of the John Rylands University Library*
BTB	*Biblical Theology Bulletin*
CBQ	*Catholic Biblical Quarterly*
DSS	*The Dead Sea Scrolls*, G. Vermès. 3rd ed. London: Penguin Books, 1987.
ET	*Evangelische Theologie*
GS	*The Gnostic Scriptures: A New Translation*. Edited and translated by B. Layton. Garden City, N.Y.: Doubleday & Co., 1987.
HBT	*Horizons in Biblical Theology*
HTR	*Harvard Theological Review*
HUCA	*Hebrew Union College Annual*
IDB	*The Interpreter's Dictionary of the Bible*. Edited by G.A. Buttrick. 4 vols. Nashville: Abingdon Press, 1962.
IDBS	*The Interpreter's Dictionary of the Bible*, Supplementary Volume. Edited by G.A. Buttrick. Nashville: Abingdon Press, 1976.
JBL	*Journal of Biblical Literature*
JJS	*Journal for Jewish Studies*
JSJ	*Journal for the Study of Judaism*

JSNT	*Journal for the Study of the New Testament*
JTS	*Journal of Theological Studies*
NHL	*The Nag Hammadi Library in English.* Edited by J.M. Robinson. San Francisco: Harper & Row, 1977.
NovT	*Novum Testamentum*
NTA	*New Testament Apocrypha*, E. Hennecke. Edited by W. Schneemelcher; English translation edited by R. McL. Wilson. 2 vols. Philadelphia: Westminster Press, 1963–1965.
NTS	*New Testament Studies*
OTP	*The Old Testament Pseudepigrapha.* Edited by J.H. Charlesworth. 2 vols. Garden City, N.Y.: Doubleday & Co., 1983, 1985.
PGM	*Papyri Graecae Magicae.* Edited by K. Preisendanz. 3 vols. Leipzig: Teubner, 1928–1941.
RSR	*Religious Studies Review*
SBL	Society of Biblical Literature
SBLDS	SBL Dissertation Series
SBLMS	SBL Monograph Series
SecC	*Second Century*
SJT	*Scottish Journal of Theology*
TDNT	*Theological Dictionary of the New Testament.* Edited by G. Kittel and G. Friedrich. 10 vols. Grand Rapids: Wm. B. Eerdmans Publishing Co., 1964–1976.
TU	Texte und Untersuchungen
USQR	*Union Seminary Quarterly Review*
VC	*Vigiliae christianae*
ZNW	*Zeitschrift für die neutestamentliche Wissenschaft*

Dead Sea Scrolls

CD	Cairo Damascus Document
1QapGen	Genesis Apocryphon of Qumran Cave 1
1QpHab	Pesher on Habakkuk from Qumran Cave 1
1QM	*Milhamah* (War Scroll)
1QS	*Serek hayyahad* (Manual of Discipline)

Works of Philo

Abr.	*De Abrahamo*
Cher.	*De Cherubim*
Heres	*Quis Rerum Divinarum Heres*
Immut.	*Quod Deus immutabilis sit*

Leg. All.	*Legum Allegoriae*
Migr.	*De Migratione Abrahami*
Mut.	*De Mutatione Nominum*
Post.	*De Posteritate Caini*
Praem.	*De Praemiis et Poenis*
Sac.	*De Sacrificiis Abelis et Caini*
Sobr.	*De Sobrietate*
Spec. Leg.	*De Specialibus Legibus*
Virt.	*De Viritutibus*

1

Introduction

Problem and Proposal

In Romans 11:28–29 Paul, a Jewish Christian, writes to the Gentile Christians of the church at Rome (cf. 11:13) in order to show them that although most Jews had not accepted Jesus as the Christ, still God had not thereby reneged on the promise to non-Christian Jews: "As regards the gospel they are enemies of God, for your sake; but as regards election they are beloved for the sake of their forefathers. For the gifts and the call of God are irrevocable." The Jews had opposed the Christian message, especially as it made room for Gentiles apart from covenantal law observance. But God would remain faithful to the patriarchal promises, the promises made to Abraham and his descendants. The Jews, even non-Christian Jews, remained the children of Abraham for Paul, although he saw them as disobedient children for rejecting Jesus as the Christ. They had not stumbled so as to fall, so as to be disinherited of God's promises to Abraham and his children.

One hundred years later, in his *Dialogue with Trypho the Jew*, the apologist Justin Martyr, a Gentile Christian, had a rather different view of the Jews and their status before God than that expressed by Paul. In *Dialogue* 119 Justin says to Trypho the Jew: "And we [Christians] shall inherit the Holy Land together with Abraham, receiving our inheritance for all eternity, because by our similar faith we have become children of Abraham. . . . Thus, God promised Abraham a religious and righteous nation of like faith, and a delight to the Father; but it is not you, 'in whom there is no faith' [Deut.

13

32:20]." According to Justin, the patriarchal promises do not apply to the Jews; rather, God has transferred these promises to the Christians and, as we shall see, to Gentile Christians in particular. For Justin, apart from Christ the Jews stood as a cursed people who had renounced all claim to the Abrahamic promises—indeed, a people whom God had renounced as God's children. The Jews had been disinherited.

How did it happen that in the span of a hundred years the Christian conception of Judaism and of the Jews' status before God changed so radically from Paul to Justin Martyr? How is it that while Paul acknowledged the Jews as children of Abraham, Justin Martyr denied them this status, reserving it for Christians alone? How is it that only the first half of Romans 11:28 was remembered by later generations of Christians: "As regards the gospel they are enemies of God"? But these questions point to still larger questions. How may we characterize the split between formative Christianity and early Judaism? What factors contributed to the separation of these two forms of first-century Judaism into two very different religious traditions already by the middle of the second century? When does separation begin, and when does it become complete? What controls do we have for describing and evaluating the nature and extent of early Christian controversy with Judaism? What happened and why? These are the questions that underlie the present investigation.

Two kinds of problems typically arise when one attempts to answer such questions. On the one hand, the limited number of sources makes it difficult to sketch a complete picture of what happened, when it happened, how it happened, and why it happened as it did. On the other hand, the sources we do have are so diverse that they do not present us with a unified picture. As a result, there are not many handles for gaining a comprehensive understanding of the nature and extent of early Christian controversy with Judaism. The present study seeks to provide better handles for probing this issue.

My proposal is that an analysis of the use of Abraham in Christian writings from Paul through Justin Martyr can serve as an effective heuristic device for assessing the character of early Christian controversy with Judaism. By looking at how early Christians used Abraham, we can see something of how they appropriated their Jewish heritage and how they understood their relationship to non-Christian Judaism during the formative stages of Christianity, as Christianity emerged from and split off from Judaism. We can also better understand why early Jewish/Christian relations initially developed as they did, from both social-historical and theological perspectives.

The Significance of Abraham

In a 1956 monograph on Philo's place in first-century Judaism, Samuel Sandmel wrote: "To see what the writer makes of Abraham is often to see most clearly what the writer is trying to say."[1] Ten years later, in an article on Luke-Acts, Nils Dahl referred to this observation and noted, "This statement may be applied to New Testament as well as to Jewish authors."[2]

The reason for Abraham's importance is that a variety of issues central to both early Judaism and Christianity converged around the figure of Abraham: God's covenant promises, what it means to be heirs of these promises, the eschatological realization of the promises, law, circumcision, God's relation to non-Jewish peoples, and the character of faith and righteousness. That so many concerns inherent to early Jewish and Christian identity involved the understanding of this one figure is due to the fact that both early Judaism and Christianity claimed the covenant God initiated with Abraham as their special heritage. To speak of Abraham at all was to trigger an entire complex of factors that defined one's heritage and thus one's identity as Jew and as Christian. We have reason to expect, then, that an examination of early Christian use of Abraham will also serve as an instructive heuristic device for understanding early Christian attitudes toward Judaism.

From Paul Through Justin Martyr

While it is fairly straightforward to begin with Paul,[3] some scholars might question whether Justin Martyr marks the most appropriate point to end this investigation—indeed, whether with Justin we have not already moved beyond the scope of so-called "earliest Christianity" and into the beginnings of the patristic period. For example, Adolph von Harnack saw Justin's *Dialogue with Trypho* as a watershed in Christian controversy with Judaism.[4] At issue, however, is the character of this watershed. Surely Justin is a transitional figure, but does he mark the beginning of a new era or the end of an old era? Harnack argued the former; I shall argue the latter.

In Harnack's estimate the New Testament writings show active discussion and debate between Christians and Jews, whereas by the time of Justin such discussion and debate are essentially over. Indeed, Harnack concludes: "The *Dialogue with Trypho* is in reality the monologue of the victor. The opponent no longer speaks for himself; Justin speaks for him."[5] For Harnack, by the time of Justin any real Christian debate with Judaism no longer exists; Christians merely prop up Jewish opponents as straw characters to knock down. Christianity has ceased to define itself primarily over against Judaism. Instead, secure of its own identity in the aftermath of having conquered Judaism, Christianity now turns to conquer the pagan world.

In recent years, however, Harnack's conclusions have been increasingly challenged.[6] There has been a growing awareness that the relationship between early Judaism and Christianity stands in need of reevaluation.[7] One aim of the present study is to show not so much that Justin illustrates a lack of dialogue and debate between Christianity and Judaism as that he represents the arrival of early Christianity at a stagnant plateau on which later Christian polemics against Judaism have been constructed.[8] Justin marks the end of an era, the culmination of a process in formative Christianity that had begun much earlier, as our examination of early Christian use of Abraham will demonstrate.[9]

Procedures and Qualifications

The procedure that I will use for this study will be to work through all Christian writers from Paul through Justin who use Abraham, focusing our attention on how their appeals to Abraham illuminate the question of Christian controversy with Judaism.[10] Although I am seeking to present these authors' uses of Abraham in chronological order, I will try to avoid too facile an understanding of the progressive influence of one author upon another. Attempts to trace such influences are notoriously difficult and are beset with problems of control. As we will see, many traditions concerning Abraham were in general circulation in the first century C.E. Understanding these traditions is important in setting the stage for early Christian use of Abraham, but one is hard-pressed to know when an author is indebted to a specific source and when an author is simply picking up on traditions in general circulation. It is often next to impossible to know exactly from where an author draws his use of Abraham, although when this information can be obtained it adds to our understanding. At any rate, my concern is not so much from where an author draws Abraham traditions but with why and how an author uses Abraham and what that use tells us about early Christian controversy with Judaism. In other words, my primary interest revolves around how an author's use of Abraham reflects what is going on in that author's particular situation.

This investigation, then, will take us through the writings of Paul (Romans 4; 9–11; Galatians 3–4; and 2 Cor. 11:22); Matthew (1:1, 2, 17; 3:9; 8:11; 22:32); Hebrews (2:16; 6:13; 7:1, 2, 4, 5, 6, 9; 11:8, 17); James (2:21, 23); the two volumes of Luke-Acts (Luke 1:55, 73; 3:8, 34; 13:16, 28; 16:22–30; 19:9; 20:37; Acts 3:13, 25; 7:2–32; 13:26); the Gospel of John (8:31–59); the Epistle of Barnabas (6:8; 8:4; 9:7, 8; 13:7); the letters of Ignatius (Phil. 9:1); the Gospel of Philip (82:26); the Apology of Aristides (Greek, ch. 14; Syriac, ch. 2); Marcion (in Origen); Heracleon (in Irenaeus); and Justin's *Dialogue with Trypho.*[11] I will also survey the use of Abraham in other second-century Christian writings.[12]

The only New Testament passages in which Abraham is mentioned that will not receive special attention are Mark 12:26 and 1 Peter 3:6, both of which are minor references to Abraham. I will deal briefly with Mark 12:26 in discussions of Matthew 22:32 and Luke 20:37, both of which are based on Mark 12:26, Mark's only reference to Abraham (see pp. 85–86, 114–115 below). In 1 Peter 3:6, Abraham is mentioned within the context of a household code (3:1–7), in which Christian women are encouraged to imitate Sarah by obeying their husbands (an allusion to Gen. 18:1–15) and so become Sarah's children (*tekna*). There is simply not much more to say about Abraham in 1 Peter 3:6.[13]

Early Jewish Uses of Abraham

Long before Christianity came on the scene a rich variety of Abraham traditions had developed and enjoyed wide circulation in early Judaism.[14] Although a complete survey of these traditions lies beyond the scope of the present study, it is still helpful to have a general sense of the kinds of traditions that would have been current in Judaism at the beginning of the first century C.E. Throughout the study, I will refer to pertinent early Jewish uses of Abraham insofar as they provide a context for a better understanding of a Christian author's use of Abraham, yet a brief sketch here can serve to set the stage for early Christian appeals to Abraham.[15]

The question of Jewish use of Abraham has been addressed many times.[16] Two problems arise in a discussion of the place of Abraham in early Judaism. The first problem revolves around the dating of sources. Which sources truly come from early Judaism? The dilemma here is that the rabbinic materials from the Targums, the Mishnah, and especially the Talmud have a fair amount to say about Abraham. But most of these writings come from the time period of the early third century through the sixth century C.E., later than the time period of early Judaism under examination here. Because of the lateness of the sources, it is prudent for us to exclude most rabbinic sources from consideration, since our endeavor is to describe the contours of early Jewish use of Abraham in order to provide a general context for understanding early Christian usage.[17]

The second problem in presenting Jewish use of Abraham has been the quandary of how to organize the relevant material from early Jewish tradition. Scholars have usually adopted one of two approaches in presenting the materials. On the one hand, some scholars have organized the traditions by summarizing the respective views of important and representative individual Jewish authors from the Greco-Roman period.[18] On the other hand, some scholars, using the same sources, have taken a thematic approach in order to highlight common elements in the use of Abraham across the various traditions.[19]

Both of these approaches are legitimate, and each has advantages and disadvantages. The basic strength of the first approach is that it points out the specificity of each author's use of Abraham. A basic weakness is that it can lead to a rather fragmented understanding of early Jewish use of Abraham.[20] The basic strength of the second approach is that it presents a cohesive picture of the ways in which Abraham was used in early Judaism across a broad range of traditions. A basic weakness is that it can lead to an oversimplified and artificial understanding of the tremendous complexities in early Jewish use of Abraham.[21]

For our purposes, the second approach proves more useful in seeking to sketch early Jewish use of Abraham in broad terms. In adopting this approach, I would draw attention to three themes in early Jewish use of Abraham: (1) God's promises to Abraham, (2) the faith of Abraham, and (3) the status of Abraham as intermediary. Although I shall use these three categories as a way of organizing early Jewish traditions about Abraham, it is important to remember that there is quite some overlap between these themes.

God's Promises to Abraham

The promises to Abraham recorded in Genesis (e.g., 12:1–3; 13:14–17; 15:1–6, 18–20; 17:1–21; and 22:15–18) provided the foundation for the identity of Israel as a people set apart. God promised that Abraham would have countless descendants, that these descendants would be given a special land, and that they would also be a blessing to other nations. In addition, these promises indicate that Abraham would be the father of many nations. Reference to these promises recur throughout the Hebrew Scriptures.[22] In early Jewish writings from various perspectives the promises also figure significantly, although they are often unspoken assumptions and can be drawn into view by a mere allusion.[23]

At times the covenant promises to Abraham are referred to in passing. So, for example, Ezekiel the Tragedian, a Hellenistic Jewish author from the second century B.C.E., has God address Moses:

> God am I of those, your fathers three,
> of Abram, Isaac, Jacob, I am He.
> Mindful of my promises to them,
> to save my Hebrew people I am come.[24]

A writing from the Qumran community can mention the "covenant with our fathers."[25] Or 4 Ezra, a first-century C.E. Palestinian Jewish writing, can speak about Abraham rather simply in an address to God: "You made with him an everlasting covenant, and promised him that you would never forsake his descendants."[26]

But the promises also find more explicit statement. References to the multitude of Abraham's descendants run throughout early Jewish writings. In the context of recounting the story of Balaam, Pseudo-Philo, a writing that "seems to reflect the milieu of the Palestinian synagogues at the turn of the common era,"[27] has God remind Balaam: "I spoke to Abraham in a vision, saying 'Your seed will be like the stars of the heaven.'"[28] Or, in the Testament of Abraham, a late-first-century C.E. writing that "represents a kind of lowest-common-denominator Judaism,"[29] God says regarding Abraham, "I have blessed him more than the sand of the sea and as the stars of heaven."[30] Similar statements are found among the Qumran writings, for example in the Genesis Apocryphon, where God says to Abraham, "And I will multiply your seed like the dust of the earth which no man can number; neither shall any man number your seed."[31]

Thus the theme of Abraham's many descendants occurs regularly.[32]

The promise of the land also occurs explicitly in early Jewish writings. For example, in the book of Jubilees, a Palestinian Jewish writing from the second century B.C.E., we read that "the Lord made a covenant with Abram, saying 'To your seed I will give this land from the river of Egypt to the great river, the Euphrates River.' "[33] Again in the Genesis Apocryphon from Qumran, Abraham tells of a vision he has had:

> And God appeared to me in a vision at night and said to me, 'Go to Ramath Hazor which is north of Bethel, the place where you dwell, and lift up your eyes and look to the east and to the west and to the south and to the north; and behold all this land which I give to you and your seed for ever.'[34]

Sometimes the reference to the land is in allegorical terms. For example, Philo, a Hellenistic Alexandrian Jew writing in the first century C.E., deals with the promise of the land in this way. In commenting upon God's promise of land in Genesis 15:18, Philo states, "What land does he mean, but that which was mentioned before to which he now refers, the land whose fruit is the sure and steadfast apprehension of the wisdom of God?"[35] Whether referred to in literal or allegorical terms, the promise of the land occurs in various early Jewish writings.[36]

The blessing of the nations through Abraham's offspring is also explicitly mentioned in early Judaism but plays a less significant role, probably due to the political and social situations of most Jews in the first century C.E., in Palestine and in the Diaspora.[37] Jubilees 12:23 repeats God's promise to Abraham: "and all the nations of the earth will bless themselves by you." In a similar manner, Sirach, a Palestinian Jewish wisdom writing from around the time of the Maccabean uprising in the second century B.C.E., relates that "the Lord assured him by an oath that the nations would be blessed through his posterity."[38] Abraham was thus seen as the father of many nations. Indeed, Abraham was treated as the father of Jews and Gentiles alike, especially in Hellenistic Jewish apologetic literature.[39] On the other hand, some early Jewish writers expressed a less inclusive attitude toward the blessing of the nations. In the Psalms of Solomon, for example, a first-century B.C.E. Palestinian Jewish writing, the psalmist addresses God and says, "You chose the seed of Abraham rather than all the nations."[40]

The promises to Abraham regarding the descendants, the

land, and the blessing to the nations thus receive some explicit attention in various early Jewish writings, although they are rarely the topic of extended discussion. Even if they were understood in somewhat different ways, the promises to Abraham did provide significant common ground for diverse expressions of Jewish faith, and they were a unifying bond for the Jewish people. A passage from Sirach can help summarize a general understanding of God's promises to Abraham. In Sirach 44:19–21, Abraham is praised along with other famous individuals from Israel's past:

> Abraham was the great father of a multitude of nations,
> and no one has been found like him in glory;
> he kept the law of the Most High,
> and was taken into covenant with him;
> he established the covenant in his flesh,
> and when he was tested he was found faithful.
> Therefore the Lord assured him by an oath
> that the nations would be blessed through his posterity;
> that he would multiply him like the dust of the earth,
> and exalt his posterity like the stars,
> and cause them to inherit from sea to sea
> and from the River to the ends of the earth.

Such early Jewish appropriations of the promises to Abraham provide a general context within which to understand some of the early Christian approaches to Abraham. In early Christianity the promises to Abraham also had a significant place. Indeed, as we shall see, they play a pivotal role in the writings of Paul (Rom. 4:13–20; 9:4–9; 15:8; Gal. 3:14–29), and they figure prominently in the reflections of Luke-Acts (Luke 1:55, 72; 3:7–9; Acts 3:25; 7:1–8; 13:32), Hebrews (6:12–17; 7:6; 11:9–17), Barnabas (13:1–7; 14:4–5), Justin Martyr (throughout the *Dialogue*), and others. For the early Christians, the question of the identity of the true descendants of Abraham becomes a crucial issue (e.g., Romans 4; Galatians 3; Luke 3:7–9; Justin's *Dialogue* 11.5; 25.1; 43.1; 44.1). The land is also a topic of discussion (e.g., Acts 7:1–8; Heb. 11:8–16; Justin's *Dialogue* 16.2; 40.2; 80.5). And the promise that Abraham's descendants would be a blessing upon the nations is assigned a special place (e.g., Romans 4; Galatians 3; Acts 3:25; 13:26, 32, 47; Justin's *Dialogue* 11.5; 119.3–6; 130.3–4). Just as in early Jewish references to the Abrahamic promises, however, early Christians did not consistently incorporate all of the promises. Because they too chose to emphasize particular facets of the promises, we

will consider their specific appropriations of the Abrahamic
promises as these arise within their respective contexts.[41]

The Faith of Abraham

If the promises indicate the blessings that God will bestow
on Abraham and his descendants, the faith of Abraham indicates his response to God's promises.[42] Abraham's faith was a
regular topic of discussion in early Jewish writings, because
his faith was exemplary. Indeed, his faith was considered to be
heroic. References to Abraham's faithfulness encompass a variety of topics, ranging from his enduring trials, to his rejection of idol worship, his hospitality, and his obedience to God,
as expressed in his circumcision, in his law observance, and in
his offering up of Isaac. All of these characteristics point to his
righteousness before God and make him an ideal figure to
emulate.

Abraham was famous for his faithfulness amidst various trials. Sometimes the trials come from God. For example, in Jubilees 17:17–18 we read:

> And the Lord was aware that Abraham was faithful in all of his
> afflictions because he tested him with his land, and with famine.
> And he tested him with the wealth of kings. And he tested him
> again with his wife, when she was taken (from him), and with
> circumcision. And he tested him with Ishmael and with Hagar,
> his maidservant, when he sent them away. And in everything in
> which he tested him, he was found faithful. And his soul was not
> impatient. And he was not slow to act because he was faithful
> and a lover of the Lord.

At other times Abraham is subject to tests from the unfaithful.
For example, the Testament of Levi tells how "they persecuted Abraham when he was a nomad" (6:9), and Pseudo-
Philo relates how Abraham was faithful even when a malicious
leader "took Abram and threw him along with the bricks into
the fiery furnace" (6:16; 23:5), from which God saved Abraham. Similarly, both 1 Maccabees 2:52 and Sirach 44:20 state
that "when he was tested he was found faithful."[43] Such faithfulness despite adversity was regularly seen as exemplary.[44]

Related to his endurance of trials was Abraham's faithfulness in his rejection of idol worship, even though his own
father, Terah, made idols. For example, Abraham tells that
when Terah "heard my speech he became furiously angry
with me, because I had spoken harsh words against his
gods."[45] And in his farewell to Isaac, Abraham says, "I hated

idols, and those who serve them I have rejected."[46] Similarly, Josephus relates that Abraham "was thus the first boldly to declare that God, the creator of the universe, is one."[47]

Abraham's faithfulness was further associated with his hospitality. For example, at the very outset the Testament of Abraham states that "the righteous man was very hospitable."[48] And Philo speaks about Abraham's "splendid and magnificent exchange of hospitality."[49]

Most important, however, was Abraham's obedience. For example, Jubilees 15:23–34 discusses at length Abraham's faithfulness in having his whole household circumcised. Similarly, Sirach 44:20 states that Abraham "established the covenant in his flesh." Not only does Abraham obey God's command to circumcise but he observes the law as a whole, even before it was given to Moses. For example, 2 Baruch speaks of "the fountain of Abraham and his generation. . . . For at that time the unwritten law was in force among them, and the works of the commandments were accomplished at that time."[50] Likewise, the Damascus Rule from Qumran states that Abraham "was accounted a friend of God because he kept the commandments of God and did not choose his own will."[51] Finally, Abraham was seen as most faithful in his willingness to offer up his only son, Isaac, as a sacrifice to God. Thus Josephus comments that Abraham was faithful even in this, "deeming that nothing would justify disobedience to God and that in everything he must submit to His will."[52] Similarly, the seven brothers who die as martyrs in 4 Maccabees encourage and exhort one another: "Remember whence you came, and the father by whose hand Isaac would have submitted to being slain for the sake of religion" (13:12).[53] And Philo states that Abraham's offering of Isaac, "though not followed by the intended ending, was complete and perfect, and the record of it as such stands graven not only in the sacred books but in the minds of the readers."[54]

Abraham's faith was thus legendary in early Judaism. His faith and righteousness were considered exemplary. Like the traditions about the promises, these early Jewish appeals to Abraham's faith provide a general context within which to understand early Christian reflections on Abraham. The faith of Abraham was also important for early Christianity, although this theme was developed in rather different ways by various early Christian authors. As we shall see, the theme of Abraham's faith plays a crucial role in the writings of Paul in particular (Romans 4; Galalatians 3–4). But it also figures in the accounts of Matthew (8:5–13), Hebrews (11:9–17), James

(2:18–24), Luke-Acts (Acts 7:1–8), and Barnabas (13:6–7), among others. As was the case in early Jewish writings, so in early Christian writings the authors discuss Abraham's faith in connection with manifestations of that faith. For example, we will see that Paul addresses the relationship between Abraham's faith and his observance of circumcision and of the law (Rom. 4:9–12; Gal. 3:6–18). Hebrews and James, on the other hand, refer to Abraham's faith in the light of his obedience in offering up Isaac (Heb. 11:17–19; James 2:21). Yet we shall also see that in talking about the manifestations of Abraham's faith, early Christian authors sometimes move in new directions as they seek to appropriate the patriarch as the forefather of Christianity.

The Status of Abraham as Intermediary

One final aspect of early Jewish use of Abraham that we will discuss involves the role he frequently played as an intermediary between humanity and God. Insofar as God gave the promises to Abraham, Abraham mediated the promises to his descendants, which is one reason why both Jews and Christians considered it so important to establish some close connection to Abraham. Overall, Abraham's intermediary status can be seen in descriptions of him as a seer, as a priestly figure, and as a prophetic judge.

Intimations that Abraham saw visions appear already in the Genesis accounts. Genesis 15:12–16 relates that, after "a deep sleep fell on Abram," God reveals to Abraham what will happen to his descendants. Throughout various early Jewish writings Abraham is portrayed as one who has special dreams. For example, the author of Jubilees tells that "the word of the Lord came to Abram in a dream, saying, 'Don't fear, Abram. I am your defender and your reward (will be) very great.'"[55] The Genesis Apocryphon from Qumran relates that Abraham had a dream regarding the danger he faced from the Egyptians because of Sarah's beauty.[56] And in an address to God, the author of 4 Ezra states that God chose Abraham: "and you loved him and to him only you revealed the end of the times, secretly by night."[57]

Not only does Abraham have revelatory dreams but he also can predict the future through his reading of the stars. Abraham's astrological prowess was a common subject of discussion among early Jewish authors, perhaps derived from references in Genesis to God's call for Abraham to "look toward heaven, and number the stars" (Gen. 15:5; cf. Gen.

22:17).[58] For example, Pseudo-Eupolemus remarks that Abraham "sought and obtained the knowledge of astrology and the Chaldean craft."[59] Josephus boasts that Abraham taught the laws of astronomy to the Egyptians, from whom the Greeks in turn learned.[60] The author of Jubilees states that "Abram sat up during the night on the first of the seventh month, so that he might observe the stars from evening until daybreak so that he might see what the nature of the year would be with respect to rain."[61] Yet this aspect of Abraham's role as an intermediary also met with some criticism in early Jewish writings. Jubilees 12 proceeds to relate that Abraham questioned himself and apparently thenceforth gave up his astrological practices. Similarly, Philo criticizes Abraham's early venture into astrology:

> In this creed Abraham had been reared, and for a long time remained a Chaldean. Then opening the soul's eye as though after profound sleep, and beginning to see the pure beam instead of the deep darkness, he followed the ray and discerned what he had not beheld before, a charioteer and pilot presiding over the world and directing in safety his own work, assuming the charge and superintendence of that work and of all such parts of it as are worthy of the divine care.[62]

Whether welcomed or criticized, however, the idea that Abraham had special astrological skills had a significant place in early Jewish portraits of Abraham as a seer.

Abraham's status as an intermediary also found expression in depictions of the patriarch in a priestly role. Thus early Jewish authors sometimes show Abraham asking for God's mercy on behalf of others. The Genesis accounts already had presented Abraham in this light, when he petitioned God on behalf of the Sodomites in Genesis 18:22–33. Early Jewish authors picked up on this scriptural motif. For example, in the Apocalypse of Zephaniah, a mid-first century C.E. Hellenistic Jewish writing, an angel identifies three individuals praying for people in torment as being Abraham, Isaac, and Jacob. They beseech God: "We pray to you on account of those who are in all these torments so that you might have mercy on all of them."[63] In the Testament of Levi, Levi warns his sons that "unless you had received mercy through Abraham, Isaac, and Jacob, our fathers, not a single one of your descendants would be left on the earth."[64] And in the Testament of Abraham, Abraham says to the archangel Michael:

> I beg you, archangel, heed my plea; and let us beseech the Lord

yet (again) and let us prostrate ourselves for his compassion and beg his mercy on behalf of the souls of the sinners whom I previously, being evil-minded, cursed and destroyed.[65]

Abraham's priestly function can also be seen in texts where the name of Abraham is invoked as a way to ensure God's favor. For example, the Prayer of Jacob, a Hellenistic Jewish writing possibly from the first century C.E., addresses God as the "father of (the) Patria[rch]s," and "He who showed favor to [Abr]aham by [giving the] kingd[om to him]."[66] Pseudo-Philo relates that before he slung his stones at Goliath, David "took seven stones and wrote on them the names of his fathers (those of Abraham, Isaac, and Jacob, Moses and Aaron) and his own and the Most Powerful."[67]

In his priestly role, Abraham also offers sacrifices to God, as he had in the Genesis accounts (Gen. 12:7–8; 15:9–11, 17; 22:1–14). For example, both Jubilees and Josephus relate Abraham's sacrifice from Genesis 15.[68] In addition, the Testament of Levi shows Abraham as one who taught Levi how to make certain offerings.[69]

Finally, Abraham acts in a priestly manner by receiving the faithful in the afterlife.[70] The author of 4 Maccabees is confident that martyrs will be welcomed: "After our death in this fashion Abraham and Isaac and Jacob will receive us, and all our forefathers will praise us."[71] Other early Jewish authors also state that Abraham will be present in God's kingdom, celebrating at God's victory.[72]

In addition to portraits of Abraham as a seer and as a priestly figure, accounts of Abraham as a prophetic judge also attest to the patriarch's role as an intermediary in early Jewish writings. In this case, however, Abraham is a mediator on behalf of God. In 2 Baruch, Abraham is aligned with the origin of "belief in the coming judgment."[73] First Enoch 93:5 states that "a (certain) man shall be elected as the plant of the righteous judgment." According to Ethiopian commentators, this man was Abraham.[74] Finally, the Testament of Abraham shows Abraham as a ruthless judge who condemns all sinners. After Abraham condemns a host of people, God intervenes:

And immediately a voice came down from heaven to the Commander-in-chief, speaking thus, "O Michael, Commander-in-chief, command the chariot to stop and turn Abraham away, lest he should see the entire inhabited world. For if he were to see all those who pass their lives in sin, he would destroy everything that exists. For behold, Abraham has not sinned and he has no mercy on sinners."[75]

Although Abraham later shows mercy to the sinners, this passage indicates that he could function as a prophetic judge.

Early Jewish authors thus appealed to Abraham as an intermediary by depicting him as a seer, a priestly figure, and a prophetic judge. Once again, these early Jewish uses of Abraham provide a broad context for understanding similar reflections by early Christian authors. Although early Christian references to Abraham as an intermediary are less prominent than references to other aspects of Abraham, still they are present. As we shall see, Paul (Rom. 11:28–29) and Luke (1:54–55, 72–75; 16:19–31) use Abraham in appeals to God for mercy. Matthew (8:11–12; 22:31–32) and Luke (13:28–29; 16:19–31; 20:37–38) refer to Abraham in connection with the afterlife and prophetic judgment (Matt. 8:11–12; Luke 13:28–29). John, Barnabas, and Justin all refer to Abraham as one who saw Christ (John 8:56; Barn. 8:1–4; 9:7–9; Justin, *Dialogue* 55–59).

In sum, studying the various uses of Abraham in early Judaism provides us with significant contexts for understanding early Christian uses of Abraham. At times, early Christian authors depart little or not at all from traditional Jewish usage. At other times, they shape the traditions in dramatically new ways. In either case, how early Christians use Abraham indicates something about their assessment of their Jewish roots and their vision of the relation between emerging Christianity and formative Judaism.

Projections

To anticipate my conclusions, we will see that early Christians used Abraham to discuss who belongs to God's people and who is excluded, especially in the light of God's action in Christ. We will observe that Paul used Abraham to stress Gentile inclusion within God's promises, at the same time safeguarding Jewish inclusion, while a hundred years later Justin used Abraham to argue for Jewish exclusion from God's promises, at the same time emphasizing the specifically Gentile character of Christianity.[76] My study will suggest that, in the main, the use of Abraham in early Christian controversy with Judaism moved away from appealing to Abraham as the father of Jew and Gentile alike and moved increasingly toward the portrayal of a Christian Abraham who has abandoned and disinherited his children, the Jews.

2

The Father of Jews
and Gentiles Alike:
Abraham in the Letters
of Paul

Abraham occupies a pivotal position in Paul's exposition of the faith, particularly in connection with the relation between Christians and Jews. The figure Abraham occurs a total of nineteen times in only three of the undisputed letters of Paul: Romans (9x), Galatians (9x), and 2 Corinthians 11:22. In Romans, seven of the nine occurrences fall in one chapter — Rom. 4:1, 2, 3, 9, 12, 13, and 16, with the other two at 9:7 and 11:1.[1] Similarly, in Galatians eight of the nine occurrences fall in one chapter — Gal. 3:6, 7, 8, 9, 14, 16, 18, and 29, with the remaining reference at 4:22. Paul never refers to Abraham elsewhere. Nor do any of the deutero-Pauline letters mention Abraham.

When we ask about Paul's use of Abraham, then, our discussion is essentially restricted to Romans and Galatians, the two letters in which Paul extensively addresses significant issues between Jewish and Gentile Christians and the larger conflict between Jews and Christians. In letters to Christian communities where little apparent controversy exists between Jews and Gentiles, Paul does not appeal to Abraham.[2] A close correlation exists, then, between the appearance of Jewish/Christian disputes in the communities addressed by Paul and the appearance of Abraham in Paul's letters. This correlation leads us to surmise that Paul thinks that a consideration of Abraham will be singularly effective both in addressing the relationship between Jewish and Gentile Christians and in reflecting upon questions regarding the relationship between non-Christian Jews and Christians.[3] We will better understand why Paul believes this after looking at how Paul uses Abraham.

Before we move directly to an investigation of Paul's use of Abraham, it is appropriate to issue a few caveats regarding problems encountered in any such examination. The problems are of two kinds. On the one hand, they come from our end as interpreters; on the other hand, they are inherent in Paul's writings.

From our end, when we look at Paul's use of Abraham in Galatians and Romans from a vantage point twenty centuries later, we are liable to misunderstand what Paul is saying to those whom he addresses. This is so for three reasons. First, we view Christianity and Judaism as two separate religions. Paul did not. No matter how much we may stress Paul's understanding of the essential congruity and continuity between Jewish and Christian faith, we still find ourselves again and again hurdling twenty centuries of essential incongruity and discontinuity that has characterized relations between Jews and Christians. Second, we tend to read Galatians and Romans together because they correspond on various levels. But Paul wrote these two letters addressing different situations with nearly opposite problems. Certainly, we are obliged to understand in what ways Galatians and Romans cohere. But our first task must be to understand each letter on its own terms, lest we mistakenly settle for a flat reading of both.[4] And third, just as Krister Stendahl has demonstrated our propensity to read modern concerns back into Paul's letters,[5] similarly so much of the Christian, and especially the Protestant, heritage has been preoccupied with Paul's emphasis on "justification by faith" that we have tended to forget Paul's preoccupation with the relationship between Jews and Gentiles before God. Attention has too often focused on Paul's use of Abraham in service to the theme of "justification by faith," at the expense of fully appreciating Paul's use of Abraham in negotiating the relationship between Jews and Gentiles.[6]

From Paul's end, we encounter two related difficulties when attempting to understand his use of Abraham as a whole. First, in Galatians and Romans, Paul appears to advocate inconsistent and contradictory positions regarding Abraham.[7] Second, Paul's exposition of the significance of Abraham is very compact and dense in both Galatians and Romans.[8] Romans 4 and Galatians 3 require careful explication in order for the interpreter to understand fully the broad range in Paul's use of Abraham.

The above caveats having been issued, we aim to explore broadly three questions regarding Paul's use of Abraham. First, how does Paul use Abraham? Second, why does Paul use

Abraham as he does? And third, what light does Paul's use of
Abraham shed on our understanding of the nature and the
extent of the disputes among Jewish and Gentile Christians,
and among non-Christian Jews and Christians, in the first generation of Christianity? This final aspect has the most significance within the larger context of the study, but we will be
able to make sound judgments in this regard only after addressing the first two questions.

We will proceed by (1) examining Abraham in Galatians;
(2) considering Abraham in 2 Corinthians 11:22; (3) examining Abraham in Romans; (4) proposing a coherent way of
reading Galatians and Romans together; and (5) drawing conclusions from Paul's use and understanding of Abraham regarding the nature and the scope of Paul's controversy with
Judaism.

Abraham in Galatians

Galatians ranks among the most polemical letters of Paul,
along with his stinging letter to the Corinthians preserved in 2
Corinthians 10–13. The letter as a whole addresses a Gentile-
Christian community established by Paul (Gal. 4:12–20) that
has come under the influence of a Jewish-Christian law-
observant missionary group, a group that Paul sees as opponents preaching a rival and "perverted" gospel (1:7; cf. 1:6–
9; 3:1–5; 5:7–12; 6:12–13).[9] In response to this situation,
Paul appeals to Abraham in Galatians 3–4 in a positive manner
to remind the Galatians of the terms in which they initially
received the gospel (apart from the law) and in a negative
manner to counter the position of the Teachers, those he
views as opponents, who stress the need for the Galatians to
observe the law, especially circumcision (5:2–12; 6:12–13).
In order to understand more clearly Paul's argument in Galatians, we need first to understand the identity of the rival
Teachers in Galatia.

The Rival Teachers in Galatia

Paul alludes several times in Galatians to a group of Christians who have come to Galatia proclaiming what Paul considers a rival gospel that stresses the necessity of circumcision
and law observance (1:6–9; 3:1; 4:17; 5:7–12; 6:12–13). Apparently, the Galatians were accepting this message (1:6; 3:1–
3). Exactly how Paul has become aware of the situation in
Galatia or how long the Teachers were active in Galatia is not

immediately clear. Nevertheless, Paul responds to this turn of events in the strongest possible terms, appealing to Abraham to argue against the position of the Teachers.

Several perplexing questions arise when we consider the Teachers in Galatia: Who were they? Why had they come to Galatia? How did they view themselves in relation to Paul? Had they appealed to Abraham in convincing the Galatians to observe the law? What was their understanding of the gospel? Did they consider themselves opposed to Paul? Did they know that Paul was opposed to their mission? Were they aligned with the Jerusalem apostles whom Paul refers to in Galatians 2:1–10? Did Paul understand them to be aligned with the Jerusalem church? Was Paul responding to specific arguments made by the Teachers?

In attempting to answer these questions, we find ourselves in an equally perplexing methodological predicament. We can only reach conclusions about the Teachers by attempting to mirror-read Paul's statements in Galatians, our sole primary source.[10] This kind of mirror-reading is rendered all the more difficult because of the polemical cast of the letter.[11] We have few controls for determining how much distortion has entered into the refraction Paul has offered of the Teachers.[12] And to make matters more difficult, we cannot always tell when Paul is responding directly to the Teachers, when he is raising unrelated issues of old business with the Galatians, or when he is initiating new lines of discussion altogether.[13] We simply do not have access to an extended collection of correspondence between Paul and the Galatians that allows us great confidence in sketching the dynamics between them, such as we do have with the Corinthian correspondence.[14] Further, the polemical tone of the letter may have as much to do with Paul's constant battling with the Galatians as it does with the specific problem of the Teachers who have gained at least a foothold in the community, as 1:9 and 4:19 may indicate.

Still, it is possible to arrive at some relatively firm conclusions regarding the Teachers in Galatia.[15] Most probably, the Teachers were Jewish-Christian missionaries who were advocating circumcision and the observance of the law as essential for Gentile Christians.[16] It is also highly probable that these Teachers have introduced scripture passages regarding Abraham to support their position regarding law observance in general and circumcision in particular, as we shall see.

The most important observation regarding the Teachers is that they were Jewish *Christians*. There is no evidence in Galatians to suggest that they were non-Christian Jews. This ob-

servation is important, because it signals that Paul's fight is an
intramural battle between rival *Christian* understandings of
the gospel and not in the first place an expression of conflict
between Paul and non-Christian Judaism. We will take up this
observation more extensively below.

We can also see that the Teachers were *Jewish* Christians
from several pieces of evidence. First, Paul's repeated reference to the Teachers' advocacy of circumcision (2:3, 7–9, 12;
5:2, 3, 6; 6:12, 13, 15) already suggests their Jewish roots.
Second, their association with circumcision suggests that Paul
sees them aligned with the "circumcision party" (2:12) from
James in Jerusalem, whom Paul terms "false brethren" (2:4).
If this is the case, then the Teachers may have close ties with
the Jerusalem church, a stronghold for Jewish Christians.
Third, by twice employing an emphatic use of *hēmeis* ("we")
in 2:15–16, Paul stresses that he and his associates, "who are
Jews by birth," know that justification does not come through
works of the law but through believing in Christ. Paul seems
to have the Teachers in view here, which would suggest that
they too are "Jews by birth."

Further, these rival Jewish Christians (for Paul too is a Jewish Christian) have been evangelizing among the Galatians, a
development that appears to have particularly irked Paul.
They are "preaching" the gospel (1:8–9), although Paul
terms it a "different gospel" (1:6). Paul seems especially angered by their missionary activity, because from his perspective it was common knowledge that the Gentile territory
belonged to him (2:7–8; and Barnabas, 2:9), while the Jewish
territory belonged to Peter (2:7–8) and others from the Jerusalem church (James and John, 2:9). Paul's understanding
that he was the proprietor of the Gentile mission is evident in
Galatians 1:16. God's purpose for revealing Christ to him
was "in order that I might preach him among the Gentiles."
Thus God had called Paul to the Gentile mission and the
Jerusalem pillars had recognized and confirmed this call.
Paul could only have viewed the presence of other Jewish-
Christian missionaries in Galatia as intrusive. For Paul, these
Jewish Christians were usurping his territory. He may even
have interpreted their rival mission as an intentional slap in
the face from the Jerusalem pillars, with whom he thought he
had an agreement.[17] At the very least the presence of rival
Jewish-Christian missionaries in Paul's territory indicates
that some segments of Jewish Christianity viewed Paul's missionary work among the Gentiles as less than adequate, because he failed to inculcate among the Gentile Christians the

necessary understanding of and observance of the law, especially circumcision.

Finally, in order to convince the Galatians that circumcision in particular and law observance in general were necessary components of Christian faith, the Teachers most probably appealed to scripture texts regarding Abraham.[18] Four pieces of evidence indicate that Paul's references to Abraham in Galatians 3–4 form part of his response to scriptural arguments advanced by the Teachers.

First, the convoluted character of Paul's discussion throughout Galatians 3 should tip us off that he presumes that his readers already have an interpretive framework for understanding his line of reasoning. His argument is not intentionally opaque. Rather, he is engaged in midrashic debate with the Teachers in Galatia whose positions the Galatians know full well. We find the argument difficult to follow because we are hearing only one side of the debate, in contrast to the Galatians, whom Paul can assume will understand the points he is making—indeed, or so Paul hopes, the points he is scoring. Paul's argument does not come across as straightforward, because in all likelihood he is taking up only the issues in the scriptural debate that he thinks will persuade the Galatians.

Second, after Paul has introduced Abraham in Galatians 3:6 by appealing to the scriptural proof text from Genesis 15:6, he draws the inference in Galatians 3:7 that "it is men of faith who are the sons of Abraham" (*hoi ek pisteōs, houtoi huioi eisin Abraam*). In formulating this deduction, Paul uses the demonstrative pronoun *houtoi* ("these") where he could simply have written "those of faith are the sons of Abraham" (*hoi ek pisteōs eisin huioi Abraam*). With the use of *houtoi*, the sentence literally reads: "those of faith, *they* are the ones who are sons of Abraham." By employing this construction, Paul appears to be intentionally countering a different understanding of who the "sons of Abraham" are. In 3:7 Paul is probably challenging the rival view he assigns to the Teachers, that it is those "who rely on works of the law" (*hoi ex ergōn nomou*) who are sons of Abraham, a position he introduces in 3:10.

Third, when Paul in 3:16 refers to "the promises . . . made to Abraham and to his offspring" (*tō spermati autou*), taking up a passage from Genesis 13:15 and 17:8,[19] he begins his discussion by saying first what "to his offspring" does *not* mean. By starting with a denial of what the passage means, it sounds as though Paul is responding directly to what the Teachers have been saying the passage *does* mean, of which he is aware.[20] Paul is hoping to offer a different interpretation of the passage that undercuts the position held by the Teachers.[21]

And fourth, it seems more than just coincidence that Paul's introduction of Abraham in 3:6 follows as a proof text directly after 3:1–5, where Paul refers explicitly to the Teachers in 3:1, "O foolish Galatians! *Who* has bewitched you?" Paul's appeal to Abraham so closely after this cry of frustration probably indicates that the Teachers managed to "bewitch" the Galatians in part by convincing them from the scriptural example of Abraham that circumcision was central to Christian faith and practice.

These considerations lead us to conclude that Paul has taken up discussion of Abraham because he knows the Teachers have been using Abraham to argue for the necessity of circumcision and law observance. From what we know of early Jewish interpretation, the Teachers' use of Abraham stands in line with an understanding that saw Abraham as evidence of the need for both circumcision and law observance. The practice of circumcision began with Abraham and was the sign of the covenant. In addition, tradition held that Abraham himself observed the law.[22] If these Gentile Galatian converts to Christianity really wanted to be counted as heirs of God's promises to Abraham, then they must be fully incorporated among the descendants of Abraham (*sperma Abraam*; Gen. 13:15; 17:18; Gal. 3:16) and so be circumcised and observe the law.[23]

One curious problem remains. Why does Paul not refer to Abraham's circumcision in countering the Teachers' use of Abraham? This omission is especially surprising, since elsewhere (Rom. 4:11–12) Paul makes a particular point of drawing attention to Abraham's circumcision, arguing that since Abraham was reckoned righteous by faith *before* he was circumcised, then circumcision had no bearing on his status before God. Such a point would seem to serve Paul well in Galatians also, but he does not make it. The most we can say is that perhaps Paul thought that even mentioning Abraham's circumcision would play into the hands of the Teachers, whereas in Romans 4:11–12 Paul has no such fears.

Having considered the identity of the Teachers and the probability that they have appealed to Abraham in order to convince the Galatian Gentile Christians of the need for circumcision and law observance, we can now consider more fully Paul's response to the Teachers' use of Abraham. As we will see below, part of Paul's response is to appeal positively to Abraham to remind the Galatians of what they should already know, namely, that their faith in Christ fulfills God's age-old promise to Abraham regarding the extension of God's blessing to the Gentiles (3:8, 14). Paul identifies the central feature of this fulfillment as their faith in Christ.

Galatians 3:1–4:7

Before we turn directly to Abraham in 3:1–4:7 a few observations are in order regarding the larger literary context of this section.[24] In Galatians 2, Paul has rehearsed his own defense of the gospel for the Gentiles against any insistence upon law observance (2:1–10), in which context he has related his rebuke of Peter's hypocritical behavior (2:11–14). Paul concludes Galatians 2 by reminding the Galatians that even the Jewish Christians, among whom Paul numbers himself, realize that justification comes from faith in Christ and not from works of the law (2:15–21). In 3:1 Paul turns directly to confront the Galatians, who have been convinced by others that law observance is necessary (3:1–5). Paul then appeals to Abraham to counter their newfound conviction regarding the significance of law observance (3:6–4:7). In 4:8–20 Paul moves beyond his consideration of Abraham per se, although in 4:21–31 he returns to Abraham for a final time.

Galatians 3:1–4:7 forms a distinct literary unit within the letter. Structurally, I divide Galatians 3:1–4:7 into five main units: 3:1–5/6; 3:6/7–14; 3:15–18; 3:19–25; and 3:26–4:7.[25] In 3:1–5/6 Paul raises his basic problem with the Galatians, whether they have received the Spirit by works of the law or by hearing with faith. [26] In 3:6 Paul introduces Abraham as scriptural support for the latter position. Then in 3:6/7–14 Paul develops God's promise to Abraham regarding Gentile inclusion, advancing the position that faith forms the necessary basis of this inclusion and offering a critique of the position that law observance has anything to do with Gentile inclusion. In 3:15–18 Paul gives an analogy based on the human example of a will to establish further his case that the Abrahamic promise of Gentile inclusion in Christ does not come about by law observance. In 3:19–25, then, he makes a slight digression regarding the purpose of the law. Finally, in 3:26–4:7 Paul considers who are truly sons of God and thus sons of Abraham. We will look at each of these sections in turn.

Galatians 3:1–5/6

A twice-repeated question governs Paul's introduction of Abraham into the discussion in Galatians 3. In 3:2 Paul writes,

"Let me ask you only this: Did you receive the Spirit by works of the law, or by hearing with faith?" In 3:5 he restates the question: "Does he who supplies the Spirit to you and works miracles among you do so by works of the law, or by hearing with faith?" The questions are rhetorical, for Paul's answer is clear: the Galatians have received the Spirit, and God is active among them through the Spirit, by their hearing with faith. By focusing on the Spirit, Paul calls their attention to the manifestation of God's power, which they apparently have already experienced.[27]

Paul begins to develop an answer to his twice-repeated rhetorical question (3:2, 5) by citing Genesis 15:6 in Galatians 3:6, Paul's first reference to Abraham: "Thus Abraham 'believed God, and it was reckoned to him as righteousness.'" Paul's nearly verbatim citation of Genesis 15:6 accomplishes two things. First, by introducing the citation with the conjunction "thus" (*kathōs*), Paul indicates that he sees Genesis 15:6 as a scriptural proof text supporting the obvious answer to his rhetorical question posed to the Galatians in 3:2–5.[28] Their reception of the Spirit came about (3:2) and still comes about (3:5) through faith. The term "faith" (*pistis*) provides the point of contact between Genesis 15:6 and Galatians 3:1–5. As Abraham's faith put him in right relation to God, resulting in his rectification, so the Galatians' faith puts them in right relation to God, resulting in their reception of the Spirit. For Paul, the case of Abraham supports his argument that faith is the true basis of one's relation to God. Receiving and participating in God's Spirit, receiving the gospel, depends on hearing with faith.

Second, the introduction of Abraham's faith invites an extended consideration of who the "sons of Abraham" are (*huioi Abraam*), developed sporadically throughout Galatians 3 and 4 (3:7–9, 29 [*sperma*]; 4:1–7, 21–31). From his citation of Genesis 15:6 in Galatians 3:6, Paul infers 3:7: "So you see that it is those of faith who are the sons of Abraham" (*houtoi huioi eisin Abraam*).[29] Faith thus mediates not only one's relationship to God but also one's kinship to Abraham. Abraham has a paradigmatic function. What one says of Abraham also applies to his children. Paul uses the reference to Abraham in Genesis 15:6, then, both to confirm what he has said in Galatians 3:1–5 and to anticipate his discussion in Galatians 3:7–9.

Galatians 3:6/7–14

The use of Genesis 15:6 to lift up the primacy of faith and the character of Abrahamic sonship arises from Paul's fundamental concern with the basis of God's inclusion of the Gentiles. Paul is not concerned about Abrahamic sonship in general; he is preoccupied with Gentiles as "sons of Abraham" in particular. This keynote comes to the fore as Paul moves from Galatians 3:7 to 3:8. In 3:8 Paul goes so far as to equate the gospel with God's blessing upon the Gentiles. The gospel was preached beforehand to Abraham, "that God would justify the Gentiles by faith." Paul then cites a mixture of Genesis 12:3 and Genesis 18:18, where God addresses Abraham, to support his point: "In you shall all the nations (*ta ethnē*) be blessed" (Gal. 3:8). [30] Paul defines the gospel here in terms of the promise of Gentile inclusion within God's blessing upon Abraham. Paul equates the blessing upon Abraham with Gentile justification by faith (3:8). Those who have faith "are blessed with Abraham who had faith" (3:9). The promised inclusion of the Gentiles by faith has now been realized in Christ, according to Paul.[31] Thus, not only does Paul identify the Gentiles as recipients and heirs of the promise to Abraham in Christ (cf. 3:29) but Paul also sees Gentile inclusion in the blessing of Abraham as part of the substance of the promise itself.[32] The Gentiles are both the recipients of the promise and the subject of the promise.

In receiving the promise, the Gentiles accept in Christ God's acceptance of themselves as Gentiles, apart from the law. Indeed, the law is conspicuously absent from Paul's initial discussion of the promise to Abraham in 3:6–9.[33] Since the promise was made before and apart from the law, the Gentiles participate in the promise apart from the law. Since the promise was mediated to Abraham through faith, the Gentiles participate in the promise through faith. The law has no essential bearing on the Gentiles' relation to God, except that the law itself points to the incorporation of the Gentiles in Christ (3:8).

Of course, Paul's discussion of the promise without reference to the law in 3:6–9 begs the question of the function of the law, which Paul begins to address in 3:10–14. Whereas in 3:6–9 Paul considers the rightful recipients of God's blessing upon Abraham, in 3:10–14 Paul moves to consider the curse that comes upon those who rely not on faith but on works of the law to secure God's blessing.[34] For our purposes here it is enough to notice that in 3:10–14 Abraham has little to do with the law, just as the law has little to do with Abraham in 3:6–9.[35] For Paul, it is God's activity in Christ Jesus, not the law, that mediates the blessing of Abraham to the Gentiles.[36] Galatians 3:14 functions as a summary statement referring

back to Paul's discussion of Abraham in 3:6–9. In 3:14 Paul
points again to the blessing of Abraham that comes to the
Gentiles in the form of the reception of the Spirit mediated
through faith in Christ. Thus throughout 3:6–14 Paul has in
mind the extension of God's blessing upon Abraham to the
Gentiles (3:8, 14).

In the first two sections of Galatians 3, then, Paul appeals
positively to Abraham to remind the Gentile Christians in Galatia of the basis on which they received the Spirit and to show
them that this blessing fulfills what God had spoken to Abraham. Of course, that Paul has to remind the Galatians of how
they received the gospel at all indicates that they are turning
from the gospel he preached and turning to another gospel
(1:6, 9; 3:1).

Galatians 3:15–18

In 3:15–18 Paul picks up on 3:14, which refers to Christ as
the promised blessing of Abraham that has come upon the
Gentiles. To begin, Paul identifies this promise with the covenant (diathēkē) that God made with Abraham.[37] Paul plays
here on the dual meaning of diathēkē, which can mean either
"will" or "covenant."[38] By taking diathēkē as "will," Paul's
argument works as "a human example," since everyone
knows that "no one annuls even a man's will (diathēkē), or
adds to it, once it has been ratified" (3:15). By analogy, taking
diathēkē as "covenant," Paul can assert that the law, which
was added four hundred and thirty years after God's covenant
with Abraham, "does not annul a covenant (diathēkē) previously ratified by God, so as to make the promise void"
(3:17). Thus one should not evaluate God's covenant with
Abraham from the perspective of the Mosaic law, which was
added later; rather, one should evaluate the Mosaic law from
the perspective of God's prior covenant with Abraham.

Paul goes on in 3:16a to make a further point: "The
promises were made to Abraham and to his offspring." Immediately, in 3:16b, Paul makes a qualification regarding the
meaning of "offspring" (to sperma): "It does not say 'And to
offsprings' [tois spermasin], referring to many; but, referring
to one, 'And to your offspring' [tō spermati], which is Christ."
Thus "the offspring" (to sperma) does not refer to all of Abraham's descendants; rather, Paul construes the offspring to be
Abraham's singular descendant, Christ.[39] In disqualifying a
reading that would take the singular to sperma as a generic
singular, Paul rules out a traditional understanding of this pas-

sage, one that he himself accepts in Romans 4:16–18 and 9:6–7.[40] Paul can make this move because of the ambiguity of the word *to sperma* ("the offspring"). Grammatically the word is a neuter singular, although it is often understood as a generic singular that refers to a collective group, as in English. Paul plays on the technicality of the singular form to stipulate a singular offspring, Christ.

Christ, as Abraham's singular offspring, is the recipient of God's covenant with Abraham regarding the blessing of the Gentiles. Or to use the analogous language that Paul has introduced of a human will, Christ is the *executor* of Abraham's will. But Paul does not have in mind just any aspect of this covenant/will. Rather, Paul has in view God's covenant promise regarding the blessing of the *Gentiles*, as 3:8 and 3:14 make clear. By picking up on 3:14 in 3:15–18, Paul continues to focus predominantly on God's blessing of the Gentiles promised to Abraham. Paul's point is that this blessing takes place through Christ, the inheritor and executor of Abraham's will, not through the law, which has no bearing whatsoever on God's blessing of the Gentiles. In 3:18 Paul hammers this point home. Inheritance by the law and inheritance by the promise are mutually exclusive. But God gave this inheritance of Gentile blessing to Abraham by the promise, which is negotiated through Christ in faith.

Why does Paul go out of his way to restrict the meaning of "offspring" to Christ and not to the descendants of Abraham as a generic group? The best explanation has to do with an observation we noted above (pp. 33–34), namely, that Paul is countering a position advocated by the rival Teachers in Galatia. Otherwise it is difficult to explain why Paul stresses what "offspring" does *not* mean. How would the Teachers have employed *to sperma* ("offspring") as a generic singular to support their case? As we argued above, 3:7 indicates that the Teachers maintained the need for Gentile-Christian law observance in order for them to be reckoned among the "sons of Abraham." The most significant feature of this law observance was circumcision, as Paul's constant reference to it in Galatians shows (2:3, 12; 5:2, 6, 11, 12; 6:12, 13, 15). To support their argument for Gentile-Christian circumcision the Teachers probably pointed to Abraham's circumcision and God's command for Abraham to circumcise all of his offspring (Gen. 17:9–14, 23–27; 21:4).[41] If the Gentile Christians wanted to be numbered among the descendants of Abraham as heirs of the promises, then they too needed to be circumcised. The case for circumcision having been established, it was but a little step to advocate law observance in general. Thus the Teachers in Galatia equated "sons of Abraham" (*huioi Abraam*, 3:7) with "offspring of Abraham" (*sperma Abraam*, 3:16).

In 3:7 Paul had undercut the Teachers' argument that the "sons of Abraham" are so designated by virtue of law observance. Rather, the "sons of Abraham" are those who, like Abraham, believe God. Now in 3:16–18 Paul undercuts the Teachers' implicit argument that the "offspring of Abraham" refers to all those who are rightful heirs to the Abrahamic promise by virtue of circumcision. Rather, the "offspring of Abraham" is a singular reference to Christ, who is the singular heir to the Abrahamic promise and who through faith mediates this promise to the Gentiles, the focus of Paul's attention throughout this section.

Paul makes it exceedingly clear to the Galatians that the only basis on which they may find a real connection to God's promise to Abraham is their relationship to Christ. Gentile inclusion in God's promise to Abraham comes not through law observance but in Christ through faith.[42] Thus Paul uses the very Abraham employed by the Teachers in order to combat the Teachers' understanding of the gospel and to counter the hold they appear to have over the Gentile Christians in Galatia.

Galatians 3:19–25

Having undercut the significance of law observance for Gentile inclusion, Paul has to take up again the place of the law, which he does in 3:19–25. As Hans Dieter Betz points out, Paul makes a slight digression here.[43] His discussion of the law is an extension of his response to the position advocated by the Teachers regarding Abraham. Whereas the Teachers had closely linked Abraham to the law, Paul distances Abraham from the law. As Abraham did not figure into Paul's discussion of the law in 3:10–13, so again Abraham does not come into view in Paul's discussion of the law in 3:19–25.

There are three connecting links between 3:15–18 and 3:19–25: reference to "the law" (*ho nomos*) in 3:17–18 and 3:19, reference to "the offspring" (*to sperma*) in 3:16 and 3:19, and reference to "the promise" (*hē epaggelia*) in 3:18 and 3:19.[44] In brief, Paul correlates these three in the following manner. The law was an intermediate stopgap measure (a "custodian," 3:24) instituted until *the* offspring, Christ, should come to mediate the promised faith (3:19, 22–

25).[45] Appropriately, 3:19 states that "the law," which functioned as an intermediate step on the temporal horizontal plane, "was ordained by angels," which function as intermediaries on the spatial vertical plane, "through an intermediary," probably a reference to Moses.[46]

Despite his attack on the Teachers' emphasis on the works of the law, however, Paul does not here engage in an all-out assault on the law or on law observance itself. He states explicitly that the law is not against the promises of God (3:21).[47] Indeed, Paul's statements in Galatians 5:6 and 6:15, that neither circumcision nor uncircumcision makes any difference, indicate that Jewish-Christian observance of the law is a matter of relative indifference to Paul. Paul does not attack Jewish Christians who continue to observe the law after coming to faith in Jesus. Indeed, Paul himself may well have observed the law so as not to violate the scruples of fellow Jews (cf. 1 Cor. 9:20–23).

Law observance ceases to be a matter of indifference, however, when Jewish Christians mandate similar observance from Gentile Christians, as they did in Galatia. The Teachers' insistence on law observance and their exaltation of the law enrage Paul, and so he is forced to address the issue of the law. The law has a positive role for Gentile Christians only insofar as it functions as scripture, "foreseeing that God would justify the Gentiles by faith" (3:8). Abraham received the promise of Gentile inclusion, and this promise has been fulfilled in Christ (3:15–18). For the Galatians to give in to law observance shows that they are seeking to be justified by the law and so abrogates God's blessing upon them through Christ (5:4) and bars them from participating in the Abrahamic blessing.

But again, the law itself stands neither in opposition to the promises God gave to Abraham nor in opposition to the inclusion of the Gentiles within these promises (3:21). Rather, Paul's apparent denigration of the law in 3:17–19 and his anguish over the Galatians' observance of the law throughout the letter (e.g., 4:8–10; 5:1–12) are a function of his attack on the position of the Teachers in Galatia. Paul's polemical style of argumentation results from the gravity of the situation he is addressing.[48] He apparently feels that the pendulum has swung so far in the direction of the Teachers that the only way he can counter the hold they have over the Gentile-Christian community in Galatia is by stating his case in the strongest terms possible (cf. 5:12!).

The *chronological priority* of Christ inherent in God's prom-

ise to Abraham (3:17) indicates the *ontological priority* of
Christ to the law and so further undercuts any soteriological
significance the Teachers might assign to the law. Paul is thus
forced to denigrate that which the Teachers elevate. The law
is certainly not contrary to God's promise to Abraham, but the
law does not constitute the promise (3:21–22). The law
changes nothing regarding the basis of Gentile blessing which
was already established in God's covenant promise to Abraham and was fulfilled in the coming of Christ (3:15–18).

In short, the Teachers are saying that Gentiles find inclusion
in the gospel in the same way that Jews do, by observing the
law. By contrast, Paul is saying that the Gentiles are included
in the gospel in the same way that true Jews always have been
included, by hearing with faith, the prime example being
Abraham. The difference is that Gentiles now have access in
Christ to the promises that God made to Abraham, whereas
before Christ they had no such access.

Galatians 3:26–4:7

Galatians 3:26–4:7 falls into two smaller units: 3:26–29 and
4:1–7. In 3:26–29 Paul summarizes the whole of his discussion from 3:6–29 by turning to address the Galatians directly,
as indicated by the shift from the "we" in 3:23–25 to the
"you" in 3:26–29. He begins in 3:26 by reaffirming that they
find the basis for their relation to God in Christ through faith:
"for in Christ Jesus you are all sons of God (*huiou theou*),
through faith." Paul again sees Christ the Son of God (cf.
2:20) as *the* central figure who coordinates the relationships
between God, Abraham, the Jews, and the Gentiles. Believers
become "sons of God" through faith in Christ the Son of
God.[49]

In 3:27 Paul picks up on baptismal language of being incorporated into Christ. [50] In 3:28 Paul refers once again to Gentile inclusion in Christ, stressing that fundamental distinctions
between Jew and Greek have no place in Christ. Finally, in
3:29, Paul comes full circle from 3:6–7 where he had spoken
about who the "sons of Abraham" (*huioi Abraam*) are. Only
now, Paul speaks about the Gentiles as "offspring of Abraham" (*tou Abraam sperma*). Just as the Teachers in Galatia had
equated "sons of Abraham" with "offspring of Abraham" on
the basis of law observance, so now Paul equates "sons of
Abraham" with "offspring of Abraham" on the basis of faith in
Christ. Whereas earlier in 3:16 Paul had disqualified a generic
singular understanding of *sperma Abraam* ("offspring of Abra-

ham"), here Paul explicitly appeals to a generic understanding of *sperma* as referring to all who are in Christ through faith. *Sperma Abraam* still has a christological focus, but having established Christ as the singular offspring of Abraham, Paul now allows those in Christ to be termed collective offspring of Abraham.

In 4:1–7 Paul picks up on his final comment in 3:29, that the Gentile Christians in Galatia are "heirs according to promise" (*kat' epaggelian klēronomoi*). Paul's purpose in 4:1–7 is to explain what he means by this language (4:1, *legō de*, "I mean"). He particularly wants to comment on the significance of the term "heir" (*klēronomos*), as 4:1 indicates: "I mean that the heir, as long as he is a child, is no better than a slave, though he is the owner of all the estate." As Paul had given "a human example" in 3:15, so again here he provides an example from human experience that his readers would readily understand, the relationship between the heir who owns the estate and the guardian who oversees the estate until the heir comes of age at the time designated by the father.[51] For Paul, this image applies to the situation of Christians. The child is the person before Christ's coming. The estate is the promise of divine adoption, of sonship, that God made to Abraham and to his offspring (3:26–29). The guardian is the law (4:5; cf. 3:24–25). The coming of age designated by the father coincides with God's sending his son in the fullness of time (4:4; cf. 3:23–25).

With the sending of God's son comes the reality of adoption in Christ through faith, thus fulfilling God's promise to Abraham (4:4–5). And because those in Christ are sons of God, God sends into their hearts the Spirit of sonship—indeed, the Spirit of his son (4:6). By referring to the Spirit in 4:6 Paul comes full circle, reminding us of how he began the entire discussion in 3:2: "Let me ask you only this: Did you receive the Spirit by works of the law, or by hearing with faith?" Whereas in 3:1–5 Paul stresses that the reception of the Spirit comes about by faith, in 4:1–7 he stresses that the sending of the Spirit comes about as a result of receiving adoption as God's sons. Thus faith and divine adoption are coterminous. Both lead to experiencing the power of God's Spirit (3:4; 4:6; cf. 3:14).

Paul concludes his discussion in 4:7: "So through God you are no longer a slave but a son, and if a son then an heir." As heirs, Christians have begun to come into possession of the estate that God promised to Abraham and to his offspring. For Paul, reception of the Spirit provides no small evidence of this reality. Yet it is significant for Paul that Christians are in the midst of falling heir to the promise (3:29), for the possibility still exists that Christians can forfeit their inheritance by renouncing their sonship (3:18; cf. Rom 4:14). Paul's agony with the Galatians is that by submitting to the Teachers regarding circumcision and law observance they are thereby relinquishing their adoption as sons of God (4:8–11, 19–20). By so doing, far from becoming "sons of Abraham" and "offspring of Abraham" as the Teachers suggest, they surrender their inclusion among the offspring of Abraham, which inclusion God had purposed for the Gentiles in the promise to Abraham (3:8).

Two points remain. First, the position of the Teachers seems to have been that the Gentile Christians in Galatia could only qualify as true Christians by first becoming true "offspring" or "children of Abraham," that is, by being circumcised and observing the law. Paul's argument, however, runs in the opposite direction, as 3:29 indicates. The Gentile Christians in Galatia qualify as true "offspring" or "children of Abraham" only by first becoming Christ's through faith. If they meet the condition of being Christ's (*ei de hymeis Christou*), then they are Abraham's offspring (*ara tou Abraam este*). Thus, whereas for the Teachers Abrahamic sonship (understood in terms of law observance) mediates incorporation into Christ, for Paul incorporation into Christ (understood in terms of hearing with faith) mediates Abrahamic sonship.

Second, the entire consideration of Abraham in Galatians 3:1–4:7 is a function of a debate between Paul and the Teachers regarding the bearing of law observance upon Gentile inclusion in God's covenant promises to Abraham. We have seen this explicit focus on Gentile inclusion at the beginning (3:8), middle (3:14), and end (3:28–29) of Paul's discussion. Paul's whole concern revolves around the Gentile question. His discussion of the law, circumcision, and the Jews is purely a function of his dispute with the Teachers regarding the basis of Gentile inclusion.

Galatians 4:21–31

The only reference to Abraham in Galatians outside chapter 3 occurs in 4:22. Here Paul appeals to Abraham in introducing an allegory on the sons of Abraham by Hagar and Sarah (4:21–31).[52] A distinction can be drawn between Paul's use of Abraham in 3:1–4:7 and 4:21–31. In Galatians 3:1–4:7 Paul discussed the figure of Abraham himself, developing Abraham's belief, Abraham's righteousness, God's promise to

Abraham, Abraham's blessing, and Abraham's descendants. In Galatians 4:21–31 Paul considers another of the Abraham stories (Gen. 16:15; 21:2–10) but focuses his attention on Hagar and Sarah and their children as representative figures rather than on Abraham himself. The two passages are similar, however, as in both Paul seeks to demonstrate his position from scripture (3:8; 4:21), and in both Paul addresses the issue of who the sons/offspring/children/heirs of Abraham are (3:7, 16, 29; 4:22, 31).

To begin, is there any evidence that the Teachers in Galatia had used this story of Abraham, Hagar/Sarah, Ishmael/Isaac? As we saw above, they probably had used other Abraham traditions to which Paul responded. Is he responding to them again? Although there is a strong possibility that the Teachers used this story also, it is less probable than with the other Abraham traditions. First, we find no telltale signs that Paul is refuting another interpretation of the story, as we found in 3:1–18. Second, it is not immediately clear how the Teachers would have used the story of Hagar and Sarah to convince the Galatians of the need for law observance, if indeed they used the story to that end. To be sure, Paul employs the story to attack the position of the Teachers, but whether or not he is responding to their use of the story is less evident.[53]

In turning to look at Paul's interpretation of the story, we notice first that he specifically refers to Abraham having two sons (4:22), which reminds us of the discussion in 3:6–14. In 3:7 Paul had concluded that those of faith are the sons of Abraham. But in 4:21–31 the faith of Abraham's two sons is simply not raised. Indeed, the noun "faith" or the verb "to believe" does not occur in this passage. Rather, Paul develops the notion of Abrahamic sonship in a different way here. Sonship is either a function of the flesh (*kata sarka*, 4:23, 29) or of the promise (*di' epaggelias*, 4:23, 28). Sonship according to the flesh is bound in slavery, just as Ishmael was born to Abraham as a result of his own activity in union with the slave Hagar. By contrast, sonship through the promise is characterized by freedom, just as Isaac was born to Abraham as a result of God's activity in keeping his promise to Abraham and the free woman Sarah.

The two women and their sons stand for two covenants (4:24). The slave Hagar represents Mt. Sinai, a clear allusion to the Mosaic law. She corresponds to the present Jerusalem and is in slavery with her children (*tekna*), Paul's way of referring to his contemporaries who advocated law observance for the Gentile Christians (4:25). The free woman Sarah represents the Jerusalem above, probably an allusion to the new age inaugurated in Christ, but continuous with God's covenant promise to Abraham (4:26).[54] Paul's use here of covenant language (*diathēkē*) reminds us of his discussion of "covenant/will" (*diathēkē*) in 3:15–18. Although the reference to Hagar (present Jerusalem) and Sarah (Jerusalem above) is new, they correspond to the two different covenants he alludes to in 3:15–18. The Mosaic law, "which came four hundred and thirty years afterward" (3:17), is now represented by the slave Hagar. The "covenant previously ratified by God" with Abraham (3:17) is now represented by the free woman Sarah.

In 4:28–29 Paul applies this interpretation of Hagar and Sarah to the situation in Galatia. Paul lets the Gentile Christians there know that they are to identify with the children of the promise, with Isaac, because they have received the promise (3:14, 29). As Ishmael "persecuted" Isaac,[55] so now the advocates of law observance, a reference to the Teachers in Galatia, are persecuting those who advocate Gentile inclusion in Christ apart from the law, Paul's reference to himself. Significantly, in 4:29 Paul refers to Ishmael and Isaac no longer by name but by the realities they represent: "he who was born according to the flesh" and "him who was born according to the Spirit." In his description of Ishmael as one born "according to the flesh" (*kata sarka*), Paul aligns the law with the flesh and slavery. Likewise, in his description of Isaac as one born "according to the Spirit" (*kata pneuma*) Paul aligns the promise with the Spirit (4:23, 29) and freedom, and he recalls again the importance of the Galatians' experience of the Spirit (3:2, 5, 14).

By alluding to the Teachers in Galatia as those who preach law observance and persecute Paul, he identifies the Teachers with the circumcision party in Jerusalem, who likewise "persecuted" Paul by seeking to "spy out" Paul's freedom and bring him "into bondage," and so showing themselves to be "false brethren" (2:4–5, 12–13). In addition, Paul's allegorical identification of Hagar with "the present Jerusalem," whose children are enslaved, is probably also a literal reference to the Jewish Christians from the circumcision party in Jerusalem who have opposed Paul.

Having applied the Abraham/Hagar/Sarah story to the situation in Galatia, Paul concludes in 4:30–31. He takes his conclusion from the end of the Genesis story itself, citing Genesis 21:10 (LXX): "'Cast out the slave and her son; for the son of the slave shall not inherit with the son of the free woman.'" On the surface it appears that Paul wants the Galatians to cast out the Teachers who have been "persecuting" them and leading them astray.[56] Although Paul does not explicitly say so, this could be implicitly understood from his choice of scripture citations.[57] The appeal to scripture would give his judgment more authority. As Abraham cast out the slave Hagar and her son Ishmael at the bidding of Sarah, so the Galatians should cast out the Teachers who would enslave them by pressing circumcision and law observance upon them, robbing them of their Abrahamic sonship (3:7; 4:17; 5:10).

Three factors, however, may indicate that Paul does not intend his citation of Genesis 21:10 to be a suggested course of action for the Galatians in regard to the Teachers. First, from Paul's letter it sounds as though the Teachers have established themselves as authoritative leaders in the community. It is unlikely that Paul was in any position of authority to issue such a command to the Galatians. He must first persuade them that their submission to circumcision and law observance is contrary to the gospel.

Second, immediately after citing Genesis 21:10 Paul does not conclude by saying, "Therefore, cast out these would-be sons of Abraham!" Rather, in 4:31 we read: "So, brethren, we are not children of the slave but of the free woman." Paul appears to be focusing not on the first half of the citation, but on the second half regarding who is the true heir of the promises to Abraham, an important theme throughout 3:1–4:31 (3:14, 18, 22, 29; 4:1, 7, 23, 28). For Paul, Genesis 21:10 provides further evidence that the Gentile Christians in Galatia are children of the free woman, children of promise.

And third, in 5:1 Paul explicitly states his concluding exhortation on the basis of the Hagar/Sarah story: "For freedom Christ has set us free; stand fast therefore, and do not submit again to a yoke of slavery." As children of the free woman, the Galatians should act accordingly. By submitting to circumcision and law observance, the Galatians align themselves with the children of the slave.

For Paul, the allegory in 4:21–31 highlights the contrast between the gospel he has preached to the Galatians and the "other gospel" the Teachers have advanced among the Galatians. Paul wants the Galatians to see the implications of the choice they are making to follow the adherents of the law.

Summary and Conclusions

In summary, how does Paul use Abraham in Galatians? Paul appeals to Abraham primarily to ground the inclusion of the

Gentiles in Christ in the promises God made to Abraham. The
law has no bearing on God's promise to Abraham (3:8, 29).
Why does Paul use Abraham in this way? Paul has a twofold
purpose in appealing to Abraham: first, to remind the Galatians of the true basis of their inclusion in Christ; and second,
to counter the arguments of the Teachers in Galatia, who have
also appealed to Abraham.

Finally, what implications may we draw regarding Paul's
view of non-Christian Judaism from his use of Abraham in
Galatians? The most important conclusion is that Paul's fight
in Galatians is not with non-Christian Jews but with a rival
group of Christians whom he views as opponents because of
their understanding of the law's centrality to the gospel. Indeed, Paul's dispute with the Teachers appears to have been
primarily over the necessity of law observance for Gentile
Christians.[58]

This dispute points to the deeper issue of the relationship
between Christ and the law. For Paul, Christ relativizes the
law and puts the law in proper perspective, whereas for the
Teachers in Galatia the law seems to relativize Christ and
place Christ in proper perspective.[59] Again, however, it is crucial to state clearly here that this dispute represents rival Jewish-Christian interpretations of the gospel, Paul's and the
Teachers', and the significance of the gospel for Gentiles.

This observation raises an important question. Is Paul's fight
with the Jewish-Christian Teachers in Galatia indicative of his
fight with non-Christian Judaism? Can his assertions in Galatians be taken as categorical statements that can be abstracted
from their contingent situation and that can be seen as direct
evidence for his view of non-Christian Judaism? Many interpreters have answered yes to these questions, equating Paul's
polemic against the Jewish-Christian Teachers with a polemic
against non-Christian Judaism as well.[60]

In my view, however, Galatians at best provides indirect and
secondary evidence of Paul's controversy with non-Christian
Judaism. First, Paul is addressing in Galatians an *intramural* dispute between rival groups of Christians. He does not address
the issue of non-Christian Judaism.[61] Before one can extrapolate
Paul's views on non-Christian Judaism from Galatians, one must
take account of this internal dispute. We should be wary of
too readily taking Paul's explicit statements about a form of
Jewish Christianity as implicit statements about non-Christian
Judaism.[62]

Second, Paul appears to be on the losing side of the fight
with the Teachers in Galatia, and so he engages in what can

only be termed "overkill," a common feature of polemical argumentation. He thus utilizes arguments that are designed for the specific situation he is addressing, arguments he would not use elsewhere (e.g., Christ as the singular *sperma Abraam* in Gal. 3:16; Paul's apparent denigration of the law in 3:17–19). These arguments do not appear to be generally representative of Paul's positions, and one takes them as categorical statements regarding non-Christian Judaism only at the risk of distorting Paul's larger perspective on this issue as it finds expression elsewhere, especially in Romans.

Still, having issued these qualifications, we see that Paul's statements in Galatians do have ramifications for his view of non-Christian Judaism, especially regarding allegiance to the law. The implications of his statements about the law leave the distinct impression that Paul views non-Christian Judaism as enslaved to the law (2:4; 3:15–16; 4:21–31). Further, Paul denies that the law has any soteriological capacity (3:21). Finally, Paul's statements regarding who are truly children of Abraham imply that Paul does not count non-Christian Jews among Abraham's children (3:7, 29), at least not among Abraham's free children (4:31). In general, a relatively negative, if implicit, picture emerges from Galatians regarding Paul's view of non-Christian Judaism.

In assessing the significance of Paul's use of Abraham in Galatians for Paul's view of non-Christian Judaism, then, we should avoid two extremes. First, we should avoid the extreme of equating Paul's attack on the Jewish-Christian Teachers with an attack on non-Christian Judaism. It is important to remember that Paul's complaint in Galatians is not with Jews and Judaism per se but with Jewish Christians who are preaching what Paul considers a bastardized gospel that exacts law observance at the price of freedom in Christ. To see Paul's use of Abraham in Galatians 3–4 as direct evidence for Paul's position on jews and Judaism, therefore, is to apply mistakenly his polemic against certain Jewish Christians in Galatia to Jews as a group and so to misunderstand both the identity of the Teachers and the substance of his argument.[63]

Thus, although it has become a standard term, it is not quite accurate to call the Teachers in Galatia "Judaizers," as if they were trying to convert the Galatian Christians to non-Christian Judaism.[64] While it seems clear that the Teachers are calling on Gentile Christians to observe the Jewish law, it seems equally clear that they have aligned themselves with the Christian community. They appear to have some stake in confessing Jesus to be the Christ, which would certainly put them at odds with non-Christian Jews. Perhaps a term such as "nomistic Christianity" or "nomistic imperialism" better characterizes their approach. The term "Judaizers" connotes an attempt to persuade Gentiles to become Jews. But Paul does not dispute the Teachers' belief in Jesus as the Christ. Rather, he argues that their nomistic commitment undermines the salience of their belief in Christ.

Second, although Paul's primary argument in Galatians is not with Judaism, we should avoid the opposite extreme of saying that his use of Abraham in Galatians shows that for him the Christ has in effect no direct bearing on the status of the Jews' covenant relationship with God. This position, which has been advocated in particular by Lloyd Gaston and John Gager, does not deal adequately with Paul's statements in Galatians.[65] Paul does undercut the significance of the law in Galatians 3–4, both for Gentile Christians who would keep the law and, by implication, for non-Christian Jews.[66] As we will see below, however, this is not Paul's final statement on non-Christian Judaism.

Abraham in 2 Corinthians 11:22

The only reference to Abraham in Paul's letters outside Galatians and Romans occurs in 2 Corinthians 11:22: "Are they Hebrews? So am I. Are they Israelites? So am I. Are they descendants of Abraham [*sperma Abraam*]? So am I."[67] Here Paul compares himself to Jewish-Christian rivals who have come to Corinth (10:12–18; 11:4–6) and have apparently made inroads among the Christian community he had established there.[68]

Second Corinthians 10–13, often identified with Paul's so-called "painful" or "tearful" letter to the Corinthians (in reference to 2 Cor. 2:2–4), forms the larger context of his appeal to Abraham in 11:22.[69] In this letter to the Corinthians, Paul engages both in polemic against rival apostles there and in apologetic defense of himself against various charges.

The narrower context is 11:1–12:13, the "fool's speech"[70] that Paul makes in comparing himself to the "superlative apostles" (11:5) who have usurped his ministry in Corinth. Paul uses Abraham in the technical term "descendants of Abraham," along with two other terms stressing Jewish heritage, "Hebrews" and "Israelites." In the present context the three terms are almost interchangeable, functioning to identify the Jewish heritage of both Paul's opponents in Corinth and Paul himself.

Paul introduces Abraham because his opponents apparently had boasted of their Jewish stock, including their descent from Abraham (11:21b). This appeal to Abraham raises a question regarding the identity of these rivals and of Paul's use of Abraham in responding to them. Paul says a great deal about his opponents (10:2, 7, 10–11, 12; 11:5–6, 12–15, 18–20, 21b–23a; 12:11). For our purposes, however, it is sufficient to note that they are Jewish Christians.[71] There is no indication that Paul polemicizes against their use of Abraham per se, nor that their appeal to Abraham extends beyond their desire to establish their Jewish heritage. Indeed, Paul concedes their claim to be descendants of Abraham. Rather, Paul's reference to Abraham in 11:22 functions as part of his apologetic defense against the rival apostles' claims of superiority over Paul, which claims the Corinthians appear to have accepted (11:4–6). If the Corinthians want to compare the credentials of the rival apostles to those of Paul, Paul will humor them in this foolish game. Paul points out that his Jewish credentials are just as good as those of his opponents, for he also is a descendant of Abraham.

In many ways Paul's situation in 2 Corinthians 10–13 corresponds on a general level to what we find in Galatians. In both letters Paul addresses an adverse situation in which his authority has been challenged. Both letters indicate that Jewish-Christian outsiders have established themselves as leaders in churches that Paul had founded. Both letters show that the opponents see their Jewish heritage, and thus their Abrahamic descent, as an important feature in their work among Gentile Christian communities. Both letters suggest that Paul's opponents identify their Jewish heritage as a central component of their Christian faith. In both letters Paul refers to his opponents' preaching as a "different gospel" (Gal. 1:7; 2 Cor. 11:4).

In terms of their specific use of Abraham, however, the two letters differ in several important ways. First, whereas the Galatians appear to be concerned with how they are *sperma Abraam* (Gal. 3:29), we find no evidence that the Corinthian Christians have a similar concern. Second, whereas Paul's opponents in Corinth are boasting of their Abrahamic descent, we find no evidence that the Teachers in Galatia are making similar boasts. Third, whereas in 2 Corinthians, Paul stresses his Jewish heritage and descent from Abraham, in Galatians he distances himself from his acknowledged Jewish heritage

(Gal. 1:13–15) and never refers to his descent from Abraham. Fourth, and most important, whereas the Jewish-Christian Teachers in Galatia are pushing the Gentile Christians to be circumcised and to obey the law, there is no evidence that Paul's Jewish-Christian opponents in Corinth are advocating either circumcision or law observance. Indeed, it appears unlikely that the Teachers in Galatia have any connection to the Jewish-Christian teachers in Corinth.

How, then, does Paul use Abraham in 2 Corinthians 11:22? Paul appeals to Abraham to establish that his Jewish credentials are just as good as those of his opponents. Why does Paul use Abraham in this way? Paul wants to show, first, that such boasting is foolish (11:21, 30) and, second, that being a servant of Christ in weakness is more important than being a Hebrew, an Israelite, or a descendant of Abraham (11:23, 30). In his Jewish credentials Paul is equal to his opponents. In what really counts, however, in his service of Christ, Paul is better than his opponents and he can demonstrate this fact by reminding the Corinthians of the sufferings he has endured as a servant of Christ (11:23–29).

What does Paul's use of Abraham in 2 Corinthians 11:22 tell us about Paul's controversy with non-Christian Judaism? As was the case with Galatians, so Paul's appeal to Abraham in 2 Corinthians tells us nothing directly about Paul's controversy with non-Christian Judaism. Similarly, the methodological restrictions hampering any abstraction of Paul's polemical statements from the contingent situation that we found in Galatians apply also to his apologetic statements in 2 Corinthians. An implication one can draw from this passage, however, is that, for Paul, being a descendant of Abraham (*sperma Abraam*) in and of itself counts for little or nothing. What matters is the extent to which one is a servant of Christ. Thus from Paul's use of Abraham in 2 Corinthians we find corroborating evidence that mere physical descent from Abraham does not establish any special status before God.

Abraham in Romans

Just as paying attention to Paul's purpose in writing Galatians and 2 Corinthians helps us understand the larger contexts behind his references to Abraham, so a brief look at Paul's purposes in writing to the Romans will assist us in situating his use of Abraham in the letter. We can identify two basic reasons behind the writing of this letter.[72] First, since Paul has never visited the Roman congregation and is now making plans to do so, he is concerned to tell the Romans something about his situation. He accomplishes this task by detailing his travel plans (Rom. 1:10; 15:22–29), by expressing his hopes for the upcoming visit (1:11–15), by communicating his understanding of his own mission (1:1, 13–15; 11:1), and by relating his conception of the gospel message (1:16–17; 3:21–31; 10:9). In these ways Paul hopes both to prepare the Roman church for his arrival and to dispel any disturbing rumors about him they may have heard.[73]

Second, Paul appears to know something of the situation in the Roman church, in spite of the fact that he has never been there, and so he addresses the tensions of which he is aware.[74] In particular, he speaks to strains between Jewish and Gentile Christians in the community, especially in Romans 14 and 15. He also offers an extended consideration of the relationship between non-Christian Jews and Christians (Romans 9–11), expressing his own understanding of the matter and offering constructive advice, especially to the Gentile Christians in the congregation regarding their newfound status as part of God's Israel (cf. 11:13, 25).

Both reasons cause Paul to reflect at some length upon his understanding of what God has done in Christ, upon the significance of Gentile inclusion for God's purposes with the Jews, and upon the identity of Israel. Because all of these considerations revolve around the relationship between Jews and Gentiles before God and with one another, an examination of the figure of Abraham functions as an effective way for Paul to coordinate his understanding of the status of Jewish and Gentile relationships in the light of the Christ event. This is so because Abraham was, of course, commonly understood to be the father of the Jewish faith, since he is the bearer of God's promises and since he was the first to be circumcised. Abraham provided a meaningful focus for Jewish identity. Yet Abraham was also widely considered to be the first convert to Judaism and so could likewise provide a significant focus for the identity of Gentiles who were being incorporated into this Jewish people.[75] In these ways Paul found in Abraham a figure well suited both to express his own understanding of the interrelationships among Jews and Gentiles in the light of Christ and to address the situation in the church at Rome.

Romans 4

As with Galatians 3–4, it is appropriate to make some observations regarding the literary context and structure of

Romans 4 before we turn directly to Paul's treatment of Abraham. In broad literary terms, Romans 4:1–25 serves to close off the first major section of the letter, 1:16–4:25. In Romans 4, Paul recapitulates the theme he had introduced in 1:16–17 regarding the righteousness of God revealed through faith. This same righteousness can be seen, Paul now concludes, in God's reckoning Abraham righteous on account of faith. Paul thus uses the story of Abraham to cap his argument with an appeal to scripture, a typical strategy for Paul. As 1:16–17 is confirmed by his appeal to Habakkuk 2:4, and 1:18–3:9 finds substantiation in an extended citation of scripture (3:10–18), so again Paul establishes 3:21–31 through a lengthy exploration of the story of Abraham in 4:1–25. Paul does not explicitly cite scripture again until the end of his argument in Romans 5–8 (8:36).

With 5:1 Paul moves on to show the christological foundation of justification. Even so, 4:1–25 also serves as a backdrop for this discussion. For example, the "therefore" (*oun*) of 5:1 looks directly back to 4:1–25 as having laid a secure foundation regarding justification by faith. And the motif that God justifies the ungodly (*asebē*), applied to Abraham in 4:5, is sounded again in 5:6, the only other occurrence of *asebē* ("ungodly") in Paul's writings.

For the immediate literary context of 4:1–25 we must look to 3:21–31, as 4:1–25 provides a scriptural verification for Paul's argument there. Paul begins 4:1 with a question, "What therefore shall we say?" (*ti oun eroumen*), that refers back to the whole discussion in 3:21–31 and especially 3:27–31. In 3:27–31 Paul has concluded that God is the God of both Jew and Gentile, since neither circumcision (the crux of "works of the law") nor uncircumcision has any bearing on one's status before God in terms of "righteousness." Nobody has cause to boast before God on account of works of the law, and nobody can claim righteousness on that basis. Rather, God reckons people righteous by faith. Having made his argument, Paul now appeals to the example of Abraham as a case in point, a specific instance of his claims in 3:21–31.

There are also several motifs in common between 3:21–31 and 4:1–25, for example, the law, righteousness, grace, boasting, faith, and circumcision/uncircumcision. In Romans 4 these motifs are examined by Paul in the light of Abraham. Although these terms connect 4:1–25 with 3:21–31, Paul drops explicit reference to some subjects and picks up others not developed in 3:21–31. For example, it is striking that whereas Christ is central to 3:21–31, we find no explicit mention of Christ in 4:1–25 apart from 4:24–25. By contrast, whereas the themes of "reckoning" (*logizomai*) and "promise" (*epaggelia*) play an important role in 4:1–25, they are almost entirely absent from 3:21–31, apart from *logizomai* in 3:28, which anticipates 4:3. Further, Paul moves from talking about *dikaiosynē theou* ("righteousness of God") in 3:21–31 to *dikaiosynē Abraam* ("righteousness of Abraham") in 4:1–25. With this shift Paul shows how Abraham is an example of the way in which God's righteousness works in the world. Thus, although Romans 4:1–25 is closely bound by the categories raised in 3:21–31, still Paul points these same categories in a somewhat different direction in 4:1–25 for the purpose of filling out his argument.

The literary style of Romans 4 combines elements of diatribe and scriptural exegesis. The diatribe style can be seen in the largely rhetorical question format of 4:1, 3, 9, 10. As for the exegetical style, there is broad consensus that Paul uses the rabbinical method of *gezerah šawah*, the second of Hillel's seven Middoth.[76] This is the principle of understanding one passage in the light of another in which the same word occurs. In this instance, Paul uses Psalm 31:1–2a (LXX) to interpret Genesis 15:6 because the word *logizomai* ("to reckon") occurs in both places. Paul equates *logizomai* with the forgiveness of transgressions and the covering over of sins (Rom. 4:7). Thus, being reckoned righteous means that God does not count sins.

The internal structure of 4:1–25 can be broken into four main sections: 4:1–8; 4:9–12; 4:13–22; and 4:23–25.[77] A brief sketch of the literary flow of each section will help set the stage for addressing Paul's use of Abraham per se.

In 4:1–8 Paul seeks to determine the basis on which God reckoned Abraham righteous. This is the question he asks in 4:1. The question is filled out in 4:2 by a conditional statement that clarifies Paul's understanding of the issue at hand— whether or not Abraham was justified by works. If he was justified by works, then he would have cause to boast (recalling 3:27), but not before God. In 4:3 Paul restates his opening question by pointing the reader specifically to the scriptural passage from Genesis 15:6, which he cites nearly verbatim. For Paul, this passage serves as a warrant for his understanding that God reckoned Abraham righteous by faith: "For what does the scripture say? 'Abraham believed God, and it was reckoned to him as righteousness.'"

With 4:4–5 Paul offers his interpretation of Genesis 15:6. He draws a contrast between two pairs of terms: "one who works" with "one who does not work but believes," and "due" (*opheilēma*) with "gift" (*charis*). Paul implies that Abraham was reckoned righteous as God's gift to one who did not work but believed. In 4:6–8 Paul cites a passage verbatim from Psalm 31:1–2a (LXX) because it also contains the catchword *logizomai* ("to reckon") found in Genesis 15:6. "Blessed are those whose iniquities are forgiven, and whose sins are covered; blessed is the man against whom the Lord will not reckon his sin" (*ou mē logisētai*). For Paul, this citation provides further proof from scripture for his argument that "God reckons righteousness apart from works" (4:6; cf. 4:2).

In 4:9–12 Paul picks up on David's "blessing" (*makarismos*) from Psalm 31 and uses it to sharpen the question of "works of the law" (*erga nomou*) around the issue of "circumcision" and "uncircumcision" (*peritomē* and *akrobystia*). Thus in 4:9–10 Paul restates the general question raised in 4:1 and 4:3 in terms of the specific issue of circumcision. Paul concludes that righteousness was reckoned to Abraham while he was still uncircumcised (4:10). This conclusion, in turn, begs the implicit question to which 4:11 is addressed: Then why did Abraham receive circumcision? He received it as a "sign" (*sēmeion*), a "seal" (*sphragis*) of his righteousness prior to circumcision. Why did he receive this sign and seal? Paul answers this question with a twofold purpose statement in 4:11–12: "The purpose was to make him the father of all who believe without being circumcised and who thus have righteousness reckoned to them, and likewise the father of the circumcised who are not merely circumcised but also follow the example of the faith which our father Abraham had before he was circumcised." The purpose of circumcision was that Abraham might be the one "forefather" for both the Jews and the Gentiles.

In 4:13–22 Paul shifts his focus slightly. Whereas the central question throughout 4:1–12 was the basis on which God reckoned Abraham righteous, in 4:13–22 Paul considers the "promise to Abraham" (4:13). The promise holds good not "through the law" (*dia nomou*) but "through the righteousness of faith" (*dia dikaiosynēs pisteōs*, 4:13). Paul spells out the consequences of the former position in 4:14–15. If the promise comes through the law, then faith and the promise would be null and void. In 4:16a, by means of another twofold purpose clause (cf. 4:11–12), Paul reaffirms 4:13, elaborating the reason for the grounding of the promise in faith: "That is why it depends on faith, in order that the promise may rest on grace (*kata charin*) and be guaranteed to all his descendants (*panti tō spermati*)." With 4:16b Paul picks up on the notion that the promise is to "all his descendants," taking this term as a reference to both "adherents of the law" (*tō ek tou nomou*) and "those who share the faith of Abraham" (*tō ek pisteōs Abraam*), another way of speaking about both Jews and Gentiles (cf. 4:11–12). In 4:17 Paul then grounds Abraham's fatherhood of both Jews and Gentiles with a verbatim citation from Genesis 17:5: "As it is written, 'I have made you the father of many nations.'" In 4:18 Paul highlights Abraham's faith that he would indeed be the father of many nations, referring to God's promise with a verbatim citation from Genesis 15:5: "In hope he believed against hope, that he should become the father of many nations; as he had been told, 'So shall your descendants be.'" And in 4:19–21 Paul emphasizes the strength of Abraham's faith in God's promise despite his age and Sarah's barrenness. Paul ends this section in 4:22 by returning to the initial theme of the chapter, the basis on which God reckoned Abraham righteous: "That is why his faith was 'reckoned to him as righteousness.'"

In 4:23–25 Paul concludes the chapter by applying 4:1–22 to the recipients of the letter, since the story of God reckoning Abraham righteous by faith was "written not for his sake alone, but for ours also" (4:23–24). As Abraham was reckoned righteous on account of his faith, so those who have faith "in him that raised from the dead Jesus our Lord" will be reckoned righteous for their faith (4:24). Finally, 4:25 serves to bring the whole chapter to a close with a traditional christological formula, referring to Christ "who was put to death for our trespasses and raised for our justification."

On the whole, Romans 4 is tightly constructed. The passage is so tightly put together, in fact, that Paul does not always fully complete his thoughts. What Ernst Käsemann says in regard to 4:5 holds true for the passage as a whole, that Paul does not always have "enough patience to round off his metaphors and comparisons well."[78]

One final issue remains regarding the literary dimensions of Romans 4. Whom is Paul addressing here? The options would include Jewish Christians, Gentile Christians, non-Christian Jews, and non-Christian Gentiles. In my view, Paul has primarily a Jewish-Christian audience in mind throughout Romans 4, although clearly Paul wants the Gentile component of the church at Rome to overhear this discussion.[79]

Three pieces of evidence indicate that Paul is addressing Jewish Christians in Romans 4. First, in 4:1 Paul asks about Abraham "*our* forefather according to the flesh." The first person plural "our" can only refer to those of Jewish descent, since Paul stresses descent here "according to the flesh" (*kata sarka*). Second, the discussion about circumcision in 4:9–12 makes the most sense if Paul is addressing those who would advocate circumcision, namely, those of Jewish descent. Third, the specifically Christian character of the audience can be seen from 4:24, where Paul applies the story of Abraham to "us who believe in him that raised from the dead Jesus our Lord."

Still, 4:16 indicates that Paul also has the Gentile Christians in mind, even if they are not his primary audience in Romans 4. In 4:16 Paul refers to the adherents of the law who have faith (i.e., Jewish Christians; cf. 4:12) and then to those who "share the faith of Abraham," apparently intended as a contrast to "the adherents of the law." This latter reference to those who are not adherents of the law and yet share the faith of Abraham can only be an allusion to Gentile Christians. Having referred, then, to both Jewish and Gentile Christians, Paul says that Abraham "is the father of us all" (4:16). The "us" here must be an inclusive reference to both groups of Christians in Rome.[80]

Why does Paul address Jewish Christians in this passage? As we will see in more detail below, Paul wants to show them that Jewish and Gentile Christians stand on equal footing before an impartial God.[81] Both find the basis for their relationship to God in faith, not in circumcision or, by extension, in law observance. This situation has always been the case, according to Paul. Abraham serves Paul particularly well in providing scriptural support for his claims.

Bearing in mind the literary context, the structure, and the audience of Romans 4, we can now look more closely at Paul's use of Abraham. Our literary analysis points to three elements that stand out in Paul's treatment of Abraham in Romans 4: (1) Paul stresses that Abraham is the father of all who believe, of Jew and of Gentile alike (4:11); (2) Paul identifies the content of the promise to Abraham as the inclusion of the Gentiles within the family of Abraham (4:17, 18, 20); and (3) Paul sees Abraham as an example of redemptive faith to be followed by those who believe (4:19–25).

Abraham the Father of Jew and of Gentile Alike

First, Paul hammers home the thesis that Abraham is the father of all who believe in God, of Jew and of Gentile alike (4:11, 16). In what sense, however, is Abraham their father? How is his paternity the same for Jews and for Gentiles? The answer to this question can be found in the question Paul himself asks in 4:1: "What then shall we say? Have we found Abraham to be our forefather according to the flesh?"[82] Paul develops an implicit contrast here between Abraham as father according to the flesh and Abraham as father according to faith. He is the common father of Jew and of Gentile alike according to faith alone.

Paul already anticipates this answer in 3:21–31, the section immediately preceding chapter 4 that sets the context for the material to follow.[83] In this section Paul has demonstrated that all of humanity, both Jews and Gentiles, share the same dilemma. Indeed, "there is no distinction; since all have sinned and fall short of the glory of God, they are justified by his grace as a gift" (3:22–24). Similarly, there is no distinction between the basis on which Jews and Gentiles participate in God's grace, namely, faith. "If indeed God, who will justify the circumcised on the basis of faith, is one, he will also justify the uncircumcised through faith" (3:30). Just as God is the God not only of the Jews but also of the Gentiles, so Abraham is the father in faith not only of the Jews but also of the Gentiles.

But must not the Gentiles be circumcised to be true children of Abraham? This is the question Paul anticipates in 3:31a: "Do we then overthrow the law by this faith?" Paul's answer is clear: "By no means! On the contrary, we uphold the law" (3:31b). Paul's task in Romans 4, then, is to demonstrate exactly how he upholds the law in the assertion that believing Gentiles share Abraham as their forefather, along with the Jews, apart from circumcision.[84] Paul tackles this challenge: (*a*) by addressing the relation between Abraham's faith and his circumcision and (*b*) by developing the notion of three different, but related, types of descendants from Abraham.

Abraham and circumcision. In 4:9–12, and only here in his writings, Paul speaks of the connection between Abraham's faith and Abraham's circumcision. The key question for Paul is 4:9b–10: "We say that faith was reckoned to Abraham as righteousness. How then was it reckoned to him? Was it before (*en akrobystia*) or after (*en peritomē*) he had been circumcised? It was not after, but before he was circumcised."

For Paul, the crucial factor lies in the temporal relation between Abraham's faith and his circumcision.[85] The pronouncement of Genesis 15:6 takes place before the circumcision in Genesis 17. Paul refuses to allow Abraham's

circumcision any significance apart from Abraham's prior faith
in God's promise. Abraham's circumcision was just a sign or a
seal of the faith he had before being circumcised (Rom. 4:11).
His circumcision functioned as a sign in that it was an outward
indication of an inward reality. It functioned as a seal in that it
confirmed the fact that he had already been justified by his
faith.[86] Circumcision results from faith, not faith from
circumcision.[87]

The connection between faith and circumcision in the case
of Abraham has such importance for Paul because Abraham
alone can demonstrate the priority of faith to circumcision or
to any work of the law (4:10).[88] The purpose of Abraham's
faith preceding his circumcision was so that Abraham's status
as father in faith would be the primary focus of his paternity,
and attention to his status as father in the flesh, physical descent, would be secondary at best (4:11–12).[89] To be sure,
there is some benefit and advantage to this secondary status
(3:1–2), but Paul is most concerned that the believer realize
the primary significance of faith.[90]

Thus, for Paul, the uncircumcision of the Gentiles in no way
hinders them from being true descendants of Abraham, and
the circumcision of the Jews in no way automatically makes
them true descendants of Abraham (4:11–12). Since Abraham
believed before as well as after his circumcision, he can be the
father of all who believe, both without circumcision (4:11)
and with circumcision (4:12; 3:30).

Descendants of Abraham.   Having addressed the connection between Abraham's faith and his circumcision, Paul then
develops the notion of three different kinds of descendants
from Abraham. They are (1) those who are descendants both
according to flesh and according to faith; (2) those who are
descendants according to faith alone; and (3) those who are descendants according to flesh alone.

1. *Descendants according to flesh and faith.* Paul speaks positively about those who descend from Abraham both according to the flesh and according to faith. This group consists of
Jewish Christians, whom Paul considers blessed (4:9). Paul
locates himself here (11:1). Their circumcision functions as it
was intended, as a sign or seal of the righteousness they have
in faith. These individuals are not merely circumcised but also
follow the example of faith which Abraham had even before
his circumcision (4:12).

In principle, faithful Jews before the coming of Christ
would also be included here, along with Abraham. This princi-

ple raises the question of whether or not Paul would allow for the possibility that Jews after the coming of Christ could be faithful like Abraham without believing in Christ. Although Paul does not contemplate this important question in Romans 4, he does address it in Romans 9–11, which we will consider below.

2. *Descendants according to faith alone.* Paul also speaks positively regarding those who descend from Abraham in faith alone, the Gentiles who believe apart from circumcision, the *akrobystia* (4:11, 16; 9:8). They too share in the blessing of having their sins forgiven (4:9). Their faith in Christ resembles the faith that Abraham had in God (4:19–25). Because their faith mirrors the faith of Abraham, they are counted as true descendants of Abraham.

3. *Descendants according to flesh alone.* Finally, Paul refers to those who descend from Abraham according to the flesh alone, the merely circumcised who can claim physical descent from Abraham but not the descent in faith that counts (4:12, 13, 14, 16; 9:7). These individuals emphasize physical descent and count works of the law, including circumcision, as some kind of guarantee of receiving the promises God made to Abraham. They include the adherents of the law who expect a reward as their due on account of their works, and not as God's gracious gift (4:4; cf. 10:3). They have cause to boast, but not before God (cf. 4:2). Paul appears to characterize them as confident of their own abilities to secure the promise, failing to see the promise as that which can be received only as God's gift. The guarantee of the promise comes from God's grace (4:16), which can be received only in faith. From Paul's perspective, those who have approached God in this manner have never been true descendants of Abraham; they have never been true Jews. This situation is nothing new but has always been the case.

God's Promise to Abraham of Gentile Inclusion

The second element that is central to Paul's use of Abraham in Romans 4 has to do with Paul's view of the content of God's promise to Abraham. Paul identifies this content as the inclusion of the Gentiles within the group of true descendants of Abraham (4:17–18, 20–21).[91] In 4:17 Paul cites Genesis 17:5: "'I have made you the father of many nations.'" This promise, explicitly identified as such in 4:20–21, was the object of Abraham's hope, as Paul makes clear from 4:18, this time citing Genesis 15:5. As we saw in Galatians 3:8, so again here

Paul specifies that not only do the Gentiles share in the promise to Abraham but their inclusion also in part fulfills the promise. The Gentiles are not only the recipients of the promise but also the subject of the promise. Having been incorporated into Abraham's true descendants, the believing Gentiles will now also share with believing Jews in another dimension of God's promise to Abraham, a dimension that Paul spells out in 4:13: "That they should inherit the world."

In contrast to Galatians 3:16, however, Paul does not in Romans 4:18–21 equate the promise of "descendants of Abraham" (*sperma Abraam*) with the advent of Christ. Rather, in 4:18 Paul explicitly identifies the descendants of Abraham from Genesis 15:5 with the advent of the many Gentiles whose father Abraham will become (*patera pollōn ethnōn*).[92] Indeed, the christological dimension of Gentile inclusion comes to expression only in 4:23–25. And even here, Paul emphasizes faith in *God's* action in raising Jesus from the dead, a theocentric focus. This observation is not meant to imply that Paul thinks one can believe in the God who raised Jesus from the dead without believing in Jesus. However, it does raise questions about the character of Abraham's faith, which Paul describes in 4:16–21 and to which we now turn.

The Example of Abraham's Redemptive Faith

The third element that characterizes Paul's use of Abraham in Romans 4 has to do with the way in which Abraham provides an example of faith for later generations of Christians. How is Abraham's faith similar to the faith that Paul advocates for Christians, Jewish and Gentile alike? According to Paul, Abraham believed in the God who gives life to the dead and calls into existence the things that do not exist (4:17). He believed that God was able to do what God had promised (4:20–21). Similarly, Christians believe in the God who raised Jesus from the dead (4:23). As Abraham believed God's promise and was reckoned righteous, so Christians believe God's promise that they will be reckoned righteous for their faith in God's action in Christ (4:24). In short, we find three similarities between Abraham's faith and Christian faith: (1) the theocentric focus of belief; (2) the emphasis on God's power to make the dead alive; and (3) the trusting attitude of the believer, who in hope believes against hope (4:18).

Interestingly enough, however, in developing the similarities between the faith of Abraham and the faith of Christians, the object of God's enlivening action differs for Abraham and for Christians. Abraham did not believe in the resurrection of Jesus.[93] Rather, Abraham believed that God would enliven *his own* dead body to give birth to an heir (4:17–19). In contrast, Christians believe God has raised *Jesus* from the dead (4:24–25). Despite this difference in the content of their belief, however, both Abraham and Christians are reckoned righteous. We can conclude, then, that it suffices for Paul that the *structure* of their faith is similar, namely, that they both believe in the God who makes the dead alive.[94] This conclusion is not meant to imply that after the advent of Christ, belief in the God who makes the dead alive can be separated from the one whom God has raised from the dead. It is meant, however, to stress the limits of Paul's comparison of the faith of Abraham to the faith of Christians.

This comparison raises a question for us, even if it did not for Paul. If Abraham was reckoned righteous and was forgiven his sins on account of his faith (4:5–8), how does Christ add anything to the substance of faith for Paul? If true faith—that is, rectifying faith—has always been a possibility after the example of Abraham, then why was the Christ necessary?

This is not, however, the way Paul himself puts the question. Rather, he asks a related but very different question: Why then the law? Paul assumes the solution of the Christ and examines the nature of the problem from the perspective of the need for the Christ. Paul never considers the possibility that the rectifying faith of Abraham could make sense apart from how it illumines faith in Christ. Paul notices Christian faith as a type of Abrahamic faith only because of his belief in Christ. If Christ were not necessary, then God would not have sent him to die and to be raised.[95] Indeed, Paul seems to skip from Abraham to Christ, with the need for Christ being found in the way the power of sin has co-opted the law (Rom. 7:11–13) and in Christ's becoming the occasion for Gentile inclusion apart from the law.

Thus, just as Paul stressed in Galatians 3 that Abraham's faith was essentially independent of the law, so Paul stresses in Romans 4 that Abraham's faith was essentially independent of circumcision, which for Paul functions as an expression of the law. This observation brings us back full circle to Paul's starting point in discussing the faith of Abraham. Long before the giving of the law and before his circumcision, Abraham's faith became the ground of his relationship to God. Paul sees Abraham's faith as scriptural evidence supporting his argument that God is the God of both Jew and Gentile through faith in Christ (3:29–30).

Paul's concern to undergird the legitimacy of Gentile faith in Christ on its own terms apart from the law, while upholding the law, thus forms the heart of his appeal to Abraham in Romans 4. The Gentiles are reckoned righteous in faith apart from circumcision because Abraham was reckoned righteous in faith apart from circumcision (4:10). The Gentiles are true children of Abraham because faith is the determining factor in identifying Abraham's true children (3:30; 4:11–12). The Gentiles share in the promise God made to Abraham because they were in part the subject of God's promise to Abraham (4:17–21). The Gentiles' belief in the God who raised Jesus from the dead is legitimate because Abraham also believed in the God who makes the dead alive (4:17–25). Because Abraham's faith preceded his circumcision and so the law, because Christian faith parallels Abraham's faith in several regards, and because Abraham's faith in God's promise is central to Paul's understanding of Gentile inclusion, Paul finds the story of Abraham singularly helpful in expressing his own understanding of Christian faith and in addressing problems he is aware of between Jewish and Gentile Christians in Rome.

Abraham in Romans 9–11

Paul refers explicitly to Abraham only twice in Romans 9–11 (9:7; 11:1), compared to seven references in Romans 4, although he also alludes twice to Abraham (9:5; 11:28). Despite the relatively few references to Abraham in this section, Paul assigns Abraham a prominent role, as we shall see.

The place of Romans 9–11 within the larger context of Romans has long been disputed.[96] There has been increasing agreement, however, that Romans 9–11 forms the climax of Romans rather than being an appendix or an excursus.[97] Although a full treatment of Romans 9–11 lies beyond the scope of our present investigation, several observations regarding the literary structure of the passage and Paul's intended audience in this section are pertinent to an understanding of his use of Abraham.

Abraham occupies an important place within the larger structure of Romans 9–11.[98] In 9:1–5 Paul introduces the topic of chapters 9–11, the refusal on the part of most Jews to believe the gospel. This refusal has caused Paul great anguish and sorrow (9:2). He is especially troubled because as Israelites they have been well prepared for receiving the gospel, since "to them belong the sonship, the glory, the covenants, the giving of the law, the worship, and the promises; to them belong the patriarchs (*pateres*), and of their race, according to the flesh, is the Christ" (9:4–5). Even in this introductory section Paul mentions four factors central to Jewish identity that allude to Abraham. These include sonship, the covenants, the promises, and the patriarchs. Already in Romans 4 Paul has discussed Abrahamic sonship, showing that those who share a faith like Abraham are Abraham's true descendants. Similarly, Paul has spoken about the covenant promises of God to Abraham throughout 4:13–25. The reference to the patriarchs in 9:5 further recalls the figure of Abraham.[99]

Immediately after his introductory remarks in 9:1–5 Paul launches into a consideration of Abraham in 9:6–9 to demonstrate his claim in 9:6 that the word of God has not failed, despite the unbelief of many Jews. In this section Paul refers once again to Abrahamic sonship ("children of Abraham," 9:7) and the covenant promises with Abraham (9:8–9). After a passing reference to Abraham in 11:1, Paul again alludes to Abraham in 11:28b, "as regards election they [the Jews] are beloved for the sake of their forefathers" (*dia tous pateras*).

Paul's references and allusions to Abraham in 9:1–5, 6–9, and 11:28 are particularly significant when one is considering the literary structure of Romans 9–11, because Paul uses the figure of Abraham at the beginning and at the end of this whole section. The figure of Abraham thus frames the entire discussion, even though Paul only alludes to him in 11:28.

At the beginning of the discussion Paul shows that the true descendants of Abraham include those who are the children of the promise. The children of the promise in turn are those whom God has called and chosen apart from works (9:11). Later on in chapter 9, then, we learn that God has also called and chosen from among the Gentiles (9:24–26). Thus the Gentiles appear to be children of the promise and so are true descendants of Abraham. Paul's appeal to Abraham at the beginning of Romans 9–11 sets up his discussion of Gentile inclusion through faith (9:30). At the end of the discussion in 11:25–32 Paul shows that even those Jews who do not believe the gospel are nevertheless still called and chosen by God "for the sake of their forefathers," that is, on account of the patriarchs and God's covenant promises with Abraham (11:27–28).[100] "For the gifts and the call of God are irrevocable" (11:29). Paul's appeal to Abraham at the end of Romans 9–11 thus confirms his discussion of non-Christian Jewish inclusion in the ultimate mercy of God (11:30–32).

Paul has assigned Abraham a significant role in the structure of Romans 9–11, then, by positioning him at the beginning and at the end of his discussion. In this way Paul seeks to establish his argument regarding Gentile and Jewish inclusion within God's salvific purposes. Accordingly, Paul hopes to answer the theological problem of Israel's unbelief, maintaining both the centrality of faith in Christ and the integrity of God's covenant faithfulness.[101]

There are several clues as to the audience that Paul has in mind in Romans 9–11. First, in 9:23–24 Paul speaks of the "vessels of mercy," which God has prepared beforehand for glory, "even us whom he has called, not from the Jews only but also from the Gentiles." And in 9:25–26 Paul cites passages from Hosea 2:25 (LXX; MT, 2:23) and 2:1 (LXX; MT, 1:10) as scriptural support for the inclusion of the Gentiles as "sons of the living God." (While the citation from Hosea 2:25 does not match the LXX exactly, Paul's citation of Hosea 2:1 does match the LXX version exactly.) The "us" in 9:24, then, appears to refer particularly to Gentile Christians, with whom Paul identifies.

Second, and more explicitly, in 11:13 Paul says flatly, "Now I am speaking to you Gentiles." This specific address to the Gentiles continues through the rest of Romans 11, as Paul exhorts the Gentile Christians directly, repeatedly admonishing them as "you" in 11:17, 18, 19, 20, 21, 22, 24, 25, 28, 30, and 31. Further, in the preceding section of 9:1–11:12, nothing suggests that Paul does not have the Gentile Christians particularly in mind there also, since 9:1–11:10 sets the stage for Paul to resolve in 11:11–32 the problem of Jewish unbelief in the face of Gentile belief.

Thus, whereas Romans 4 was addressed primarily to Jewish Christians, now in chapters 9–11 Paul speaks especially to Gentile Christians.[102] In chapter 4, speaking in particular to the Jewish component of the Roman church, he had appealed to God's promises to Abraham to establish Gentile inclusion in faith apart from works of the law. In this way he addressed the concerns of Jewish Christians who may have been uneasy with Gentile inclusion apart from law observance. Now, in chapters 9–11, speaking in particular to the Gentile component of the Roman church (most explicitly in chapter 11), Paul invokes God's covenant faithfulness to the promises to Abraham regarding the election of even non-Christian Jews (11:28). In this way he addresses Gentile Christians who may have been tempted to see their Christian faith as a reason to boast over Judaism (11:17–21) and to view Judaism as having been discarded by God. Such a response would easily have led, and in fact did lead, to Gentile Christians' viewing their faith as divorced from or incongruous with Judaism rather than to viewing their faith as the realization of God's long-standing promises that were central to Jewish faith, as Paul understood it.

In the light of the above comments on the literary structure and audience of Romans 9–11, we can probe more deeply into the substance of Paul's use of Abraham in this section. In the course of the discussion we will pay particular attention to 9:6–9; 11:1–6; and 11:25–32, the passages in which Paul refers to or alludes to Abraham.

Despite the anguish Paul expresses in 9:1–5, he begins his discussion in 9:6 with a positive affirmation in the face of what appears on the surface to be a negative outcome, the Jewish rejection of the gospel. "But it is not as though the word of God had failed. For not all who are descended from Israel (*hoi ex Israēl*) belong to Israel." This thesis statement sets up a distinction Paul draws in 9:6–9 between two types of descendants from Abraham, those who are merely physical descendants according to the flesh and those who are descendants according to the promise. In making this distinction, Paul contrasts "descendants of Abraham" (*sperma Abraam*) with "children of Abraham" (9:7, *tekna Abraam*),[103] although Paul mixes his language in distinguishing between the terms.

Paul's point is simply that not all those who are physically descended from Abraham (*sperma Abraam, tekna tēs sarkos*) are reckoned by God as true descendants of Abraham (*tekna [Abraam], tekna tou theou, tekna tēs epaggelias, logizetai eis sperma*). In 9:7–8 Paul shows that those who are children of the promise are reckoned (*logizetai*) as true descendants, just as those who are reckoned by faith are true descendants (4:13–16).[104] This observation has significance for Paul because it demonstrates that God has been true to God's word, namely, to the promise (9:8–9). Paul cites Genesis 18:10, 14 in Romans 9:9 to show that God had kept the promise. God had promised to return to Sarah and give her a son, and so it had happened. Thus God's word has not failed but still stands.

But not all have responded to God's word, to the fruition of God's promise in the gospel (10:14–17). In particular, not all of Abraham's descendants according to the flesh, the Jews, have accepted the words of the gospel that have been preached to them. Indeed, most have rejected it, while the Gentiles have accepted it (10:18–21). This is the basic dilemma Paul addresses.

Does Jewish rejection of the gospel mean that God has rejected them? Paul asks and responds to this question in 11:1, where he next refers to Abraham: "I ask, then, has God rejected his people? By no means! I myself am an Israelite, a descendant of Abraham, a member of the tribe of Benjamin."[105] In referring to himself as a descendant of Abraham (*sperma Abraam*), Paul numbers himself among the children of the promise (9:7–8), which for him implicitly means having accepted the gospel of Christ through faith (10:17). Paul sees his own case as further proof that God has not rejected his people. Just as during the time of Elijah there was a faithful remnant, so now in Paul's time there is a remnant chosen by God's grace, namely, a group of Jews who have accepted the gospel of Christ (11:2–5).

But why do so many of Paul's fellow Jews not believe? Paul attributes their unbelief to their misguided notions regarding how righteousness comes about. They do not believe, because they seek righteousness through works of the law rather than through faith (9:32). In other words, they do not believe, because they never believed. Their failure to believe results from their failure to see that righteousness comes only from God's action, not from one's own actions (9:11; 10:3).

But for Paul this is not the end of the matter. Rather, he goes on to attribute the unbelief of some Jews to the activity of God, who has hardened part of Israel, referring to those Jews who do not now believe in Christ but will eventually be among those whom God saves (11:8–9, 25–26). Why has God hardened a portion of the Jews? God has done this so that their disobedience, their disbelief (11:23), would bring about salvation to the Gentiles (11:11–12, 30–31), although Paul does not state explicitly how this dynamic works.

How long will they remain hardened? They will continue in their disobedience until the full number of Gentiles come in (11:25), although Paul never specifies exactly what this "full number" means.[106] The belief of the Gentiles, in turn, will bring about jealousy among some of the hardened Jews, which in turn will bring about their belief in Christ (11:13–15, 23–24, 30–32). Thus Paul leaves us with the paradox that the preaching of Christ to the Jews has brought about the belief of the Gentiles; the preaching of Christ to the Gentiles, in turn, will bring about the belief of the Jews (9:30–31; 10:18–21; 11:13–14, 30–31).

The point here is that Paul thinks that there are contemporary Jews who do not believe in Jesus as the Christ but who will nevertheless be saved by God in due course (11:25–32).[107] This does not mean that they will be saved apart from Christ, for Paul seems to envision that they will come to believe in Christ (11:23).[108] Presently, however, because these Jews do not believe the gospel of Christ, they appear to be enemies of God (11:28a). But their disobedience and unbelief serve the inclusion of the Gentiles in Christ. Indeed, the most striking aspect of Paul's discussion is that he develops here a soteriological dimension to the Jews' unbelief in the gospel, not for themselves but for the Gentiles. They thus serve to bring about the salvific inclusion of the Gentiles in spite of, perhaps because of, their unbelief.

But God has not abandoned these unbelieving Jews, according to Paul. Rather, God has chosen them and still loves them on account of their forefathers (11:28b), an implicit reference to the patriarchs Abraham, Isaac, and Jacob.[109] This verse appears to be an expression of the Jewish notion of "the merits of the fathers," that despite its disobedience Israel remains beloved by God.[110] Despite Israel's faithlessness, God remains faithful to Israel (cf. 3:3–4).[111]

Why has God made this provision for unbelieving Jews? Paul provides the rationale for 11:28b in 11:29: "For the gifts and the call of God are irrevocable." To what is Paul referring by "gifts" and "call"? When we examine Paul's use of "gifts of God" (*charismata tou theou*) elsewhere in Romans, we see that they function as instruments of salvation, especially in association with Christ. Thus in 5:16 the gift of God in Christ brings justification. Similarly, in 6:23 the "free gift of God (*charisma tou theou*) is eternal life in Christ Jesus our Lord."

What, then, are the gifts that God has given to the Jews? If the gifts of God function as instruments of salvation, then the catalog in 9:4–5 of what God has given to the Jews would seem to indicate the kind of gifts Paul has in mind in 11:29. In particular, the coordination of the gifts of God with the patriarchs in 11:28–29 recalls the coordination of the covenants, the promises, and the patriarchs in 9:4–5. These gifts are irrevocable, according to Paul.

Further, Paul sees Christ as God's crowning gift (9:5), in whom the fulfillment of the promises to the patriarchs has been realized. If God's gifts bring about salvation, then despite the current disbelief and disobedience of some Jews, these gifts will ultimately bring about their salvation also. The promises to Abraham apply not only to the salvation of the faithful remnant that *has* believed—namely, to Paul and other Jewish Christians—but also to the salvation of the hardened portion of Israel that *will* believe.[112] At least, Paul is convinced that in the mystery of God's wisdom such salvation will come about (11:25–26, 30–36).[113]

Similarly, God's call (*klēsis*) is irrevocable. Paul seldom uses this term (elsewhere only in 1 Cor. 1:26; 7:20; Phil. 3:14; cf. Rom. 9:11–12), but it appears to refer to God's choosing Israel even if Israel does not reciprocate God's calling by obediently believing in Christ. Indeed, in Romans 9:11–12 God's calling is closely tied to God's purpose of election. By referring to God's irrevocable call, Paul again speaks of God's faithfulness.

This irrevocability of God's gifts and call to non-Christian Jews has a significant implication for Paul's view of Abraham. According to Paul, God's blessing upon Abraham[114] functions in a way that is slightly different for Jews than for Gentiles. Although Christ is God's culminating gift to Jews and to Gentiles alike (9:5), the gifts and call of God, located especially in God's covenant and promise to Abraham (9:4–5; 11:28–29), will lead to God's blessing upon these hardened Jews as well, expressed in terms of their salvation and God's taking away of their sins (9:26–27). Thus God's covenant promises to Abraham, implied in 11:28b, function as the basis for God's mercy upon hardened Jews in a way that does not appear to be the case for Gentiles. At least Paul never speaks about hardened Gentiles in this manner.

For Paul, God remains faithful to God's covenant election of Israel despite Israel's unfaithfulness. The Jews still have a special place in God's eyes simply because God chose them to receive the oracles (3:2) and gifts and call (11:29; 9:1–5). God's word has not failed (9:6) but will eventually bring about the salvation even of those Jews whom God has now hardened. To be sure, Paul characterizes God's plan as mysterious (11:25, 33–36), but he has confidence that at least some Jews, and perhaps all (11:26), who do not now appear to be true children of Abraham, children of the promise (9:7), will in God's mercy be included among the true children of Abraham.

Thus we may conclude that, for Paul, there are really two groups of descendants of Abraham both according to the flesh and according to faith. The first group consists of Jewish Christians, the faithful remnant among Israel who have come to faith in Christ (11:5). The second group consists of hardened non-Christian Jews, those who will be included at the fullness of Gentile inclusion (11:8, 25, the fullness of time?). The first group is actual. The second group is potential. Both, however, are in accord with God's purposes.

If in Romans 4, then, Paul drew attention to the way in which Abraham demonstrates the legitimacy of Gentile inclusion within God's people, in Romans 9–11 Paul draws attention to the way in which Abraham points to God's continued election of the Jews.

One final passage in Romans that alludes to Abraham occurs in 15:7–9.

> [7]Welcome one another, therefore, as Christ has welcomed you, for the glory of God. [8]For I tell you that Christ became a servant to the circumcised to show God's truthfulness, in order to confirm the promises given to the patriarchs, [9]and in order that the Gentiles might glorify God for his mercy. As it is written, "Therefore I will praise thee among the Gentiles, and sing to thy name."

In Romans 14 Paul had addressed tensions in the Roman community regarding ritual observance in diet, whether one day of the week is better than another for honoring the Lord, and some individuals in the church passing judgment on others regarding such matters. Tensions have developed between the "strong" and the "weak" (15:1), probably referring at least to some extent to tensions among Gentile and Jewish Christians in Rome.[115]

In 15:1–6 Paul has encouraged the Christians in Rome to bear with one another and to promote harmony in the community (15:5). Paul continues along the same lines in 15:7 by exhorting them to welcome one another. That Paul has in mind tensions between Jewish and Gentile Christians in Rome seems evident from his remarks in 15:8–9, where he speaks of the circumcised (Jewish Christians) and of the Gentiles. In this context Paul refers to Christ's servanthood as a confirmation of "the promises given to the patriarchs" (*tas epaggelias tōn paterōn*, 15:8). By referring to the patriarchal promises, Paul again calls to mind God's covenant promises with Abraham that he had discussed in Romans 4, in 9:1–9, and in 11:28–29. And as he had done in chapter 4 and in chapters 9–11, Paul applies these promises both to the Jews (15:8) and to the Gentiles (15:9).

Summary and Conclusions

In summary, how does Paul use Abraham in Romans? Paul appeals to Abraham to argue for Gentile inclusion, on the one hand (4:16–18; 15:9), and to assert God's continued election of non-Christian Jews for the sake of God's promises to faithful Abraham, on the other hand (11:25–36; 15:8). Why does Paul use Abraham in this way? Paul's purpose is twofold.

First, he wants to demonstrate that righteousness has always been reckoned on the basis of faithfulness, with Abraham as the prime example (4:1–12, 22–25). Second, however, Paul is determined to counter Gentile Christians in Rome who appear to suggest that Jewish rejection of the Christ means Jewish exclusion from God's promises (11:13, 25). On the contrary, Paul goes out of his way to affirm the place of non-Christian Jews within God's people (11:11–12, 28–32).

Finally, what implications may we draw regarding Paul's view of non-Christian Judaism from his use of Abraham in Romans? In contrast to Galatians, where Paul battles Christians proclaiming a rival form of the gospel, Paul takes care in Romans to safeguard God's continued faithfulness to non-Christian Jews even in their disobedience and failure to believe in Christ. Indeed, this abiding faithfulness results in part from the character of Abraham's faith, through which he was reckoned righteous and through which he received the covenant promises. At the same time, Abraham's faith foreshadows the faithfulness of Jesus, whose death and resurrection become the occasion for God's rectifying those who believe in him (4:23–25).

Because the death and resurrection of Jesus occupy center stage in Paul's understanding of the gospel, Paul views the Jewish rejection of Jesus as the Christ in tragic terms (9:2; 3:3–4). By failing to believe in Jesus the Jews have stumbled and have been disobedient (10:21; 11:11). At the same time, however, this rejection is not the end of the story, for Paul believes that non-Christian Jews will yet find full inclusion (11:12, 25–26). Just as the Gentiles were formerly disobedient but now have received God's mercy, so those non-Christian Jews who are presently disobedient will receive God's mercy in the mystery of God's will (11:30–36).

Reading Galatians and Romans Together

I have attempted to demonstrate the various dimensions of Paul's use of Abraham in Galatians and Romans, without falling into the trap of reading one through the other. This task having been completed, we are now in a position to compare and contrast the use of Abraham in Galatians and in Romans and to inquire into the nature of Paul's use of Abraham as a whole. What are the tensions between the function of Abraham in Galatians and Romans, respectively? Does either provide us with a more holistic understanding of Abraham in Paul?

A comparison of the use of Abraham in Galatians and in

Romans shows several similarities.[116] In both letters, Paul appeals to Abraham as a scriptural demonstration of his argument. In both, Paul uses Abraham to discuss the basis for being in right relation to God, and in both, he contrasts works with the faith of Abraham. In both, Paul uses Abraham to demonstrate the priority of hearing with faith over works of the law (over circumcision in Romans). In both, Paul addresses the connection between Christians and Abraham, arguing that Christians are children of Abraham. And, most significant, in both, Paul appeals to God's promise to Abraham as the basis for Gentile inclusion.

Despite these similarities, however, Paul uses Abraham to make very different points in Galatians and Romans.[117] In Galatians, Paul uses Abraham in a polemical manner to combat Jewish-*Christian* opponents who are preaching a rival gospel. In Romans, however, Paul uses Abraham to address relations between *non-Christian* Jews and Christians.[118] These different agendas result in the following contrasts. In Galatians, Paul identifies Christ as the singular child of Abraham, and believers become children of Abraham only by participating in Christ. In Romans, however, Paul emphasizes the way in which all who believe like Abraham are children of Abraham, with no reference to Christ as a child of Abraham. In Galatians, the emphasis falls upon the discontinuity between Christian faith and the Jewish law (Gal. 3:19, 23–25). In Romans, however, the emphasis falls upon the continuity between Christian faith and the Jewish law (Rom. 3:31). In Galatians, Paul stresses that Christian faith inherits God's promises to Abraham, appearing to imply that Jews outside Christ have no standing at all before God. In Romans, however, Paul stresses that God has not in any way abandoned non-Christian Jews, and he spells out God's purposes concerning the salvation of non-Christian Jews (Romans 9–11).

How are we to account for these differences? The underlying cause of the disparity can be attributed to the different purposes for which Paul was writing Galatians and Romans. Paul wrote Galatians as a strong corrective letter to the Gentile Christians in Galatia, who were turning to a false form of the gospel. Paul engages in polemic throughout this letter, and so by engaging in overkill he overstates his case. By contrast, Paul wrote Romans as a letter introducing himself firsthand to the Roman church he hoped to visit soon, hoping also in this letter to address tensions he was aware of between Jewish and Gentile Christians in Rome and the relationship between Christians and non-Christian Jews.

Given the contrasts between Paul's use of Abraham in Galatians and Romans, as well as the different purposes that help account for these contrasts, how are we to gain an overall understanding of Paul's view of the significance of Abraham? Should we simply accept these contradictions and tensions as constant features of Paul's position, as H. Räisänen suggests in regard to Paul's view of the law?[119] Perhaps such resignation could be our last resort, but it should not be our first. Rather, I believe that the very character of the differences between Galatians and Romans suggests that we must let Romans guide our reading of Galatians. In Romans, Paul develops the significance of Abraham without polemic and in much clearer terms than in his stylistically terse exposition of Galatians 3. Since in Galatians we find Paul engaged in the heat of battle against his opponents, we must rely on Romans to provide us with Paul's self-conscious, more carefully stated, and fuller position on what significance Abraham holds for Christians and Jews and why he has this significance.

In particular, when assessing Paul's use of Abraham as a clue to his understanding of non-Christian Judaism, we must remember that only in Romans does Paul explicitly and intentionally deal with the question of non-Christian Judaism. This is in no way his concern in Galatians. It only makes sense to use Paul's explicit statements in Romans regarding non-Christian Judaism as an interpretive guide when trying to understand the potential implications of his statements in Galatians regarding Jewish-Christian rivals for his view of non-Christian Judaism.

Reading Galatians and Romans together, then, we see first of all a strong emphasis on Gentile inclusion in both letters, based on God's promise to Abraham. Second, however, in Romans Paul provides us with an equally strong emphasis on God's fidelity to Jews. This fidelity finds foremost expression in the faithful remnant that has accepted the gospel concerning Christ. But it also stands out in God's continued call to the hardened and unfaithful portion of Israel. Paul is confident that this call will be answered in the ultimate salvation of all Israel (Rom. 11:26). We should not allow the harsh polemic against Jewish Christians in Galatians to undercut Paul's hopeful vision for non-Christian Jews in Romans.

Abraham in Paul's Controversy with Judaism

Finally, we are in a position to draw conclusions about the significance of Abraham for determining the nature and the scope of Paul's controversy with non-Christian Judaism. In brief, from Galatians we learn little direct information regarding his view of non-Christian Judaism. Rather, we learn something regarding Paul's intramural struggles with law-observant Jewish Christianity. By contrast, from Paul's use of Abraham in Romans we do gain some direct information regarding his view of non-Christian Judaism. Although Paul considers non-Christian Jews as disobedient and misguided for pursuing righteousness through the law (Rom. 10:2–3), he believes they will eventually receive salvation because God is faithful (3:3–4), because of Abraham's faithfulness (11:28), and because God's irrevocable gifts and call, now crowned by Christ, are effective (9:4–5; 11:29). They remain chosen and beloved.

Paul's use of Abraham, then, suggests a surprisingly positive assessment of Judaism. At the same time, however, we should not be misled into thinking that Paul had no controversy with non-Christian Judaism. Far from it. Paul obviously felt that Christ had come in fulfillment of God's promises to Abraham, for Jew and Gentile alike (Rom. 15:8–9; 1:16; 2:9–10; 3:9, 29; 9:24; 11:11–12). We must understand, however, that the center of Paul's controversy with non-Christian Judaism was the question of Gentile inclusion within the purposes of God. Paul's use of Abraham points exactly to this issue. Indeed, he appeals to Abraham in both Galatians and Romans primarily to establish in God's promise to Abraham the inclusion of the Gentiles through their faith in Christ, apart from law observance (Gal. 3:8; Rom. 4:11–12, 17–18). This emphasis on Gentile inclusion provides *the* constant feature in Paul's use of Abraham.

Gentile inclusion, then, is that aspect of Paul's use of Abraham which governs everything else he says about the patriarch. The basis of this inclusion is simply God's promise to Abraham. Paul is persuaded that the advent of Christ has inaugurated the fulfillment of God's promise simply because Paul has been called to preach to the Gentiles and the Gentiles have responded in faith (Gal. 1:16; 2:7–8; Rom. 1:5).

Paul's complaint with non-Christian Jews is their failure to recognize Gentile inclusion through Christ apart from the law. To put it another way, Paul's complaint is with the failure of non-Christian Jews to see the faithfulness of Gentiles and so to miss out on the fulfillment of God's promises in Christ. The failure to recognize Christ results in the failure to recognize Gentile faithfulness. The failure to recognize Gentile faithfulness results in the failure to recognize Christ. The two failures go hand in hand.

For Paul, Christ indeed has significance for Jew and Gentile alike. What is new in Christ is Gentile inclusion apart from the law, and this inclusion is in keeping with God's promise to Abraham. But this Gentile inclusion does not come at the expense of Jewish exclusion from God's promise to Abraham. This very implication, which some Gentile Christians in Rome seem to be drawing, provides the whole reason why Paul has to spell out explicitly that God has not rejected his people (11:1–6) and that they remain his people in the mystery of God's election (11:25–36). In this way Paul addresses the concurrent realities of Gentile inclusion and Jewish unbelief in a manner that maintains simultaneously the significance of Christ and the covenant faithfulness of God.

Thus in Galatians and Romans, we see Paul addressing two concerns. In Galatians, Paul uses Abraham to oppose Jewish Christians for stressing law observance at the expense of recognizing the inclusion of faithful Gentiles in Christ. While Paul makes a similar point in Romans, he also emphasizes that Gentile inclusion in Christ does not come at the expense of the abrogation of God's covenant to non-Christian Jews, despite their current disobedience at the advent of Christ.

3

Jewish Traditions Revised: Abraham in Matthew, Hebrews, and James

In the preceding chapter we examined the use of Abraham in the writings of Paul, a first-generation Jewish Christian. In the present chapter we turn to the use of Abraham in the writings of second-generation Jewish Christians, that is, in the Gospel of Matthew, in Hebrews, and in James.[1] I roughly group these writings together not so much because they use Abraham in exactly the same ways but because, unlike Paul, they make fairly restricted use of Abraham in primarily Jewish-Christian contexts.

In speaking of "Jewish-Christian contexts," however, it is important to be aware of potential problems of definition. With this phrase I do not mean to infer that there were no Gentile Christians in the communities addressed by Matthew, Hebrews, and James. Indeed, the danger of flatly distinguishing between "Jewish Christian" and "Gentile Christian" is on a par with the absolute contrast between "Palestinian Judaism" and "Hellenistic Judaism." By calling Matthew, Hebrews, and James "Jewish-Christian" I simply mean that the authors in all likelihood come from a Jewish heritage and that they make significant use of this heritage in their writings. The communities they are addressing have in large part probably also come to Christian faith from Jewish contexts.[2] We will consider each writing in turn.

Abraham in the Gospel of Matthew

Matthew refers to Abraham a total of only seven times (1:1, 2, 17; 3:9 [2x]; 8:11; and 22:32). Three of the references oc-

77

cur in the genealogy (1:1–17; cf. Luke 3:23–38), two in the Q
tradition regarding John the Baptist (3:7–12; cf. Luke 3:1–8),
one in the context of the Q story of Jesus healing a centurion's
servant (8:11; cf. Luke 13:28–29), and one in the triple tradition about Jesus' dispute with Sadducees regarding the resurrection (22:32; cf. Mark 12:26; Luke 20:37).[3] In all, then,
there are four passages in which Matthew gives Abraham a
role to play: 1:1–17; 3:7–10; 8:5–13; and 22:23–33. In each
instance the Matthean passages correspond directly to Lukan
parallels. By contrast, the Gospel of Luke refers to Abraham
fifteen times, including five passages without any parallel in
Matthew (Luke 1:55; 1:73; 13:16; 16:22–23; 19:9). In comparison to the Gospel of Luke and the Gospel of John (where
Abraham dominates John 8), then, Matthew assigns Abraham
a fairly limited place in his Gospel. An examination of the four
passages in which Abraham appears will clarify exactly what
part he does play in Matthew.

Abraham in the Matthean Genealogy (1:1–17)

Matthew gives Abraham more of a role to play in the genealogy than anywhere else in the Gospel.[4] Indeed, Abraham
occupies a significant place in the genealogy. Matthew makes
a connection between Abraham and Jesus in the very first line
of the Gospel (1:1), at the beginning of the genealogy (1:2),
and in the summary at the end of the genealogy (1:17). For
Matthew, Abraham is the starting point of the genealogy, the
most ancient of Jesus' ancestors.[5] Jesus is a "son of Abraham"
(*huiou Abraam*, 1:1). The question, of course, is why Matthew
emphasizes Abraham to this degree in the genealogy. I would
suggest two reasons for his strategic positioning of Abraham in
the genealogy at the very outset of the Gospel: (1) to establish
a close connection between Jesus and the Jewish heritage represented by Abraham and (2) to hint at the inclusion of faithful Gentiles among God's people, a reflection of the situation
faced by Matthew's predominantly Jewish-Christian church.[6]

Abraham and Jesus

Matthew places the story of Jesus squarely within the story
of Jewish salvation history.[7] He does this by presenting a genealogical link especially between Jesus and two figures who
represent turning points in this history: Abraham and David.[8]
By linking Jesus to Abraham, Matthew establishes a connection between Jesus and *the* forefather of the Jewish people.

Thus, the genealogical appeal to Abraham situates Jesus broadly within the Jewish tradition. By beginning with this genealogy, emphasizing Jesus' connections to Jewish history, Matthew shows that he is addressing a primarily Jewish-Christian audience, for whom the genealogy would hold special significance.

Yet the cornerstone of Matthew's genealogy is not Abraham but David.[9] The claim to descent from Abraham really goes without saying; Jesus has this status simply by virtue of being a Jew. What matters more for Matthew is to show that Jesus comes as the fulfillment of Jewish messianic hopes. This he does by linking Jesus to David the king (1:1, 6, 17), which gives him a right to the messianic title "Son of David."[10] This connection can be seen throughout Matthew's Gospel. Jesus is regularly called "Son of David" (1:1; 9:27; 15:22; 20:30, 31; 21:9, 15; 22:42), more in Matthew than in any other Gospel. And Matthew has the birth of Jesus take place in Bethlehem, the ancestral town of David (2:1–12; cf. Luke 2:8–20). Overall, Matthew refers to David fifteen times in his Gospel (1:1, 6 [2x], 17 [2x], 20; 9:27; 12:3, 23; 15:22; 20:30, 31; 21:9, 15; 22:42, 43, 45), more than twice as often as he refers to Abraham. Thus Matthew subordinates Abraham to the figure of David, both in the genealogy and in the Gospel at large. Still, it is significant that Matthew grounds the genealogy of Jesus in Abraham, for it relates Jesus to the father of the Jews.

Abraham and the Gentile Connection

Raymond E. Brown, among others, has suggested that reference to Abraham in the genealogy may also function as a hint at the inclusion of Gentiles within Matthew's community.[11] Brown sees the reference to the "son of Abraham" in conjunction with the inclusion of foreign women in the genealogy (Tamar, 1:3; Rahab, Ruth, 1:5; the wife of Uriah [Bathsheba], 1:6) as an indication that, according to Matthew, Jesus was intended to be the savior of Gentiles as well as of Jews. Thus, by calling Jesus a "son of Abraham," Matthew may be alluding to God's promise that in Abraham's seed (i.e., Jesus) the nations of the earth would find blessing and would then be included in God's salvific purposes (cf. Gen. 12:3; 18:18; 22:18).

Such Gentile inclusion finds further support from the birth narrative in Matthew 2:1–12, where magi from the East, presumably Gentiles, come to pay homage to Jesus.[12] Passages elsewhere in the Gospel make clear that Matthew is moving directly toward Gentile inclusion.[13] Still, one cannot conclude that Matthew's reference to Jesus as "son of Abraham" (or other indications of Gentile inclusion within the Gospel) signals either an extensive Gentile presence in Matthew's community or an aggressive Gentile mission that had long been undertaken by the Matthean community. Jesus never seeks out Gentiles in the Gospel, and when he sends his disciples off on a missionary journey he explicitly tells them, "Go nowhere among the Gentiles, and enter no town of the Samaritans, but go rather to the lost sheep of the house of Israel" (10:5–6; cf. also 15:24). Therefore, rather than serving as a mandate for a Gentile mission, Matthew's reference to Jesus as "son of Abraham" once again simply locates Jesus within the Jewish tradition, ties Jesus to the pregnant promises associated with Abraham, and as yet only hints at Gentile inclusion.

Abraham in Matthew 3:7–10

Immediately after the birth narrative of Matthew 1 and 2, Matthew introduces John the Baptist in 3:1–12 as the precursor to Jesus. In the context of preaching repentance, John the Baptist warns his hearers (3:8–9), "Bear fruit that befits repentance, and do not presume to say to yourselves, 'We have Abraham as our father' (*patera echomen ton Abraam*); for I tell you, God is able from these stones to raise up children to Abraham (*tekna tō Abraam*)." Matthew derives John the Baptist's preaching from Q material (cf. Luke 3:7–9). Indeed, the parallel between Matthew and Luke here is nearly exact. A significant difference, however, arises between Matthew and Luke in how each introduces the preaching of John the Baptist. In Luke 3:7, Luke has John address "the multitudes that came out to be baptized by him." Matthew agrees that large anonymous crowds came to be baptized, specifically referring to "Jerusalem and all Judea and all the region about the Jordan" (3:5; perhaps following Mark 1:5). But in Matthew 3:7, the parallel to Luke 3:7, Matthew has John the Baptist speak to "many of the Pharisees and Sadducees coming for baptism." Matthew thus specifies that John's warning is especially for the Pharisees and the Sadducees.[14] By reserving this warning for the Pharisees and the Sadducees in particular, Matthew introduces a motif of contempt for the Pharisees and the Sadducees that will be repeated throughout his Gospel.[15] This contempt arises in response to the opposition of the Pharisees and the Sadducees to Jesus and his followers.[16]

The warning in 3:9 indicates that mere reliance upon one's

Jewish heritage does not suffice for salvation. In order to lay legitimate claim to Abraham as father one must "bear fruit that befits repentance" (3:8). In effect, John the Baptist already pronounces eschatological judgment upon the Pharisees and the Sadducees (3:10–12), whom Matthew sees as unfaithful.[17] Matthew thus begins to prepare the reader for a final break with Pharisaic Judaism and sets the stage for the outcome that those who follow Jesus are truly children of Abraham, for they bear fruit (cf. 7:15–20; 21:43).[18] In making these preparations, Matthew may already have in mind the extension of the gospel to the Gentiles, as the phrase "God is able from these stones to raise up children to Abraham" perhaps indicates (3:9).[19] If one may draw such an inference only tentatively from 3:7–10, it becomes more evident in 8:5–13.

Abraham in Matthew 8:5–13

The next reference to Abraham comes in the context of Jesus' first interaction with a Gentile in Matthew.[20] The account is a miracle story, the healing of a centurion's servant, which Matthew has drawn from Q (cf. Luke 7:1–10; cf. also John 4:46b–54). In this story a centurion asks Jesus to heal his paralyzed servant. Jesus responds by saying he will come and heal the servant. But the centurion protests that he is unworthy to have Jesus come under his roof; rather, he simply asks Jesus to pronounce words that will effect the healing of his servant. After all, as a centurion he knows the power of commands, and he trusts that Jesus' command of healing will be effective. Jesus responds with amazement at the faith of this centurion. Indeed, he says to those following him, "Not even in Israel have I found such faith" (8:10). Jesus then proceeds to make a pronouncement in which he refers to Abraham: "I tell you, many will come from east and west and sit at table with Abraham, Isaac, and Jacob in the kingdom of heaven, while the sons of the kingdom will be thrown into the outer darkness; there men will weep and gnash their teeth" (8:11–12).[21] Jesus then commands that what the centurion has believed be done, and with this Jesus sends him forth. Finally, the narrator tells the reader that "the servant was healed at that very moment" (8:13).

Several observations have a bearing upon Matthew's reference to Abraham within the context of this story: (1) a comparison with Luke's version; (2) the significance of the encounter between Jesus and a Gentile centurion; and (3) the function of Jesus' pronouncement in 8:11–12.

A Comparison Between Matthew 8:5–13 and Luke 7:1–10

While Matthew 3:7–10 and Luke 3:7–9 are nearly identical in their appropriation of the Q tradition regarding the preaching of John the Baptist, in which Abraham figures, Matthew and Luke differ dramatically in their respective use of the Q story about Jesus healing the centurion's servant. For our purposes the most significant difference is that Matthew includes the pronouncement referring to Abraham in 8:11–12, whereas Luke includes the pronouncement not in the context of this story but later in Luke 13:28–29. This difference indicates that the Q saying was probably not originally part of the healing story but has been added by Matthew at this point (8:11–12) as an interpretive comment to the story.[22] In contrast, Luke has taken the saying and incorporated it into a very different context, which deals with how many will be saved.[23]

In addition to placing the saying in different contexts, Matthew and Luke also diverge in how they present the exact content of the saying, as the following comparison shows:

Matthew 8:11–12	*Luke 13:28–29*
[11]I tell you, many will come from east and west and sit at table with Abraham, Isaac, and Jacob in the kingdom of heaven, [12]while the sons of the kingdom will be thrown into the outer darkness; there men will weep and gnash their teeth.	[28]There you will weep and gnash your teeth, when you see Abraham and Isaac and Jacob and all the prophets in the kingdom of God and you yourselves thrust out. [29]And men will come from east and west, and from north and south, and sit at table in the kingdom of God.

In both Matthew and Luke the saying has two parts. One part has to do with inclusion, with people coming from various directions and sitting at table in the kingdom of God. The other part has to do with exclusion, with people being cast out of the kingdom and, as a result, weeping and gnashing their teeth.

Three differences stand out in how Matthew and Luke present the saying itself. First, Matthew and Luke present the two parts of the saying in reverse order. Matthew begins with the phrase regarding people coming from east and west to sit at table in the kingdom (8:11), while Luke begins with the phrase regarding people being cast out of the kingdom and weeping and gnashing their teeth (13:28). Second, Matthew and Luke likewise associate Abraham with different parts of the saying. Matthew aligns Abraham with those included at table in the kingdom (8:11), while Luke mentions Abraham

when referring to those who have been cast out of the kingdom and weep and gnash their teeth upon seeing Abraham in
the kingdom (13:28). Third, although both Matthew and Luke
have Jesus speak in direct discourse, in the saying about exclusion from the kingdom Matthew has Jesus speak in the third
person regarding "the sons of the kingdom" who will be cast
out, whereas Luke has Jesus speak in the second person directly to those who object to being cast out: "There *you* will
weep . . . when *you* see Abraham . . . in the kingdom of God
and *you yourselves* thrust out" (13:28).

As to the first difference, it is difficult to determine whether
Matthew or Luke has inverted the order of the two-part saying. The logic of the story in Matthew 8:5–10 moves from
Jesus' surprise at the faith of the Gentile centurion to a comment regarding the absence of such faith in Israel. Matthew
8:11–12 has a similar progression, as it begins by referring to
the inclusion of many from east and west (an allusion to Gentile inclusion?) and ends by pointing to the exclusion of "the
sons of the kingdom," presumably a rather direct allusion to
the expulsion of those Jews who are not faithful. The significance of the second and third differences is uncertain.
Clearly, in both Matthew and Luke, Abraham is in the kingdom. Although only Matthew specifies that he sits at table,
perhaps this is implicit in Luke. The second person address in
Luke makes the statement more direct than in Matthew, but
Matthew's third person reference to "the sons of the kingdom" makes the identity of those cast out of the kingdom less
ambiguous.

The Encounter Between Jesus and the Gentile Centurion

In the account of Jesus and the centurion three important
issues stand out for Matthew. First, Jesus marvels at the faith
of this Gentile (8:10). Jesus' surprise may indicate that from
Matthew's perspective such expressions of Gentile faithfulness were more the exception than the rule.[24] Second, however, by telling this story Matthew clearly gives a foretaste of
Gentile inclusion, perhaps setting the stage for the inaugura-
tion of a larger Gentile mission that comes to the fore only at
the end of Matthew's Gospel, in 28:16–20. Third, and most
significant, by contrasting the faithfulness of the Gentile centurion with that of Israel in 8:10, Matthew has Jesus implicitly
critique the faithlessness among the Jews in Israel. The faith
of the Gentile becomes an occasion for commenting upon the
failure of faith in Israel. Thus, in summary, Matthew uses this

story to anticipate Gentile inclusion, on the one hand, and to allude to Israel's faithlessness, on the other hand.

The seeds of Gentile inclusion can be seen not just in this story but also in the only other encounter between Jesus and a Gentile in Matthew, the story of Jesus and the Canaanite woman in 15:21–28 (par. Mark 7:24–30). In both stories, the individuals seek out Jesus and ask him to heal another individual (8:5–6; 15:22, 25). In both instances, Jesus appears surprised at the faithfulness of the individuals (8:10; 15:28). And in both stories, Jesus grants the healing with the command, "Be it done for you as you have believed [8:13]/as you desire [15:28]." Even though Jesus restates his mission to Israel during his conversation with the Canaanite woman (15:24), still he grants her request because of her faith. In both accounts, then, Matthew appears to be opening the door for the recognition of Gentile faithfulness.

The Function of Jesus' Pronouncement in Matthew 8:11–12

In 8:11–12 the two dimensions of the story that we have already noticed, the critique of faithless Jews and the hint at Gentile inclusion, become more clear. The implicit judgment of faithless Israel in 8:10 becomes an explicit statement of exclusion in 8:12 — "the sons of the kingdom will be thrown into the outer darkness." The hints of Gentile inclusion in the story find confirmation in 8:11 — "many will come from east and west and sit at table with Abraham, Isaac, and Jacob in the kingdom of heaven." Thus, by inserting this Q pronouncement precisely at 8:11–12, as a commentary on 8:5–10 and a prelude to 8:13, Matthew makes his own position obvious. The Jews who do not demonstrate faith will be cut off from the kingdom, while the Gentiles who do exhibit faith will find themselves included in the kingdom and will sit at table with Abraham.

Matthew 8:5–13 develops further two motifs that we have already seen in connection with the reference to Abraham in 3:7–10. First, the Pharisees and the Sadducees cannot rely solely on their relationship to Abraham for salvation (3:8–9). Unless they bear fruit worthy of repentance, that is, unless they are faithful, they will find themselves as trees good only for cutting down and being thrown into the fire (3:10). Similarly, because they have not demonstrated their faithfulness, the "sons of the kingdom" will be thrown out into the darkness (8:12).[25] Second, as John the Baptist declares, God is able to raise up children to Abraham even from stones (3:9). Perhaps Matthew is suggesting in 8:11 that indeed God is raising up new children to Abraham from "stones," that is, from Gentiles. Some Gentiles are already bearing fruits of faith, leading in 8:5–13 and 15:21–28 to healings.

In conclusion, in 8:5–13 we find Matthew using Abraham in a context in which Jews are criticized for not having faith and Gentiles are introduced as having the potential for faith. Ironically, in Matthew, Jesus does not find faithfulness where he would most expect it, that is, in Israel, and he does find faithfulness where he would least expect it, that is, among the Gentiles.

Abraham in Matthew 22:23–33

When, in 8:11–12, Matthew has Jesus refer to those who "sit at table with Abraham, Isaac, and Jacob in the kingdom of heaven," the resurrection of the dead is assumed; otherwise it makes little sense to refer to sitting at table with Abraham in the kingdom. What is assumed in 8:11–12, however, becomes a matter of dispute between the Sadducees and Jesus in 22:23–33.[26]

The Pharisees had just challenged Jesus regarding paying taxes to Caesar (22:15–22), and now Matthew gives the Sadducees a turn at stumping Jesus.[27] The Sadducees believe there is no resurrection (22:23), and so they present Jesus with a dilemma in order to show that the notion of the resurrection is ridiculous. The Sadducees begin by quoting the law of levirate marriage from Moses (Matthew 22:24; cf. Deut. 25:5–10), which says that if a man dies childless, his brother must marry the widow and raise up children for his brother (cf. Gen. 38:1–11). On the basis of this law they then present a scenario of seven brothers who all, in turn, were married to the same woman and then died. The question is finally put (22:28): "In the resurrection, therefore, to which of the seven will she be wife?"

By way of response Jesus quotes Exodus 3:6 back to them: "And as for the resurrection of the dead, have you not read what was said to you by God, 'I am the God of Abraham, and the God of Isaac, and the God of Jacob'? He is not God of the dead, but of the living" (22:31–32). Since God is alive, and since God identifies himself as the God of Abraham, Isaac, and Jacob, then Abraham, Isaac, and Jacob must be alive with God (cf. 4 Macc. 16:24–25; 18:23). Thus there is a resurrection from the dead. Matthew concludes the story by noting that the crowd was astonished at his teaching (22:33).

In this passage, Matthew has Jesus refer to Abraham in passing with Isaac and Jacob. The significance of this reference is that Matthew links Abraham to the future resurrection, as he had in 8:11–12. Abraham is already alive in the resurrection life. By implication, those who are faithful will share in this resurrection (22:30–31).[28]

Conclusion: The Significance of Abraham in Matthew for Christian Controversy with Judaism

As we noted at the beginning of this chapter, Abraham plays a fairly limited role in the Gospel of Matthew.[29] Still, we can make some concluding remarks about the role he plays in Matthew, especially in terms of continuity and of discontinuity with Jewish tradition. We can point to two aspects of continuity. First, Matthew refers to Abraham in the genealogy (1:1–17) in order to help provide a context for the birth of Jesus. As a descendant of Abraham, Jesus stands in continuity with Jewish hopes and expectations. Second, an appeal to Abraham can also confirm fairly standard Jewish beliefs about the resurrection life (22:23–33). Thus, in Matthew, Abraham figures both in discussions of roots (1:1, 2, 17; 3:9) and of destiny (8:11–12; 22:32). The faithful can look back to him and they can look forward to him. He encompasses the whole of salvation history, from beginning to end.

There are also two aspects of discontinuity with Jewish tradition. Although Matthew refers to Abraham only a few times, when the patriarch appears he is introduced into disputes with Jewish leaders: with the Pharisees and the Sadducees in 3:7–10, perhaps the same in 8:11–12 (with reference to "sons of the kingdom"), and with the Sadducees in 22:23–33. Matthew has Abraham appear in passages that oppose the positions of the Pharisees and the Sadducees, whether these positions find explicit (22:23–33) or implicit (3:7–10; 8:5–13) formulation. Second, Matthew appeals to Abraham in order to hint strongly at Gentile faithfulness and Gentile inclusion within the kingdom of God and, by extension, in the Matthean community as well, especially at 8:5–13 (and possibly at 1:1–17 and 3:7–10).

Thus we find as much continuity as discontinuity with Jewish tradition in Matthew's use of Abraham. Both the continuities, insofar as Matthew addresses the identity of Jesus, and the discontinuities, insofar as Matthew hints at Gentile inclusion, show that Matthew also implicated Abraham in his controversy with Judaism.

Abraham in Hebrews

The author of Hebrews refers to Abraham a total of ten times (2:16; 6:13; 7:1, 2, 4, 5, 6, 9; 11:8, 17). From the perspective of Abraham's role in early Christian controversy with Judaism, the most significant passage is 7:1–10, where the author refers to Abraham in the context of a discussion about the priesthood of Melchizedek, who was explicitly introduced in 5:5–10 and mentioned again in 6:20. The remaining occurrences of Abraham in Hebrews are less significant, if not unimportant. Abraham is mentioned in passing at 2:16. In 6:13 Abraham appears in a discussion of God's promise (6:13–20) that leads up to the introduction of Melchizedek in 6:20. Finally, in 11:8–19 Abraham figures in a presentation of faithful heroes of old, a fairly stock role for the patriarch in early Jewish literature, as we shall see.

Before we turn to these passages, it is helpful to articulate some broad themes of Hebrews in order to set a general context for examining Abraham's role. As a "word of exhortation" (13:22), Hebrews seeks to uplift a community of Christians who have grown weary. They have "drooping hands" and "weak knees," and their faith verges on being "lame" (12:12). They appear to be in danger of drifting away from their Christian commitment (2:1–4; 3:7–4:13). Hebrews exhorts them to endure with patience (10:19–39). In order to admonish this community, the author reminds them that Jesus is superior to all that has come before in God's dealings with the people of Israel. Jesus is superior to the angels (1:5–14) and to Moses (3:1–6). Indeed, Jesus is best described as the perfect high priest who offers himself for sins on behalf of the people (4:14–10:39). The image of Jesus as "high priest" in fact is the single most important role for Jesus in Hebrews (cf. 3:1; 4:14, 15; 5:1, 5, 10; 6:20; 7:26, 27, 28; 8:1, 3; 9:7, 11, 25; 13:11). Thus, finally and most significant, Jesus is superior to the Levitical priesthood that had formerly besought God in mediating the forgiveness of the people's sins (5:1–10; 7:15–8:7; 10:11–18). For these reasons, the Christians addressed should hold fast in their faith to what God has accomplished among them through Christ (10:19–25). In the light of this background we can turn to Abraham's place in Hebrews.

Hebrews 2:16

In 2:16 we read, "For surely it is not with angels that he [Jesus] is concerned but with the descendants of Abraham" (*spermatos Abraam*). This reference to Abraham occurs within the context of 2:14–18, where the author discusses why Jesus shared in the flesh and blood of humanity. The primary reason for the incarnation was so that by being "like his brethren in every respect, . . . he might become a merciful and faithful high priest in the service of God" (2:17). Since Jesus suffered as a human being, he can be effective in bringing salvation to suffering humanity, especially as a high priest who advocates for humanity before God. This is the first time Jesus is called a "high priest" in Hebrews. Jesus' priesthood is not on behalf of angels (cf. 1:5–14) but for the sake of the "descendants of Abraham."[30]

Does the expression "descendants of Abraham" here refer exclusively or primarily to physical descendants of Abraham, that is, to Jews? It is difficult to decide, but in all likelihood the phrase can be understood to refer to both Jews and Gentiles, although this is not explicitly stated. Two reasons point in this direction. First, Hebrews conceives of Christ as inaugurating a new covenant (8:1–13) that renders the old covenant obsolete (7:12; 8:13). The old covenant was but a shadow of the covenant established in Christ (8:5), and now it is "ready to vanish away" (8:13). As an expression of the old covenant, the law too was but a shadow (10:1). Thus the law has also faded and has been written on the hearts of the believers who now cling to Christ in faith (8:10; 11:1–12:2). The constant emphasis on faith and on the new covenant relationship points beyond an exclusively Jewish–Christian congregation, although the community for the most part probably had Jewish roots. Gentiles would thus appear to be included as potential partakers of this new covenant, even apart from observing the old ritual law. Second, in 2:10, the author states that Jesus brings "many sons to glory" (*pollous huious*), perhaps suggesting that the Christian community includes all those who share faith in Christ. In this way, the author would be in accord with the sentiments of Paul expressed in Galatians 3:7: "It is men of faith who are the sons of Abraham."[31]

Further, it should be noted that Hebrews does not lay stress on distinguishing between physical and spiritual descendants of Abraham. Elsewhere in Hebrews, the only references to "descendants" (*sperma*) occur at 11:11 and 11:18 in the context of a discussion about Sarah, who conceived and gave birth to Isaac, and in whom Abraham's descendants would be named. In general, then, there is nothing to suggest that *sperma Abraam* ("descendants of Abraham") in 2:16 connotes exclusively or primarily physical descendants. Rather, it simply refers to those who are numbered among the faithful in the new covenant, allowing it to refer to Jew and Gentile alike.

By saying that Christ is concerned with the "descendants of Abraham," the author implicitly points to Christ as the realization of the covenant promises that God made to Abraham and to his descendants.[32] Already in 2:16, then, the author states what will become more explicit in 6:13–15; 7:6; 11:9, 17.

Hebrews 6:13

In 6:13–15 the author of Hebrews states, "For when God made a promise to Abraham, since he had no one greater by whom to swear, he swore by himself, saying, 'Surely I will bless you and multiply you.' And thus Abraham, having patiently endured, obtained the promise." This reference to Abraham occurs within the context of 6:9–20, and it functions as a transition from 6:9–12 to 6:16–20. In 6:9–12 the Christians addressed have been encouraged to maintain their faith with hope and patience, for God takes heed of their work and love (6:10). The author exhorts them not to be sluggish but to be "imitators of those who through faith and patience inherit the promises" (6:12). God's promises are reliable, and the people must patiently endure until the promises in Christ are finally obtained. In 6:13–15, then, Hebrews offers Abraham as an example to be imitated, since Abraham endured patiently in faith (6:15) and thus obtained the promise that God made to him in Genesis 22:17, which Hebrews cites in 6:14.[33] (Hebrews will again appeal to Abraham as a primary example of faithfulness in 11:8–22, where this motif is more fully developed.) Having provided Abraham as an example, the author then turns in 6:16–20 to explore further the dependable character of God's promise. In Christ, God has given Christians "a sure and steadfast anchor of the soul" (6:19), for Christ is the ultimate high priest on their behalf "after the order of Melchizedek" (6:20). Following the introduction of Melchizedek again in 6:20 (cf. 5:6, 10), Hebrews moves in chapter 7 to develop more fully the image of Christ as an eternal high priest after the order of Melchizedek.

Abraham thus serves as a model of the faithful individual who obtains the promise after waiting with patience and forbearance (6:15).[34] What promise did Abraham obtain? Hebrews does not explicitly spell out what Abraham obtained,

but from the reference to Genesis 22:17 we may infer that
he obtained many descendants through Isaac (cf. 11:12, 17).[35]
The statement in 6:15, that "Abraham . . . obtained the promise," appears to be contradicted later in Hebrews by 11:13,
where Abraham is included among those who "died in faith,
not having received what was promised [*mē labontes tas epaggelias*], but having seen it and greeted it from afar." Similarly, in
11:39 Abraham is included among those who, "though well
attested by their faith, did not receive what was promised."
These statements, however, do not contradict the affirmation of
6:15. Both 11:13 and 11:39 refer to God's eschatological
promises in Christ, which Abraham saw from afar but did not
yet obtain.[36]

Hebrews 7

In 2:16 and 6:13 we have seen that Abraham has a fairly
limited role. He is the recipient of God's promises and an
example of faithfulness. Abraham has a more significant place
in Hebrews 7, where he is introduced in connection with the
priestly figure of Melchizedek. Abraham receives more attention here than anywhere else in Hebrews (7:1, 2, 4, 5, 6, 9).
Still, it is important to note that Abraham enters into the discussion solely because of his association with the Melchizedek
story in Genesis 14:17–20. Abraham's significance here rests
only in his relationship to Melchizedek. In Hebrews 6:20 the
high-priestly order of Melchizedek was mentioned in relation
to the activity of Jesus. Now in 7:1–28 the attention turns to
the priesthood of Melchizedek. Indeed, Hebrews 7 presents
the most developed discussion of Melchizedek, who plays a
central role in developing the high-priestly identity of Jesus.[37]
It is not simply coincidence that Hebrews 7 also stands as the
pivotal chapter of Hebrews.[38] Rather, Hebrews 7 serves as the
climax precisely because it develops the identity and the significance of Jesus' high priesthood.

The earlier references to Melchizedek in Hebrews 5:6, 10 are
based on Psalm 110:4.[39] Although the influence of Psalm 110
is evident in the section of Hebrews 7 where Abraham figures
(7:1–10; cf. 7:3), Hebrews 7:1–10 is basically a midrash on
the only other Old Testament reference to Melchizedek, Genesis 14:17–20.[40] Hebrews 7:1–10 falls into two parts. In
7:1–2a the author retells the story of Genesis 14:17–20. In
7:2b–10 the author provides an interpretation of the passage.
This interpretation leads the author in 7:11–28 to conclude
that Christ's priesthood is infinitely superior to the Levitical

priesthood. A closer examination of 7:1–10 shows how the author reaches this conclusion.

Hebrews 7:1–2a

To begin, a comparison between Genesis 14:17–20 and Hebrews 7:1–2a proves instructive.

Genesis 14:17–20	*Hebrews 7:1–2a*
[17]After his return from the defeat of Chedorlaomer and the kings who were with him, the king of Sodom went out to meet him at the Valley of Shaveh (that is, the King's Valley). [18]And Melchizedek king of Salem brought out bread and wine; he was priest of God Most High. [19]And he blessed him and said, "Blessed be Abram by God Most High, maker of heaven and earth; [20]and blessed be God Most High, who has delivered your enemies into your hand!" And Abram gave him a tenth of everything.	[1]For this Melchizedek, king of Salem, priest of the Most High God, met Abraham returning from the slaughter of the kings and blessed him; [2a] and to him Abraham apportioned a tenth part of everything.

From the comparison above, we can see that Hebrews focuses on three items in its summary of Genesis 14:17–20. First, Melchizedek was priest of the most high God; second, Melchizedek blessed Abraham; and third, Abraham gave Melchizedek a tenth of all his spoils from his victory over the kings. These three observations figure prominently in the author's interpretation of this passage in 7:2b–10. It is significant that Hebrews makes no reference to Melchizedek bringing out bread and wine (Gen. 14:18), nor does the author call attention to the vindication of Abraham's enemies (Gen. 14:20).[41]

Hebrews 7:2b–10

The midrash on Genesis 14:17–20 begins by picking up on observations that find no explication in the passage itself. In Hebrews 7:2b–3 the author points out the symbolic meaning of Melchizedek's name and calls attention to the omission of any genealogy. This latter observation leads the author to conclude that Melchizedek "has neither beginning of days nor end of life, but resembling the Son of God he continues a

priest for ever" (7:3). The final comment draws not from Genesis 14 but from Psalm 110:4, which states, "You are a priest
for ever after the order of Melchizedek."

After signaling Melchizedek's special status and function as
an eternal priest, the author proceeds to discuss the relationship between Abraham and Melchizedek (7:4–10). At this
point the three considerations we noted above come into play.
Hebrews picks up first on the tithe that Abraham gave to Melchizedek (Gen. 14:20; Heb. 7:4). As the law says, the Levitical priests receive tithes from the people, even though the
priests, like the people, are descendants of Abraham (7:5).
But the priestly Melchizedek, who is not an Abrahamic descendant, received tithes from Abraham; and furthermore,
Melchizedek blessed Abraham (Gen. 14:19–20; Heb. 7:6).
Since "the inferior is blessed by the superior" (7:7), it follows
that Melchizedek is superior to Abraham. Similarly, since the
Levitical priests are descendants of Abraham, "one might
even say that Levi himself, who receives tithes, paid tithes
through Abraham" to the priest Melchizedek (7:9–10). Consequently, the priesthood of Melchizedek must be superior to
the Levitical priesthood. In fact, the Levitical priesthood has
been surpassed and even replaced by the priesthood after the
order of Melchizedek. Because the author of Hebrews had
already determined that Jesus was a high priest after the order
of Melchizedek (5:5–10; 6:19–20), the author concludes that
the high priesthood of Christ infinitely surpasses the Levitical
priesthood (7:11–19).

The crucial link in the argument of Hebrews comes therefore at 7:9. When Abraham paid a tithe to Melchizedek, he
did so as a representative of the Levitical priesthood that was
to come from his seed. Abraham functions first and foremost
as a representative of the later Levitical priesthood. His relationship to Melchizedek serves as an indicator of the Levitical
priesthood's relationship to Christ. The logic works as follows:
Melchizedek is a type for Christ, and Abraham is a type
for the Levitical priests; since Melchizedek is shown to be
greater than Abraham, then Christ by necessity is shown to
be greater than the Levitical priests. The comparison does not
stop there, however. For just as Christ's priesthood is superior
to the Levitical priesthood, so the covenant inaugurated in
Christ is superior to the covenant under which the Levitical
priests served. Or, as Hebrews puts it, "This makes Jesus the
surety of a better covenant" (7:22).

One final point must be made regarding the use of Abraham
in Hebrews 7. Whereas previously the author of Hebrews had

argued directly for the superiority of Christ to the angels (1:4) and to Moses (3:3), such is not the case with Christ and Abraham. Hebrews' point is not to show that Christ is superior to Abraham but to enlist Abraham in demonstrating that Christ's priesthood is superior to the Levitical priesthood. The superiority of Melchizedek to Abraham functions on a secondary level in service to the proof that Christ's priesthood is superior to the Levitical priesthood. Christ and Abraham do not meet directly in Hebrews, nor are they compared directly. At most they meet indirectly, insofar as Christ in the person of Melchizedek "meets" Abraham. But it is not really Abraham that Christ meets, but the Levitical priesthood, which Abraham here represents. The relationship between Abraham and Melchizedek simply shows, for Hebrews, that Christ's priesthood supersedes the Levitical priesthood.

Hebrews 11:8–19

In 10:19–29 the author of Hebrews has exhorted and warned the audience to maintain their fidelity to the covenant promises in Christ. Now in Hebrews 11 the author proceeds to give a long list of exemplary heroes of the faith from of old. Not surprisingly, Abraham figures prominently in this recollection of faithful individuals among Israel's forebears. Indeed, Hebrews discusses Abraham's faith in two sections, 11:8–12 and 11:17–19.

Hebrews 11:8–12

After presenting the faithfulness of Abel (11:4–5), Enoch (11:5–6), and Noah (11:7), the author turns to consider Abraham's faith. The author lifts up three features of Abraham's faith. First, "by faith Abraham obeyed when he was called to go out to a place which he was to receive as an inheritance; and he went out, not knowing where he was to go" (11:8). Second, "by faith he sojourned in the land of promise, as in a foreign land" (11:9). And third, by faith Abraham and Sarah were able to conceive a child (*sperma*), even in their old age (11:11–12). The author stresses Abraham's obedience in faith (11:8) and his endurance in faith (11:9–12) as he held fast to the promises. God's promises to Abraham are understood as consisting of the land (11:9) and many descendants (11:12; cf. 6:13–14). Even when the fulfillment of the promises appeared to be in jeopardy and was threatened by the death of Abraham and Sarah, literally and figuratively (11:11–12), still

Abraham believed and saw the initial realization of the promises (cf. 6:15).

Hebrews' appeal to Abraham's faith is very traditional within early Jewish circles, and one finds abundant parallels.[42] Indeed, there is nothing particularly Christian about the emphasis on Abraham's faithful obedience and endurance in the face of death.[43] To be sure, the author invokes the example of Abraham for the purpose of encouraging Christian faith, which faith Hebrews sees as in keeping with Abrahamic faith, but there are no christological overtones in 11:8–12 per se.

Hebrews 11:17–19

After 11:8–12 the author makes a brief digression in 11:13–16, in which he provides the reader with an interpretive guide to the preceding and following remarks about Abraham. Having pointed to the faithfulness of Abraham and the other forebears in 11:2–12, Hebrews stresses that Abraham and the others died without having fully received what was promised (11:13), despite their faith. They only saw the ultimate realization of the promises from afar. But since they knew that they were sojourning as strangers and exiles who awaited a homeland beyond this mere earth, they remained faithful and endured to the end (11:14–16).

The remarks in 11:13–16 indicate a somewhat spiritualized understanding of the promises that God made to Abraham. Already in 11:10 the author had hinted that the promised land was not primarily physical land to be possessed but a heavenly city "whose builder and maker is God." This spiritual dimension of the land finds explicit expression in 11:13–16. The true promised land refers to a heavenly city (11:16) in an eschatological future. As we shall see in 11:17–19, spiritual overtones are also present in Hebrews' understanding of the promised descendants.

Hebrews considers the character of Abraham's faith for the last time in 11:17–19. The author sees the greatest indicator of Abraham's depth of faith in the story of the Akedah, where Abraham offers up Isaac in obedience to God's command (Genesis 22).[44] Abraham saw the initial fulfillment of God's promise of descendants in the birth of Isaac. He had believed in the face of his own death that God would honor the promise of descendants (11:11–12). Now he believes in the face of death again, although this time in the face of the death of Isaac, the promised son. The potential death of Isaac becomes the supreme test of Abraham's faith, for God has commanded

Abraham himself to offer Isaac up in sacrifice. But Abraham "was ready to offer up his only son" (11:17).[45] In 11:19 the author provides the reason why Abraham was ready to offer up his son: "He considered that God was able to raise men even from the dead; hence, figuratively speaking, he did receive him back." According to Hebrews, Abraham believed even in the face of Isaac's death by Abraham's own hand that God would keep God's promises. If it meant that God had to raise Isaac from the dead in order to keep the promise, so be it. Thus, for Hebrews, Abraham actually did offer Isaac up. He intended to sacrifice Isaac and he tried to carry out the sacrifice. In that sense the sacrifice was complete, even though at the last second God called to Abraham to prevent the actual sacrifice. Thus Hebrews can conclude that "figuratively speaking (*en parabolē*), he did receive him back" from the dead.[46]

The spiritual overtones in Hebrews' understanding of the descendants promised to Abraham can now be discussed in the light of the treatment he gives to the Akedah. Although J. Swetnam may be correct that the sacrifice of Isaac in Hebrews 11:19 is an allusion to Christ's death and resurrection, Hebrews does not make this connection explicit.[47] It would be reading too much into the text to conclude that Hebrews here spiritualizes Isaac as a descendant (*sperma*) of Abraham who is a type for Christ.[48] Swetnam is more on target in calling attention to another aspect of Hebrews' spiritualizing the descendants promised to Abraham when he states:[49]

> The "seed" which was promised to Abraham seems to have been realized in the eyes of the author of Hebrews not merely in the numerous offspring which come to Abraham through Isaac and his physical descendants as a result of a promise, but in the spiritual "seed" composed of all those who, like Abraham, have faith when they are tested in God's power to raise from the dead.

This appears to be the case especially in the light of the exhortative context provided for Hebrews 11 in 10:32–39, and in the light of 11:39–40, where Hebrews connects the faith and hopes of the heroes of old to the faith and realization of the promises among the Christians whom the author is addressing. They are counted among the true descendants of Abraham if, like Abraham, they endure with faith. As heirs of the promise they will inherit the heavenly homeland that Jesus has prepared for them (10:19–25).

One final point must be made about the appearance of

Abraham in both 11:8–12 and 11:17–19. Although Abraham's exemplary faith has an important place in the author's exhortation, even this faith is subordinate to the reliability of God's promise. The trustworthiness of God's promises had already been raised in connection with Abraham in 6:13–20. In 6:13–14 we read, "For when God made a promise to Abraham, since he had no one greater by whom to swear, he swore by himself, saying, 'Surely I will bless you and multiply you.'" The author comments on this oath in 6:17: "So when God desired to show more convincingly to the heirs of the promise the unchangeable character of his purpose, he interposed with an oath." Abraham could have faith in God's promises because God's promises are truly reliable. Similarly in 11:10 Abraham could confidently look forward to a heavenly country (11:16) because the city there "has foundations, whose builder and maker is God." Finally, in 11:17–19 the only reason Abraham has faith that his sacrifice of Isaac will not annul God's promises is that "he considered that God was able to raise men even from the dead" (11:19). For the author of Hebrews, God's trustworthiness provides the foundation for Abraham's faith. Likewise, God's faithfulness provides the basis for faithfulness on the part of the audience that Hebrews addresses.[50]

Conclusion: The Significance of Abraham in Hebrews for Christian Controversy with Judaism

To what extent does Hebrews use Abraham in Christian controversy with Judaism? As was the case with Matthew, we can get some clues to answer this question by noting elements of continuity and discontinuity with Judaism in Hebrews' use of Abraham. In terms of continuity, the author of Hebrews points to Abraham in a rather stock manner as the most exemplary model of constant faith in the face of long-suffering (6:13–15; 11:8–12). There is nothing particularly novel or Christian about this use of Abraham. This continuity does not come as a surprise, given that the author here uses Abraham for pastoral rather than polemical purposes. He seeks to exhort a congregation, providing the people with a strong model of faith they can look to amidst their struggles.

What is new, however, indicating some tension and discontinuity with the Jewish heritage of the audience addressed, is the use of Abraham to critique the Levitical priesthood as inferior to Christ's priesthood (Hebrews 7). By employing Abraham to highlight the superiority of Melchizedek's priesthood, the author of Hebrews shows his depreciation of Jewish faith and practice apart from Christ. The coming of Christ has cast the whole of Judaism in a new light, revealing the obsolete character of Jewish worship and ritual after the Levitical order. Depending on how one dates Hebrews, one can argue either that this depreciation of the Levitical priesthood is restricted to the Temple cult or that it applies equally to emergent post-70 C.E. rabbinical Judaism. Yet Hebrews' criticism of the Levitical priesthood would seem to apply to any non-Christian Jew who would recognize the legitimacy of the Temple cult, either before or after the destruction of the Temple. We should stress, however, that this use of Abraham to criticize non-Christian Judaism takes more the form of in-house exhortation than of a polemic or an apologetic addressed directly at nonbelievers.

Hebrews' tendency to spiritualize the promises to Abraham also implies a degree of critique of non-Christian Judaism. To dissociate the promised land from physical land and to weaken the connection between the promised descendants and physical descendants is to challenge deep-seated Jewish beliefs. Yet once again, the main aim of the author is not to critique non-Christian Judaism directly but to exhort the audience to stand firm and not to sink into a lame faith (12:12). Christians can take solace in the idea of the heavenly city promised to Abraham (11:13–16). They can also rest assured that Jesus cares for those who show themselves to be descendants of Abraham through faith. If they endure patiently, they shall receive the rest that Christ has once and for all secured (10:19–39). Like Abraham, the faithful must have confidence that God is able to raise the dead (11:17–19). They must trust that Jesus is concerned with the descendants of Abraham (2:16), on which account Jesus took on human suffering.

Moreover, if any direct critique of non-Christian Judaism is absent from Hebrews, so is any explicit appeal to Abraham to argue for Gentile inclusion such as we saw in Paul and Matthew. Yet Hebrews does appear to assume Gentile inclusion by means of the author's spiritualized notion of the promises to Abraham and especially the descendants of Abraham. Thus Hebrews certainly makes room for Gentile inclusion. Why this theme, so important in Paul (and, as we shall see, in Luke-Acts, in Barnabas, and in Justin), does not appear to be an issue for Hebrews it is difficult to say.

We turn, finally, to examine what James's use of Abraham might tell us about the place of the patriarch in early Christian controversy with Judaism.

Abraham in James

James refers to Abraham in 2:20–24:

> [20]Do you want to be shown, you shallow man, that faith apart from works is barren? [21]Was not Abraham our father justified by works, when he offered his son Isaac upon the altar? [22]You see that faith was active along with his works, and faith was completed by works, [23]and the scripture was fulfilled which says, "Abraham believed God, and it was reckoned to him as righteousness"; and he was called the friend of God. [24]You see that a man is justified by works and not by faith alone.

This passage has probably received more attention than any other in James, because the use of Abraham here seems to be directly opposed to Paul's contention that Abraham was indeed justified by faith apart from works of the law (cf. Rom. 3:28; 4:2–3; Gal. 2:16; 3:6).[51] As we shall see, however, the discussion of faith and works in James is less comparable to Paul's discussion of faith and works than might at first appear.

The references to Abraham occur within the immediate literary context of 2:14–26.[52] In 2:14 James introduces the topic of faith and works: "What does it profit, my brethren, if a man says he has faith but has not works?"[53] Yet the content of this section is also related to the preceding material in 1:19–27 and in 2:1–13.[54] In 1:19–27 James discusses the relation between hearing and doing. He tells his audience in 1:22, "But be doers of the word, and not hearers only, deceiving yourselves."[55] Similarly, in 2:12 the author encourages his audience to speak and to act as befits the faith. The distinction between hearing and doing in 1:22 parallels the contrast between faith and works developed in 2:14–26. Similarly, the author's desire that his audience both speak and act faithfully (2:12) finds further development in 2:14–26, where faith apart from action is shown to be empty faith. Thus, as 1:19–2:26 indicates, what matters for James is that one's faith find active expression in specific deeds. Passive faith, a faith that does not act, is really no faith at all, for it is dead (2:17, 20, 26). True hearing leads to doing (1:19–27). True faith leads to works (2:14–26). The question in 2:14, then, further develops the prior discussion.

The motif of faith and works in 2:14–26 arises again with related language in 3:13: "Who is wise and understanding among you? By his good life let him show his works in the meekness of wisdom." Here the notion of "works in the meekness of wisdom" is akin to the statement in 2:22 that "faith was active along with [Abraham's] works." Wisdom and faith go hand in hand for James.[56] We see, then, that the discussion of faith and works, so dominant in 2:14–26, relates to the preceding material and to what follows. In general, James is concerned with the relation between words and deeds, speech and action, confession and practice.

Within the structure of 2:14–26, the reference to Abraham in 2:20–24 functions as a proof from scripture, as 2:20 explicitly indicates.[57] The example of Abraham shows that he was justified by a working faith (2:21–22). Curiously, the author refers to Abraham's "works" in the plural (*erga*, 2:21) but then proceeds to discuss one work only, Abraham's offering of "Isaac upon the altar" (2:21).[58] In all likelihood, the reference to the "works" of Abraham is governed by the general referral to "works" already in 2:14, 17, 18, and 20. Indeed, throughout his discussion in 2:14–26, James never refers to the singular form "work" (*ergon*).[59] For James, the offering of Isaac was Abraham's crowning work, his ultimate trial, and could be seen as representative of his works in general.[60] Having referred to this one work, he has no need to mention any others, although he could. For example, the reference to Rahab's hospitality in 2:25 would clearly call to mind Abraham's hospitality, especially since hospitality and merciful deeds are the subject in 2:14–17.[61]

After emphasizing Abraham's justifying works in 2:21, James connects Abraham's works to his faith in 2:22. The connection is obvious to James, as his introductory remark in 2:22 ("You see that") indicates. The author makes two observations regarding the relationship between Abraham's works and his faith. First, Abraham's "faith was active along with (*sunērgei*) his works."[62] Second, Abraham's "faith was completed (*eteleiōthē*) by works." Both observations show that James considers faith to be intimately connected to works. Indeed, faith finds its fruition and completion in works. Faith actively manifests itself in works. The opening remarks of James in 1:3–4 provide further evidence for this inseparable connection: "knowing that the testing of your faith brings about endurance; and let endurance do its whole work, so that you may be whole and complete, lacking in nothing."[63] As in 2:22 James states that faith is completed (*eteleiōthē*) by works, so in 1:3–4 the author exhorts his readers to let their faithful endurance be effective in perfect work (*ergon teleion*).[64] Faith is the source that leads to works, and works are the completion of faith.[65] For James, faith and works stand completely unified. The one is a reflection of the other.[66] Ac-

cording to James, one has either both faith and works or neither faith nor works.

The unity of faith and works in Abraham's case is confirmed
by Genesis 15:6, which James cites in 2:23. The pronouncement of Abraham's righteousness in Genesis 15:6 thus anticipates his faithful action in Genesis 22. By making this
connection, James stands in agreement with 1 Maccabees
2:52, where Mattathias reminds his sons of Abraham's faithful
deeds: "Was not Abraham found faithful when tested, and it
was reckoned to him as righteousness?"[67] Because God
counted Abraham righteous on account of his faithful actions,
James concludes that Abraham "was called the friend of God"
(2:23), a common notion in early Judaism.[68] In his appeals to
Abraham's faith and works, James thus shows his thoroughly
Jewish understanding of the relation between faith and
works.[69]

Since James does not allow a distinction between faith and
works, however, where does he come up with such a distinction? Is he refuting the position of a real opponent, or is he
merely setting up an imaginary position for the sake of discussion? As M. Dibelius has shown, the text allows for both possibilities.[70] On the one hand, for example, in 2:18, James states
that "some one will say (*erei tis*), 'You have faith and I have
works.'" Perhaps this differentiation between faith and works
comes from real opponents. On the other hand, it would be
more logical that the position of the opponents would be the
opposite of 2:18, namely, that "I have faith and you have
works." Thus, it can be argued that the position of 2:18 "does
not seem to come at all from one who is an opponent of our
author."[71] The problem, then, is that the very distinction between faith and works throughout 2:14–26 begs the question
of where James came across this contrast. Yet at the same time
one need not hypothesize any real opponent in order to account for 2:18.

Some scholars have argued that the distinction between
faith and works makes sense only in the light of Paul's letters,
as he articulates such a contrast in Galatians 3 and Romans 4.[72]
This is not to say that James has read Paul's letters; rather,
James responds in general to the separation of faith and works
as a dangerous position. It is also possible that he was responding to a misrepresentation of Paul's position.[73] Other scholars
have argued against this view, noting especially that Paul and
James mean different things by "works."[74] Paul speaks about
"works of the law," whereas James has "works" of mercy in
mind.[75] In the light of these difficulties, it is best to maintain

that James and Paul are not quite comparable.[76] At most, we can conclude that the separation of works from faith, which position James opposes, may well derive from Paulinist circles. At the same time, we can see that James and Paul would agree on the need for "faith working through love" (Gal. 5:6).[77]

Finally, to what extent does James use Abraham in Christian controversy with Judaism? Clearly, James does not use Abraham in any way to issue a specifically Christian critique of Judaism. Rather, we have seen that James is completely indebted to a traditional Jewish understanding of the patriarch as an individual who demonstrates his faithful righteousness through his actions, and whom God counts as a friend. Abraham's active faith exemplifies the kind of behavior that James seeks to promote among his audience. If James employs Abraham at all to combat opponents, those opponents are Christians and not Jews.

Conclusion

In this chapter we have explored the use of Abraham in the writings of three second-generation Jewish-Christian authors: Matthew, Hebrews, and James. We have found that Matthew does use Abraham in controversy with Judaism, especially to call into question the claims of Jewish leaders regarding the significance of physical descent from Abraham apart from inward faith. Matthew also appeals to Abraham to hint at Gentile inclusion, at the same time using such inclusion to criticize Jewish faithlessness. The author of Hebrews uses Abraham to critique the Levitical priesthood but otherwise makes rather traditional appeals to Abraham as an exemplar of faithful endurance. Similarly, James's use of Abraham is completely traditional. This author does not even use Abraham in implicit Christian controversy with Judiasm.

We see, then, two features in the use of Abraham by second-generation Jewish Christians. First, Hebrews and James in particular refer to Abraham in keeping with traditional Jewish usage. Thus we see in their appeals to Abraham a great deal of continuity with their Jewish heritage. We noted such continuity in Matthew as well. Second, however, Matthew and Hebrews in particular use Abraham in order to differentiate emerging Christianity from non-Christian Jewish expressions of faith. They appeal to Abraham in order to say something about the identity of Jesus as the Christ. In Matthew, Jesus comes as the Davidic messiah, the culmination of

Abraham's descendants. In Hebrews, Jesus comes as the eternal high priest after the order of Melchizedek, the priest who blessed Abraham and to whom Abraham paid tithes. If with Paul we saw Abraham used in the initial rupture between Christianity and Judaism, with Matthew and Hebrews we see Abraham used to mark a further separation between Christianity and Judaism. And if we saw Paul use Abraham also to safeguard the status of non-Christian Jews before God, with Matthew and Hebrews we find such safeguards withdrawn.

4

The Father
of the Outcast:
Abraham in Luke-Acts

In turning to an examination of the use of Abraham in Luke-Acts, we move to a writing in early Christian literature that uses Abraham to point to the common heritage of Christians and Jews, specifically of Gentile Christians and Jews. In this chapter, I will seek to demonstrate that Luke-Acts uses Abraham in order to show that Gentile Christians have a legitimate claim to Abraham as their father, on the same terms as Jews, and thus they have a share in the promises to Abraham along with the Jews.

Luke makes his case in two ways. First, in the Gospel, Abraham appears in contexts that emphasize God's mercy toward pious poor Jews who are on the fringe of society and toward Jews who are repentant. Luke's use of Abraham thus challenges any presumption of special status before God on the basis of physical descent from Abraham. Second, in Acts, Abraham appears in contexts in which Luke argues for the inclusion of Gentiles as part and parcel of God's purposes in Christ. Jews who welcome Gentile inclusion in Christ honor God's covenant with Abraham. Jews who oppose Gentile inclusion in Christ oppose the fulfillment of God's purposes.

In the first half of this chapter, I will examine the use of Abraham in Luke under four rubrics: (1) Abraham in the birth narrative (Luke 1:55, 73); (2) Abraham and his descendants (Luke 3:8, 34); (3) Abraham and the character of his children (Luke 13:16; 19:9); and (4) Abraham and the afterlife (Luke 16:22–30; 13:28; 20:37). My focus in each instance will be on the use of Abraham and the significance of this use for early Jewish/Christian relations, not an exhaustive analysis of the myriad other questions that each passage raises. The second half of this chapter will then examine the use of Abraham in three missionary speeches by Luke's heroes, each addressed to Jews: (1) Peter in the Temple (Acts 3:12–26); (2) Stephen in Jerusalem (Acts 7:2–53); and (3) Paul in Pisidian Antioch (Acts 13:26–41).

At the outset, some introductory comments about Abraham in Luke-Acts are in order.[1] Luke refers to Abraham twenty-two times (fifteen in Luke; seven in Acts), which is more than any other New Testament author and accounts for nearly one third of all the references to Abraham in the New Testament. (By comparison, Paul, with the second largest number of references, appeals to Abraham nineteen times.) Luke's appeals to Abraham are scattered throughout the Gospel, appearing in hymns of praise (Luke 1:55, 73), the preaching of John the Baptist (3:8), a healing story (13:15), a parable (16:19–31), a story of repentance (19:9), and Jesus' teaching about inclusion in the heavenly kingdom of God (13:28; 20:37; see also 16:19–31). In Acts, the appeals to Abraham are grouped in three missionary speeches to Jews in the first half of the book (Acts 3:13, 25; 7:2, 16, 17, 32; 13:26).[2]

The Use of Abraham in the Gospel of Luke

Abraham in the Birth Narrative

Two passages come into consideration here: the Magnificat of Mary (1:46–55) and the Benedictus of Zechariah (1:68–79). In both the Magnificat and the Benedictus three factors give specific shape to Luke's use of Abraham: the probable origin of the hymns in Jewish (or Jewish-Christian) Anawim piety, the Old Testament background, and the motif of promise/fulfillment.

Abraham in the Magnificat (Luke 1:46–55)

1. Raymond E. Brown, in his exhaustive analysis of the infancy narratives, has argued that the origin of the hymns is best found within communities of Jewish Anawim who had been converted to Christianity.[3] The term "Anawim" initially referred to those who were physically poor but came to refer more broadly to those on the fringe who were destitute because of sickness or being widowed, orphaned, socially outcast, and so forth. The Anawim looked to the power of God for deliverance.[4] From this perspective, Mary's hymn of

praise can be seen to reflect the response of such a group to God's actions in the birth of Jesus, Mary herself being a prime example of a pious individual on the social fringe. That Luke would borrow this hymn and incorporate it into his own account indicates his sympathies with the ideals of the Anawim.

It is no accident that Abraham appears in the culminating and concluding line of the Anawim hymn in 1:55. His appearance here indicates that the hopes of the pious among the social fringe are grounded in God's "remembrance of his mercy, as he spoke to our fathers, to Abraham and to his posterity (*tō spermati autou*) for ever" (1:54–55).[5] The hymn thus aligns Abraham with the God who is on the side of "those of low degree" (1:52). That which God spoke to Abraham provides the source of mercy and power to Abraham's posterity.

By claiming Abraham, the hymn claims the mercy that God communicated to him. Abraham almost takes on the role here of a mediator of God's mercy, for by appealing to Abraham in the hymn Luke claims access to that power and mercy of God which Abraham symbolizes. Appealing to Abraham is a shorthand way for claiming God's salvation and redemption. Indeed, as we will see, Luke makes explicit connections between Abraham and the poor not only in the Magnificat but also in the story of poor Lazarus, who rests in the bosom of Abraham (16:19–31), and in the account of the repentant Zacchaeus, designated by Jesus as a "son of Abraham" immediately after Zacchaeus promises to give half of his goods to the poor (19:1–9). In the Magnificat, Luke claims God's salvation on behalf of Mary and of all those who, like her, are of low degree.

2. The Old Testament allusions in 1:54–55 also align Abraham with those whom God saves. In particular, as Brown points out,[6] the hymn recalls Isaiah 41:8–9, which reads, "You, O Israel, my servant Jacob whom I chose, seed of Abraham (*sperma Abraam*) whom I loved, whom I have helped from the ends of the earth." Mary's thanksgiving in Luke 1:54–55, then, implies that the election, love, and help of God, which were promised to Abraham's seed in Isaiah, are made accessible through Jesus. Again, Abraham provides the connection with the manifestation of God's love in Jesus.

3. Although the hymn does not refer explicitly to God's specific promises to Abraham, Luke portrays the hymn as Mary's response to God's fulfillment of the promises in general.[7] The clearest indication of this comes in 1:45, where Elizabeth blesses Mary for believing "that there would be a fulfillment of what was spoken to her from the Lord." Just as

Mary believes in God's fulfillment of what has been spoken to her, so her faith is grounded in God's remembrance of his mercy, "as he spoke to our fathers, to Abraham and to his posterity for ever" (1:55). As God accomplished the promise spoken to Abraham, so the promise will find further fulfillment in God's dealings with Mary through the birth of Jesus. As we will see, the promise to Abraham implicit in the Magnificat becomes explicit in the Benedictus.

Abraham in the Benedictus (Luke 1:68–79)

Abraham plays a special role in the Benedictus beyond the reference to him in 1:73. As many commentators have pointed out, the situation of Zechariah and Elizabeth (cf. 1:5–7) in many ways is patterned after the story of Abraham and Sarah (Gen. 16:1; 18:11).[8] The righteousness of Zechariah also parallels that of Abraham, as does God's faithfulness in giving a son to Zechariah in a remarkable way. In addition, we can make the same three observations about the Benedictus that held for the Magnificat, regarding its origin in Anawim piety, the Old Testament background, and the motif of promise/fulfillment.

1. Here Zechariah, a Temple priest, expresses a piety similar to Mary's in the Magnificat, praising God for redeeming God's people from their enemies. The origins of the Benedictus, like the origins of the Magnificat, may be found within the general milieu of Jewish-Christian Anawim piety. In agreement with Brown, J. A. Fitzmyer notes that "traces of Temple piety in v. 75 suggest a plausible background in the Jewish Christian Anawim of the early community."[9] Again, "the oath which he swore to our father Abraham" (1:73) expresses a central theme of this piety.

2. As was the case with the Magnificat, Old Testament allusions provide important background for interpreting the reference to Abraham. In particular, 1:72–73 recalls Micah 7:20; Exodus 2:24; Psalm 105:8–9; and Genesis 26:3, all of which make reference to remembering God's covenant with Abraham.[10] Luke does nothing terribly new in making these connections, but by tying the prophecy of Zechariah so closely to God's covenant with Abraham he anchors his claim and in effect states that what is taking place in the birth of Jesus stands in direct fulfillment of this covenant.

3. The nature of God's promise to Abraham takes on sharper definition in the Benedictus than in the Magnificat. The "holy covenant, the oath which he swore to our father

Abraham" (1:72–73) is spelled out in explicit terms in 1:74–75. Two components stand out: deliverance from enemies (1:74a; also 1:71) and serving (*latreuein*) God in holiness and righteousness (1:74b–75).[11] Deliverance from enemies in 1:74 is syntactically subordinated to proper service, indicating that true service becomes possible only after deliverance. For Luke, salvation and service characterize the nature of God's covenant promise with Abraham. Jesus comes to fulfill this promise by giving knowledge of salvation (cf. 1:77) and in turn becomes the focus for proper service of God.[12]

In sum, the origin of both hymns in Anawim piety, the Old Testament allusions they contain, and the theme of promise/fulfillment give specific shape to Luke's use of Abraham. Both the Old Testament allusions and the theme of promise/fulfillment ground the event of Jesus' birth in God's long-standing promise to Abraham. The promise focuses on salvation through forgiveness of sins (God's action) and the consequent response of true service/worship before God (humanity's action).

Luke thus begins to redefine the nature of God's promise to Abraham, a redefinition that he will continue throughout Luke-Acts. The traditional notion of the promise to Abraham in terms of descendants, land, and being a blessing to the nations (Gen. 12:1–3; 22:15–18) begins to take on a new shape. At the same time, Luke stresses the continuity of God's current dealings with God's actions of old. Luke touches on the descendants of Abraham (1:55) but never explicitly refers to them as part of the promise per se. The promise of the land is absent from view but will be developed in Acts 7 within the context of Stephen's speech.[13] The promise of being a blessing to the nations will be developed in Peter's speech in Acts 3:12–26.[14]

The significance of Abraham in Luke's birth narrative lies especially in his connection with the pious Jews who are marginalized, who feel some kinship with the ethos of the Anawim. These individuals find an ally in Abraham, and, as we will see in our examination of the remaining appeals to Abraham in Luke-Acts, Luke continues to place Abraham in close proximity to those on the fringe.

Finally, we should simply observe that by appealing to Abraham already in two hymns in the first chapter of his Gospel, Luke assigns a significant place to Abraham and thereby shows his concern to hold fast to the central pillar of Jewish identity. By associating the very beginning of his gospel story with Abraham, Luke puts down the deepest roots he can and claims Abraham as a primary link to God's covenant promises with Israel.

Descendants of Abraham

Luke refers explicitly to physical descent from Abraham in two passages in the Gospel, 3:8 and 3:34. In 3:8 Luke has John the Baptist deny that physical descent from Abraham has any bearing on salvation. In 3:34 Luke's placement of Abraham in the genealogy of Jesus again allows no significance to descent from Abraham, in stark contrast to the Matthean genealogy. We turn now to examine each passage more fully, paying attention to the Matthean parallels as they arise.

In 3:7–9 Luke has taken over a Q tradition that reports the eschatological preaching of John the Baptist in preparation for Jesus' ministry.[15] In this context John the Baptist either quotes a slogan or anticipates an objection that could have been used to undercut his call to repentance. It seems more likely that he is quoting a slogan of some kind, as we find a parallel tradition in John 8:39, an independent saying in which the Jews respond defensively to John the Baptist by appealing to their Abrahamic descent (cf. Rom. 4:1).[16] Luke rules out completely the notion that mere physical descent from Abraham gives one a special claim on God's mercy. Only repentance and ethical behavior that demonstrates this repentance count before God.[17] Physical descent from Abraham makes no difference at all, for "God is able from these stones to raise up children (*tekna*) to Abraham" (3:8).[18] To attach any significance to physical descent is, for Luke, to misconstrue the proper way in which the relationship with Abraham (and by implication with God) is to be established.

As we saw in chapter 3 above, Luke's use of the Q tradition (Luke 3:7–9) is nearly identical to that of Matthew (Matt. 3:7–10) in reporting the preaching of John the Baptist.[19] Yet a significant difference occurs in the way each evangelist introduces John's preaching. Matthew has John address "many of the Pharisees and Sadducees" (Matt. 3:7), whereas Luke has John address in a more general way "the multitudes" (*tois ochlois*). Some have seen in this a Lukan tendency toward universalizing, a hint at the Gentile scope of Luke's vision already present in the preaching of John the Baptist.[20] But this assertion undercuts the significance of John's warning to the crowd not to rely on descent from Abraham, which makes sense only if John is addressing Jews. At the most, one can conclude that Luke is referring here to the Jewish people in general, not to the Pharisees and the Sadducees specifically.[21]

Regardless, Luke uses the Q saying of John the Baptist regarding Abraham *not* in order to denigrate Abrahamic descent but to qualify it radically by denying any special standing before God on the basis of such descent. Luke refuses to link Abraham and salvation in terms of ethnicity; rather, as we saw above in our consideration of the Magnificat and the Benedictus, Luke establishes this connection in terms of God's covenant promise to Abraham.

Luke further lessens the significance of genetic descent by his treatment of Abraham in the genealogy of Jesus (Luke 3:23–38). This depreciation of physical descent stands out most clearly in contrast to Matthew's genealogy (Matt. 1:1–17). As we saw above, Matthew refers to Abraham three times in his genealogy: in a summary statement at the beginning (Matt. 1:1), as the very source of the genealogy (Matt. 1:2), and in the summary statement at the end (Matt. 1:17).[22] Abraham has a very important place in Matthew's genealogy. By contrast, Luke's genealogy refers only once in passing to Abraham (Luke 3:34). Further, Luke, unlike Matthew, lists Abraham's nineteen ancestors, ending with Adam and finally God. Abraham appears as merely one among seventy-seven names and gets buried in the list. Whereas Matthew is concerned to draw an explicit connection between Jesus and Abraham, who stands out as the patriarch of the Jews, Luke's concern is to establish the connection between Jesus and Adam, the patriarch of the entire human race, and ultimately between Jesus and God.[23] For Luke, Abraham's importance is not to be found in any physical kinship.

By making Abraham out to be merely one ancestor among dozens of others, Luke puts the status of Abrahamic descent in perspective. The focus of Jesus' identity is not Abraham, as in Matthew's genealogy, but Adam and ultimately God. As has often been noted, Luke's appeal to Adam shows his concern to move beyond any exclusive Jewish claims on God and to anticipate Gentile inclusion in God's dealings with humanity through Jesus.[24] As Adam is the patriarch of all humanity, so Jesus is the savior of all humanity. Abraham has no special place as Jesus' ancestor.

Luke's use of Abraham in both 3:8 and 3:34 addresses the issue of the significance of physical descent from Abraham. By means of the statement of John the Baptist in 3:8 and Abraham's lack of prominence in 3:34 Luke clearly makes the point that physical descent from Abraham makes no difference at all before God. Already in his Gospel, then, Luke's use of Abraham has a leveling effect, placing Jew and non-Jew on the same plane before God.

Children of Abraham

If, for Luke, physical descent from Abraham does not distinguish one as a true child of Abraham, then what does? Luke provides an answer to this question by giving two examples of true children of Abraham, even explicitly labeling them as such. In 13:10–17 Luke recounts the story of the healing of a crippled woman on the Sabbath, whom Jesus calls in 13:16 "a daughter of Abraham" (*thygatera Abraam*). In 19:1–10 Luke tells the story of a repentant Zacchaeus, whom Jesus subsequently calls "a son of Abraham" (*huios Abraam*, 19:9). We turn now to look at each story in more detail, concentrating on Luke's use of Abraham in each case.

The Healing of a Crippled Woman: Daughter of Abraham

While most commentators focus on the controversy between Jesus and the ruler of the synagogue in this story,[25] which is told only by Luke, our interest is in the healing of the woman and in why Jesus calls her "a daughter of Abraham."

This miracle story is rather typical of the genre, with the significant exception that the woman never makes a request for healing. Rather, Jesus initiates the healing. The woman's physical ailment is obvious. Luke emphasizes her suffering by twice specifying that she has been ill for eighteen years (13:11, 16), that she is bent over, and that she cannot straighten herself.[26] While he is teaching in the synagogue, Jesus sees her, calls to her, pronounces her free from her infirmity, places his hands upon her, and heals her. Jesus initiates all the action. Thus Luke stresses both the suffering of the woman and the initiative of Jesus in healing her.

The healing on the Sabbath leads to a dispute with the ruler of the synagogue. As most commentators note,[27] Jesus uses the principle of *qal wahomer* (from minor premise to major premise) to argue that if one is permitted to show mercy to animals on the Sabbath by giving them water, then surely Jesus should be permitted to show mercy to this woman by healing her on the Sabbath.

In this context Luke has Jesus call the woman "a daughter of Abraham." Why? She is clearly Jewish, since she is in a synagogue, and so perhaps Luke has Jesus use the phrase in order to point to her physical descent from Abraham. Jacob Jervell has taken this position. He asserts: "What is decisive is not that she is a woman who suffers, but that she is an Israelite, a Jewess, one of the elect people who is suffering. According to Luke, salvation belongs first and above all to Israel." But Jervell's interpretation runs against Luke's double emphasis upon her eighteen-year affliction (13:11, 16) and against Luke's linking of Abraham with the suffering ones who receive God's mercy, as I have shown from the Magnificat and the Benedictus.[28] The woman is not a "daughter of Abraham" simply because she is Jewish, which should be clear from 3:8, where Luke disallows the attaching of significance to physical descent.

The synagogue setting on the Sabbath does, however, point to another feature that indicates why Luke considers the woman a "daughter of Abraham." Luke establishes a worship setting in this story, although he does not develop it. The woman, despite her suffering, has come to worship God. She exemplifies true piety, and so shows herself as a genuine child of Abraham. It is in the context of the woman rendering service to God, then, that Jesus heals her (cf. 1:74). The woman responds with an act of worship by praising God (13:14). By calling her a daughter of Abraham, Luke has Jesus identify the woman as a long-suffering pious individual who becomes the object of God's special mercy. The woman does appear to be faithful, but still the initiative rests with God. The woman represents the kind of person for whom God demonstrates God's care in an extraordinary way.

The connection here to the use of Abraham in the Magnificat and the Benedictus is striking. The healing of the crippled woman is an example and fulfillment of Mary's song of praise: "He has . . . exalted those of low degree; . . . he has helped his servant Israel, in remembrance of his mercy, as he spoke to our fathers, to Abraham and to his posterity for ever" (1:52–55). As Mary praises God for exalting those of low degree, so Jesus exalts this woman in a literal fashion by healing her so that she may stand straight. The healing also recalls Zechariah's song of praise (1:71–74):

> that we should be saved from our enemies, and from the hand of all who hate us; to perform the mercy promised to our fathers, and to remember his holy covenant, the oath which he swore to our father Abraham, to grant us that we, being delivered from the hand of our enemies, might serve him without fear.

As Zechariah praises God for deliverance from enemies, so

Jesus delivers the woman from the bonds of Satan, who has afflicted her with this infirmity. The woman in turn praises God. She may now serve God without hindrance. The use of Abraham in the story of the healing of the crippled woman confirms what we already saw in the use of Abraham in the Magnificat and the Benedictus, that Luke aligns Abraham with God's mercy toward the pious poor and lowly.[29]

The Repentant Zacchaeus: Son of Abraham

Like the account of the healing of the crippled woman, the story of Zacchaeus (19:1–10) occurs only in Luke's Gospel. As Jesus called the woman "a daughter of Abraham," so the story of Zacchaeus ends with Jesus calling him "a son of Abraham" (19:9).

The story tells of Zacchaeus's transformation from a sinful chief tax collector (19:2, 7) to one who repents and receives salvation (19:8–9). His repentance is indicated, though not explicitly stated, by his declaration in 19:8: "Behold, Lord, the half of my goods I give to the poor; and if I have defrauded any one of anything, I restore it fourfold." The response of Jesus to this pronouncement confirms this interpretation: "*Today* salvation has come to this house, since he also is a son of Abraham. For the Son of man came to seek and to save the lost" (19:9–10, emphasis mine). Before this day, apparently, salvation had not come to Zacchaeus's house and he was numbered among the "lost."

Although the story seems to tell of Zacchaeus's repentance, there exists a division among commentators regarding whether or not he actually does repent. Some hold that he does repent and that this is one more of Luke's stories about the salvation of the social outcast.[30] Others hold that Zacchaeus does not repent, because he is already righteous; this is a story of vindication rather than of salvation.[31] According to this interpretation, the crowd presumes that Zacchaeus is a sinner simply because he is the chief tax collector. However, although this story does not clearly show Zacchaeus repenting or expressing faith, Luke himself appears to see this as a story of repentance. Three reasons support this conclusion: (1) The story is grouped with other stories of repentance and salvation in chapters 15–19; (2) 19:9–10 indicates the coming of salvation to Zacchaeus's house; and (3) 19:10 implicitly identifies Zacchaeus as one of the lost (19:10).[32]

If one allows this as a story of the repentance of Zacchaeus, why does Jesus call him "a son of Abraham"? Just as the use of the appellation "daughter of Abraham" becomes clearer when viewed in the light of the Magnificat and the Benedictus, so the use of the appellation "son of Abraham" becomes clearer when viewed in the light of the preaching of John the Baptist in 3:7–9. The key is John's statement in 3:8: "Bear fruits that befit repentance, and do not begin to say to yourselves, 'We have Abraham as our father.'" Bearing fruits of repentance, not the mere claim of physical descent, aligns one as a child of Abraham, for Luke.

Just as the healing of the pious crippled woman exemplifies God's mercy coming to the lowly and suffering, so the story of the repentance of Zacchaeus exemplifies God's salvation coming to those who truly repent. Jesus makes his pronouncement of 19:9 only *after* Zacchaeus receives Jesus joyfully and promises to give half of his goods to the poor and to restore fourfold anyone he has defrauded.[33]

In contrast, however, to the story of the crippled woman, where the initiative rested with Jesus, in the story of Zacchaeus the initiative rests with Zacchaeus. He sought to see Jesus (19:3), ran ahead and climbed up into a tree to see him (19:4), and at Jesus' word made haste, came down, and received Jesus joyfully. The response of Jesus to Zacchaeus's initiative (19:5) leads in turn to the penitent response of Zacchaeus to Jesus' receptiveness (19:6–8). Zacchaeus demonstrates his repentance by giving his possessions to the poor. He is a "son of Abraham" because he has born fruits befitting repentance, as John the Baptist had called for in his preaching.

In addition, Zacchaeus's repentance extends further mercy to the poor, as he gives half of his goods to the poor and restores fourfold anyone he has defrauded.[34] The one who becomes a "son of Abraham" through repentance recognizes the child of Abraham who is poor as his or her brother or sister. Luke makes a connection, then, between the different children of Abraham.

In conclusion, we see here two different but related types of true children of Abraham: those pious individuals on whom God bestows mercy and salvation because they are poor or downtrodden (e.g., the crippled woman) and those individuals who receive God's mercy and salvation because they repent and bear fruits of repentance (e.g., Zacchaeus). Luke, then, uses Abraham to confirm two patterns of the way in which God brings about salvation: through mercy to the pious poor and through the fruitful repentance of sinners. Both are children of Abraham.

Abraham and Afterlife

The final group of passages in Luke that refer to Abraham has to do with the afterlife: 13:28; 20:37; and 16:19–31.[35] In 13:28 and 20:37 Luke mentions Abraham in passing along with Isaac and Jacob.[36] In 16:19–31, however, we find a parable in which Abraham plays a more developed role. We will examine each passage in turn.

The theme of 13:22–30 is indicated by the question that an unidentified person asks of Jesus in 13:23: "Lord, will those who are saved be few?" Luke has pulled together material from various sources to form 13:22–30, a block of material that addresses this question of salvation and judgment.[37] A comparison of Luke 13:22–30 with parallels in Matthew 7:13–14, 22–23, and especially 8:11–12 proves to be helpful in highlighting Luke's use of Abraham.[38]

In Matthew 8:11–12 Abraham is associated with those coming from east and west to sit at table in God's kingdom. The expulsion of "the sons of the kingdom" into the outer darkness is not linked to Abraham. In Luke 13:28–29, however, Abraham is linked to those who are thrust out of the kingdom of God. Those who are thrust out will *see* Abraham and Isaac and Jacob and all the prophets in the kingdom; when they see this they will weep and gnash their teeth. Luke then has the saying about people coming from east and west and north and south to sit at table in the kingdom of God, but Abraham is not explicitly referred to as being at table, in contrast to the description in Matthew.

These differences have some significance for understanding Luke's use of Abraham. Previously, we have seen Luke appeal to Abraham in contexts that deal with the inclusion of the marginalized; here, however, Luke links Abraham explicitly to the exclusion of those who thought they were insiders. As J. A. Fitzmyer notes, "Verse 28 expresses in terms of exclusion what v. 29 does in terms of inclusion."[39]

As we saw above, in Matthew the saying serves to comment on the specific faith of the Gentile centurion.[40] Luke knows the story of the Gentile centurion (7:1–10) but does not link it to Jesus' saying regarding inclusion/exclusion. In Luke, the saying occurs within the general context of Jesus stressing the need for repentance (13:3, 5), contrasting the hypocrisy of the Pharisees with the faith of the pious crippled woman (13:10–17), and speaking about the kingdom of God (13:18–21). Immediately after the saying, Jesus laments over Jerusalem, which kills the prophets (13:31–35). The saying in Luke

13:28–30 speaks of the inclusion of the outcast within God's kingdom[41] and the exclusion of the unrepentant insiders who show themselves to be "workers of iniquity" (13:27; the hypocritical Pharisees and Jerusalem which kills the prophets). In this way, "some are last who will be first, and some are first who will be last" (13:30). Those who are first, yet fail to repent, will find themselves outside looking in (13:28), while those who are last, the pious poor and the repentant, will be admitted to sit at table in God's kingdom (13:29).[42] Insiders and outsiders reverse roles. As earlier Luke identified Abraham with two patterns of salvation (mercy and repentance), so now he identifies Abraham with those in God's kingdom and contrasts him with those who have been shut out (cf. 3:8).

While 13:22–30 deals with the issue of salvation and judgment in the afterlife, 20:27–40 addresses the question raised by the Sadducees about the nature of the resurrection life, explicitly referring to Abraham in 20:38. Luke's account is based on a parallel passage in Mark 12:18–27 (cf. Matt. 22:23–33).[43]

Following his Markan source, Luke has Jesus cite Exodus 3:6, which functions as a proof text for the resurrection. The inference drawn from Exodus 3:6 is that since the Lord is the God of the living and not of the dead (20:38), and since the Lord identifies himself as the God of Abraham, Isaac, and Jacob, then they in turn must be alive, that is, in the resurrection life.[44] Therefore the reality of resurrection life cannot be called into question, as the Sadducees seek to do.

While following Mark fairly closely (though not as closely as Matthew), Luke makes some significant changes in his source. In 20:36 Luke alone refers to those in the afterlife as "sons of God, being sons of the resurrection," associating them then with Abraham, Isaac, and Jacob.[45] For Luke, the term "sons of God" equals the term "sons of the resurrection" (20:36). Since Abraham, Isaac, and Jacob have entered the resurrection life, they too are "sons of the resurrection." It follows, then, that those who are "sons of the resurrection" are by implication children of Abraham. For Luke, Zacchaeus (a "son of Abraham," 19:9) and the bent woman (a "daughter of Abraham," 13:16) would seem to exemplify "those who are accounted worthy to attain to that age and to the resurrection" (20:35).[46] The pattern established in this life for being a child of Abraham finds eternal confirmation in the resurrection life (20:36).

We turn, finally, to Luke 16:19–31, the so-called parable of the rich man and Lazarus.[47] Whereas the two previous references to Abraham in the afterlife (13:28; 20:37) had synoptic parallels, Luke 16:19–31 has no parallel account in the other Gospels.[48] In addition, whereas the two previous references to Abraham were more in passing, the story of the rich man and Lazarus grants a more developed role to Abraham than any other passage in Luke, or for that matter in the Synoptic Gospels. Indeed, this passage contains many of the elements that we have seen Luke develop in regard to Abraham already and so may provide a summary of sorts for Luke's use of Abraham in the Gospel.

As we have seen, Luke appeals to Abraham in developing a twofold pattern of salvation. In the first pattern, God extends salvation to those who are poor and downtrodden, whom Luke explicitly links to Abraham. In the second pattern, God extends salvation to those who repent. We have seen the first pattern in the Magnificat and the Benedictus and in the story of the bent woman. We find this pattern again in the present story in Luke's portrayal of Lazarus. He is poor, wants only scraps from the rich man's table, and is full of sores, which the dogs lick. His life has been full of evil things (16:25). When he dies, the angels carry him to the bosom of Abraham (*eis ton kolpon Abraam*, 16:22, 23).[49] Having lived in misery, he now finds comfort in God's kingdom. The pattern of salvation to the poor is confirmed when Lazarus, another son of Abraham, finds rest in the bosom of Abraham.

Regarding Lazarus's reception into God's kingdom, B. Schein writes,[50]

> Lazarus has evidently repented even as the crowd had been warned to repent in 3:8, while the rich man has relied on a kinship that seems to guarantee salvation, given his blessed state of wealth.

There is no evidence, however, that Lazarus has repented of anything. Just as the bent woman was healed through no initiative of her own (13:10–17), so here Lazarus appears to be worthy of God's kingdom merely because of his long-suffering (cf. 20:35). In Luke, God extends mercy in a special way to those who endure a life of hardship.

The rich man of the story demonstrates, if in a negative way, the second pattern of salvation tied to Abraham, in which God extends mercy to those who show signs of repentance. We have seen this pattern in the preaching of John the Baptist and in the story of Zacchaeus. We find this pattern in the present story in Luke's portrayal of the rich man, whose life shows no sign of the necessary repentance.

The rich man is well clothed and well fed, has received good things in his lifetime, and ignores poor Lazarus. Having lived sumptuously, he finds himself in torment in Hades after his death. In the midst of his suffering he looks up and sees Abraham with Lazarus in his bosom. This scene calls to mind Luke 13:28, where those cast out of God's kingdom see Abraham. The rich man sees Abraham and seeks mercy from him, twice addressing him as "Father" (16:24, 27); Abraham in turn calls the rich man "child" (*teknon*, 16:25).[51] The rich man provides an example of one who has not heeded the warning of John the Baptist in 3:8: "Do not . . . say to yourselves, 'We have Abraham as our father.'" The rich man did not repent in his life, as is evident from his treatment of poor Lazarus, and so he is not truly a "son of Abraham," even though Abraham calls him "child" (*teknon*). In contrast to the unrepentant rich man, Zacchaeus demonstrated his repentance by his treatment of the poor (19:8) and so is deemed a "son of Abraham" (*huios Abraam*, 19:9).

The rich man still has not truly repented even in Hades. This can be seen from the way in which he continues to view Lazarus as a servant who should do his bidding. Thus he asks Abraham first to send Lazarus to bring him water (16:24), then to send Lazarus to warn his brothers (16:27–28). The rich man looks to Abraham as a mediator between the heavenly realm and Hades in the afterlife. But Abraham turns down both of the rich man's requests. The pattern of reversal here is permanent. Because the rich man did not repent and did not use his wealth to show mercy to the poor, no mercy is shown to him in the afterlife. Lazarus, by contrast, finds eternal comfort.

Thus in 16:19–31 we find the two patterns of salvation associated with Abraham brought together in one story. Lazarus fits the pattern of the poor on whom God has mercy. The rich man fits the pattern of the one standing in need of repentance. These two patterns of salvation are integrally related, as the reality of repentance finds expression in the extension of mercy to the poor.[52] Since the rich man in his lifetime did not act on behalf of the poor man Lazarus, neither can Lazarus act on behalf of the rich man in the afterlife.

In summary, Luke develops a rather full composite picture of Abraham and appeals to him in a variety of contexts: in the announcement of Jesus' birth, which fulfills the promise to Abraham (1:55, 73); in the proclamation of John the Baptist, which prepares the way for Jesus and denies any significance to physical descent from Abraham (3:8, 34); in Jesus' ministry, which shows who the true sons and daughters of Abraham are (13:10–17; 19:1–10); and in stories concerning the resurrection and afterlife, where Abraham is present (13:28; 20:37; 16:19–31). Luke closely associates Abraham with two patterns of salvation: mercy to the poor and mercy to those showing signs of repentance. By making these connections, Luke stresses God's acceptance of the outcast: those on the margin of society, on the one hand, and those sinners on the margin of God's kingdom who repent, on the other hand. Being Jewish has little or nothing to do with either pattern of salvation. Like Paul before him, Luke refuses to grant significance to physical descent from Abraham. By downplaying the significance of any Jewish claim on Abraham and by universalizing the scope of the promise to Abraham, Luke in his Gospel anticipates the explicit move he makes in Acts of tying Abraham directly to Gentile inclusion in God's kingdom. We turn now to an examination of Luke's use of Abraham in Acts.

The Use of Abraham in Acts

Abraham in Peter's Speech at the Temple (Acts 3:11–26)

In the Gospel of Luke we saw Abraham regularly associated with a twofold pattern of salvation: God's mercy to the lowly and God's mercy to those showing signs of repentance. The first time Luke refers to Abraham in Acts (3:13), in Peter's Temple speech (3:11–26), we see this pattern continued. We will see, however, that Luke introduces here a new feature in his references to Abraham: the explicit inclusion of the Gentiles within God's promises to Abraham.

Peter's speech follows the healing of a lame man (3:1–10).[53] Luke has Peter attribute this healing to the power of "the God of Abraham and of Isaac and of Jacob, the God of our fathers" (3:13). Just as Luke linked Abraham to God's mercy to the poor and the outcast in his Gospel (1:55, 73; 13:16; 16:22–30), so this pattern continues in the first healing story of Acts (3:1–10). As with the stories of the crippled woman (Luke 13:16) and Lazarus (Luke 16:22–30), there is no indication here that the lame man repents or exhibits faith in Jesus before the healing takes place.[54] Just as Jesus had initiated the healing of the crippled woman, so Peter initiates the healing of this lame man. As Jesus called the crippled woman "the daughter of Abraham," so here Peter attributes the healing of the lame man to the power of "the God of Abraham, Isaac, and Jacob." God extends mercy in a special way to those who are poor and outcast, and Luke associates this mercy with Abraham.

Further, just as Luke linked Abraham to those showing signs of repentance in the Gospel (3:8; 19:9), so this pattern continues in Acts as Luke has Peter refer to Abraham in the context of a sermon (3:12–26) calling for repentance (3:19, 26). Just as Jesus calls Zacchaeus a "son of Abraham" (19:9) because of his repentance, so Peter calls upon the crowd to repent if they wish to live up to their status as "sons of the covenant" (*hoi huioi tēs diathēkēs*) which God gave to Abraham (3:25).[55]

Later in the same speech, however, Luke goes on to have Peter introduce the new feature of Gentile inclusion in connection with God's covenant promises to Abraham. God's covenant was intended to become a blessing to the Gentiles, which Luke spells out in 3:25. Luke here cites Genesis 22:18 (LXX): "and in your seed [*tō spermati sou*] shall all the families of the earth be blessed."[56] There is general agreement among scholars that Luke's purpose in quoting Genesis 22:18 is to point clearly to the inclusion of Gentiles in the promises of God to Abraham.[57] This purpose stands out for two reasons: (1) because of the covenant promise regarding the blessing of all the people of the world (3:25) and (2) because Israel is specified as the "first" to whom God sent Jesus, implying that God has sent Jesus to people beyond Israel as well (3:26).

One critical issue in 3:25 is whether *tō spermati sou* ("your seed") refers to Israel or to Christ. At stake here is the construal of the promise to Abraham. If *tō spermati sou* ("your seed") refers to Christ,[58] then salvation to the Gentiles is not mediated through God's blessing on Israel but comes only through Christ, independently of Israel. The promise to Abraham would then be not Gentile inclusion in a reconstituted Israel but a new people altogether with only indirect ties to the Israel of old. The blessing would come not from being connected to Israel but only from relation to Christ. If, on the other hand, *tō spermati sou* ("your seed") refers to Israel,[59] then salvation to the Gentiles would be directly mediated through God's blessing on Israel, which culminates in the coming of Christ. The promise to Abraham would then indicate the turning of Israel to Christ as the means through which God would extend salvation to the Gentiles.

Although commentators tend to see these two positions as mutually exclusive, I think Luke affirms both. In favor of taking "seed of Abraham" as a reference to Christ, two points can be made. First, the verses preceding the reference to "seed of Abraham" focus on Christ, whom God has appointed for Israel (3:20). Second, Luke makes it clear that God has sent Christ to bless Israel (3:26), perhaps seeing Israel here as among the recipients of God's covenant promise to Abraham (3:25).

Two reasons also support the position that "seed of Abraham" refers to Israel. First, as Jacob Jervell observes, elsewhere in Luke's writing "seed of Abraham" never refers to Christ or the church (Luke 1:55; 7:5–6; see also Acts 13:23) but refers instead consistently to Israel. Second, as Jacques Dupont notes, the emphasis in 3:26 that God sent Christ *first* to the Jews to bless them, which shows the priority of the Jews in salvation history, indicates that the blessing of all the families of the earth (3:25) comes through Israel's having received the blessing of Christ. Israel is thus the very source of Christ, and all the families of the earth are blessed because of Abraham's seed, that is, Israel. Otherwise the priority of the Jews in 3:26 would make little sense.

Thus, I would argue, the covenant with Abraham is God's promise that through the blessing of Israel in Christ the Gentiles will find blessing. Christ is the focus of this covenant promise for both Israel and the Gentiles, but Christ also comes from Israel. By repenting and receiving God's intended blessing, Israel in turn becomes the vehicle for God's blessing upon the nations. Oddly enough, however, for Luke Israel's rejection of Christ also leads to God's blessing upon the nations (e.g., Acts 18:6).

To summarize this section, we see in Acts 3:12–26 that the twofold pattern of God's mercy to the Jews in Luke's Gospel now has implications for the Gentiles in Acts. Just as Abraham serves as a focal point for the extension of God's salvation to the outsiders among the Jews in Luke's Gospel (Luke 1:55, 73; 13:16; 16:22–30) and is referred to in Acts 3 with reference to the healing of the lame man, so Peter's speech reaches its climax in 3:25–26 with the assertion that God is extending his mercy to the Gentiles, the outsiders par excellence, in fulfillment of God's covenant promise to Abraham in Genesis 22:18.[60] And just as Abraham serves as a focal point for salvation coming to those who show signs of repentance in Luke's Gospel (Luke 3:8; 19:9; 16:22–30) and is referred to in Peter's call for repentance in Acts 3, so the repentant in Israel receive God's blessing from Christ and in turn become the means by which this same blessing is made available in Christ to the Gentiles (3:25–26). The Jews show signs of their repentance by welcoming Gentiles in Christ into the people of God. Luke, then, extends this dual pattern of salvation associated with Abraham from the Jews to the Gentiles in Acts.[61]

Abraham in Stephen's Speech (Acts 7:2–8)

The use of Abraham in connection with the twofold pattern of salvation coming to the outsiders and to the repentant, so prominent in Luke's Gospel and in Acts 3, takes a new turn in Stephen's speech in Acts 7:2–53. Although attention must be given to the speech as a whole, our focus will be on that section of the speech which appeals to Abraham, 7:2–8.[62] Since this is the only place in Acts where Luke develops the figure of Abraham at any length, this passage has particular importance for understanding Luke's use of Abraham.

A number of elements stand out in Stephen's speech to the Jewish leaders regarding Abraham in 7:2–8. As Nils Dahl and B. W. Bacon have pointed out, the speech curiously leaves out summary references to Abraham in Egypt, to Abraham and Lot, to Hagar and Ishmael, to the destruction of Sodom, and, most striking, to the sacrifice of Isaac.[63] Instead, the speech focuses on the migration of Abraham (7:2–4), the promise of the land (7:5–7), and, in passing, the covenant of circumcision (7:8) and the birth and circumcision of Isaac (7:8).

Luke highlights in particular the relationship between Abraham and the land, but he does so in such a way that he actually undercuts the significance of the promise of the land per se.[64] Luke accomplishes this undercutting in two ways. First, by relating the story of the migration of Abraham—or rather, God's moving Abraham—from Mesopotamia to Haran, and then from Haran to Canaan ("this land in which you are now living," 7:4), Luke stresses that God dealt with Abraham in a land not his own. Second, even when he arrives in the promised land (7:4), "yet he gave him no inheritance in it, not even a foot's length, but promised to give it to him in possession and to his posterity after him, though he had no child" (7:5). Even when Abraham migrated to the land that God showed him, he did not receive an inheritance in it.

Thus we find Abraham in an anomalous position. When Abraham is in another land, God promises to show him a land he will receive; yet when he arrives in the land that God has shown him, he receives no inheritance in the land. Rather, God gives the land not to Abraham alone, but to Abraham and his posterity. The reception of the land as an inheritance depends on Abraham having heirs, which he does not yet have in

7:5 but does have in 7:8. Despite the prominence of land in Luke's recounting of the story of Abraham, Abraham himself appears landless. His posterity will receive the land only after they themselves are slaves in an alien land for four hundred years; only then will they come out to the land that God had shown Abraham (7:7).

The motif of "Abraham and the land" thus serves as the focus for Luke's entire portrayal of the Abraham story. At several points Luke's account varies from the stories about Abraham in Genesis,[65] but at one point in particular, Acts 7:7, Luke tips his hand about his attitude toward Abraham. Luke first recounts the way in which God had called Abraham from Mesopotamia and had promised land to him and his posterity (7:2–6). Although his posterity would endure four hundred years of slavery in a land belonging to others (7:6; Gen. 15:13), in 7:7 Luke has Stephen recall God's words: "'But I will judge the nation which they serve,' said God, 'and after that they shall come out and worship me in this place.'" The scripture citation conflates two passages, Genesis 15:14 and Exodus 3:12, as the following comparison shows:

Genesis 15:14	*Acts 7:7*	*Exodus 3:12*
But I will bring judgment on the nation which they serve, and afterward they shall come out with great possessions.	But I will judge the nation which they serve, said God, and after that they shall come out and worship me in this place.	When you have brought forth the people out of Egypt, you shall serve God upon this mountain.

Luke changes the end of the citation of Genesis 15:14, so that whereas Genesis 15:14 concludes, "and afterward they shall come out *with great possessions*," Acts 7:7 concludes with the end of Exodus 3:12 (conforming it to the syntax of Gen. 15:14), "and after that they shall come out *and worship me* in this place." The effect of this change is to redefine the nature of the promise from focusing on Israel's *possessions* to Israel's *worshiping* in the promised land. The function of the land is to be a vehicle for free and true worship of God, not something else Israel will possess.[66]

Another change occurs in Luke's adaptation of Exodus 3:12, where "upon this mountain" (*en tō orei toutō*) becomes "in this place" (*en tō topō toutō*). At issue is the meaning of "this place." Does it refer to the land in general, Jerusalem, or, given the context of Stephen's speech, to the Temple (6:13, 14)? Against John Kilgallen and others, I think that "this place" here refers to the promised land in general, not to the Temple or Jerusalem.[67] The immediate antecedent of "this place" in 7:7 is not the Temple but the land, which is the repeated subject of 7:2–6. Kilgallen mistakenly identifies "this place" in 7:7 with the Temple, because he sees the antecedent as being "this place" in 6:14. This identification begs the question, however, of why 7:7 should refer back to the charges of 6:13–14 when the rest of this section (7:2–8) does not do so. Such a position requires, further, an explanation as to why the immediate antecedent, the land, does not suffice.[68]

The answer to the question of whether "this place" refers to the land, Jerusalem, or the Temple determines the extent to which Stephen's speech can be seen as using Abraham in an anti-Temple or anti-Jerusalem polemic. If the reference were to the Temple or Jerusalem, Luke would be using Abraham to attack the very centers of Judaism that Jews claim to be grounded in the promises to Abraham.[69] That some early Christians used Abraham in such a way cannot be doubted, as the preceding chapters of this study indicate. At issue, however, is the question of whether or not Luke-Acts uses Abraham in anti-Jewish polemic.

I contend that the appeal to Abraham in the Stephen speech functions not to denigrate the Temple but to point to the purpose of God's giving the land in the first place—true worship.[70] The focus on *true* worship rather than the *place* of worship becomes clearer when attention is drawn to the parallels between Acts 7:6–7 and the Benedictus in Luke 1:68–75.[71] In Luke 1:72–75 Zechariah praises God, who in Christ has been faithful

> to perform the mercy promised to our fathers, and to remember his holy covenant, the oath which he swore to our father Abraham, to grant us that we, being delivered from the hand of our enemies, might serve him without fear, in holiness and righteousness before him all the days of our life.

The purpose of being delivered from one's enemies is service and worship (*latreuein*, 1:74). This purpose parallels almost exactly the salvation history retold by Stephen in Acts 7:6–7, where after four hundred years of slavery God delivers the people to the promised land, "and after that they shall come out and worship me in this place" (7:7). Just as the crippled woman in Luke 13 worships God after being delivered from Satan, so Israel is to worship God after being delivered from its enemies.

The promise to Abraham finds its fulfillment not in the possession of the land per se but in the worship and service rendered to God by God's people. The inheritance of the land only functions as a means to this end, and true worship does not depend on this inheritance. Worship fulfills God's purpose for giving the land; true worship is not incidental to the giving of the land but is the whole reason God gives Israel the land.[72]

At the same time, God's presence is not limited to any specific land.[73] Thus Luke stresses that God is present to Abraham in Mesopotamia, Haran, and Canaan (7:2–4). The promise to Abraham regarding the land is transformed by Luke into a promise that finds fulfillment in the expression of worship, and worship, according to Luke, is localized now in Christ, even if this is only implicit in Stephen's speech.[74] Thus true worship transcends the promised land and takes on a new focus in Christ, who transcends the boundaries between Jews and Gentiles and Samaritans.

Further, Stephen himself exemplifies the worship about which he speaks. Luke connects Stephen to Abraham by his narration of Stephen's martyrdom. Just as at the beginning of Stephen's speech he says that "the God of glory" (*ho theos tēs doxēs*) appeared to Abraham to lead him on his pilgrimage (7:2), so at the end of the speech Luke tells us that Stephen, "full of the Holy Spirit, gazed into heaven and saw the glory of God" (*doxan theou*, 7:55). But Stephen also sees "Jesus standing at the right hand of God" (7:55). When Stephen relates his vision and the crowd responds by stoning him, Stephen then prays directly to Jesus: "Lord Jesus, receive my spirit" (7:59), even praying the prayer that Jesus prayed on the cross (Luke 23:34): "Lord, do not hold this sin against them" (7:60). Both Abraham and Stephen experience God's glory, Abraham in the promise given by God and Stephen in the fulfillment of that promise in Christ. [75] Luke demonstrates the new focus on Christ by portraying Stephen's vision of Christ and prayer to Christ, both features of worship.

In Stephen's speech, Luke uses Abraham in a different way from what we have seen before in Luke-Acts. The emphasis falls on redefining the promise of the land in terms of worship rather than on the dual pattern of mercy to those who repent and to those who are on the fringe. Nor is the emphasis on Gentile inclusion per se. However, the way in which Luke transforms the thrust of the promise to Abraham away from possession of the land to worship has two direct implications for Gentile inclusion. First, as Dahl points out, the "Jewishness of Abraham is not concealed but emphatically pronounced."[76] Simply by beginning the salvation history of

Israel with the figure of Abraham, Luke makes the fulfillment of God's promises to Abraham the basis of all that is to follow. The promises are mediated from Abraham through Israel, culminating in Christ. Second, however, by redefining God's promise to Abraham regarding the land in terms of worship, Luke undercuts the significance of the promised land as a special possession of the Jews. What matters in being an heir of the Abrahamic promise is not possession of any land but worshipful service of God. Gentiles can become true heirs of Abraham by worshiping God in holiness and righteousness (1:75). This worship is accessible to them in Christ, regardless of their locale. Worship sanctifies the land; it is not possession of the land which sanctifies worship. Gentiles can participate in the promise to Abraham on the same basis as Jews.

Finally, the very placement of the Stephen speech in Acts as the final witness to the Jews in Jerusalem, followed by the preaching in Samaria and the beginning of the Gentile mission, has the effect of dovetailing the mission to the Gentiles with the salvation history of Israel. Gentile Christians stand in continuity with the promises of God made to Abraham.

Abraham in Paul's Speech at Pisidian Antioch
(Acts 13:13-52)

The movement toward the Gentiles becomes explicit in Paul's speech at Pisidian Antioch (13:13–52), which contains the last references to Abraham in Luke-Acts (13:17, 26, 32).[77] As in Acts 7, we find here a recapitulation of Israel's history. In this instance, however, there is no separate section on the Abraham story. Rather, a summary statement in 13:17 includes a reference to Abraham: "The God of this people Israel chose our fathers."

In 13:26 Luke has Paul appeal to the people by addressing them as "Brethren, sons of the family of Abraham" (*huioi genous Abraam*). In the same breath Paul addresses "those among you that fear God" (*hoi en hymin phoboumenoi ton theon*), referring to Gentile adherents of Judaism. Paul's message is that "we bring you the good news that what God promised to the fathers, this he has fulfilled to us their children by raising Jesus" (13:32–33). The promise to Abraham, implicit in reference to "the fathers," finds fulfillment in Jesus. As was the case in Peter's speech in Acts 3, Paul calls for repentance in this speech. The rejection of the message means rejecting one's identity as a true child of Abraham, since one rejects the fulfillment of the promise made to Abraham (13:46). As the promise to Abraham is linked with inclusion of the Gentiles in Acts 3:25–26, so in 13:47 this theme is reiterated by Paul: "I have set you to be a light for the Gentiles, that you may bring salvation to the uttermost parts of the earth." The Gentiles hear and gladly receive this message of salvation (13:48). Thus the speech beginning with the last reference to Abraham in Acts, a speech to Jews and Gentiles, concludes with the preaching of Gentile inclusion and with Gentile reception of the gospel.

Conclusion

Our examination of the use of Abraham in Luke-Acts has pointed to the inclusion of the outcast. Luke has developed this use in several ways. First, in the Gospel, we saw Luke appeal to Abraham in two related patterns: God's mercy to the pious poor (in the Magnificat, the Benedictus, the healing of the crippled woman, and Lazarus); and God's mercy to those showing signs of repentance (the preaching of John the Baptist, Zacchaeus, and the rich man). We saw in Acts how Luke continued appealing to Abraham in terms of these patterns: Peter's speech following the healing of the lame man; and the calls for repentance in the speeches of Peter, Stephen, and Paul.

We also saw the way in which Luke appealed to Abraham in terms of this twofold pattern as a springboard for the extension in Acts of God's salvation to the outcasts par excellence, the Gentiles. The promises to Abraham are redefined in such a way as to point directly to Gentile inclusion. The promise of the land, which would potentially militate against Gentile inclusion, is redefined so as to focus on true worship of God, a worship now localized in Jesus and accessible to all, Jew and Gentile alike.

What ramifications, then, does Luke's use of Abraham have for our understanding of early Christian controversy with Judaism? First, when Luke refers to Abraham, his primary concern is inclusion of the outcast, climaxing in the incorporation of the Gentiles in God's promises. This inclusion is consistent with the Jewish heritage, according to Luke. Indeed, Luke sees the coming of Christ as the culmination of the Jewish heritage, since Christ becomes the vehicle for the fulfillment of God's promises to Abraham.

Yet, what about the Jews? Luke does not use Abraham to argue for the exclusion of the Jews as God's people, although he does use Abraham to qualify Jewish inclusion. He qualifies

Jewish inclusion by moving away from one traditional ground of such inclusion, physical descent. Instead, he moves toward inclusion on the basis of pious poverty and repentance. He also qualifies Jewish inclusion by calling non-Christian Jews to belief in Christ, especially in Acts. Yet he does not go so far as categorically to exclude Jews who do not evidence belief in Christ. Thus Luke shows some degree of ambiguity regarding the issue of Jewish inclusion.

As we shall see in the next chapter, however, for John there is no ambiguity on this point.

5

The True Children
of Abraham:
Abraham
in the Gospel of John

Of all the early Christian literature that uses Abraham in controversy with Judaism, the Gospel of John takes the most polemical stance, perhaps because it stands closer to the heat of Jewish/Christian controversy than any of the other extant literature.[1] In the Gospel of John we encounter a Christian community embroiled in Jewish/Christian controversy, shaping its identity in relation both to Judaism and to other forms of Christianity. By and large, the struggle of the Johannine community with non-Christian Judaism represents this community's birth pangs as it emerged from Judaism toward the end of the first century C.E. That the Fourth Gospel comes from a community whose origin lies in Jewish Christianity can no longer be called into question. But the relationship of Johannine Christianity to non-Christian Judaism remains the focus of much debate. In this chapter we will see how Abraham figured in the Jewish/Christian controversy that the Gospel of John reflects.

Our discussion will center on John 8:31–59, the only passage in which John refers to Abraham explicitly.[2] John 8:31–59 has been approached from many different angles. While there are only a few full-scale works that address this passage, it has also been the focus of several special studies and has received a variety of treatments in the standard commentaries.[3] In spite of all the different approaches to this passage in the secondary literature, there appears to be a measure of consensus that it presents the greatest conflict between the Jews and Jesus during his public ministry.[4]

For the purposes of my argument, this consensus is rather

significant, because John assigns to the figure of Abraham a prominent role precisely at the height of the tension between Jesus and the Jews. In John 8:31–59 the Jews first take specific steps to kill Jesus, by picking up stones (8:59), after Jesus states "Before Abraham was, I am" (8:58). Thus, in the passage in which Jesus and the Jews stand most sharply over against each other in the Gospel of John, the argument revolves around the figure of Abraham (8:39–44), who is mentioned here by name eleven times (and nowhere else in the Gospel). Is this accidental, or does what Samuel Sandmel said about Philo, and Nils Dahl about Luke-Acts, also apply here: What a writer says about Abraham provides the basic clue to what he wants to say?[5] We will see that in the midst of intense conflict between Jesus and the Jews, the use of Abraham provides a clue regarding what John wants to say.

We will proceed in two steps, the first addressing the literary dimensions of John 8:31–59, the second addressing the specific use of Abraham in 8:31–59. The first step will help us understand some of the nuances of John's use of Abraham in the second step. In the first step, we will establish the character of John 8:31–59 as a discrete literary unit, look at the larger literary context (John 7–8), and see how 8:12–30 sets the stage for 8:31–59. In the second step, after some general comments on 8:31–59, we will survey John's use of Abraham, focusing on the terms "descendants of Abraham" (*sperma Abraam*) and "children of Abraham" (*tekna Abraam*) and on the relationship between Abraham and Jesus. By way of summary and conclusion we will assess the role of Abraham in the Johannine community's controversy with Judaism.

Literary Dimensions of John 8:31–59

John 8:31–59 as a Discrete Literary Unit

One overriding factor shows that 8:31–59 is a coherent literary unit: references to Abraham. As we noted above, only in this section does John refer to Abraham (8:33, 37, 39 [3x], 40, 52, 53, 56, 57, 58). The section clearly ends in 8:59, as the scene changes completely in 9:1, where new characters are introduced (the blind man, Jesus' disciples) in a new context (Jesus passing by, after he went out of the Temple), introducing a new story (the healing of the blind man).

Determining where the section begins is more difficult. All of John 8 contains a series of loose discourses by Jesus and controversy dialogues between Jesus and the Jews (8:12–20;

21–30; 31–47; 48–59).[6] Abraham begins to figure into these discourses and dialogues at 8:33, where the Jews appeal to Abraham in responding to Jesus' statement in 8:31–32. These are not just any Jews, however. They are "the Jews who had believed in him" (8:31). But this reference picks up, in turn, on 8:30: "As he spoke thus, many believed in him." As it stands, however, 8:30 functions as a summary statement to 8:21–29, and 8:31 begins a new subsection within John 8. As the final form of the text has come down to us, then, 8:31–59 stands as a coherent block of material in which the figure of Abraham plays a dominant role.[7]

John 7–8 as the Larger Literary Context

John 7–8 hangs together as the larger literary unit within which 8:31–59 functions. Two themes tie all of John 7 and 8 together. First, and most important, throughout John 7–8 we find the motif of the Jews seeking to kill Jesus, as C. H. Dodd has shown.[8] In 7:1 Jesus avoids Judea, because the Jews are seeking to kill him.[9] In 7:19 Jesus asks the Jews, "Why do you seek to kill me?"[10] In 7:25 Jesus is referred to as "the man whom [the Jews] seek to kill."[11] In 8:28 Jesus clearly anticipates his death by saying that the Son of man will be lifted up. In 8:37 and 40 Jesus says to the Jews, "You seek to kill me." This statement is borne out at the end of the chapter, in 8:59, where the Jews do indeed try to stone Jesus. The motif of the Jews seeking to kill Jesus is thus sharply drawn and ties John 7 and 8 together.[12]

The second theme that ties John 7 and 8 together is the Feast of Tabernacles.[13] In 7:2 we hear that the Feast of Tabernacles is at hand. In 7:8 Jesus turns down his brothers' advice to go up to the feast, but right after this, in 7:10, he goes up to the feast secretly. In 7:14 we are told that in the middle of the feast Jesus went up to the Temple and taught. In 7:37 we read: "On the last day of the feast, the great day, Jesus stood up and proclaimed, 'If any one thirst, let him come to me and drink.'" The motif of thirst/drinking refers to a prominent feature of the Feast of Tabernacles, water-libation ceremonies.[14] The pronouncement of Jesus in 8:12 also appears to take place on the last day of the Feast of Tabernacles: "I am the light of the world." Like water, the motif of light takes on special significance against the backdrop of the Feast of Tabernacles, in which a lamplighting ceremony played an important part. After the pronouncement in 8:12, the Feast of Tabernacles setting does not appear again explicitly. Sufficient notice has been taken of this feast throughout John 7 and 8, however, that it still serves as a broad unifying theme for both chapters. In addition, throughout John 7 and 8 Jesus teaches in the Temple (7:14, 28; 8:20), where special rituals of the feast were observed. Jesus does not leave the Temple until 8:59.[15] Thus two themes bind John 7 and 8 together as the larger literary context for 8:31–59: the Jews' intention to kill Jesus and the Feast of Tabernacles.[16]

John 8:12-30—Setting the Stage for 8:31-59

Although John 8 functions within the larger literary unit of John 7 and 8, a new scene opens with 8:12. This change of scene is signaled in three ways. First, after the pronouncement of Jesus in 7:37–38 and the editorial comment in 7:39, the spotlight shifts away from the dialogue between Jesus and the Jews to a discussion among the Jews as to whether or not Jesus is the Christ (7:40–44). This intra-Jewish discussion continues to 7:52; then in 8:12 Jesus suddenly reappears. Second, there is physical movement, as the officers who had been sent by the chief priests and the Pharisees to arrest Jesus in 7:32 return empty-handed at the end of the chapter (7:45–52). And third, the reader is told in 8:12 that Jesus resumes speaking to the people.

The scene shift in 8:12 introduces the term "Father" (*patēr*, 8:18–19) and with it the notion of paternity, which is a prominent theme that anticipates 8:31–59.[17] This theme distinguishes 8:12–59 from what precedes and from what follows.[18]

In addition, beginning with 8:12 the Jews no longer dispute with one another regarding the identity of Jesus (as in 7:25–27, 32, 35–36, 40–52); rather, the dialogue is exclusively between Jesus and the Jews, identified either as Pharisees (8:13) or simply as "Jews" (8:22). Throughout 8:12–30 the Johannine Jesus deepens the rift between himself and the Jews by contrasting himself with the Jews. In 8:14 Jesus knows where he comes from and whither he is going, but he tells the Jews, "You do not know whence I come or whither I am going." In 8:15 Jesus judges no one, but he tells the Jews, "You judge according to the flesh." In 8:18 Jesus and the Father bear witness to Jesus, but he tells the Jews, "You know neither me nor my Father" (8:19). In 8:23 Jesus says he is from above, but he tells the Jews, "You are from below." Jesus and the Jews operate on completely different levels, and this explains why the Jews do not understand him (8:27) and consequently do not believe him (8:24).

John 8:12–30 thus sets the stage for 8:31–59 in two ways. First, by introducing "the Father" into the discussion, it anticipates the theme of paternity revolving around Abraham in 8:31–59. Second, by contrasting Jesus with the Jews, it builds up the tension between Jesus and the Jews, which culminates in Jesus' statement regarding Abraham in 8:58 that, in turn, prompts the Jews to pick up stones to throw at Jesus in 8:59.

Abraham in John 8:31–59

General Comments

While there is widespread agreement about dividing John 8:12–59 into three sections (8:12–20, 21–30, 31–59), there is little agreement regarding the structure of 8:31–59 and especially of 8:31–47. Most commentators treat 8:48–59 as a single unit.[19] I think it best to structure 8:31–59 in two parts: 8:31–47 and 8:48–59. There are two basic reasons for this structuring: the thematic use of Abraham and the identity of the Jews in dialogue with Jesus. First, the appeals to Abraham in 8:31–47 revolve around the Jews' claim to be descendants and children of Abraham (8:33, 37, 39), contesting Jesus' statement in 8:31–32. This theme is absent from 8:48–59. The appeals to Abraham in 8:48–59 revolve around the Jews' claim that even Abraham died (8:52, 53, 57), contesting Jesus' statement in 8:51. The thematic use of Abraham in 8:31–47 differs from that in 8:48–59.

Second, in 8:31 the Jews who are addressed by Jesus are identified as "the Jews who had believed in him." This group responds to Jesus in 8:39, with no explicit mention of their identity. It is understood that they are the same as those addressed in 8:31. But in 8:48 explicit reference is made to "the Jews," perhaps suggesting a different group from "the Jews who had believed in him" of 8:31. Otherwise, it is unclear why they are explicitly identified, breaking the pattern of 8:39.[20] While the shift in 8:48 to "the Jews" does not provide conclusive evidence of a different group from 8:31, it is a strong possibility.

The different thematic use of Abraham and the identity of the Jews thus point to a seam between 8:47 and 48, which most commentators recognize. Perhaps, then, 8:31–47 and 8:48–59 were originally two separate controversy dialogues that have been joined together in John. Even though a seam exists between 8:47 and 48, it does not have a dramatic effect upon how we should understand 8:31–59 as a whole, since both halves involve appeals to Abraham by a group of Jews in controversy with Jesus.[21]

We may start a more detailed examination of 8:31–59 by observing the flow of thought in this section, with the expectation that it will provide us with some initial clues regarding John's use of Abraham. The passage begins (8:31) with Jesus addressing Jews who purportedly believed in him (8:30). Jesus claims that if they abide in his word, they will be his disciples, know the truth, and be free.[22]

This claim is followed by Jewish reaction in the form of a counterclaim that appeals to Abraham and provides the basis for a question regarding freedom (8:33). Jesus responds first to their question about freedom with another pronouncement in 8:34–35, which connects the Jews' bondage with slavery to sin, a theme to which he had earlier referred (8:21, 24). In 8:36 Jesus essentially restates the initial claim of 8:31. Only then does he go on in 8:37 to address the counterclaim (8:33) made by the Jews regarding their Abrahamic heritage. He concedes that they are descendants of Abraham but then states that his word does not dwell within them. Jesus appears to arrive at this conclusion because of their objection in 8:33. Thus they do not meet the general condition stated by Jesus in 8:31 and are not truly his disciples.

In 8:38 Jesus then makes an implicit distinction between two contrasting fathers: the father of Jesus ("I speak of what I have seen with my Father") and the father of the Jews ("and you do what you have heard from your father"). In response to this distinction the Jews reiterate the claim they made in 8:33: "Abraham is our father" (8:39). Jesus, in turn, responds with an awkward conditional sentence, in which he challenges their status as children of Abraham (8:39b). The extent to which their actions parallel those of Abraham provides the criterion for assessing their claim to be children of Abraham. Since they seek to kill Jesus, they are not Abraham's children, for this is not what Abraham did (8:40). Rather, they do the works of their true father (8:41a).

The Jews respond much as they did in 8:39, except now they claim not only Abrahamic sonship but also divine sonship (8:41b). With this the Jews appeal to higher ground, making explicit the implication of their claims regarding Abraham. Abraham is their father in an earthly sense. They are his physical seed and share in his heritage. But this relationship actually symbolizes on a deeper level their relationship to God as Father. The Jews' appeal to Abraham in 8:31–40 has now led to a discussion of paternity at a depth level (8:41b).

Jesus responds to this higher claim in 8:42, and so begins a short polemical discourse that ends in 8:47, in which Abraham is absent from the discussion. Just as Jesus had denied that Abraham was their father with the conditional sentence in 8:39, so now Jesus denies that God is their Father with the contrary-to-fact condition in 8:42. Just as their actions demonstrated that Abraham was not their father (8:39), so their actions demonstrate that God is not their Father (8:42). Their rejection of Jesus finds expression in their failure to love Jesus, which shows that God is not their Father (8:42).

The Johannine Jesus then goes on to analyze the theological roots of their rejection of him and their inability to hear his word. It is not mere stubbornness or hard-heartedness. Rather, their incapacity arises from the very core of their being, for they have another father than God, a father whose will they seek to do over against the will of God. This father can be none other than the devil (8:44), as is revealed by their desire to kill the one sent by God. Because they align themselves with the one who opposes God's purposes, they show themselves to be in collusion with the devil and in fact children of the devil.[23]

If, as Jesus concedes in 8:37, they are descendants of Abraham, at the same time they are children of the devil. They cannot hear or see the truth which Jesus speaks because it is not in their nature to do so. In this polemic, John has moved far beyond accusing the Jews of having mistakenly decided against Jesus because of a false notion of allegiance to the one true God. Rather, they were *never* God's children, as has now been revealed by their hostile reaction to Jesus. These Jews are not of God; they are of the devil, and so their claims about Abraham as earthly father and God as heavenly Father can be seen for the lies that they are. *It is not their rejection of Jesus that has placed them on the side of the devil; rather, it is because they are on the side of the devil that they have rejected Jesus and have sought to kill him.*

The Jews respond by accusing Jesus of having a demon, a charge that Jesus denies (8:48–50). In 8:51 Jesus makes another pronouncement: that the one who keeps his word will not see death (parallel to the statement about abiding in Jesus' word in 8:31). Just as in 8:33, so in 8:52 the Jews appeal to Abraham by way of rejecting Jesus' claim. Even Abraham, the greatest of the fathers, died. Surely, they add, Jesus is not claiming to be greater than Abraham (8:53)! But that is exactly what the Johannine Jesus is claiming, as becomes clear in 8:56–58, at the conclusion of which the Jews attempt to stone

Jesus. The controversy dialogue ends with Jesus hiding himself and escaping (8:59).

The movement of the passage as a whole is one of increasing antagonism and polemic on the part of both Jesus and the Jews. At the outset we are told that Jesus was addressing Jews who had believed in him (8:31). But in the course of the controversy the escalating claims of the Jews in response to Jesus (8:33, 39, 41b, 53) are met with harsher and harsher statements by Jesus in response to the Jews (8:39, 41a, 42, 44). The Jews, in turn, make increasingly polemical statements regarding Jesus (8:41, 48, 52–53, 57, 59). As a whole, 8:31–59 creates the following effect: the very Jews who at the beginning of the dialogue had in some way believed in the Johannine Jesus are shown at the end of the dialogue to be his most vehement enemies.

The two appeals to Abraham (8:33, 52) are introduced by the Jews as evidence against Jesus' claims regarding freedom (8:32) and death (8:51).[24] In 8:31–47 the relation of the *Jews* to Abraham is at issue, and Jesus uses Abraham to turn the tables on them, showing that they are merely genetic descendants of Abraham (*sperma Abraam*) but that they do not belong to the true Abrahamic heritage as children of Abraham (*tekna Abraam*). In 8:48–59 the relation of *Jesus* to Abraham is at issue, and Jesus shows that he is indeed greater than Abraham. In both instances Jesus uses the very Abraham to whom the Jews appeal in order to drive home his point regarding their alienation from Abraham, on the one hand, and Jesus' own priority over Abraham, on the other hand.

For John, to speak of one's relation to Abraham is to speak at the same time of one's paternity. In turn, to speak of one's paternity reveals one's basic identity. In 8:31–47 the paternity of the Jews is at issue and thus their identity (8:33, 38, 39, 42, 44). In 8:48–59 the paternity of Jesus is at issue and thus his identity (8:53, 58). The issue of the Jews' paternity raised by Jesus in 8:19 ("You know neither me nor my Father") and 8:39/42 ("If you were Abraham's children" / "If God were your Father") finds its resolution in 8:44 when Jesus tells them, "You are of your father the devil." The demonic paternity of the Jews reveals their demonic identity. The issue of Jesus' paternity raised by the Jews in 8:19 ("Where is your Father?") and 8:53 ("Are you greater than our father Abraham?" / "Who do you claim to be?") finds its resolution in 8:58, when Jesus proclaims "Before Abraham was, I am." The divine paternity of Jesus reveals his divine identity.

Our examination of Abraham in 8:31–59 has shown the paternity of the Jews and the paternity of Jesus to be primary concerns of John. In regard to Abraham and the Jews, we have seen an initial contrast between the Jews as descendants of Abraham (*sperma Abraam*) and as children of Abraham (*tekna Abraam*). We turn now to investigate this contrast further, after which we will look more closely at the relationship between Jesus and Abraham in John.

Sperma Abraam and tekna Abraam

The distinction in John 8:31–59 between *sperma* ("descendants") and *tekna* ("children") has often been noted in passing by interpreters, but it has not been given its due weight.[25] I would argue that for John the contrast between *sperma Abraam* ("descendants of Abraham") and *tekna Abraam* ("children of Abraham") points to the heart of the dispute in John 8:31–47. The contrast is set up with 8:33, where the Jews respond to Jesus' claim of 8:31–32 with a counterclaim of their own: "We are descendants of Abraham [*sperma Abraam*], and have never been in bondage to anyone."[26] Jesus does not deny their status as "descendants of Abraham"; indeed, he concedes it in 8:37: "I know that you are descendants of Abraham (*sperma Abraam*)." Jesus goes on, however, to draw a distinction between his own actions (8:38) and the actions of the Jews (8:37–38) on the basis of an implied distinction between two different fathers.

The Jews respond by reiterating in a different fashion the claim they made in 8:33, this time claiming not that they are "descendants of Abraham" (which Jesus had allowed) but that "Abraham is our father" (*ho patēr hēmōn Abraam estin*). It is this claim that Jesus denies (8:39). But how can Jesus acknowledge that they are "descendants of Abraham" while at the same time denying that Abraham is their father? While he has conceded that they have a genetic link to Abraham as "descendants" (according to the flesh, cf. 8:15), he denies that this makes Abraham their father in any meaningful way. Genetic descent has no bearing on paternity.

At this point the term *tekna Abraam* ("children of Abraham") comes into play. Jesus states, "If you were Abraham's children, you would do what Abraham did" (8:39, RSV; *ei tekna tou Abraam este, ta erga tou Abraam epoieite*). The RSV translation treats 8:39 as a contrary-to-fact condition: "If you were . . . , you would do." The implication is that the Jews in fact do not do what Abraham did, and so they are not "chil-

dren of Abraham." The Greek at this point, however, is more
ambiguous and technically falls under the category of a mixed
condition, which does not have the customary *an* in the
apodosis.[27] Accordingly, Raymond E. Brown translates 8:39 to
reflect the mixed condition: "If you are really Abraham's children, you would be doing works worthy of Abraham." The
implication, as Brown points out, is that "the Jews are really
Abraham's children, but are denying it by their actions."[28]
Although by strict grammatical rules Brown is correct, both
the introduction of 8:40 with the adversative expression *nun
de* ("but now") and the content of the verse make it clear that
by seeking to kill Jesus, the Jews do not do what Abraham did
and so are not really Abraham's children. Thus, even if the
grammatical construction of 8:39 is a mixed condition, strictly
speaking, the force of 8:40 makes it read as a contrary-to-fact
condition.[29] Although Jesus will concede that the Jews are
sperma Abraam ("descendants of Abraham," 8:37), he does
not allow that they are *tekna Abraam* ("children of Abraham,"
8:39–40).

For the Jews in John, spiritual descent goes hand in hand
with physical descent; the one brings the other. It is this connection which Jesus denies. The Jews are portrayed as placing
a premium on genetic descent (*sperma*), assuming that the
status of being children of Abraham (*tekna*) goes along with it.
But for John, physical descent has no necessary connection to
paternity. The only thing that matters to the Johannine Jesus
is whether or not one is a *teknon Abraam* ("child of Abraham"), which is equivalent to being a *teknon theou* ("child of
God"), as we will see below.

This usage of *tekna* ("children") in contrast to *sperma* ("descendants") becomes clearer when we look at both terms elsewhere in John. The key verse is 1:12: "But to all who received
him, who believed in his name, he gave power to become
children of God (*tekna theou*)." Identity as a *teknon* ("child")
is granted only by God. It is granted only to those who receive
Jesus and believe in him, which is equivalent to remaining
in Jesus' word (8:31). To be "children of Abraham" (8:39)
means to be "children of God" (1:12). For just as Jesus denies that the Jews are "children of Abraham," that is, that
Abraham is their father (8:39), so he denies the claim of the
Jews that God is their Father (8:41–42). One's relationship to
Abraham is a sign of one's relationship to God, since Abraham
demonstrates the definitive relationship with God in Jewish
tradition. Attention to 1:12 informs our understanding of
8:39: being a child of God[30] comes as a gift from God and is

not inherited.[31] It is not a birthright. Instead, it is given to those who believe in Jesus and remain in his word. The one other reference to *tekna* ("children") in John also refers to believers: "and not for the nation only, but to gather into one the children of God (*ta tekna tou theou*) who are scattered abroad" (11:52). This passage is part of an editorial insertion explaining the real meaning of Caiaphas's prophecy regarding the significance of Jesus' death. Here "the children of God" refers to believers scattered about, perhaps both Jewish and Gentile believers.[32] This usage is consistent with 1:12 and 8:39 in referring to believers as "children" on the basis of their relationship to Christ.

The use of the terms *tekna Abraam* ("children of Abraham") and *tekna theou* ("children of God") as designations for Christians over against unbelieving Jews stands out more clearly in the light of the one other use of *sperma* ("descendants") in John. In 7:42 the Jews are disputing as to whether or not Jesus is the Christ. Some who deny he is the Christ ask, "Has not the scripture said that the Christ is descended from David (*ek tou spermatos Dauid*), and comes from Bethlehem, the village where David was?" Here some of the Jews claim that physical descent from the seed of David is a necessary requirement which the Messiah must fulfill. Since Jesus comes from Galilee, he cannot be the Messiah (7:41). Just as physical descent from Abraham (*sperma Abraam*) gives one a special status before God, according to the Jews in John (8:33), so the physical descent "from the seed of David" (*ek tou spermatos Dauid*) is the distinguishing mark of the Messiah. John does not allow either claim to stand. Just as physical descent from Abraham has no bearing on one's relationship to God, so physical descent from David has no bearing on Jesus' messianic status for John. What matters is that Jesus is from God and has been sent by God, an origin that John never tires of mentioning.[33]

The Johannine distinction between "children" and "descendants" has some important theological ramifications. From the perspective of the Fourth Gospel, one becomes a child of God (*teknon theou*) only through divine agency (cf. 1:12), not through any human agency or genetic heritage (*sperma*). According to the Fourth Gospel, the Jews fail to recognize and to respond to the divine agent who comes to them as Christ in Jesus. Apart from Christ, one has no claim to being a "child of God" and no access to God. The Jews mistakenly hold their status as "descendants of Abraham" to be a divine right to the status of "children of God." They confuse human agency with divine grace and so are not open to God's working in their midst. Thus they show themselves not to be of God (8:47). Instead, by opposing God to preserve their false status, they turn out in fact to be children of the devil (8:44). Their attempt to claim the status of "children of God" by appealing to their heritage as "descendants of Abraham" reveals their true identity as "children of the devil" (*tekna diabolou*), as murderers and liars in the likeness of their father.[34]

Finally, it is significant that the issue of Abrahamic paternity has evidently been raised not by John but by "the Jews who had believed" in Jesus, probably a reference to Christian Jewish "opponents."[35] In both 8:33 and 8:39 the Johannine Jews sound their proud boast in response to Jesus' statement in 8:31–32. Thus Abraham functions as a litmus test for the would-be believers, who in the end show themselves to be adversaries of Jesus and of John. John turns the table on them by appealing to their slogan (8:33, 39) and discounting it, showing that even as "descendants of Abraham" they are not "children of Abraham."

Abraham and Jesus

With the pronouncement of Jesus in 8:51 and the Jews' appeal to Abraham in challenging Jesus' claim (8:52), the relationship between Abraham and Jesus becomes the focal point, whereas in 8:31–40 the issue was the relationship between Abraham and the Jews and consequently between God and the Jews (8:41–47). By developing the narrative in this way, the author of the Fourth Gospel assigns a significant, indeed central, role to the figure of Abraham. The relationship of Abraham to the Jews, on the one hand, and of Abraham to Jesus, on the other hand, shows the nature of the relationship between Jesus and the Jews. The identity of each (Jesus and the Jews) becomes manifest in the relationship of each to Abraham. Again, Abraham functions as a heuristic device by which the true nature and identity of Jesus and of the Jews are revealed.

The Fourth Gospel communicates the real significance and identity of Jesus in relation to Abraham by reversing the position taken by the Jews. The Jews appeal to Abraham as the standard of greatness by which Jesus is measured. John turns this model on its head and instead shows that Jesus is the standard by which even Abraham is measured. In 8:51 Jesus makes a solemn pronouncement that whoever guards his word will not see death. To challenge this claim, the Jews point out

that even Abraham died (8:52), and on this basis they ask
Jesus whether he is greater than "our father Abraham," ex-
pecting a negative answer (indicated by the introductory *mē*
in 8:53).

The response of Jesus in 8:54–56 shows a movement similar
to the movement from 8:31–40 to 8:41–47, where the discussion moved from the relationship between the Jews and
Abraham to the relationship between the Jews and God. Similarly, the relationship between Jesus and Abraham (8:51–53)
points to the relationship between Jesus and God (8:54–55).
Jesus' greatness cannot be compared to that of Abraham, for
his greatness, his glory, comes from his Father, God, whom
the Jews falsely claim to be their Father also (8:54–55).

The statement of Jesus in 8:55 harks back to his pronouncement in 8:51. Just as whoever guards Jesus' word will not see
death, so Jesus guards the word he has received from his Father. The pattern of the relationship between Jesus and his
Father provides the pattern for the relationship between Jesus
and the believer. Jesus is not subordinate to Abraham; Abraham is not the standard by which Jesus can be measured.
Rather, only God the Father is the standard of Jesus' greatness
and glory, and Abraham is subordinate to Jesus.

This interpretation is confirmed by 8:56: Abraham rejoiced
to see Jesus' day. The response of the Jews in 8:57 shows that
they persist in judging the greatness of Jesus by the standard
of Abraham rather than the reverse: "The Jews said to him,
'You are not yet fifty years old, and have you seen Abraham?'"
The Jews fail to see that Abraham bears witness to Jesus, not
Jesus who bears witness to Abraham.[36]

The more the Jews protest, failing to comprehend and believe who Jesus is, the greater become the claims of Jesus in
relation to Abraham. The movement from 8:51 to 8:54–56 to
the climax in 8:58 progressively subordinates Abraham to Jesus. With Jesus' pronouncement in 8:58 the reversal is complete: "Truly, truly, I say to you, before Abraham was, I am."
As Raymond E. Brown observes, "No clearer implication of
divinity is found in the Gospel tradition."[37] The suspicion of
the Jews that Jesus was claiming greatness on a par with Abraham is outstripped by the radical leap here beyond Abraham
to *God*. Not only is Jesus greater than Abraham, but Jesus
existed before Abraham. The only thing more scandalous than
the claim that Abraham had a vision of Jesus and rejoiced to
see his day is the still greater claim that Jesus existed before
Abraham was born and is thus divine. The response of the
Jews in 8:59 ("So they took up stones to throw at him") dem-

onstrates for John the truth of Jesus' statements in 8:40 and 8:44.

The bridge that links the section on "Abraham and the Jews" to the section on "Abraham and Jesus" is 8:39, where the Johannine Jesus gives the criterion for assessing who truly is a "child of Abraham." The one who does "the works of Abraham" (*ta erga tou Abraam*) shows himself or herself to be a "child of Abraham" (8:39). What, then, are "the works of Abraham" to which John refers? First, it is important to note that the phrase "the works of Abraham" (*ta erga tou Abraam*) does not appear to be a technical term that was common in early Jewish or early Christian literature. Indeed, I have been unable to find any other occurrence of this phrase.[38]

Although the Fourth Gospel does not seem to be redefining a common Jewish tradition, some scholars have seen allusions here to Abraham's hospitable reception of the divine messengers in Genesis 18.[39] Although this is a possibility, there is no evidence to make it more than a possibility. A few scholars have suggested that 8:39 can be understood in the light of the Akedah tradition of Genesis 22 (the binding of Isaac) and the Isaac-Ishmael stories in general, with an implicit comparison of Isaac with Jesus and Ishmael with the Jews.[40] Having suggested the presence of the Akedah tradition, it requires only a short step to see an implicit Isaac/Ishmael typology at work, especially in the light of early Jewish traditions about Ishmael threatening the life of Isaac. The problem, however, is that neither Isaac nor Ishmael is ever explicitly mentioned in the Fourth Gospel.[41]

To what, then, does "the works of Abraham" refer? The answer is given in 8:56: "Your father Abraham rejoiced that he was to see my day; he saw it and was glad." For John, "the works of Abraham" refers to Abraham's rejoicing at seeing Jesus' day. One difficulty raised by this passage is that Jesus calls Abraham "your father," a relationship he seemed to deny to the Jews in the conditional statement of 8:39. I would suggest, however, that "your father Abraham" can be understood to mean "Abraham, whom you *claim* to be your father." It could also be understood as a concession again to their identity as descendants of Abraham but not to their identity as true children of Abraham.

According to 8:56, then, the work of Abraham consists of his witness to Jesus, as he sees Jesus and is glad. Indeed, John appears to portray Abraham as believing in Jesus.[42] In this way, Abraham is seen as fulfilling the statement of Jesus in response to his disciples' question: "Then they said to him,

'What must we do, to be doing the works of God (*ta erga tou theou*)?' Jesus answered them, 'This is the work of God, that you believe in him whom he has sent'" (6:28–29). As John the Baptist (1:19–27; 3:25–30), Isaiah (12:41), and Moses (5:39) bear witness to Jesus, so Abraham, the exemplary father of the Jews, functions exclusively as a witness to Jesus as the Christ: "Abraham rejoiced that he was to see my day; he saw it and was glad" (8:56).

The other side of his witness is that he is an accuser against those who renounce his testimony. The Jews' rejection of Abraham's testimony to Jesus is at the same time a rejection of the one who bears witness. By rejecting Jesus, the Jews renounce any claim to Abraham, who lived to point to Jesus, according to the Fourth Gospel.

Thus Abraham has an exclusively christological function for John. The differentiation between the *tekna* ("children") and the *sperma* ("descendants") of Abraham in the end shows itself to be a christological issue. One's relationship to Abraham is determined solely by whether or not one shares in the witness of Abraham to Christ. This is the work that all true "children" do but that the Jews fail to do (8:40, 45, 46). Whereas Abraham rejoiced to see Jesus' day, the Jews dishonor Jesus (8:49). Whereas Abraham was glad at seeing Jesus, the Jews attempt to kill him (8:40, 59).

Conclusion: Abraham in Johannine Controversy with Judaism

In the course of this chapter we have seen the way in which the Jewish opponents of the Johannine community, both Jews who had believed in Jesus (8:31–47) and other Jews (8:48–59), appealed to Abraham in order to dispute the claims made by the Johannine Christians regarding the status of the Jews and the significance of Jesus. We have also seen how these appeals were turned back upon their proponents by the Johannine Christians, so that Abraham served both to substantiate Johannine christological claims about Jesus and to attack positions held by the opponents of the Johannine community.

In the end, Abraham himself takes on the appearance of a "disciple of Jesus" (8:31; 6:27–28), because of his witness and self-subordination to Jesus. Abraham is a "child of God" because of his relationship to Jesus. The Jews who staked a special claim on their self-designation as "descendants of Abraham," conceded by John, find themselves abandoned in the Fourth Gospel. They have no legitimate claim to being "children of Abraham," and so stand in opposition to God the Father. On the other hand, the very ones who make no claim based on genetic descent, and who might not qualify as "descendants of Abraham," are seen to be "children of Abraham," genuine children, on account of their belief in and witness to Jesus as the Christ. In this way, Abraham plays a pivotal role at the height of Johannine Christian controversy with Judaism at the end of the first century C.E.

6

Spiritualizing
and Gnosticizing Abraham
in the Second Century

The goal of this chapter is to examine the use of Abraham in early Christian writings after the Gospel of John and before Justin's *Dialogue with Trypho*, again with special reference to the use of Abraham in Christian controversy with Judaism. Before we look at the primary literature from this perspective, it is important that we first identify the pertinent literature between about 100 and 150 C.E. Of all the Christian writings that can be dated between Justin and John with some degree of probability,[1] I count fourteen that refer explicitly to Abraham:

1. Epistle of Barnabas
2. Ignatius to the Philadelphians
3. Gospel of Philip
4. Apology of Aristides
5. 1 Clement
6. Apocalypse of Peter
7. Christian Sibyllines (Book 2)
8. Protoevangelium of James
9. Epistula Apostolorum
10. Hellenistic synagogal prayers preserved in the Apostolic Constitutions
11. Testaments of the Twelve Patriarchs
12. Greek Magical Papyri
13. Kerygmata Petrou
14. Gospel of the Nazaraeans

As I am most interested in how early Christians used Abraham in controversy with Judaism, however, not all of these writings are of equal significance. The most important sources are those in which a Christian author explicitly uses Abraham in controversy with Judaism. These sources may show either direct interaction between Christians and Jews (as in the Gospel of John or in Justin Martyr) or indirect contact. The Epistle of Barnabas, Ignatius to the Philadelphians, and the Gospel of Philip[2] all probably bear witness to direct interaction between Christians and Jews, while the Apology of Aristides probably gives evidence of indirect contact. Thus we will pay special attention in this chapter to Barnabas, Ignatius, the Gospel of Philip, and the Apology of Aristides.

There are, however, other writings in which explicit reference is made to Abraham but not in the context of any explicit or even implicit Christian controversy with Judaism. Of course, this distinction raises the question of what characterizes explicit Christian controversy with Judaism. This is not easily answered. For my purposes, explicit controversy is evident wherever a Christian writing unambiguously engages in polemical discussion with or about Jews or Judaism. For example, it is hard to get much more explicit than John 8, where Jesus denies the Jews' claim that Abraham is their father and asserts instead, "You are of your father the devil" (8:44). The same is the case with Justin, as we shall see, who in *Dialogue* 119 claims the Abrahamic heritage for the Christians and denies it to the Jews. To be sure, for some early Christians, using Abraham in contexts not explicitly critical of Jews or Judaism may still have offered an implicit critique — but it is very difficult to determine this with a degree of certainty.

Thus, although the early Christian sources we have studied so far all demonstrate explicit controversy with Judaism in their use of Abraham, to greater or lesser degrees, when we turn to literature after the Gospel of John we find that it does not always evidence clear controversy with Judaism in connection with Abraham. Even though my primary interest is in explicit early Christian controversy with Judaism, these writings are worth mentioning because they show that Abraham was also used in other contexts important to the life of early Christian communities. Writings that do not demonstrate explicit controversy with Judaism include 1 Clement, the Apocalypse of Peter, the Protoevangelium of James, the Kerygmata Petrou, the Gospel of the Nazaraeans, the Epistula Apostolorum, the Greek Magical Papyri, Christian appropriation of the Sibylline Oracles (Book 2), the Testaments of the Twelve Patriarchs, and the Hellenistic synagogal prayers, many of which writings are liturgical and apocalyptic in genre. We will examine the use of Abraham in these writings toward the end of this chapter.

In addition to the problem of dating the primary sources, then, there are two additional problems we must bear in mind when considering the use of Abraham in early-second-century Christian controversy with Judaism: the limited sources and the limited role of Abraham in the extant literature. Both of these issues merit a few additional comments.

With the possible exceptions of Barnabas, the Gospel of the Nazaraeans, and the Pseudo-Clementines (which contains the Kerygmata Petrou), none of the writings between Justin and John clearly come from Jewish Christian authors engaged on a primary level in controversy with Jews. Rather, for the most part, the extant Christian writings function within and point to primarily Gentile-Christian settings that seem to belong to a stage of Christianity already largely divorced from Judaism. This makes their authors dissimilar to Paul, Matthew, Hebrews, James, Luke, John, and Justin, all of whom were engaged in direct discussion with Jews. Almost all of the literature that can with some probability be dated between John and Justin seems to address either Gentile-Christian congregations[3] or pagans.[4] We thus have very little direct information about the controversy between Jews and Christians in the early second century to the mid-second century.

Further, Abraham plays a very limited role in the extant literature, perhaps in part because it does not come from Christians who were directly engaged in controversy with Judaism. Appeals to Abraham are infrequent. In the Apostolic Fathers he is mentioned only in 1 Clement, Barnabas, and Ignatius to the Philadelphians. Among the apologists before Justin, Abraham appears only in the Apology of Aristides. Abraham also figures, often in passing, in the Apocalypse of Peter, the Gospel of the Nazaraeans, the Epistula Apostolorum, the Gospel of Philip, the Protoevangelium of James, the Greek Magical Papyri, the Pseudo-Clementines, the Christian appropriations of the Hellenistic synagogal prayers, the Testaments of the Twelve Patriarchs, and the Sibylline Oracles (Book 2).[5]

As a result of these problems, conclusions concerning the way in which Abraham was used in Christian controversy with Judaism between Justin and John can at best be tentative. Nevertheless there is sufficient material in these writings to make a thorough investigation worthwhile. Two additional observations about the use of Abraham between John and Justin are appropriate. First, Abraham appears in different streams of Christian-

ity, from the "mainline" epistles of Ignatius and Clement, to
the Jewish-Christian Pseudo-Clementines and Gospel of the
Nazaraeans, to the Valentinian gnostic Gospel of Philip. It is not
surprising that all seem to be perfectly comfortable referring to
Abraham and counting him as their father. Second, in addition
to crossing boundaries that separated early Christian circles,
Abraham also crosses boundaries of genre. He is used in gospels, apocalypses, letters, prayers and hymns, histories, testaments, and apologies. Abraham was thus referred to in a wide
variety of early Christian contexts, from preaching to praying to
history. Both of these factors point to yet another problem in
trying to analyze the use of Abraham in Christian writings between about 100 and 150 C.E. Whereas Justin's *Dialogue with
Trypho* and the Gospel of John are discrete literary sources that
are extensive enough to permit separate treatment, this is not
the case for the literature between Justin and John. A picture of
how Abraham functions for this diverse literature must be
culled from materials ranging widely in provenance, date,
genre, and author. One may not, however, indiscriminately col-
lapse all the various sources together to produce a flat composite. The method for examining these sources must rather be
commensurate with the nature of the sources and with the difficulties they pose.

Finally, by way of introductory concerns, there are a few
primary sources from about 100 to 150 C.E. in which a Christian author appears to be engaged in some controversy with
Judaism but does not explicitly refer to Abraham. Into this
category I would place the Epistle to Diognetus,[6] the Kerygma Petrou[7] (both apologetic writings), the Gospel of
Thomas,[8] and the Martyrdom of Polycarp.[9] These writings obviously do not provide direct evidence for early Christian use
of Abraham in controversy with Judaism, but they do help to
provide a larger interpretive framework for understanding
early Christian disputes with Judaism in general, and we will
use them to that end.

We will examine early-second-century Christian use of
Abraham, then, in three groupings: (1) Abraham in the Epistle
of Barnabas, Ignatius to the Philadelphians, and the Apology
of Aristides; (2) Abraham in the Gospel of Philip and other
gnostic-Christian sources: reports of Irenaeus about Marcion
and reports of Origen about Heracleon; and (3) Abraham in
other early-second-century Christian writings (apart from
Christian controversy with Judaism). The reason for this division is due to the nature of the sources at hand. Only Barnabas, Ignatius, and Aristides can be dated with some certainty

before Justin, while the Gospel of Philip and other gnostic-Christian works that mention Abraham can only tentatively be dated before Justin Martyr.

Abraham in the Earliest Church Fathers and Apologists: Barnabas, Ignatius, and Aristides

The Epistle of Barnabas[10]

Barnabas refers to Abraham seven times (6:8; 8:4; 9:7, 8; 13:7 [3x]), including three times in citations from the Old Testament (6:8; 9:8; 13:7), more than any other Christian writing between Justin and John. First, Barnabas appeals to Abraham in 6:8, where he cites Exodus 33:1, 3 regarding God's promise of the land to Abraham and his descendants. For Barnabas, the Christians become heirs of the promised land (6:8). This "land flowing with milk and honey" is a parable (6:10) that refers to the new creation, the second creation (6:13, 14), which God has wrought by renewing the hearts of the believers through Christ's death and resurrection. "We then are they whom he brought into the good land" (6:16). "Thus therefore we also, being nourished on the faith of the promise and by the word, shall live and possess the earth" (6:17). In seeing the land as the inheritance of the Christians, Barnabas anticipates a similar move made by Justin a generation later, as we will see in the next chapter.

In Barnabas 8:1–4, in the context of discussing typological foreshadowings of the Christ in the Old Testament, Barnabas makes the following connection:

> [1]But what do you think that it typifies, that the commandment has been given to Israel that the men in whom sin is complete offer a heifer and slay it and burn it, and that boys then take the ashes and put them into vessels and bind scarlet wool on sticks (see again the type of the Cross and the scarlet wool) and hyssop, and that the boys all sprinkle the people thus one by one in order that they all be purified from their sins? [2]Observe how plainly he speaks to you. The calf is Jesus; the sinful men offering it are those who brought him to be slain. Then there are no longer men, no longer the glory of sinners. ["Glory" seems to be the only possible translation, but the text must surely be corrupt.] [3]The boys who sprinkle are they who preached to us the forgiveness of sins, and the purification of the heart, to whom he gave the power of the Gospel to preach, and there are twelve as a testimony to the tribes, because there are twelve

tribes of Israel. [4]But why are there three boys who sprinkle? As a testimony to Abraham, Isaac, and Jacob, for these are great before God. [See Numbers 19.]

For Barnabas, Abraham bears witness to the salvific meaning of the death of Jesus. Indeed, represented typologically by one of the three boys, Abraham preached the forgiveness of sins and the purification of the heart through Christ. Abraham was among those who received the power of the gospel to preach and so bears direct witness to Christ. Just as Christ is spoken of in hidden ways in the Old Testament, so also Barnabas sees references to Abraham in places where he is not explicitly mentioned. He functions as a pointer to Christ.[11]

We see Abraham again as a witness to Christ in one of the most celebrated passages from the Epistle of Barnabas, in chapter 9. In the context of a discussion about circumcision, Barnabas contrasts the true spiritual circumcision which Christians receive to the false physical circumcision of the Jews (Barn. 9:3d–4):[12]

> So then he circumcised our hearing in order that we should hear the word and believe. But moreover the circumcision in which they [the Jews] trusted has been abolished. For he declared that circumcision was not of the flesh, but they erred because an evil angel was misleading them.

Barnabas goes on to raise a possible objection (9:6): "But you will say, surely the people has received circumcision as a seal?" He answers this objection by explaining why Abraham received circumcision (9:7–9):

> Learn fully then, children of love, concerning all things, for Abraham, who first circumcised, did so looking forward in the spirit to Jesus, and had received the doctrines of three letters. For it says, "And Abraham circumcised from his household eighteen men and three hundred" [Gen. 17:23; 14:14; in Greek the number 318 is *TIĒ*]. What then was the knowledge that was given to him? Notice that he first mentions the eighteen, and after a pause the three hundred. The eighteen is *I* (=ten) and *Ē* (=8) — you have Jesus [*IĒSOUS*] — and because the cross was destined to have grace in the *T* he says "and three hundred." So he indicates Jesus in the two letters and the cross in the other. He knows this who placed the gift of his teaching in our hearts. No one has heard a more excellent lesson from me, but I know that you are worthy.

From this striking lesson the author of Barnabas shows that

although Abraham circumcised the flesh, he did so "looking
forward in the spirit to Jesus." This is evident from the number of men from his household whom Abraham had circumcised — 318.[13] Thus for Barnabas the sole function of
Abraham's circumcision, along with that of his servants, was as
a spiritual witness of the grace to come through the death of
Jesus, not as a seal of a grace already given. Spiritual circumcision alone has value, not circumcision of the flesh. The latter
interpretation was the error into which an evil angel led the
Jews. For Barnabas, there is no question why Abraham circumcised the flesh, for he sees it as a clear pointer to the
sacrificial death of Jesus on the cross. Rather, he is critical of
the Jews who persist in circumcising the flesh and thus miss
the true meaning of Abraham's circumcision. Because of its
witness to Christ, Abraham's physical circumcision had a
unique spiritual value that does not apply to any other fleshly
circumcision. Thus the Jews wrongly ascribe any value to
their physical circumcision, since they do not bear witness to
Christ thereby but instead demonstrate a false confidence in
the flesh.

Finally, in 13:6–7, Barnabas uses Abraham not to bear witness to Christ, as he did in the previous two passages, but to
prove that God's covenant now belongs exclusively to Gentile
Christians and not to the Jews at all. Indeed, this is one of the
central themes that runs throughout the whole writing. Barnabas does not distinguish between God's promises under the
Abrahamic covenant and under the Mosaic covenant. Instead,
he speaks rather generically of "*the* covenant" (*hē diathēkē*).
Abraham is simply one more witness that the heirs of the covenant are Gentile Christians.

> See who it is of whom he ordained that this people is the first
> and heir of the covenant. If then besides this he remembered it
> also in the case of Abraham, we reach the perfection of our
> knowledge. What then does he say to Abraham, when he alone
> was faithful, and it was counted him for righteousness? "Behold
> I have made thee, Abraham, the father of the Gentiles (*patera
> ethnōn*) who believe in God in uncircumcision."

Moses had received this covenant on behalf of the Jews, but
"they were not worthy," and so "the Lord himself gave it to
us, as the people of the inheritance" (14:4; see also 13:1).
God has abandoned the Jews for the Gentiles (4:14; 5:7).
Barnabas does not develop the threefold promises to Abraham per se; rather, he speaks repeatedly in general terms of

Christians being "the heirs of the covenant" (*klēronomoi tēs diathēkēs*, 6:19; 4:3; 13:1, 6; 14:4, 5).

In sum, then, we may say that Barnabas uses Abraham to show that the Jews have been abandoned by God in favor of Gentile Christians. Abraham preached the gospel and bore witness to the atoning significance of Jesus' death. Abraham's circumcision, in Judaism the seal of God's covenant, is inverted by Barnabas and reinterpreted as a typological foreshadowing of the covenant in Christ's blood through his death on the cross. The promises to Abraham are handed down to the only truly legitimate heirs, "the Gentiles who believe in God in uncircumcision" (13:7). For Barnabas, Abraham functions exclusively as a witness to Christ and God's covenant through Christ's death with the Gentiles. Abraham is the father of the Gentiles, not of the Jews.

Ignatius to the Philadelphians[14]

Ignatius refers to Abraham only once (Philadelphians 9:1), and then in passing, but it is nevertheless a significant reference, for he connects Abraham to Christ and does so in the context of a letter in which he is engaged in some controversy with Judaism. In 6:1 Ignatius warns the Philadelphian Christians: "But if anyone interpret Judaism to you, do not listen to him; for it is better to hear Christianity from the circumcised than Judaism from the uncircumcised." Ignatius seems to refer here to disputes between Jewish Christians and Gentiles who are either proselytes to Judaism or sympathizers with Judaism.[15] In the broad context of such disputes Ignatius states in 9:1, referring to Christ, "He is the door of the Father, through which enter Abraham and Isaac and Jacob and the Prophets and the Apostles and the Church. All these are joined in the unity of God." Just as "the blessed prophets had a message pointing to him" (9:2), so the implication is that Abraham and the other patriarchs also point to Christ and approach God the Father only through the door of Christ.[16] Through Christ, Abraham is united before the Father with the prophets, apostles, and the church. For Ignatius, then, Abraham seems essentially to be a Christian. The polemics of Ignatius against Judaism lead one to doubt that he would have allowed the Jews any appeal to Abraham as father.

Apology of Aristides[17]

While Barnabas and Ignatius use Abraham to bear witness to Christ, and essentially make him out to be a Christian

rather than a Jew, Aristides uses Abraham to distinguish between Jews and Christians in another way. Aristides refers to
Abraham only once (ch. 14 in the Greek; ch. 2 in the Syriac),
noting that while Jews trace their race back to Abraham,
Christians find the origin of their religion in Christ:

> Let us proceed then, O King, to the Jews also, that we may see
> what truth there is in their view of God. For they were descen-
> dants of Abraham and Isaac and Jacob, and migrated to Egypt.
> . . . Then when the Son of God was pleased to come upon the
> earth, they received him with wanton violence and betrayed
> him into the hands of Pilate the Roman governor. . . . For they
> deny that Christ is the Son of God; and they are much like to the
> heathen, even although they may seem to make some approach
> to the truth from which they have removed themselves. So
> much for the Jews. Now the Christians trace their origin from
> the Lord Jesus Christ. (Apology of Aristides 14:1–15:1; *ANF*,
> 9:275–276; Greek recension)

The Syriac recension has much the same information but in an
earlier chapter:[18]

> This is clear to you, O King, that there are four classes of men in
> this world:—Barbarians and Greeks, Jews and Christians. . . .
> The Jews, again, trace the origin of their race from Abraham,
> who begat Isaac, of whom was born Jacob. And he begat twelve
> sons who migrated from Syria to Egypt; and there they were
> called the nation of the Hebrews, by him who made their laws;
> and at length they were named Jews. The Christians, then, trace
> the beginning of their religion from Jesus the Messiah; and he is
> named the Son of God Most High. (Apology of Aristides 2; *ANF*,
> 9:264–265; Syriac recension)

In both cases, the physical descent of the Jews as a race is
traced back to Abraham and is distinguished from the Christians' origin in Christ. While both Jews and Christians are
referred to as races,[19] there seems to be a difference in the nature of the descent ascribed to each. While Jews trace the
genealogical origin of their race from Abraham, Christians
trace the *religious* origin of their race from Christ. The primary factor that constitutes the Jews as a race is their physical, genealogical bond; only those who share this bond are
responsible for observing the religious statutes of Judaism.
The primary factor that constitutes the Christians as a race,
however, is their religious bond, which has no necessary relationship to physical descent.

This contrast highlights how early-second-century Christianity developed the distinction between spiritual and physical descent from Abraham, a distinction that we have already seen in Paul, Matthew, Luke, and John. Abraham functions in the Apology of Aristides to emphasize this distinction. Physical descent may be important for the Jews but not for the Christians, who are a new race altogether.[20]

Abraham in Gnostic Christianity:
Marcion, Heracleon, and the Gospel of Philip

Three gnostic-Christian sources, broadly defined, refer explicitly to Abraham: the Gospel of Philip, citations of Heracleon's Commentary on John recorded by Origen in his own commentary, and reports by Irenaeus on Marcion's teachings.[21] Both the Gospel of Philip and Heracleon are at least to some extent representative of Valentinian Gnosticism in the mid-second century C.E.[22] Marcion falls in a class by himself.[23]

Gospel of Philip[24]

The Gospel of Philip refers to Abraham only once, but this is a significant passage. In 82.26 (*NHL*, 149) we read: "When Abraham [rejoiced] that he was to see what he was to see, [he circumcised] the flesh of the foreskin [*akrobystia*], teaching us that it is proper to destroy the flesh."[25] The connection of the passage to its present literary context is not immediately clear, and the saying may stand by itself. But when we look more closely at the literary context of the passage, certain possibilities do arise, which might help to interpret the saying.

The preceding section speaks of brides and bridegrooms in the mystery of the bridal chamber, and the following section relates how things live as long as they are hidden, for example, trees and their roots. Just as a pure marriage is consummated in the secrecy of the bridal chamber, and the life force of things in the world is hidden (tree roots, the viscera of human beings), so Abraham's circumcision is a visible, fleshly reality veiling a hidden, spiritual sense. Abraham destroys the flesh to attain the spirit. If one wishes to attain true gnosis, that which is fleshly must give way to that which is spiritual. Abraham teaches this lesson by means of his own circumcision.[26]

Why does Abraham circumcise his flesh? He is motivated to do so out of joy "that he was to see what [or whom] he was to see," clearly a reference to Christ. For the Gospel of Philip, Abraham's action anticipates the meaning of Christ's spiritual advent.

The use of Abraham here is in keeping with the Valentinian gnostic appropriation of the Old Testament evident throughout the Gospel of Philip.[27] The treatment of Abraham provides an implicit critique of Judaism, which becomes clearer when seen along with the other polemical statements the document makes against Judaism.[28] Thus, in a section on the anti-Judaism that is reflected in Christian gnostic writings from Nag Hammadi, John Gager can rightly conclude, "Only in the *Gospel of Philip* is there a conscious effort to separate the community of the gospel from the Jews."[29]

Heracleon

Heracleon was a student of Valentinus and wrote a commentary on John which is preserved in part through Origen's citations from it in his own commentary.[30] Of special interest are Heracleon's comments on John 8, where Abraham figures in a major way.[31] As Elaine Pagels notes, for Heracleon, John 8 has to do primarily with psychics.[32] According to Heracleon, the three different fathers in John 8 (the devil, Abraham, and God the Father) represent the fathers of the hylics, psychics, and pneumatics, respectively. Those who hate Jesus and do not hear him are "of (their) father the devil" (John 8:44).

Those who respond in a neutral way still have a chance to attain pneumatic status. "Heracleon concludes that these are 'children of Abraham,' that is, of the demiurge. They are psychics, and . . . have a capacity for salvation . . . so that they may come to faith and truth."[33] Only those who are of God the Father have true salvation. Although Abraham still has a place in Heracleon's scheme of things, it is as the father of the psychics, a notch below the highest truth and knowledge. This lower rung is the level on which the Jews operate. Heracleon thus uses Abraham to show the difference between Jews and Christians but in a way distinct from any of the other writings we have examined so far. Rather than elevating Abraham from the status of a Jew to that of a Christian, Heracleon disassociates Abraham from true, gnostic Christianity. All who count Abraham as their father show themselves to be merely psychic. Christ has come to lead the way to the real Father, God. Even Abraham has not found the way. Far from asserting that Abraham bears witness to Christ and that he is father of the Christians rather than of the Jews, Heracleon is content to let the Jews and the non-gnostic Christians have Abraham as their father. Their descent from Abraham proves that they are mere psychics.

Marcion

In keeping with his denigration of the Old Testament and of Judaism in general, Marcion appears to have singled out Abraham for disinheritance. In *Against Heresies* 4.8.1, Irenaeus defends Abraham against Marcion's attack:[34]

> Vain, too, is [the effort of] Marcion and his followers when they [seek to] exclude Abraham from the inheritance, to whom the Spirit through many men, and now by Paul, bears witness, that "he believed God, and it was imputed unto him for righteousness" [Rom. 4:3]. And the Lord [also bears witness to him,] in the first place, indeed, by raising up children to him from the stones, and making his seed as the stars of heaven, saying, "They shall come from the east and from the west, from the north and from the south, and shall recline with Abraham, and Isaac, and Jacob in the kingdom of heaven" [Matt. 8:11]; and then again by saying to the Jews, "When ye shall see Abraham, and Isaac, and Jacob, and all the prophets in the kingdom of heaven, but you yourselves cast out" [Luke 13:28]. This, then, is a clear point, that those who disallow his salvation, and frame the idea of another God besides Him who made the promise to Abraham, are outside the kingdom of God, and are disinherited from [the gift of] incorruption, setting at naught and blaspheming God, who introduces, through Jesus Christ, Abraham to the kingdom of heaven, and his seed, that is, the Church, upon which also is conferred the adoption and the inheritance promised to Abraham.

Since Marcion disinherits Abraham from the promises that God made to him, Marcion is in turn disinherited himself, according to Irenaeus. (Like Ignatius, Irenaeus speaks of Abraham entering God's kingdom through Christ.) This passage also shows that already by the time of Irenaeus proof texts from the New Testament were being offered to show Abraham as the father of the Christian faith (Rom. 4:3; Matt. 8:11; Luke 13:28).

Irenaeus reports another element of Marcion's teaching regarding Abraham that is striking, because it contrasts sharply with many contemporary Christian writings that speak of the heavenly Abraham (see below). Marcion puts Abraham in hell and leaves him there even after Christ's visit:

> In addition to his blasphemy against God Himself, he [Marcion] advanced this also, truly speaking as with the mouth of the devil, and saying all things in direct opposition to the truth,— that Cain, and those like him, and the Sodomites, and the Egyp-

tians, and others like them, and, in fine, all the nations who walked in all sorts of abomination, were saved by the Lord, on His descending into Hades, and on their running unto Him, and that they welcomed Him into their kingdom. But the serpent which was in Marcion declared that Abel, and Enoch, and Noah, and those other righteous men who sprang from the patriarch Abraham, with all the prophets, and those who were pleasing to God, did not partake in salvation. For since these men, he says, knew that their God was constantly tempting them, so now they suspected that He was tempting them, and did not run to Jesus, or believe His announcement: and for this reason he declared that their souls remained in Hades.[35]

For Marcion, Christianity's complete separation from Judaism necessarily entails a complete separation from Abraham also. Abraham not only does not bear witness to Christ, he even refuses Christ's salvation!

Thus while the Gospel of Philip treats Abraham as a positive example of seeing Christ and responding accordingly, neither Heracleon nor Marcion allows Abraham any place in true Christian faith, according to the evidence preserved by Origen and Irenaeus. Perhaps the Gospel of Philip allows Abraham a positive place because of its ties to Jewish Christianity, despite its criticism of Judaism in other regards.[36] Heracleon and Marcion, on the other hand, show the very different treatment that Abraham received at the hands of at least some representatives of gnostic Christianity. For them, association with Abraham shows a lesser spirituality than that which Christ both reveals and calls for.

Abraham in Christian Writings Apart from Controversy with Judaism

As we noted at the outset of this chapter, Abraham also figures in other Christian writings between John and Justin where there is no direct evidence of controversy with Judaism. He appears in four contexts: (1) as the otherworldly Abraham, (2) in liturgical settings, (3) as a witness to Christ, and (4) as a figure who exemplifies Christian virtues.

The Otherworldly Abraham

In several apocalyptic writings Abraham functions as a figure in heaven and/or in hell. In the Christian Sibyllines[37] (Book 2.238–246; *OTP*, 1:351), we read:

> When Sabaoth Adonai, who thunders on high, dissolves fate
> and raises the dead, and takes his seat
> on a heavenly throne, and establishes a great pillar,
> Christ, imperishable himself, will come in glory on a cloud
> toward the imperishable one with the blameless angels.
> He will sit on the right of the Great One, judging at the tribunal
> the life of pious men and the way of impious men.
> Moses, the great friend of the Most High, also will come,
> having put on flesh. Great Abraham himself will come.

Abraham, then, appears in heaven for God's apocalyptic judgment. In the Apocalypse of Peter,[38] Peter takes a slight detour from his tour of hell. On this detour he asks to go to the holy mountain, the scene of the transfiguration. The following scene takes place:

> And I approached God Jesus Christ and said to him, "My Lord who is this?" And he said to me, "These are Moses and Elias." And I said to him, "(Where then are) Abraham, Isaac, Jacob and the other righteous fathers?" And he showed us a great open garden. (It was) full of fair trees and blessed fruits, full of the fragrance of perfume. Its fragrance was beautiful and that fragrance reached to us. And of it . . . I saw many fruits. And my Lord and God Jesus Christ said unto me, "Hast thou seen the companies of the fathers? As is their rest, so also is the honour and glory of those who will be persecuted for my righteousness' sake." (Apocalypse of Peter 16; *NTA*, 2:681–682; Ethiopic recension)

Again in the Epistula Apostolorum[39] we find Abraham in another world. Christ tells his disciples:

> But to those who have loved me and do love me and who have done my commandment I will grant rest in life in the kingdom of my heavenly Father. . . . And on that account I have descended and have spoken with Abraham and Isaac and Jacob, to your fathers the prophets, and have brought to them news that they may come from the rest which is below into heaven, and have given them the right hand of the baptism of life and forgiveness and pardon for all wickedness as to you, so from now on also to those who believe in me. (Epistula Apostolorum 26–27; *NTA*, 1:209; Ethiopic recension)

Here Christ invites Abraham, along with other fathers, to come from "the rest below" into the rest of heaven.[40]

In addition to the above-mentioned writings, the Epistula Apostolorum (Coptic recension, ch. 27), the Apocalypse of

Peter (Ethiopic recension, ch. 16), the Christian Sibyllines
(Book 2.238–251), and the Testaments of the Twelve Patriarchs (e.g., Testament of Levi 18:6–14) all refer to the res-
urrected/heavenly Abraham.

Abraham in Liturgical Use

Abraham was renowned for his advocacy with God, owing
largely to the accounts of his appeal to God for mercy upon
Sodom in Genesis 18:22–33. In Jewish tradition he had also
earned God's merit by offering up Isaac.[41] Abraham thus often
figures in prayers to God and hymns of praise, where he is
used to invoke God's power and compassion. A clear example
of this usage can be found in the Hellenistic syngagogal
prayers preserved in the Apostolic Constitutions.[42] In 7.33.2–
7 we find a prayer in which God is praised:

> For from the beginning of our forefather Abraham's laying claim
>   to the way of truth,
> you led (him) by a vision,
>   having taught (him) what at any time this world is.
> And his faith traveled ahead of his knowledge,
>   but the covenant was the follower of his faith.
> . . . .
> O Fighter on behalf of Abraham's race,
> blessed are you forever!

Abraham is mentioned in similar contexts elsewhere in the
Apostolic Constitutions (7.37.1–5; 7.39.2–4; 8.5.1–4;
8.12.6–27; 8.40.2–4; 8.41.2–5; *OTP*, 2:677–697).

In the Protoevangelium of James 19.3–20.2 (*NTA*, 1:385),[43]
Salome appeals to Abraham in her prayer to God for healing:
"O God of my fathers, remember me; for I am the seed of
Abraham, Isaac and Jacob." God hears her prayer and heals
her.

In several Greek Magical Papyri we find evidence of Abraham's role in prayers and magical formulas that were used in
Christian circles and popular religious culture in general between Justin and John.[44] Abraham frequently appears in a
catena of names being invoked by the petitioner. For instance, in *PGM* XII, 287 (vol. 2, p. 77), we read: "Greatest
God, who surpasses every power, I call upon you, Iao, Saba-
oth, Adonai, Eiloein . . . Saphtha, Nouchitha, Abraam, Isak,
Iakkob . . . ." That Abraham was used to invoke God's pro-
tection is also apparent from Origen's *Contra Celsum*.[45] Celsus was apparently a contemporary of Justin,[46] and so his

observations of Christianity and Judaism probably come from the mid-second century. In *Contra Celsum* 1.22 Origen criticizes Celsus for believing reports from certain Egyptians rather than from Moses regarding the origin of circumcision. In this context he also attacks the use of Abraham in magical formulas:

> For many also of those who chant incantations for daemons use among their formulas "the God of Abraham"; they do this on account of the name and the familiarity between God and this righteous man. It is for this reason that they employ the expression "the God of Abraham" although they do not know who Abraham is.

Origen also defends the Jewish patriarchs against an attack by Celsus in *Contra Celsum* 4.33:

> It is clear that the Jews trace their genealogy back to the three fathers Abraham, Isaac, and Jacob. Their names are so powerful when linked with the name of God that the formula "the God of Abraham, the God of Isaac, and the God of Jacob" is used not only by members of the Jewish nation in their prayers to God and when they exorcise daemons, but also by almost all those who deal in magic and spells. For in magical treatises it is often to be found that God is invoked by this formula, and that in spells against daemons His name is used in close connexion with the names of these men.

That such use of Abraham was common in popular society before Justin is clear from Justin's own confession in *Dialogue with Trypho* 85: "If any man among you should exorcise them [demons] in the name of the God of Abraham, and the God of Isaac, and the God of Jacob, they will, perhaps, become subject to you."[47]

Finally, I call attention to a *phylaktērion*, a benediction or blessing, found on a papyrus fragment that was placed at the entrance to a room or a house.[48] Although the fragment is early, dating it exactly is almost impossible. Still, this *phylaktērion* demonstrates the sort of role Abraham no doubt played in popular religious culture before the time of Justin. On both sides of the papyrus the blessing reads:

> The power of our God is strong and the Lord patrols the door and does not allow the destroyer to enter in. Abraham dwells here. Blood of Christ, put evil to an end!

Thus Abraham played a significant, if not major, role in Christian liturgical life between Justin and John. In this regard, Christian tradition is very similar to Jewish liturgical traditions from around the same time.[49]

Abraham and Christ

References occur to Abraham as a witness to Christ not only in early Christian controversy with Judaism but also in early Christian writings where Jewish/Christian relations do not appear to be at issue. In the Epistula Apostolorum 27 (Ethiopic), Christ descends to the resting place of Abraham (and of Isaac and Jacob) and gives him "the right hand of the baptism of life and forgiveness" on account of his belief in Christ. In the Hellenistic synagogal prayers embedded in the Apostolic Constitutions, a clear Christian interpolation in the Jewish *Grundschrift* can be made out in 8.12.23: "You are the one who delivered Abraham from ancestral godlessness, and appointed him heir of the world, *and showed to him your Christ.*"[50]

The Exemplary Abraham

In 1 Clement,[51] Abraham is held up as an example of faithful living, especially on account of his hospitality (Gen. 18:1–8).[52] In 9:2 Clement sets out his task for the next several chapters: "Let us fix our gaze on those who have rendered perfect service to his excellent glory." The whole of chapter 10 is then devoted to recounting Abraham's faithful obedience and righteousness. Clement concludes, "Because of his faith and hospitality a son was given him [Abraham] in his old age, and in his obedience he offered him as a sacrifice to God" (10:7). And again in 17:2 Abraham's humility is exemplary: "Great fame was given to Abraham, and he was called the Friend of God, and he, fixing his gaze in humility on the Glory of God, says 'But I am dust and ashes.'" Finally, in 31:1–2 Clement again holds Abraham up as an example:

> Let us cleave, then, to his blessing and let us consider what are the paths of blessing. Let us unfold the deeds of old. Why was our father Abraham blessed? Was it not because he wrought righteousness and truth through faith?

Clement clearly considers Abraham "our father" and repeatedly uses him as an example for Christian faith and piety.

Thus we have seen that Abraham was used in several contexts in early Christian literature about 100–150 C.E. other than controversy with Judaism. It remains striking, however, that neither the promises to Abraham nor his circumcision is a subject for discussion in this literature. These two topics appear to have functioned almost exclusively in Christian controversy with Judaism.

Conclusion

What, finally, can we conclude about the use of Abraham in Christian literature between John and Justin, especially in contexts of Christian controversy with Judaism? We must avoid two extremes in drawing conclusions on the basis of the evidence surveyed in this chapter. First, we cannot conclude that Abraham was a pivotal figure across the board. We have only four primary sources from about 100 to 150 C.E. which explicitly refer to Abraham in the context of Christian controversy with Judaism: the Epistle of Barnabas, Ignatius to the Philadelphians, the Gospel of Philip, and the Apology of Aristides. (The accounts from Origen on Heracleon and Irenaeus on Marcion are important, but secondary, witnesses.) Thus we must be cautious about claiming too much from the evidence we have.

Nor, however, can we conclude that Abraham played a minor role in Christian controversy with Judaism during this period. At the very least, Abraham was widely used by Christians as a witness to Christ, several times in clear controversy with Judaism (Barnabas, Ignatius, Gospel of Philip).

What we can say is that in controversy with Judaism Abraham appears in significant contexts in quite divergent Christian writings. Abraham was used by very different stripes of Christians (Barnabas, Ignatius, Aristides, Gospel of Philip, Heracleon, Marcion) in very different genres (treatise, letter, apology, gospel, commentary) to make Christian claims over against Judaism. What stands out as significant, however, is that these Christian writers in conflict with Judaism appear to have felt obliged to mention Abraham in one way or another.

At any rate, the question before us is *when* Abraham plays a role, *what* does this role indicate about early-second-century Christian controversy with Judaism? As we have seen, some authors were determined to make Abraham out to be a Christian (Barnabas, Ignatius, Philip), while others were more than willing to leave him to the Jews (Heracleon, Marcion). Making Abraham into a Christian in essence amounts to offering an implicit critique of Judaism. After all, it assumes that what the Jews have to say about the patriarch is not the final word on the subject. Leaving Abraham to the Jews indicates a break with Judaism to such an extent that one has lost interest in showing any continuity between Christian faith and Jewish tradition. In either case, we see that the figure Abraham provides us with a useful heuristic device that alerts us to the presence of Christian controversy with Judaism.

We turn, finally, to an examination of the use of Abraham in the writings of Justin Martyr, who picks up on the tendency to make Abraham a Christian. In Justin we will see the culmination of the trend to drive a wedge between the Jews and their Abrahamic heritage.

7

The Father
of Christians Alone:
Abraham in Justin Martyr's
Dialogue with Trypho

In the *Dialogue with Trypho*,[1] Justin Martyr appeals to Abraham over one hundred times (103 to be exact), in contexts that are crucial to Justin's controversy with Trypho and with Judaism as a whole.[2] To anticipate my conclusions, we will see in the present chapter that Justin uses Abraham to render the Jews orphaned, without legitimate claim to Abraham as their father in any meaningful way. The Jews do not have a future, nor do they have any true past. Justin uses the very Abrahamic heritage that the Jews claim in order to show that they are not the children of Abraham; he thus leaves them abandoned and disinherited.

The most striking passage in this regard is *Dialogue* 119.3–6. It occurs in the context of Justin restating his overall argument with Trypho in a briefer form for friends of Trypho who missed the first day of the dispute.[3] Justin is thus directly addressing Jews. The passage warrants citation in full:

> After the Just One was put to death, we blossomed forth as another people, and sprang up like new and thriving corn, as the Prophet exclaimed: "And many nations shall flee unto the Lord in that day for a people; and they shall dwell in the midst of the whole earth" [Zech. 2:11]. But we Christians are not only a people, but a holy people, as we have already shown: "And they shall call it a holy people, redeemed by the Lord" [Isa. 62:12]. Wherefore, we are not a contemptible people, nor a tribe of barbarians, nor just any nation as the Carians or the Phrygians, but the chosen people of God who appeared to those who did not seek Him. "Behold," He said, "I am God to a na-

tion which has not called upon My name" [Isa. 65:1]. For, this is really the nation promised to Abraham by God, when He told him that He would make him a father of many nations, not saying in particular that he would be father of the Arabs or the Egyptians or the Idumaeans, since Ishmael became the father of a mighty nation and so did Esau; and there is now a great throng of Ammonites. Noah was the father of Abraham, and indeed, of all men. And other nations had other ancestors. What greater favor, then, did Christ bestow on Abraham? This: that He likewise called with His voice, and commanded him to leave the land wherein he dwelt. And with that same voice He has also called of us, and we have abandoned our former way of life in which we used to practice evils common to the rest of the world. And we shall inherit the Holy Land together with Abraham, receiving our inheritance for all eternity, because by our similar faith we have become children of Abraham. For, just as he believed the voice of God, and was justified thereby, so have we believed the voice of God (which was spoken again to us by the Prophets and the Apostles of Christ), and have renounced even to death all worldly things. Thus, God promised Abraham a religious and righteous nation of like faith, and a delight to the Father; but it is not you, "in whom there is no faith [Deut. 32:20]."

We find in this passage a whole cluster of themes that are closely connected to Abraham, especially to the promises God made to Abraham regarding descendants, the land, and the nations. Further, Justin attributes to Christ the call to Abraham to leave his homeland.[4] Abraham thus already responds to Christ's voice, to Christ's call. This same voice now calls Christians. Because their faith is similar to the faith of Abraham, Christians have become children of Abraham. The only conclusion Justin can draw from this argument is that the Christians, not the Jews, comprise the religious and righteous nation, which God promised to Abraham. Indeed, he states explicitly to Trypho as the representative of the Jews: "It is not you (*all' ouch hymas*), 'in whom there is no faith.'"

Justin's appeal to Abraham in this passage gives an indication of the thorough manner in which he takes over the traditions about Abraham for his own purposes in his controversy with Judaism in the mid-second century. Nor is this appeal an isolated instance, for Abraham figures prominently throughout the *Dialogue*. In addition to the promises made to Abraham and his witness to Christ, the most important contexts in which Abraham appears revolve around discussions about circumcision, which is not mentioned in the passage cited above. Justin's use of Abraham results in the radical separation of the father of the Jews from any essential connection with the Jews. In the *Dialogue*, Abraham stands as a witness for Christianity against Judaism. We will explore Justin's appeals to Abraham under three headings: (1) circumcision: blessing or curse?; (2) the promises redefined; and (3) Abraham and Christ.

Circumcision: Blessing or Curse?

Justin refers to Abraham most frequently in the context of discussions about circumcision (*Dialogue* 11; 16; 19; 23; 26; 27; 33; 43; 46; 47; 92; 113; 114). Indeed, Justin seems preoccupied with circumcision.[5] In *Dialogue* 10.1, Justin summarizes the gist of the Jews' complaint against the Christians when he asks: "My friends, is there any other accusation against us than this, that we do not observe the Law, nor circumcise the flesh as your forefathers did, nor keep the sabbaths as you do?"[6] Indeed, in *Dialogue* 10.3–4 (cf. 19.1), Justin then has Trypho concede:

> This is what surprises us most, that you who claim to be pious and believe yourselves to be different from the others do not segregate yourselves from them, nor do you observe a manner of life different from that of the Gentiles, for you do not keep the feasts or sabbaths, nor do you practice the rite of circumcision. You place your hope in a crucified man, and still expect to receive favors from God when you disregard His commandments. Have you not read that the male who is not circumcised on the eighth day shall be cut off from his people? This precept was for stranger and purchased slave alike. But you, forthwith, scorn this covenant, spurn the commands that come afterwards, and then you try to convince us that you know God, when you fail to do those things that every God-fearing person would do.

In response to Trypho's challenge, Justin begins by stating clearly the common ground between himself and Trypho (*Dialogue* 11.1):

> We do not claim that our God is different from yours, for He is the God who, with a strong hand and outstretched arm, led your forefathers out of the land of Egypt. Nor have we placed our trust in any other (for, indeed, there is no other), but only in Him whom you also have trusted, the God of Abraham and of

Isaac and of Jacob. But, our hope is not through Moses or through the Law.

They trust in the same God, but the agreement ends there, for Justin disputes with Trypho the manner in which that trust is shown. For both Justin and Trypho, the status of the law is at stake, specifically the ritual law—not a new issue in Christian controversy with Judaism.[7]

Justin repeatedly links ritual law with circumcision, so that we may see circumcision as the focal point in this dispute.[8] If circumcision falls, the rest of the ritual law goes with it. Justin and Trypho both appeal to Abraham to help adjudicate the dispute over circumcision. By making Abraham the basis of the argument, they engage the question of whether or not Moses can be bypassed and whether or not the Mosaic law stands in continuity with the Abrahamic covenant, which even the Jews acknowledge to be more ancient than the Mosaic law. Trypho, of course, says only what Justin allows him to say, but even so, it is striking that Justin allows Trypho to score a few points in appealing to Abraham. Justin probably did not think so, but he comes across on occasion as flustered with Trypho's appeal to Abraham's circumcision (e.g., 46.3).[9] Is this mere rhetorical flourish on Justin's part to keep the drama and suspense of the *Dialogue* going, or does Justin really struggle to answer Trypho adequately on this point? [10] While the former may be the case, still Justin does endeavor to answer objections and to diffuse the charges that he senses others have leveled against Christianity.

In response to criticism from Jewish quarters regarding Christian nonobservance of circumcision (and other ritual laws), Justin marshals the very Abraham to whom Jews appeal in order to demonstrate the validity of nonobservance. By appealing to Abraham against the Mosaic law, Justin engages in a rearguard action in his battle with Judaism. In so doing, Justin seeks to circumvent any Jewish attempts to draw connections between Moses and Abraham. Rather, for Justin, Abraham defines and delimits the significance of the Mosaic law. Justin, therefore, seeks to show that Abraham lines up on the side of Christianity, not of Judaism.

Like Paul before him, Justin emphasizes that Abraham was justified by faith apart from circumcision (*Dialogue* 11.5):[11]

> We have been led to God through this crucified Christ, and we are the true spiritual Israel, and the descendants of Judah, Jacob, Isaac, and Abraham, who, though uncircumcised, was approved and blessed by God because of his faith and was called

the father of many nations. All this shall be proved as we proceed with our discussion.

And again in *Dialogue* 23.3–4:

> For if circumcision was not required before the time of Abraham, and before Moses there was no need of sabbaths, festivals, and sacrifices, they are not needed now, when in accordance with the will of God, Jesus Christ, His Son, has been born of the Virgin Mary, a descendant of Abraham. Indeed, when Abraham himself was still uncircumcised, he was justified and blessed by God because of his faith in Him, as the Scriptures tell us. Furthermore, the Scriptures and the facts of the case force us to admit that Abraham received circumcision for a sign, not for justification itself.

Because Abraham was justified in uncircumcision, his circumcision takes on positive significance only when it is understood spiritually to refer to the circumcision of the heart. Justin never tires of repeating this claim, and he often supplies generous citations from the Septuagint to prove his case, especially from the prophets, and Jeremiah 31:31 in particular (e.g., *Dialogue* 11.3; 24.1; 34.1; 43.1; 67.9; 118.2). "We, indeed, who have come to God through Jesus Christ, have received not a carnal, but a spiritual, circumcision . . . by means of baptism" (*Dialogue* 43.2). Did Abraham also receive this spiritual circumcision? Although Justin never implies that Abraham was baptized, he does imply that Abraham knew the spiritual meaning of circumcision insofar as he knew Christ (as we shall see below). Indeed, in *Dialogue* 113.4–7 Justin claims:

> I have proved that it was Jesus who appeared to and talked with Moses, Abraham, and, in short, with all the Patriarchs, doing the will of the Father. . . . [It is the words of Christ] by which so many who were in error have been circumcised from their uncircumcision with the circumcision of the heart. From that time God commanded through Jesus that they who had the circumcision which began with Abraham should be circumcised again with the circumcision of the heart.

The context of this passage is a typological comparison between Joshua and Jesus. Justin refers to Joshua's circumcision of the people a second time with knives of stone (Josh. 5:2–9) and sees this as "a sign of this circumcision with which Jesus Christ Himself has circumcised us from the idols made of stone and of other materials" (*Dialogue* 113.6). Since Justin

has made explicit his view that Christians share a like faith
with Abraham, and since this faith means being circumcised in
one's heart, we may reasonably infer that, for Justin, Abraham
would qualify as knowing the circumcision of the heart.[12]
Thus, even the carnal circumcision that Abraham received
finds its true significance only in the spiritual circumcision of
his heart. Abraham's spiritual circumcision is symbolized by
his faith, according to Justin, on which account he was pronounced righteous while still in uncircumcision.

Not only does Justin appeal to Abraham's justification being
pronounced while he was uncircumcised, Justin also argues
that even after Abraham's circumcision, uncircumcision had
priority over circumcision. Justin bases his argument on the
Genesis account of the interaction between Melchizedek and
Abraham (Genesis 14). "Melchizedek, the priest of the Most
High, was not circumcised, yet Abraham, the first to accept
circumcision of the flesh, paid tithes to him and he was
blessed by him" (*Dialogue* 19.4). Since the one who blesses
must be superior to the one blessed, uncircumcision (Melchizedek) is by necessity superior to circumcision (Abraham).[13]

Justin uses Abraham, then, to show the following: (*a*) Righteousness does not come by means of circumcision, since
Abraham was pronounced righteous while in uncircumcision.
By extension, righteousness has no essential connection to the
observance of the ritual law. (*b*) Even Abraham's circumcision
has positive significance only insofar as it points to the spiritual circumcision of the heart, which comes about by faith in
Christ—as Abraham himself demonstrates through his knowledge of Christ. (*c*) The priority of uncircumcision over circumcision can be seen from the account of the uncircumcised
Melchizedek blessing the circumcised Abraham. In these
three ways Justin uses the Abraham traditions to show the
insignificance of physical circumcision when it comes to one's
status before God.

Although Justin's use of Abraham in this regard closely parallels much of what we find in Paul (Romans 4; Galatians 3),
Justin could never affirm Paul's assertion in Romans 3:1–2,
"Then what advantage has the Jew? Or what is the value of
circumcision? Much in every way!" Whereas for Paul circumcision is a sign of God's blessing and a seal of the promise, for
Justin circumcision is primarily, and strikingly, a sign of God's
curse upon the Jews. Why was circumcision given? Justin
states the following to Trypho (*Dialogue* 16.2–4):

Indeed the custom of circumcising the flesh, handed down from

Abraham, was given to you as a distinguishing mark, to set you off from other nations and from us Christians. The purpose of this was that you and only you might suffer the afflictions that are now justly yours; that only your land be desolate, and your cities ruined by fire; that the fruits of your land be eaten by strangers before your very eyes; that not one of you be permitted to enter your city of Jerusalem. Your circumcision of the flesh is the only mark by which you can certainly be distinguished from other men. Nor do I believe that any of you will attempt to deny that God either had or has foreknowledge of future events, and that He does not prepare beforehand what everyone deserves. Therefore, the above-mentioned tribulations were justly imposed upon you, for you have murdered the Just One, and His prophets before Him; now you spurn those who hope in Him, and in Him who sent Him, namely, Almighty God, the Creator of all things; to the utmost of your power you dishonor and curse in your synagogues all those who believe in Christ.

According to Justin, who lays sole responsibility for Christ's death on the Jews, circumcision was given to Abraham because of God's foreknowledge of the Jews' disobedience and disbelief. Circumcision is a mark by which God has stained those designated for just punishment. This punishment is even now being exacted by God through the Romans, who have recently put down the uprising of the Jews under Bar-Cochba, with Hadrian's conquest of Jerusalem in 135 C.E. This is not an isolated theme in Justin's *Dialogue* but is repeated several times.[14]

The emphasis falls on God's foreknowledge of the Jews' rejection of Jesus as the Christ, their responsibility for his death, and their persecution of Christians from the time of the apostles to the time in which Justin is writing. Justin sees the Roman expulsion of the Jews from Jerusalem as an example of the suffering the Jews deserve for their words and actions against Christ and Christians and thus against God. Their disobedience is nothing new, however. Rather it is the pattern of behavior that Jews have always exhibited, from their idolatrous worship of the golden calf to their killing of the prophets who looked ahead to Christ. According to Justin, the law was primarily given by Moses on account of this disobedience (e.g., *Dialogue* 12.3; 18.2; 21.1; 22.2; 43.1; 44.2; 46.5; 67.8; 92.4). Even the Sabbath was instituted so that the Jews would worship God at least one day a week (*Dialogue* 19.21; 92)!

The problem for Justin is to give a reason why *Abraham* of

all people should be the first to be circumcised. The difficulty is that Abraham was righteous and obedient—indeed, a witness to Christ—and hence did not deserve the curse of circumcision. It would have made more sense for Justin's argument if circumcision had been initiated by Moses along with the rest of the law, as God's response to the idolatry of the Jews at Sinai. Justin is at pains to solve this difficulty, and his solution is not very satisfactory. The only rationale for God giving circumcision (the mark of a curse) to Abraham is God's *foreknowledge* of what would later take place. In contrast, God gave the law through Moses only in *response* to the disobedience and hard-heartedness the Jews had already demonstrated.

In summary, in his dispute with Trypho over circumcision, which represents the whole ritual law, Justin appeals to Abraham to demonstrate that no connection exists between righteousness before God and the observance of ritual law. Further, he uses Abraham to argue that circumcision was given as a curse in God's foreknowledge of the unbelief and malice which the Jews would show toward Christ and the Christians after him. Justin thus seeks to disassociate Abraham from any essential relationship to physical circumcision. Far from being a blessing, circumcision is a curse that marks the Jews out for God's punishment. The challenge for Justin is to denigrate circumcision without at the same time denigrating Abraham. He manages to do this by presenting Abraham, the very founder of circumcision, in such a way as to divorce him from circumcision. Abraham's significance lies, rather, in his faith while uncircumcised. For Justin, Abraham is not really a Jew at all but a Gentile when it comes to circumcision.

The Promises Redefined

In addition to divorcing Abraham from any significant connection to circumcision, Justin also draws on the Genesis accounts of God's promises to Abraham, particularly Genesis 17. He takes the traditional promises regarding Abraham's manifold descendants, his posterity being a blessing to the nations, and the inheritance of the land, and redefines them in such a way that the promises are repossessed from the Jews and redirected to the Christians.[15] The Jews, who once appeared to be heirs of the promise, are now disinherited, with no place to turn outside of Christ.

In fact, from Justin's perspective it is doubtful that the Jews were ever really the intended heirs of God's promises to Abraham. Christians become the true descendants, Christians the blessing to the nations, and Christians the rightful heirs to the land. By redefining and redirecting the promises in this way, Justin seeks to preclude the Jews from making any legitimate appeal to the Abrahamic heritage, which up to now they had taken for granted. We turn now to an examination of each of the promises and Justin's treatment of them.

The Descendants: From Heirs to Abandoned Children

Justin uses primarily three terms, apparently interchangeable, to describe the descendants of Abraham in the several passages in which he makes such a reference (*Dialogue* 11.5; 25.1; 43.1; 44.1; 47.4; 66.4; 80.4; 119.5; 120.2): "race" (*genos*: 11.5; 43.1; 66.4), "children" (*tekna*: 25.1; 80.4; 119.5; 120.2), and "seed" (*sperma*: 44.1; 47.4).

Justin can speak about the descendants of Abraham in three ways: (1) in a matter-of-fact manner describing physical descendants; (2) in reference to Christians as spiritual descendants; and (3) in disclaimers of Jewish claims to be true descendants.

1. In several passages Justin refers in a seemingly neutral way to physical descendants of Abraham. Thus he speaks of Christ as being "born of the Virgin, of the race of Abraham" (*apo tou genous tou Abraam*, 43.1). Speaking again of Christ, he states, "Everyone knows . . . that of all the carnal descendants of Abraham (*en tō kata sarka Abraam*), no one was ever born of a virgin, or ever claimed to be so born, except our Christ" (66.4). Further, in a passage denying salvation to those who renounce their faith in Christ, Justin states, "The same can be said of those descendants of Abraham (*tou spermatos tou Abraam*) who follow the Law and refuse to believe in Christ to their very last breath" (47.4). Finally, in a celebrated passage in which Justin denigrates those who claim to be Christians while denying the resurrection, he tries to clarify the situation to Trypho by means of an analogous situation in Judaism: "Just as one, after careful examination, would not acknowledge as Jews the Sadducees or the similar sects of the Genistae, Meristae, Galileaens, Hellenians, and the Baptist Pharisees (please take no offense if I speak my mind), but would realize that they are Jews and children of Abraham (*tekna Abraam*) in name only . . . " (80.4).[16] In each of these passages Justin refers to Jews as physical descendants of Abraham, using alternately the terms "race," "seed," and "children."

2. In addition to assigning to the Jews the status of being merely physical descendants of Abraham, Justin also refers to Christians as the descendants of Abraham in the most important regard, their faith in Christ. "We are the true spiritual Israel, and the descendants (*genos*) of . . . Abraham" (11.5). "By our similar faith we have become children of Abraham" (*tekna tou Abraam*, 119.5).

3. In the same breath as he affirms that Christians are the spiritual descendants of Abraham, Justin denies this heritage to the Jews, granting them only the status of being physical descendants, which counts for nothing. In several passages Justin tells Trypho quite clearly that the physical descent of the Jews from Abraham is without significance. He describes as vain the efforts of those "who attempt to justify themselves, and claim that they are children of Abraham (*tekna tou Abraam*), [who] hope to receive along with us even a small part of the divine legacy" (25.1). To this, Trypho responds (25.6), "Do I understand you to say . . . that none of us Jews will inherit anything on the holy mountain of God?"[17] Although Justin answers, "I didn't say that" (26.1), he goes on to say almost exactly that: "But I do say that those who have persecuted Christ in the past and still do, and do not repent, shall not inherit anything on the holy mountain, unless they repent" (26.1). Again in 44.1 Justin says to Trypho: "You are sadly mistaken if you think that, just because you are descendants of Abraham according to the flesh (*dia to einai tou Abraam kata sarka sperma*), you will share in the legacy of benefits which God promised would be distributed by Christ." In the passages from 25.1 and 44.1 Justin adduces the statement of John the Baptist in the Q tradition (Matt. 3:9 //Luke 3:8): "Do not presume to say to yourselves, 'We have Abraham as our father'; for I tell you, God is able from these stones to raise up children to Abraham" (*tekna tou Abraam*). In its original context this is simply a warning against banking on one's descent from Abraham. Justin, however, brings the statement to a logical, if unnecessary, conclusion by construing it christologically, saying that those who do not believe in Christ are not really children of Abraham.

Perhaps the most striking passage is *Dialogue* 120.2, in which Justin offers a radical interpretation of Genesis 22:17, where the angel of the Lord says to Abraham, "I will indeed bless you, and I will multiply your descendants as the stars of heaven and as the sand which is on the seashore." Justin does not cite this passage directly, but in *Dialogue* 120.1 he alludes to it when discussing the descendants through whom Abraham's promises are continued, citing from Genesis 26:4 and 28:14, respectively:

> Notice how He makes the same promises to Isaac and Jacob. Here are His words to Isaac: "In thy seed shall all the nations be blessed." And to Jacob: "In thee and in thy seed all the tribes of the earth shall be blessed."

Justin goes on to say that this promise is not carried on through the line of Esau but comes down through Jacob and the line of Judah to David and culminates in Christ. For Justin, the division of the seed after Isaac into the lines of Jacob, the sole heir, and Esau, the disinherited, is a sign from God that foreshadows the present situation of Jews and Christians, as Justin explains to Trypho (*Dialogue* 120.2):

> Now, this was a sign that some of you Jews would be certainly children of Abraham (*tekna Abraam*), and at the same time would share in the lot of Christ; but that others, also children of Abraham (*alloi de tekna men tou Abraam*), would be like the sand on the beach, which, though vast and extensive, is barren and fruitless, not bearing any fruit at all, but only drinking up the water of the sea. Of this is a great part of your people guilty, for you all drink in bitter and godless doctrines, while you spurn the word of God.

What in Genesis 22:17 is an image of the blessed abundance of Abraham's heritage becomes in Justin's interpretation a tragic image of the disbelief of most of the Jews and their consequent desolation. Sand becomes an image not for the Jews' multitude but for their barrenness and fruitlessness, which results from their spurning the Christ. Like sand, they soak up water, drinking in "bitter and godless doctrines." Like the sand by the sea, the Jews are a wasteland, without life.

Descent from Abraham is thus determined by one's relationship to Christ. The Jews may be descendants "according to the flesh," but apart from Christ they do not belong to those descendants through whom and in whom God's promises to Abraham find their fruition. The Christians, not the Jews, are the real descendants of Abraham.

The Nations: The Gentiles a Light to the Jews

One of Trypho's chief complaints against Justin and the Christians is that "you who claim to be pious and believe yourselves to be different from the others do not segregate yourselves from them, nor do you observe a manner of life different from that of the Gentiles" (*Dialogue* 10.3). Indeed, the self-understanding of the Jews in the Greco-Roman world agrees with Trypho's assessment. By and large, the Jews considered themselves a separate race, a *genos* ("race"), set apart from all the other races. They claimed that the promise God made to Abraham — that his seed would be a blessing to the nations — was realized whenever a Gentile became a proselyte and thus was incorporated into this "race." The proselyte became part of the Jewish people through circumcision and observing the ritual law; the outsider became an insider.[18] The basis of distinction between Gentile and Jew was clear, the integrity of the Jews as a separate people sacred. But Justin destroys the traditional distinction between Gentile and Jew and sets up a new basis for distinction by making two moves, both tied to Abraham: (1) redefining how Abraham's descendants are a blessing to the nations and (2) speaking of Christians and Gentiles in synonymous language.

1. As stated above, the traditional Jewish understanding of how the Jews as a people were a blessing to the nations was that a Gentile became blessed by being incorporated into the people when he became a full convert, a proselyte. One from among "the Gentiles" (*ta ethnē*) became part of the sacred "race" (*genos*). But Justin blurs the distinction between "the Gentiles" and "race" by nullifying the significance attached to "race," physical descent. One's physical descent has no bearing on one's standing before God, since that status is now completely determined by whether or not one has faith in Christ. It makes no difference whether one is descended from Abraham or from "the Gentiles." As we have seen above, for Justin the true descendants of Abraham are those who share a similar faith. Those from among the nations become descendants by their faith in Christ. Faith in Christ is now the sole basis for distinguishing insider from outsider.

Thus the crucial distinction is no longer between "the Gentiles" and the Jews as a sacred "race" but between those who believe and those who do not. For Justin, God has formed a new "nation" (*ethnos*), a new "people" (*laos*) in Christ. This new people is the fruit of God's promise to Abraham that through his seed the nations of the world would be blessed (*Dialogue* 11.5):

> We are the true spiritual Israel, and the descendants of . . . Abraham, who, though uncircumcised, was approved and

blessed by God because of his faith and was called the father of many nations.

And again in *Dialogue* 119.3–6:

And after the Just One was put to death, we blossomed forth as another people (*laos heteros*). . . . We Christians are not only a people, but a holy people . . . nor just any nation . . . but the chosen people of God. . . . For this is really the nation (*ethnos*) promised to Abraham by God, when He told him He would make him a father of many nations . . . because by our similar faith we have become children of Abraham.

While for Judaism there was a strict distinction between the descendants of Abraham, on the one hand, and the role these descendants played in becoming a blessing to the nations, on the other hand, for Justin the true descendants in fact turn out to *be* the nations, so that God's promises to Abraham regarding descendants and the nations become nearly indistinguishable. Abraham's descendants thus become a blessing to the nations by in fact *becoming* the nations.

2. In reading the *Dialogue*, one constantly gets the impression that, from Justin's perspective, Christ came not to the Jews but to the Gentiles. The Gentiles are the chosen people, not the Jews, and this is demonstrated by the Gentiles' acceptance of Jesus as the Christ.[19] Justin never tires of citing the prophets, especially Isaiah, to show that the Gentiles are the true heirs of God's promises (e.g., *Dialogue* 26.2, 3; 28.5, 6; 29.1; 41.2; 65.4–7; 73.3–5; 109.1; 119.4; 120.3–4; 121.1, 6; 123.7–8; 130.1–4; 135.2). Indeed, Justin frequently uses the terms "Christians" and "Gentiles" as synonyms (e.g., 26.1; 29.1; 41.3; 47.1, 3; 52.4; 64.1). He is as likely to say "we Gentiles" as he is "we Christians."

Why did God at first choose the Jews and only later in Christ choose the Gentiles? Justin answers this question in *Dialogue* 130.3–4:

In the beginning God dispersed all men according to nationality and language, and from all these nations He chose for Himself yours—a useless, disobedient, and faithless nation. And He showed that those of every nationality who were chosen have obeyed His will through Christ, whom He calls Jacob, and surnames Israel, so those [Christians] should also be Jacob and Israel, as I have proved at great length. For, when He exclaims, "Rejoice, ye Gentiles, with His people [Deut. 32:43]," He gives them a share in a similar legacy and attributes to them a similar name; but by calling them "Gentiles," and stating that they rejoice with His people, He does so as a reproach to your nation. For, just as you angered Him by your acts of idolatry, so has He deemed them, though they are likewise idolaters, worthy to know His will and to share in His inheritance.

According to Justin, God chose Israel first to show the Gentiles how *not* to be faithful! Whereas Israel was consistently disobedient, the Gentiles chosen by God have been obedient through Christ. Earlier in the chapter, again in reference to Deuteronomy 32:43 (LXX), Justin says, "By these words he indicates that we Gentiles rejoice with His people, that is, Abraham, Isaac, Jacob, the Prophets" (*Dialogue* 130.2). From Justin's perspective, to be a Christian is to be a Gentile. He even has Trypho address him in the following manner: "You who come from the Gentiles . . . who are all called Christians from His name" (*Dialogue* 64.1). Although Justin is aware of and accepts Jewish Christians (e.g., *Dialogue* 46 and 47), the normative Christian for him is a Gentile.[20] To be sure, the Gentile must have faith in Christ, but this does not indicate a parity between Jews and Gentiles. As a new people, Christians claim the ancient heritage of Abraham; but for Justin there is nothing essentially Jewish in this. The promise to Abraham that through his seed the nations would be blessed is a promise to a Gentile Abraham which finds its fulfillment in a Gentile Christianity. Far from the Gentiles being incorporated into God's promises to the Jews, the Gentiles as Christians now bear witness to the Jews about God's salvation in Christ. And on this basis Justin appeals to Trypho: "Since I base my arguments and suggestions on the Scriptures and facts, you should not hesitate to believe me, notwithstanding the fact that I am uncircumcised, for there is only a short time left for conversion" (*Dialogue* 28.2). For Justin, the Gentiles have become a light to the unbelieving Jews.

The Land: Millennial Real Estate

In addition to taking over for his own purposes the promises that Abraham would have many descendants and that they would be a blessing to the nations, Justin also redefines God's promise to Abraham that he and his posterity would inherit the land. Although there are fewer references to this theme, it still occupies a significant place in his controversy with Trypho. Two aspects predominate in Justin's discussion of the land: (1) dispossession of the Jews and (2) millennial repossession by the Christians.

1. The dispossession of the Jews from the land fits into Justin's scheme as the necessary precursor to the Christian occupation of the land upon Christ's return. Justin refers several times to the ousting of the Jews from Jerusalem by the Romans (*Dialogue* 16.2; 25.5; 40.2; 92.2). Jerusalem, in fact, is the sole focus of his discussion of the land. The very setting of the *Dialogue*, whether it is historical or fictitious, points to this theme. Justin has Trypho describe himself as "a refugee of the recent war" (*Dialogue* 1.3). The war he refers to is the Jewish revolt against Rome under the leadership of Bar-Cochba, which was effectively squelched when Hadrian conquered Jerusalem in 135 c.e., thenceforth banning all Jews from the city. Justin sees the dispossession of the Jews as God's just punishment for their disobedience and disbelief (*Dialogue* 16.2). God foreknew that Jerusalem would be taken from the Jews (*Dialogue* 40.2) and that they would be expelled from the city (*Dialogue* 92.2), as was prophesied in Scripture (*Dialogue* 25.5). When Trypho asks whether Justin means to say that the Jews will not inherit anything "on the holy mountain of God" (*Dialogue* 25.6), Justin answers that "the Gentiles, who believe in Christ and are sorry for their sins, shall receive the inheritance along with the Patriarchs" (*Dialogue* 26.1). The Jews have no claim to the land that God promised to Abraham's descendants, for through Christ it has been given over to the Gentiles. All the Jews, like Trypho, are deservedly refugees. Their present status as refugees anticipates their future status at the parousia. Indeed, one gets the impression that, for Justin, their physical dispossession from the land reflects their spiritual dispossession outside Christ.

2. Justin flatly states his claim for Christians: "And we shall inherit the Holy Land together with Abraham, receiving our inheritance for all eternity, because by our similar faith we have become children of Abraham" (*Dialogue* 119.5). The land is an eternal inheritance because Christ will establish it at his second coming. Justin looks forward to "the glorious coming of Christ in Jerusalem" (*Dialogue* 85.7). For then the resurrection will take place, followed by "a thousand years in the rebuilt, embellished, and enlarged city of Jerusalem, as was announced by the Prophets Ezekiel, Isaiah and the others" (*Dialogue* 80.5). Not only does Justin find this announcement in the prophets but he also refers explicitly to "a man among us named John, one of Christ's Apostles," who "received a revelation and foretold that the followers of Christ would dwell in Jerusalem for a thousand years" (*Dialogue* 81.4; see also 24.3; 113.5; 115.2; 138.3). For Justin, the land promised

to Abraham and his descendants is that land which Christ will
secure for the Christians during his millennial reign. The Jews
have no portion in it.

In summary, we have seen how Justin takes the divine
promises to Abraham in Genesis and redefines them so that
they apply exclusively to Christians. The Jews may be physical descendants of Abraham, but since Justin reckons descent
not according to the flesh but according to the spirit, namely,
according to a faith similar to that of Abraham, the Jews are
not his true descendants. Christians, rather, are the true descendants of Abraham. The nations are blessed in as much as
the Gentiles become God's chosen people. The Gentiles become the descendants of Abraham by faith in Christ. The land
will in the near future become Christian territory, to be set-
tled during the millennium.

The Jews stand completely dispossessed. They are stripped
of their lineage from Abraham, which the Christians now
justly claim. The Jews are like a sterile wasteland. They are no
longer a light to the Gentiles; rather, the Gentiles now bear
the torch and are a light to the obstinate Jews. The Jews have
been evicted from the holy land as a result of God's just punishment, and the land is now the promised inheritance of the
Christians. Justin has no doubt that the Jews have no legitimate heritage from Abraham, nor can they lay claim to any of
God's promises to Abraham.

As we have seen above, one's relationship to Abraham and
to the promises is mediated by one's faith in Christ, or lack
thereof. We turn, then, to an examination of how Justin portrays the relationship between Abraham and Christ.

Abraham and Christ

Two scriptural passages play a crucial role in Justin's development of the relationship between Abraham and Christ:
Genesis 18 and Matthew 8:11–12. Justin argues at length in
Dialogue 55–59 for Christ's preexistence on the basis of the
account in Genesis 18 of the theophany to Abraham at
Mamre. In several other passages Justin explicitly cites Matthew 8:11–12, where Abraham figures in the eschatological
banquet and the eschatological judgment. Although Justin's
appeals to the theophany at Mamre and to the eschatological
banquet do not appear together, these two scenes describe for
Justin the essential interconnectedness of Abraham and
Christ. Just as Christ was with Abraham at Mamre, so Abraham will be with Christ at the eschatological banquet. Christ

and Abraham are together at the beginning and at the end, in the formation and the fruition of the people of God.

Abraham and Christ at Mamre

The broad context in which Justin's appeals to Genesis 18 occur consists of extensive proofs from scripture that Jesus is the promised Christ of God (*Dialogue* 48–108). In *Dialogue* 47, Justin concludes his argument that the ritual law is no longer binding. Then in *Dialogue* 48.1 a new section begins in which Trypho makes the following request:

> We have now heard your opinion on these matters [regarding the ritual law] . . . . Resume your discourse where you left off, and bring it to an end, for it seems to be entirely absurd and utterly impossible of proof. Your statement that this Christ existed as God before all ages, and then that He consented to be born and become man, yet that He is not of human origin, appears to be not only paradoxical, but preposterous.

It is to this challenge that Justin now turns his attention. Just as he has used Abraham to argue against the necessity of the ritual law and to redefine the promises, so Justin uses the story of the theophany at Mamre to place Abraham in the service of Christianity over against Judaism.[21]

In *Dialogue* 55.1, in reference to Christ, Trypho asks Justin to "prove the existence of another God, besides the Creator of all things." Justin responds by appealing at length to the theophany to Abraham in Genesis 18. He begins by rehearsing briefly in *Dialogue* 56 the account of the theophany, explicitly citing Genesis 18:1–3, 13–14, 16–17, and 20–23, 33 (56.2, 6, 17–18). He also mixes in as supporting evidence citations from Genesis 21:9–12; 19:23–25; Psalm 109:1; 44:7–8 (LXX), and Genesis 19:10, 16–25 (56.7–8, 12, 14, 19–21). Justin uses all these citations in a complicated proof that it was Christ who appeared with two angels to Abraham under the oak at Mamre, not God the Father and Creator.

Justin asks Trypho whether he believes that it was God the Father and Creator who appeared to Abraham at Mamre (*Dialogue* 56.4; cf. 114.3). Trypho answers in the affirmative. Justin then inquires whether God was one of the three who appeared to Abraham under the oak at Mamre. Trypho responds (*Dialogue* 56.5):

> No, . . . but God appeared to him before he saw the three men. Furthermore, those three whom the Scripture calls men were

angels. Two of them were commissioned to destroy Sodom, while the third was sent to impart to Sara the good news that she was to have a son (and having fulfilled his mission, he departed).

That sounds clear enough, but Justin then asks Trypho how he explains the fact that the one who made the promise to Sarah (Gen. 18:10) returns after Sarah has given birth and is then referred to not as an angel but as "God" (*theos*; Gen. 21:12). Trypho does not get a chance to answer, however, for Justin jumps in with his own explanation which preempts Trypho's interpretation of the passage (*Dialogue* 56.8):

> Do you not see, therefore, that He who promised under the oak that He would return, since He knew He would be needed to counsel Abraham to do what Sara wished [regarding Hagar], did return according to the Scriptures, and is God?

Trypho agrees with this, but he does not concede that thereby Justin has proved that Genesis 21:12 refers to another God, or another aspect of God, besides the one who appeared to Abraham at Mamre. "All you have shown is that we were mistaken in our assumption that the three who were in the tent with Abraham were all angels" (56.9). But for Justin this admission opens the floodgate. For when Trypho concedes that there were only two angels and that the third visitor was really God, even though He is called an angel, Justin can capitalize on this concession by showing that this reference to God cannot mean God the Father and Creator. Instead, it must refer to the preexistent Christ. And if Justin can show that it was Christ and not God the Father who appeared to Abraham, then on the basis of this precedent he can make the same case for every other theophany. This Justin proceeds to do (*Dialogue* 56.11):

> Let us return to the Scriptures and I shall try to convince you that He who is said to have appeared to Abraham, Jacob, and Moses, and is called God, is distinct from God, the Creator; distinct, that is, in number, but not in mind (*arithmō legō alla ou gnōmē*). For I state that He never did or said anything else than what the Creator—above whom there is no other God—desired that He do or say.

According to Justin, "the Lord" in Genesis 18 refers not to God the Father but to Christ. This Lord who accompanied the angels and appeared to Abraham at Mamre is to be distinguished from God the Father and Creator. Why? Because two Lords are mentioned in the story of the destruction of

Sodom which immediately follows the theophany at Mamre. Justin cites Genesis 19:24: "And the Lord rained upon Sodom brimstone and fire from the Lord out of Heaven" (56.12). Justin appears to distinguish the "Lord" who rains brimstone and fire from the "Lord out of Heaven." The former refers to Christ. The latter refers to God the Father and Creator. To support this interpretation, Justin cites Psalm 110:1 (Ps. 109 in the LXX), which by his time had become a standard proof text for Christ's exaltation: "The Lord said to my Lord: Sit Thou at My right hand" (56.14).[22]

Having thus shown that the angel who appeared to Abraham as a man in Genesis 18 is the same person as the one termed "God" in Genesis 21:12, and that this person in turn is identical to the one referred to in Genesis 19:24 as "Lord," Justin can finally draw his conclusion. All of these different names refer to one person, Christ, "who was at the same time Angel and God and Lord and Man, and was seen by Abraham" (*Dialogue* 59.1).[23] This is the same being who appeared to Jacob and Moses. Justin restates his claim on several occasions: "It has been conclusively proved that He who appeared to Abraham, Isaac, Jacob, and the other Patriarchs was appointed by the Father and Lord, and administers to His will, and is called God" (*Dialogue* 126.5). And in *Dialogue* 113.4 Justin states, "For I have proved that it was Jesus who appeared to and talked with Moses, Abraham, and in short, with all the Patriarchs, doing the will of the Father."

For Justin, God the Creator and Father disappears almost completely from view and is accessible only in a mediated form through Christ, from the time of Abraham to the present and into the eschatological future. This disappearance points to a central philosophical presupposition for Justin about the relationship between Christ and God the Father.[24] According to Justin (*Dialogue* 56.1), God the Creator and Father is an ineffable God who

> abides in the super-celestial sphere, who has never been seen by any man, and with whom no man has ever conversed, and whom we call Creator of all and Father.

And elsewhere (*Dialogue* 60.2) Justin states,

> No one with even the slightest intelligence would dare to assert that the Creator and Father of all things left His super-celestial realms to make Himself visible in a little spot on earth.

If God is said to have appeared to anyone, it can only be that aspect of God which is revealed in Christ. Thus for Justin all theophanies become christophanies, and all christophanies theophanies. The theophany to Abraham at Mamre is by definition an appearance of Christ to Abraham.

Abraham and Christ at the Eschatological Judgment/Banquet

In three passages from the *Dialogue* (76.4; 120.6; 140.4), Justin cites Matthew 8:11–12 (cf. Luke 13:28–29), in roughly the same form each time: "They shall come from the east and from the west, and will feast with Abraham and Isaac and Jacob in the kingdom of heaven; but the children of the kingdom will be put into the darkness outside" (140.4).[25] For Justin, this passage serves a twofold purpose. First, the reference to people coming from east and west shows the Gentile believers coming into the kingdom of heaven. Second, the casting out of the "children of the kingdom" indicates God's rejection of the unbelieving Jews.

In *Dialogue* 76.4, Justin pairs Matthew 8:11–12 with two passages that refer to God's eschatological judgment: Matthew 7:22–23 ("Many will say to me in that day, Lord, Lord. . . . And then I will say to them: Depart from me") and Matthew 25:41 ("Depart into exterior darkness"). This theme of judgment is picked up again in Justin's next appeal to Matthew 8:11–12, *Dialogue* 120.6. Before citing the passage as proof of his assertion, Justin speaks about the second coming of Christ, citing Genesis 49:10: "Until He comes for whom it is laid up; and He shall be the expectation of the Gentiles" (*Dialogue* 120.5). Justin then accuses the Jews of manipulating the wording of the Greek translation of this passage to read, "Until the things laid up for Him come" (120.4), so that it would not refer to Christ. He goes on to accuse the Jews of also having expunged from the text the words describing the death of Isaiah, "whom you Jews sawed in half with a wooden saw" (120.5).[26] The manner of death suffered by Isaiah is, for Justin, a symbol of Christ (*Dialogue* 120.5),

> who is going to cut your nation in two, and to admit the worthy half into His eternal kingdom with the holy Patriarchs and Prophets. But the rest, He has said, He will condemn to the undying flames of Hell, together with all those of all nations who are likewise disobedient and unrepentant.

To support this statement, Justin then cites Matthew 8:11–12, again with the emphasis on the judgment of the Jews, the former children of God who are now cast into the darkness. Finally, in *Dialogue* 140.2–4, Justin again cites Matthew 8:11–12 as proof that

> your teachers . . . deceive both themselves and you when they suppose that those who are descendants of Abraham according to the flesh (*apo tēs sporas tēs kata sarka tou Abraam*) will most certainly share in the eternal kingdom, even though they be faithless sinners and disobedient to God, suppositions which the Scriptures show have no foundation in fact.

Rather, "the Gentiles, who believe in Christ, and are sorry for their sins, shall receive the inheritance, along with the Patriarchs" (*Dialogue* 26.1). Referring elsewhere to Deuteronomy 32:43 (LXX; "Rejoice, O ye Gentiles, with His people"), Justin again affirms, "By these words he indicates that we Gentiles rejoice with His people, that is, Abraham, Isaac, Jacob" (*Dialogue* 130.2).

Justin thus uses Matthew 8:11–12 to support his contention that the unbelieving Jews are headed for God's damning judgment at the eschaton. The believing Gentiles are destined to share in the eschatological banquet with Abraham, the other patriarchs, and the prophets, all of whom bore witness to Christ. There is no clearer indication of the Jews' status as a disinherited people than Justin's appeal to Matthew 8:11–12.

In summary, Abraham and Christ are inseparably bound together, according to Justin. Christ appeared to Abraham at Mamre, promising to him a son who would be heir to all of God's promises. This promise finds its fulfillment in the coming of Christ, and its consummation in Christ's second coming, where the promises to Abraham will be kept. The unbelieving Jews are not children of Abraham, for they fail to believe in the very Christ to whom Abraham bore witness. As a result they will be cast out into utter darkness at God's eschatological judgment. The believing Gentiles are the true children of Abraham, and as rightful heirs they will sit and feast with him at Christ's eschatological banquet. For Justin, the Jews will receive judgment, while the Gentiles will receive a banquet.

Conclusion: Justin's Use of Abraham in Controversy with Judaism

Abraham and the Jews: Wheat Becomes Chaff

We have examined Justin's use of Abraham in the *Dialogue with Trypho*, focusing on his role in discussions about circumcision, the promises of God, and the Christ. All of these are essentially Jewish categories, central concepts deeply embedded in the heritage of Judaism, as is Abraham himself. It is all the more striking, then, that as Justin refers to Abraham in developing his arguments regarding circumcision, the promises, and the Christ, he leaves the Jews with none of them, except the curse of a carnal circumcision.

The effect of so radically divorcing Judaism from the promises and from the Christ is that the heritage of the Jews, seeming to promise so rich a harvest, becomes in Justin's hands mere chaff. Apart from the promises, the Jews have no roots in the past, no grounding. Apart from the Christ, the Jews have no hope in the future, no deliverance. Without the promises and the Christ, the Jews have no part in God, as Justin in fact claims. Apart from God, the Jews have only judgment and destruction awaiting them. In Justin's sketch of Abraham, we find a bleak picture indeed of Judaism.

Inversion as Continuity

A recurring note in our investigation is the way in which Justin uses Abraham in the "Gentilization" of Christianity. When it comes to circumcision, Abraham is a Gentile, as Justin disassociates him from the carnal circumcision of the Jews. Regarding God's promises to Abraham, Justin redefines all of them and redirects them to Gentile Christians. The traditional Jewish notions of the chosen people and the nations are inverted by Justin so that the chosen people become no people. Justin sees this inversion as continuous with God's intentions from the beginning, since the Christ existed from the beginning and all of the patriarchs and prophets bore witness to Christ. Thus, on a deeper level the Jews were never God's children at all! At best they were foster children until the revelation of God's real children, namely, those who responded faithfully to Christ. Once foster children, the Jews now stand abandoned and completely alone, with no legitimate past and with no future aside from God's wrath. For Justin, the inversion of the status of Jews and Gentiles stands in continuity with God's purposes in Christ.

8

From Gentile Inclusion
to Jewish Exclusion

This study began with various questions regarding the separation of formative Christianity from early Judaism. In an attempt to understand more clearly some of the dynamics of this split, I proposed an examination of the uses of Abraham in early Christian controversy with Judaism from about 50 to 150 C.E. We explored a wide range of early Christian writings with the thesis that their use of Abraham could serve as a heuristic device for assessing the character of early Christian controversy with Judaism. Having completed this study, we are now in a position to summarize the findings and to draw several conclusions.

We first gave some attention to early Jewish uses of Abraham, since these uses provide a general context for understanding the various roles that Abraham played in early Christianity. We saw that a broad range of traditions regarding the patriarch enjoyed wide circulation in early Judaism. These traditions revolved around the covenant promises that God had established with Abraham and his descendants, the exemplary faith of Abraham, and the intermediary status of Abraham. They provided common ground for diverse expressions of Jewish faith. To a large extent, they were taken for granted as a given heritage, a heritage that was adapted and shaped in the light of God's covenants with Moses and David.[1] The promises that Abraham had received provided a sure hope for the people despite adversities. Abraham's own enduring faithfulness provided a model to follow, and many Jews looked forward to being welcomed into God's kingdom by their father Abraham.

The belief of some first-century Jews that Jesus is the Christ, however, led to a further revisioning of the traditions regarding Abraham. Their understanding of Abraham's significance was shaped by their understanding of Jesus' identity as the Christ. Early Christians appropriated most of the early Jewish traditions about Abraham but modified them in order to give expression to their beliefs about the significance of Jesus. The earliest developed Christian understanding of Abraham is that of Paul.

We found that Paul uses Abraham primarily in two letters, Galatians and Romans. These letters represent quite different settings, and Paul's use of Abraham in these letters is accordingly significantly different. In each setting, we examined how Paul uses Abraham, why he uses Abraham as he does, and what implications might be drawn from this use for Paul's view of non-Christian Judaism.

Paul's letter to the Galatians is addressed to a community that Paul has established but one with which he has had recurring problems (Gal. 1:9; 4:19). Paul addresses churches that have fallen under the sway of rival Teachers (Gal. 1:8–9; 3:1; 4:17; 5:7–9, 12–13; 6:12–13). These Teachers have appealed to Abraham in order to convince the Galatian Christians that to be true Christians they needed to observe circumcision and the law. After all, Abraham was circumcised, and if they desired to share in the promises to the patriarch, they needed to become true children of Abraham through circumcision and the observance of the law. In response to this argument, Paul appeals to Abraham to ground the inclusion of the Gentiles apart from circumcision and the law. Paul uses Abraham as a reminder to the Galatians of the true basis of inclusion in Christ—namely, faith, not law observance. After all, Abraham was reckoned righteous and received the promises on account of his faith. If the Galatian Christians desired to share in the promises to Abraham, then they needed to hear with faith (Gal. 3:2, 29). Indeed, the inclusion of the Gentiles in Christ through faith, Paul argues, was part of God's very promise to Abraham (Gal. 3:8).

We also saw that Galatians says little directly about Paul's view of non-Christian Jews, because it reflects an intramural dispute between Christians in which Paul takes a rather polemical stance. Still, Paul's sharp attack against the Teachers and their advocacy of law observance leaves the impression that Paul views non-Christian Jews as enslaved to the law. But we should remember that Paul does not explicitly address the question of the status of non-Christian Jews.

Paul's letter to the Romans is addressed to a community he neither established nor knows, although he is probably aware of tensions between Jewish and Gentile Christians in the Roman congregation. Particularly with the Jewish Christians in view (Romans 4), Paul uses Abraham to argue for Gentile inclusion in the Abrahamic promises on the basis of faith. After all, Abraham was reckoned righteous by God before he was circumcised (Rom. 4:10). His circumcision functioned only as a sign of his righteousness (Rom. 4:11). Similarly, the Gentiles become children of Abraham and partake of these promises by following the example of Abraham's faith (Rom. 4:11–12). Indeed, the inclusion of the Gentiles was part of God's promise to Abraham (Rom. 4:17).

Then, with the Gentile Christians especially in view (Romans 9–11), Paul uses Abraham to maintain God's continued election of non-Christian Jews. He denies that Jewish rejection of Christ implies God's rejection of the Jews (Rom. 11:1, 11). Although their rejection of Christ shows their current disobedience, the Jews remain included within God's promises because God is faithful (Rom. 11:28–31). Ultimately, through God's action of including the Gentiles, God will mysteriously also show mercy to the disobedient Jews (Rom. 11:30–32).

Thus, central to Paul's use of Abraham in both Galatians and Romans is the argument for Gentile inclusion in the promises through faith, apart from the law. At the same time, Galatians and Romans differ in their use of Abraham in regard to non-Christian Jews. In Galatians, Paul does not address this issue directly, whereas in Romans he does.

In contrast to Paul, Matthew makes a limited use of Abraham. Matthew writes in a primarily Jewish-Christian setting, amidst conflict with the non-Christian Jewish synagogue. We noted that in his use of Abraham, Matthew emphasizes continuity with the Jewish heritage. Through his Abrahamic descent, Jesus stands in line with Jewish hopes that began with Abraham (Matt. 1:1–17). Similarly, in agreement with the Pharisees, Jesus believes in the resurrected life where Abraham will be present (Matt. 22:23–33). But in his use of Abraham, Matthew also points to discontinuity with his Jewish heritage and thus implicitly critiques non-Christian Judaism. References to Abraham occur in contexts of disputes with Jewish religious leaders (Matt. 3:7–10; 8:11–12; 22:23–33). Further, Matthew uses Abraham to hint strongly at Gentile inclusion within God's kingdom (Matt. 3:7–10; 8:5–13).

The author of Hebrews writes from a Jewish-Christian perspective to a community in need of encouragement. We found that the author uses Abraham in two ways. First, for Hebrews, the story of Abraham and Melchizedek indicates that since Melchizedek was greater than Abraham, so Christ's priesthood is better than the Levitical priesthood (Hebrews 7). Second, the author appeals to Abraham's faith and endurance as models to be followed by the community (Hebrews 11), in keeping with traditional Jewish appeals to Abraham's faith. The critique of the Levitical priesthood, however, offers a clear criticism of non-Christian Judaism.

Our survey of Abraham in James showed a traditional Jewish understanding of the patriarch as an example to be followed. Abraham was justified by his faithful obedience to God (James 2:21–23). Similarly, believers must demonstrate their faithfulness with concrete actions. A confession of faith is empty apart from corroborative works of mercy. Actions do speak louder than words. In James, we found no use of Abraham in controversy with Judaism. If anything, James appeals to Abraham in conflict with other Christians who emphasize faith apart from works.

We saw that Luke-Acts makes significant use of Abraham. Luke writes in a primarily Gentile-Christian setting and in his use of Abraham seeks to show God's inclusion of the outcast. In the Gospel, Luke refers to Abraham when presenting the extension of God's mercy to the pious poor (e.g., Luke 1:55, 73; the crippled woman in 13:10–17; and Lazarus in 16:22–30) and to those who repent (e.g., Luke 3:7–9; 16:22–30; and Zacchaeus in 19:1–10). In Acts, he expands upon this motif by showing that God's salvation in Christ has also come to the Gentiles, so that the promises to Abraham have been fulfilled (in the speeches of Peter, Stephen, and Paul; Acts 3:12–26; 7:2–8; 13:13–52). By universalizing God's promises to Abraham in this way, Luke undercuts any attempts to construe Abraham as the exclusive father of the Jews. Similarly, the failure of many Jews to recognize the realization of the Abrahamic promises in Christ leads Luke to criticize the Jewish leaders, especially those aligned with the Temple cult. Thus, Luke does use Abraham in controversy with Judaism, although this use forms a minor theme in his writings. Luke's major emphasis in using Abraham is to show God's inclusion of those who were formerly considered outcast, particularly the Gentiles.

We noted that the Gospel of John was written in the context of a heated dispute between Jewish-Christians and non-Christian Jews. John engages in a sharp polemic against the Jewish synagogue. Within this setting, John uses Abraham to establish claims about the christological identity of Jesus over against Jewish opponents (John 8:48–59). Abraham bears witness to Jesus. Similarly, John appeals to Abraham in order to show that non-Christian Jews, especially those Jews who had once expressed belief, cannot claim Abraham as their father, for they reject Jesus. Rather, these Jews have the devil for their father (John 8:31–47). We found no evidence to suggest that within the Johannine community Abraham functioned in discussions regarding Gentile inclusion. But we found plenty of evidence to see that John disassociates Abraham from the Jews.

In early-second-century Christian controversy with Judaism we observed two uses of Abraham. First, Barnabas, Ignatius, and the Gospel of Philip tend to Christianize Abraham in addressing primarily Gentile Christians. Barnabas in particular shows Abraham testifying to Christ (Barn. 8:1–4). Abraham's circumcision foreshadows the covenant in Christ's blood (Barn. 9:7–9), and the promises to Abraham have been realized especially in Gentile belief in Christ (Barn. 13:6–7). Second, Heracleon and Marcion, both gnosticizing Gentile Christians, take a different approach by disassociating Abraham from true Christianity and by leaving him to the Jews. Similarly, Aristides refers to Abraham in order to distinguish Jews from Christians, arguing that Abraham is the source of the Jewish race, while Christ is the source of the Christian religion. Both uses of Abraham by these early-second-century Christians indicate the exclusion of non-Christian Jews from salvation in Christ. We also noted, however, that Abraham was used in a wide variety of contexts that really have little or no relationship to Christian controversy with Judaism.

Finally, we saw that Justin Martyr makes extensive use of Abraham in his *Dialogue with Trypho*. Speaking as a Gentile Christian to Trypho, a Jew, Justin shows how the promises to Abraham have been fulfilled exclusively in Christ. The promises, in fact, have now come specifically to the Gentiles. Further, according to Justin, Abraham was obedient to Christ's voice and he bore faithful witness to Christ. As for the non-Christian Jews, Abraham's circumcision was given as a sign to mark the Jews for punishment, because they have rejected Christ. Consequently, the Jews have been severed from Abraham and have no legitimate claim on Abraham as father.

From this summary we can observe two patterns that particularly characterize the use of Abraham in early Christianity.

First, Abraham provides a focus for claims about the inclusion of people within God's salvation and the exclusion of people from God's salvation. Second, Abraham provides a focus for claims about Gentiles and Jews. In fact, various authors use Abraham to integrate these patterns around two issues that in many respects come to characterize early Christian controversy with Judaism: Gentile inclusion and Jewish exclusion.

We are now in a position to return to the original thesis that Abraham can serve as a heuristic device for assessing the character of early Christian controversy with Judaism. By tracing the issues of Gentile inclusion and Jewish exclusion as they arise in connection with Abraham, we can observe an inversion in Christian controversy with Judaism. Simply put, the various uses of Abraham from Paul through Justin Martyr show a shift in focus from Gentile inclusion to Jewish exclusion.

In order to observe this shift in early Christian controversy with Judaism it is helpful roughly to organize the authors we have studied into four generations. In the first generation, ca. 30–60 C.E., Paul has the issue of Gentile inclusion foremost on his mind as he preaches the gospel. He describes himself as an apostle to the Gentiles (Gal. 1:16; 2:7; Rom. 1:13–15) and indeed sees Gentile inclusion as part of the content of the gospel.[2] Even for the Teachers in Galatia, whom Paul opposes, the issue of Gentile inclusion is of crucial importance. As we have seen, Paul and the Teachers differ in their understanding of the basis on which Gentiles find inclusion in Christ. Yet this difference should not blind us to the fact that they agree on the centrality of the issue of Gentile inclusion.

In this first generation, the issue of Jewish exclusion also begins to be addressed by Christians, although it was not as significant as the notion of Gentile inclusion. In Romans 9–11 we saw that Paul deals with the issue of Jewish exclusion by pointing out to the Christians in Rome that God has not abandoned the Jews, indeed, by affirming that the Jews remain beloved by God on account of the patriarchs (Rom. 11:28–29).[3]

The second generation of Christians, ca. 60–90 C.E., continues to address the issues of Gentile inclusion and Jewish exclusion. Here Matthew, Hebrews, and Luke-Acts come into view.[4] Matthew uses Abraham in ways that indicate his concern for the importance of Gentile inclusion (Matt. 8:5–13). At the same time, Matthew's use of Abraham already begins to point toward an increased focus on Jewish exclusion (Matt. 3:7–10; 8:11–12; 22:32), although Matthew has not yet com-

pletely severed his ties to the synagogue. Hebrews also uses
Abraham to point toward Jewish exclusion, if more indirectly
than Matthew. Hebrews refers to Abraham in order to criticize the Levitical priesthood and so to show that the covenant
with the Jews is antiquated and inferior to God's new covenant in Christ (Heb. 7:1–10). Luke-Acts, written from a
Gentile-Christian perspective, appeals to Abraham primarily
to emphasize that in Christ God has extended the covenant
promises to Gentiles. At the same time, Luke uses Abraham to
touch on the theme of Jewish exclusion, but his position here
remains ambiguous. Still, this theme does not come to the fore
as much in Luke as it does in Matthew and Hebrews, perhaps
because Matthew and Hebrews are both written in Jewish-
Christian contexts. Thus Gentile inclusion continues to be important, especially for Luke and Matthew, but Jewish exclusion takes on a new significance with this generation.

In the third generation of Christians, ca. 90–120 C.E., the
issue of Gentile inclusion increasingly becomes a silent assumption, whereas the issue of Jewish exclusion finds more
definitive expression. Here we turn to John, Ignatius, and Barnabas. The Gospel of John does not explicitly address the issue
of Gentile inclusion, although John is clearly aware of Gentile
Christianity (e.g., John 10:16; 12:20–22). Ignatius and Barnabas tend to assume that Gentile inclusion is normative for
Christianity. Barnabas even refers to Abraham as "the father
of the Gentiles" (Barn. 13:6–7).

The issue of Jewish exclusion, however, becomes more
dominant with this generation. John in particular uses Abraham to rupture any legitimate connection between non-Christian Jews and the patriarch (John 8:31–59). As we saw, John
denies that Abraham is the true father of the Jews; rather,
their father is the devil. John thus uses Abraham to signal the
centrality of the issue of Jewish exclusion. Similarly, Barnabas
refers to Abraham in contexts that highlight Jewish exclusion
(Barn. 9:3–4; 13:6–7). In Ignatius, the use of Abraham to indicate Jewish exclusion is more implicit (Phld. 9:1), but the importance of this issue is clear elsewhere in his writings (e.g.,
Phld. 6:1; Magn. 8:1; 10:3). In the third generation of Christianity, then, Gentile inclusion appears to be taken for
granted, while Jewish exclusion finds sharper articulation than
it had before.

Finally, with the fourth generation of Christians, ca. 120–
150 C.E., these two issues on the agenda of Christian controversy with Judaism have been fully inverted. Here we can
consider Aristides, Heracleon, Marcion, Philip, and Justin

Martyr. By this time the issue of Gentile inclusion has ceased to be an issue at all, as Christianity is almost an exclusively Gentile enterprise. For example, by using Abraham to distinguish Christians from Jews in his apology to a Gentile audience, Aristides appears to presuppose that Christians are Gentiles (Greek recension, ch. 14). Similarly, Heracleon, Marcion, and the Gospel of Philip separate Christianity from Judaism. Although they do not explicitly refer to the Gentile makeup of Christianity, this situation was probably a given for them, especially for Marcion. Finally, Justin Martyr regularly uses the terms "Christians" and "Gentiles" interchangeably, a clear indication that he assumes Gentile Christianity to be the standard. Thus, when he calls Abraham the father of the Christians, he is in effect implying that Abraham is primarily the father of the Gentiles.

Whereas Gentile inclusion is fully assumed by this time, Jewish exclusion reaches the status of an explicit doctrine that becomes normative in Christian controversy with Judaism. Aristides makes this clear when, after introducing Abraham, he characterizes the Jews as having removed themselves from the truth by rejecting the Christ (ch. 14). Similarly, Heracleon, Marcion, and the Gospel of Philip see the Jews as a forsaken people that have not grasped the truth. And Justin appeals to Abraham to demonstrate that God's promises have been transferred away from the Jews to the Christians. The Jews are not true children of Abraham and so have been excluded from salvation.

In sum, then, when we trace the issues of Gentile inclusion and Jewish exclusion in early Christian discussions of Abraham, we can observe a shift in early Christian controversy with Judaism. For the earliest Christians, Gentile inclusion is the most pressing concern. These Christians appeal to Abraham in order to show that Gentiles too are heirs of the covenant promises. Later generations of Christians, however, increasingly take Gentile inclusion for granted. The idea of Jewish exclusion is also already raised by the earliest Christians but dismissed, at least by Paul, on account of God's faithfulness to the Jews. Later generations of Christians, however, increasingly emphasize that the Jews have been excluded because of their faithlessness. For later generations of Christians, Jewish exclusion becomes the most pressing concern in Christian controversy with Judaism.

Indeed, if we look at the early Christian authors where Abraham figures most prominently (Paul, Luke-Acts, John, and Justin), the following contrasts stand out:

Paul, a Jewish Christian, uses Abraham to argue for Gentile inclusion within the promises of God.

Luke, a Gentile Christian, also uses Abraham to argue for Gentile inclusion within the promises of God.

John, a Jewish Christian, uses Abraham to argue for Jewish exclusion from God's purposes.

Justin, a Gentile Christian, also uses Abraham to argue for Jewish exclusion from God's purposes.

We have already noticed the basic shift from a focus on Gentile inclusion to Jewish exclusion in early Christian controversy with Judaism. In addition, the use of Abraham in these authors points to another trend. Just as the advocacy of Gentile inclusion progresses from Jewish Christians to Gentile Christians (Paul, Luke), so the advocacy of Jewish exclusion progresses from Jewish Christians to Gentile Christians (John, Justin). Thus the following basic reversal appears: *whereas Jewish Christians initiated the use of Abraham in controversy with Judaism to argue for Gentile inclusion, Gentile Christians essentially concluded the use of Abraham in controversy with Judaism by arguing for Jewish exclusion.*

This observation is in no way meant to imply that with Justin we reach the end of Christian controversy with Judaism. Rather, Justin's use of Abraham marks the final stage of development in Christian use of Abraham against non-Christian Judaism. The many centuries of Christian controversy with Judaism following Justin simply restate in various ways the Christian conclusion that Abraham is the father of Christians and not of Jews (e.g., in Irenaeus, Tertullian, Eusebius, Chrysostom, Aphrahat).[5]

At this point, several qualifications are in order. It is likely that there were Christians, Jewish as well as Gentile, whose use of Abraham diverges from the basic shift we have observed. On the Jewish-Christian side, there were probably groups among the third and fourth generations of Christians that did not use Abraham to argue for Jewish exclusion.[6] Such Jewish Christians may even have allowed for an inclusive understanding of non-Christian Jews as children of Abraham. Yet other Jewish Christians may have been uncomfortable with the notion of Gentile inclusion and may have used Abraham to show that Christ held significance only for Jews.[7]

On the Gentile-Christian side, there may have been groups among the third and fourth generations of Christians whose attraction to Judaism led them to argue for non-Christian Jewish inclusion in God's salvation rather than exclusion from it.

Certainly Gentile Christians continued to be attracted to Judaism throughout the first two centuries. This attraction is well documented by the pastoral problems evident in the Antiochene church from the time of Ignatius to the time of John Chrysostom three centuries later.[8]

Overall, however, our observation regarding the basic shift in early Christian controversy with Judaism still holds, as these groups were at most minorities. Christian controversy with Judaism from about 50 to 150 C.E. began with Gentile inclusion and ended with Jewish exclusion. In this shift we see a nearly complete transition of Christianity from its origins as a subgroup within Judaism to its development into a full-blown Gentile religious movement outside Judaism. At the same time, we see a development of Christian controversy with Judaism to the point that Christianity completely rejects Judaism. This rejection marks a final stage in the controversy in that it is merely refined and restated in different ways by subsequent generations of Christians, even to the present time.

Given the social and theological ramifications of this shift and its end result, we may well inquire into the factors that contributed to it. Did the inherent identity of formative Christianity make such a development unavoidable, so that subsequent generations were theologically bound by its exclusivist outcome?[9] Were there historical contingencies that contributed to the movement, which would make the outcome less binding upon later generations? I would suggest the latter, since one can identify at least four factors that contributed to the shift from Gentile inclusion to Jewish exclusion.

The first factor is the diminishing emphasis upon the eschatological dimensions of the Christian faith. Paul clearly believed that Christ's parousia was close at hand (e.g., 1 Thess. 1:10; 4:15).[10] He probably also believed that the full number of Gentiles was nearly complete and therefore the inevitable salvation of all Israel was imminent (Rom. 11:25–26). But Paul's expectations failed to materialize. Christ did not return. The Jews did not en masse come to believe in Christ. The delay of Christ's parousia and the consequent decreasing emphasis on the imminence of the eschaton in Christian faith led early Christians increasingly to see non-Christian Jews not as potential converts but as opponents to the gospel. As a result, whereas Paul could affirm that "as regards the gospel they are enemies of God, for your sake; but as regards election they are beloved for the sake of their forefathers" (Rom. 11:28), later generations of Christians came increasingly to affirm only the first half of Paul's statement.

The second factor has to do with the increasingly Gentile makeup of early Christianity. Whereas Paul could speak of the Gentiles being "grafted in" like a wild olive shoot into the tree of Israel (Rom. 11:17–24), later generations of Christians more and more conceived of Gentile Christianity as the heir of Israel (cf. Barnabas and Justin). And so a century after Paul reprimanded the Gentile Christians in Rome for their presumption that they had replaced the Jews as God's people (Rom. 11:25), Justin Martyr could assume that God's people are Gentiles, not Jews.[11] The Jewish-Christian claim of Paul that Gentiles are truly children of Abraham developed eventually into the Gentile-Christian claim of Justin that Jews are not children of Abraham.

A third and related factor is the proportionally decreasing presence of Jewish Christians. The ever smaller number of Christians with Jewish roots led to theological questions regarding the status of the Jews before God. The dwindling number of Jewish Christians remaining in the church appears to have become increasingly alienated from the synagogue (e.g., Matthew and John). These Jewish Christians were eventually absorbed into an overwhelmingly Gentile Christianity.

Fourth, and finally, the increasingly invigorated and uniform expression of Judaism after the destruction of the Second Temple in 70 C.E. also contributed to more clearly defined boundaries between Jews and Christians. The Council of Jamnia and the formulation of the benediction against the heretics (*Birkat ha-Minim*), if indeed it took place already at Jamnia, helped to solidify Jewish self-definition at a time when it was sorely needed.[12] This self-definition took place, in part, as a conscious reaction against the Christian appropriation of Jewish traditions and the christological focus of Christian faith. The combination of persistent Jewish rejection of the gospel with a more vigorous and uniform expression of Judaism only led Christians, and mostly Gentile Christians at that, to identify themselves increasingly over against Judaism.

These four factors, then, all contributed to the progression from Gentile inclusion to Jewish exclusion, exemplified in early Christian use of Abraham in controversy with Judaism. Yet while we can understand the movement from Gentile inclusion to Jewish exclusion historically, we must still ask the question: Was this move theologically necessary or defensible? To put the matter quite simply: Does Gentile inclusion in God's promises necessitate Jewish exclusion?

Justin Martyr, Marcion, Heracleon, Barnabas, and Ignatius apparently did equate Gentile inclusion with Jewish exclusion.[13] Although the Gospel of John excludes the Jews quite apart from any consideration of Gentile inclusion, John's exclusion of the Jews on christological grounds would have been quite amenable to most early Gentile Christians, probably Luke-Acts included. Only Paul seems clearly to have had problems with such an equation, in fact rejecting it implicitly in Romans 4 and explicitly in Romans 9–11. Let us review Paul's position.

Paul centered his attention on the inclusion of the Gentiles in God's salvation, a salvation promised to Abraham and now fulfilled in Christ. But his emphasis in Romans 4 on the similarity of Christian faith to Abraham's faith did not extend to any explicit development of Abraham's faith in christological terms. Paul's treatment of Abraham in Romans 4 has led Hendrikus Boers to assert:[14]

> This indifference of the specific form and occasion of the faith in God clearly leaves open in principle—and that is what concerns us here—the possibility that Jews who were not Christians could have followed in the footsteps of the faith which Abraham had before he was circumcized.

From this observation, Boers concludes that in Romans 4 "Paul showed a way for a theology out of the ghetto" indeed, a way out of christological exclusivism.[15] Boers concedes, however, that Paul was probably not aware of this principle he allows in Romans 4.[16] In my opinion, Boers is correct in seeking a way for Christian theology to move "out of the ghetto" but incorrect in his conclusion that Romans 4 provides the basis for a way out of christological exclusivism, especially since he concedes that his interpretation runs against Paul's own understanding of the matter. For Paul, very simply, in the time after Jesus' death and resurrection true Jewish faith is Christian faith. Paul did not assert that Abraham had faith in Christ, but Paul did assert that faith in Christ is like Abraham's faith on this side of the resurrection.

In short, the way for Christian theology to move out of the ghetto in regard to non-Christian Judaism is not by moving out of christological exclusivism. Rather, the way out of the ghetto is to take seriously both halves of Paul's statement regarding non-Christian Judaism in Romans 11:28: "In terms of the gospel they have become enemies on your account, but in terms of election they remain beloved on account of the patriarchs."[17] In particular, the way out of the ghetto is for Christians to rehabilitate in their own theological formulations God's continued election of the Jews, which Paul expresses so clearly in Romans 11:28b. Thus it is not Paul's use of Abraham in Romans 4 that provides a way out of Christian exclusivist claims. Rather, it is Paul's use of Abraham in Romans 9–11 that provides the opportunity for Christians to make inclusive claims regarding the mercy of God, lest they be subject to Paul's warning in Romans 11:17–25.

Paul did not equate Jewish rejection of the gospel with God's rejection of the Jews. Nor would he allow such an equation to be inferred. Rather, Jewish rejection of the gospel served God's purpose of Gentile inclusion within the gospel. The Jews became enemies of the gospel so that Gentiles might be included within the gospel. Thus the Gentiles were saved by their enemies. Likewise non-Christian Jews will be saved by their enemies. This situation is the utter paradox and mystery of the gospel for Paul. God has inverted the consequence of human rebellion (death) by using humanity's rejection of God, and with it the rejection of other human beings, to bring about humanity's obedient acceptance of God, and with it the acceptance of other human beings. In short, in Christ God has turned human sinfulness resulting in death into human faithfulness resulting in salvation.

For Paul, non-Christian Jews continue to be included within God's promises simply because of God's covenant faithfulness to Abraham and the other patriarchs.[18] Thus what Paul seems to take away with one hand (denying the positive life-giving significance of the law) he gives back with the other (affirming the continued election of the Jews). Paul would not affirm the theological doctrine that became entrenched among later generations of Christians, namely, that Gentile inclusion necessitates Jewish exclusion.

Paul's use of Abraham to focus both on Gentile inclusion and on God's continued election of the Jews (Romans 4; 9–11) provides the Christian tradition with the possibility of making a move other than the equation of Gentile inclusion with Jewish exclusion. Paul could use Abraham in service of his christology (Galatians 3), but even this use does not exclude Jewish inclusion. In contrast to Paul, later Christians use Abraham to couple Gentile inclusion with Jewish exclusion, thereby closing the door on Paul's approach to non-Christian Judaism. As Paul shows, however, such a move is not theologically necessary within Christian self-understanding.

It is no accident, then, that Paul, and especially Paul's use of Abraham, has played such a significant role in contemporary discussions regarding Christian/Jewish relations.[19] Paul's unwillingness to equate Gentile inclusion in God's salvation with

Jewish exclusion from God's salvation certainly provides much ground for discussion. Regarding the developments that occurred after Paul, contemporary Christians would do well to consider the question: Can those who have been adopted as children of Abraham legitimately appeal to their adopted father in order to disinherit Abraham's other children? Or, as Nils Dahl has put it: "In America it is sometimes said about the race issue: 'It is not the black man's problem, but the white man's.' In the same way, we could say of the relation of Christianity to Judaism: 'There is no Jewish problem, but there is a Christian problem.'"[20]

Notes

Chapter 1

1. Sandmel, *Philo's Place in Judaism*, 29.

2. Dahl, "The Story of Abraham in Luke-Acts," 140. In a similar vein, Moxnes writes, "In evaluating the Jewish picture of Abraham we should always bear in mind the needs which arose from the practical situation. A reconstruction of the history of Abraham was always brought to bear upon the contemporary situation of a community, be it Jewish or Christian" (*Theology in Conflict*, 129). In the same manner, Georgi states, "The life of Abraham was understood . . . as exemplary for one's own situation" (*The Opponents of Paul in Second Corinthians*, 50).

3. Paul's letters provide the earliest Christian writings we have. The Gospels may well preserve earlier authentic sayings of Jesus regarding Abraham, but such sayings have in any case been filtered by the concerns of the Gospel writers. As a result, my interest in the Gospels has more to do with the redactional activity of their authors.

4. Harnack, *Judentum und Judenchristentum in Justins Dialog mit Trypho*.

5. Harnack, *Judentum und Judenchristentum in Justins Dialog mit Trypho*, 92.

6. Harnack argued for a radical disjuncture between the writings of the New Testament and those of Justin, associating Justin with his successors, not with his predecessors. According to Harnack, Justin shows that active discussion and debate between Christians and Jews had ended. Against this thesis, Donahue argues that the *Dialogue* shows the continuation of heated discussion and debate between Christianity and Judaism: "Justin is a figure in a transitional

period, but he belongs far more to the age which is fading away than
to that which is dawning" ("Jewish-Christian Controversy in the
Second Century," 103–04. See also Osborn, *Justin Martyr;* and Stanton, "Aspects of Early Christian-Jewish Polemic and Apologetic,"
377–392).

7. The three volumes of the McMaster symposium on Jewish and
Christian self-definition in the Greco-Roman period intend to address such issues: "We are hopeful that we can probe behind the
usual account of how orthodoxy was achieved (the evolution of the
canon, creed, and hierarchy) to the question of why Christianity
and Judaism developed the way they did" (*Jewish and Christian
Self-Definition*, vol. 1: *The Shaping of Christianity in the Second and
Third Centuries*, ed. E. P. Sanders, 1:x. See also vol. 2: *Aspects of
Judaism in the Greco-Roman Period*, ed. E. P. Sanders, Baumgarten,
and Mendelson; and vol. 3: *Self-Definition in the Greco-Roman
World*, ed. Meyer and E. P. Sanders). Although these volumes mark
an important contribution to the discussion, the conflict between
emerging Christianity and Judaism receives surprisingly little attention. As Halperin notes in his review of these volumes, "Curiously the church's self-definition over against Judaism plays a very
small role" in the volume designed to address just this issue (vol. 1)
(*RSR* 11 [1985]: 134). Indeed, not a single article looks at the significance of Justin's *Dialogue* in early Christian controversy with
Judaism. A similar effort to probe early Christian polemic against
Judaism found expression in the Canadian Society of Biblical Studies seminar on "Anti-Judaism in the Early Church." Two volumes
have been published from this important seminar: *Anti-Judaism in
Early Christianity*, vol. 1: *Paul and the Gospels*, ed. Richardson and
Granskou; and vol. 2: *Separation and Polemic*, ed. S. G. Wilson.
Finally, see Neusner and Frerichs, *"To See Ourselves as Others See
Us": Christians, Jews, "Others" in Late Antiquity*, which presents
papers from a 1984 seminar at Brown University.

8. Soon after the time of Justin, see, e.g., Melito of Sardis's pas-
chal homily in Hall, *Melito of Sardis on Pascha and Fragments*, 2–61;
and Tertullian's "Against the Jews," *ANF*, 3:151–173.

9. I think that attention only to canonical writings is method-
ologically anachronistic. I am more sympathetic to seeing the first
half of the second century as part of "New Testament times." See,
e.g., Koester, *Introduction to the New Testament*, 2:xxi–xxii. Indeed,
the early second century has too often been neglected as a no-
man's-land. As Ferguson states, "This situation may in large part be
due to the second century's being on the border of so many disci-
plines: too late for most biblical scholars, too early for most patris-
tics experts; too late for students of second-temple Judaism, too

early for specialists in rabbinics; too late for most classicists, much too early for medievalists and Byzantinists" ("A New Journal," 4).

10. Although early Jewish use of Abraham has received rather thorough attention, the situation is less satisfactory for early Christian use of Abraham. The most complete general study is that of Wieser, *Abrahamvorstellungen*. See further Démann, "La signification d'Abraham dans la perspective du Nouveau Testament," 44–67; Martin-Achard, "Abraham dans le Nouveau Testament," in *Actualité d'Abraham*, 137–160; Dahl, "The Story of Abraham in Luke-Acts"; Schein, "Our Father Abraham," 93–288; and Baird, "Abraham in the New Testament," 367–379.

The situation is different for Paul's use of Abraham, on which topic many studies have appeared, e.g., Dietzfelbinger, "Paulus und das Alte Testament," 6–41; Käsemann, "The Faith of Abraham in Romans 4," 79–101; Berger, "Abraham in den paulinischen Hauptbriefen," 47–89; Lambrecht, "'Abraham, notre père à tous': La figure d'Abraham dans les écrits Pauliniens," in Bogaert, *Abraham dans la Bible et dans la tradition juive*, 118–163; Moxnes, *Theology in Conflict*, 103–282; Gaston, "Abraham and the Righteousness of God," 39–71; and the most recent study by Hansen, *Abraham in Galatians*.

11. For early Christian use of Abraham after Justin, see Klauser, "Abraham," 1:18–27; Völker, "Das Abraham-Bild bei Philo, Origenes, und Ambrosius," 199–207; Schmitz, "Abraham im Spätjudentum und im Urchristentum," 99–123; Daniélou, "Abraham dans la tradition chrétienne," 68–87; Lanne, "La Xeniteia d'Abraham dans l'oeuvre d'Irénée"; Bacq, *De l'ancienne à la nouvelle alliance*; and Wilken, "The Christianizing of Abraham," 723–731. For the use of Abraham in Christian disputes of a much later time, see Steinmetz, "Abraham and the Reformation," 32–46.

12. In the course of this study I will, of course, draw upon the fruits of prior scholarly research on Abraham in early Judaism and in early Christianity. I do not here, however, offer a survey of the secondary literature. Those interested in such a critical survey may consult my dissertation, "Disinheriting the Jews: The Use of Abraham in Early Christian Controversy with Judaism from Paul Through Justin Martyr" (Ph.D. diss., Princeton Theological Seminary, 1989), 32–42. See also Schein's survey in his dissertation, "Our Father Abraham," 1–15.

13. Wieser (*Abrahamvorstellungen*, 92–93) sees it more as a reference to Sarah than to Abraham; also Goppelt, *Der erste Petrusbrief*, 218–220.

14. In speaking of traditions from "early Judaism," I am referring to Jewish writings that can be dated roughly between 200 B.C.E. and 200 C.E.

15. To have an awareness of these traditions does not necessarily mean that we can more readily understand the specific use of Abraham in early Christianity. See the warning sounded by Neusner, "The Absoluteness of Christianity and the Uniqueness of Judaism," 18–31.

16. For an extensive presentation of haggadic Jewish traditions about Abraham, see Beers, *Leben Abrahams*; Billerbeck, "Abrahams Leben und Bedeutung nach Auffassung der älteren Haggada," *Nathanael* 15 (1899): 43–57, 118–128, 137–157, 161–179; 16 (1900): 33–57, 65–80; Ginzberg, *Legends of the Jews*, esp. 1:183–308 and 5:207–269, which relies heavily on Beer; de Menasce, "Traditions juives sur Abraham," 96–103; Martin-Achard, "Les traditions juives sur Abraham," in *Actualité d'Abraham*, 112–137; and the "retrogressive" and "progressive" historical study by Vermès, *Scripture and Tradition in Judaism*, 67–126. For critical assessments of early Jewish traditions about Abraham from about 200 B.C.E. to 200 C.E., see especially Sandmel, *Philo's Place in Judaism*; Moxnes, "God and His Promise to Abraham: First Century Appropriations," in *Theology in Conflict*, 117–169; Wieser, "Aspekte jüdischer Abrahamtraditionen," in *Abrahamvorstellungen*, 153–179; Mayer, "Aspekte des Abrahambildes in der hellenistisch-jüdischen Literatur," 118–127; Bogaert, *Abraham dans la Bible et dans la tradition juive*; Schein, "Our Father Abraham," 1–92; and Hansen, "Appendix 2: Abraham in Jewish Literature," in *Abraham in Galatians*, 175–199. Finally, on a related topic, see Siker, "Abraham in Graeco-Roman Paganism," 188–208.

17. Thus, for example, the wealth of materials about Abraham collected by Billerbeck in his extended article "Abrahams Leben und Bedeutung nach Auffassung der älteren Haggada" for the most part includes later rabbinical reflections on Abraham and so is not directly pertinent here. This study formed the basis for the materials on Abraham that Billerbeck later presented in his *Kommentar zum Neuen Testament aus Talmud und Midrasch*, e.g., on Romans 4; see 3:186–217.

18. These surveys cover the use of Abraham in the Apocrypha and the Pseudepigrapha (e.g., Judith; Jubilees; Testaments of the Twelve Patriarchs; Testament of Abraham; Apocalypse of Abraham; 1, 2, 3, and 4 Maccabees); in the Qumran writings (Damascus Rule [CD]; Genesis Apocryphon [1QapGen]); in Philo (*De Migratione Abrahami; De Abrahamo*); in Josephus and other Hellenistic Jewish authors (e.g., Pseudo-Eupolemus; Artapanus; Demetrius); and in rabbinic literature (e.g., the targums; Genesis Rabba; Mekilta). See especially Sandmel, *Philo's Place in Judaism*, 30–95; Hansen, "Appendix 2: Abraham in Jewish Literature," in *Abraham in Galatians*, 175–199; and Martin-Achard, *Actualité d'Abraham*, 111–137.

19. Of course, different scholars have come up with different organizing themes. See especially Wieser, *Abrahamvorstellungen*, 153–179; Schein, "Our Father Abraham," 19–92; Mayer, "Aspekte des Abrahambildes," 118–127; Sandmel, *Philo's Place in Judaism*, 77–95; and Moxnes, *Theology in Conflict*, 130–164. Schein, for example, identifies five major roles assigned to Abraham: (1) the Philosopher-Sage, (2) the Missionary, (3) the High Priest, (4) the Prophet-Seer, and (5) the Righteous Man. In a related study, I found that Greco-Roman pagan authors discussed Abraham in three contexts: (1) Abraham as a wise and righteous individual, (2) Abraham as a political ruler, and (3) Abraham as one skilled in astrology and philosophy. See Siker, "Abraham in Graeco-Roman Paganism," 193–197.

20. As Schein states, in this approach "the unity in the picture of the Patriarch is lost" ("Our Father Abraham," 21).

21. Many references to Abraham are made in passing, and often an author will pick up on one or two aspects of the Abraham tradition but completely ignore others. As Schein concedes, "In fact, outside of the connected accounts of Abraham in Josephus, Philo, *Jubilees*, and the *Genesis Apocryphon*, most of the references point to only one aspect of the Patriarch or summarize his life, accenting one particular characteristic" ("Our Father Abraham," 23).

22. Cf., e.g., Gen. 28:13–15; 35:9–15; Ex. 3:7–8; 32:13; Lev. 26:42–45; Num. 32:11–12; Deut. 1:8; 4:30–31; 9:25–29; 34:4; 1 Chron. 16:15–17; 2 Chron. 20:6; 2 Kings 13:22–25; Ps. 47:10; 105:6–11; Isa. 41:8; 51:1–2; 55:3; 61:8; Jer. 32:40; Ezek. 16:60; 20:5–6; 33:24; Neh. 9:7–8.

23. Similarly, Moxnes, *Theology in Conflict*, 125; and W. D. Davies, *The Gospel and the Land*, who notes in regard to early Jewish writings that "the covenant with Abraham was at the foundation—assumed and unexpressed—of the people of Israel. Like the foundation of a building it was often hidden from view and not actively discussed" (p. 108). For a general survey on the promises to Abraham in early Jewish use, see Moxnes, *Theology in Conflict*, 117–129; and W. D. Davies, *The Gospel and the Land*, 168–179.

24. Ezekiel the Tragedian, Exagoge 104–107 (*OTP*, 2:813). (The translation is from the *OTP* edition.)

25. 1QM 13:7–8 (*DSS*, 118); similarly, the Odes of Solomon can refer rather loosely to "the promises to the patriarchs," Ode 31:13 (*OTP*, 2:763).

26. 4 Ezra 3:14 (*OTP*, 1:528).

27. D. J. Harrington, "Pseudo-Philo," *OTP*, 2:300.

28. Ps.-Philo 18:5 (*OTP*, 2:325). On Pseudo-Philo's portrait of Abraham in general, see Bogaert, "La figure d'Abraham dans les

Antiquités Bibliques du Pseudo-Philon," *Abraham dans la Bible et dans la tradition juive*, 40–61.

29. E. P. Sanders, "Testament of Abraham," *OTP*, 1:876.

30. Test. Abr. 4:11 (*OTP*, 1:884).

31. 1QapGen 21:13 (*DSS*, 256).

32. See further, e.g., Test. Abr. 8:6–7; 4 Macc. 17:6; 18:1; Sir. 44:21; Ps.-Philo 32:1; Philo, *Leg. All.* 3.39–41; 4 Ezra 3:15–17; Pss. Sol. 18:3; Jub. 12:22.

33. Jub. 14:18.

34. 1QapGen 21:8–14 (*DSS*, 256).

35. Philo, *Heres* 314. For discussion of Philo's allegorical treatment of the promises in general, see Moxnes, *Theology in Conflict*, 130–164; and Sandmel, *Philo's Place in Judaism*. Moxnes concludes that Philo, unlike the Rabbis and the Targums, "did not stress that Abraham was the ancestor of the Jews, the first to receive circumcision and a covenant" (p. 163).

36. See further, e.g., Sir. 44:21; 46:8; Ass. Mos. 1:8–9; 2:1; 2 Bar. 3:4–5; 9:2; Jub. 12:22; 13:3; 22:27; 4 Ezra 9:7–9; 13:48; Ps.-Philo 7:4; 9:3; 25:5; 1QS 8:4b–7. On the land in early Judaism in general, see W. D. Davies, *The Gospel and the Land*, 49–158. References to the land in early Jewish writings are relatively limited, although, as Davies points out, "the awareness of the land—its holiness, its possible pollution by sin, and consequent need for purification—is unmistakably clear" (Davies, *The Gospel and the Land*, 49).

37. So noted by Barrett (*From First Adam to Last Adam*), who refers to the observation by Bonsirven (*Le judaïsme palestinien*, 1:76): "It seems that the universalist promise, 'In thee shall all the families of the earth be blessed' was scarcely ever taken up [in early Judaism]. The commentaries do not develop it, or else it undergoes this significant transformation—all the blessings that God bestows upon the earth, the rain, and even creation itself, were given for Abraham's sake." Similarly, W. D. Davies comments, "Sometimes the Abrahamic blessing upon all nations was generalized to refer simply to monotheism or providence, sometimes weakened so that Abraham would serve simply as the standard of blessing or, again, sometimes confined only to proselytes. The exigencies of Jewish history—not surprisingly—had pressed upon the Abrahamic promise a 'national,' territorial stamp which often tended to obliterate its universal range" (*The Gospel and the Land*, 177).

38. Sir. 44:21; see also Test. Ben. 10:5–6 (*OTP*, 1:828), which records that Abraham gave God's commandments as an inheritance, saying, "'Keep God's commandments until the Lord reveals his salvation to all the nations.'"

39. Since he came from the Chaldeans, Abraham was occasionally considered a proselyte himself; so, e.g., Philo, *Virt.* 212–217; Jose-

phus, *Ant.* 1.7; 2.159–160. See Georgi, *The Opponents of Paul in Second Corinthians*, 49–60; Knox, "Abraham and the Quest for God," 55–60; and Kaylor, *Paul's Covenant Community*, 83–90.

40. Pss. Sol. 9:9 (my translation). A similar sentiment is found in 2 Baruch, an early-second-century C.E. Palestinian Jewish writing, which states, "We shall always be blessed; at least, we did not mingle with the nations" (2 Bar. 48:23 [*OTP*, 1:636]). See also Pss. Sol. 18:3.

41. Thus there will not be a separate section in each chapter on the promises to Abraham.

42. At times, however, God's promises were seen as a reponse to Abraham's faith, as Gen. 22:15–19 appears to indicate.

43. 1 Macc. 2:52 goes on to say, "and it was reckoned to him as righteousness."

44. See, e.g., Jub. 17:15–16; 4 Macc. 6:17–22; 9:22–23; 14:20; 16:15–23; Apoc. Abr. 1:8.

45. Apoc. Abr. 4:6 (*OTP*, 1:690).

46. Jub. 21:3.

47. Josephus, *Ant.* 1.155. See also Philo, *De Opificio Mundi*, 170.

48. Test. Abr. 1:1 (Recension A; *OTP*, 1:882).

49. Philo, *Abr.* 167; Philo also refers to Abraham's "good and wise behaviour shown in his dealings with men" (*Abr.* 208–211). See also Philo, *Mut.* 39–41. For further material on Abraham's hospitality, see Sandmel, *Philo's Place in Judaism*, 118–120; and Schein, "Our Father Abraham," 72–75. For further information on Philo's understanding of Abraham's faithfulness in general, see Sandmel, *Philo's Place in Judaism*, 138–140, 170–171.

50. 2 Bar. 57:1–2 (*OTP*, 1:641). See also Jub. 16:20–23, which states that Abraham "first observed the feast of the booths on the earth" (*OTP*, 1:89).

51. CD 3:1–3 (*DSS*, 84). Philo also saw Abraham as in some ways keeping the law, although Philo saw it more in terms of natural law. See Sandmel, *Philo's Place in Judaism*, 141.

52. Josephus, *Ant.* 1.225.

53. See further, e.g., 4 Macc. 15:28–29; 16:20; Jub. 17:16–18; 18:1–16; Ps.-Philo 18:5; 32:2–4.

54. Philo, *Abr.* 177.

55. Jub. 14:1 (*OTP*, 2:84).

56. 1QapGen 19:14. See also Ps.-Philo 23:6.

57. 4 Ezra 3:14 (*OTP*, 1:528); similarly, Ps.-Philo 18:5 (*OTP*, 2:325), where God says, "I will reveal everything I am doing to Abraham," probably an allusion to Gen. 18:17. Philo refers to Abraham's visions of God throughout his writings *De Abrahamo* and *De Migratione Abrahami*.

58. In reference to Gen. 22:17, Ps.-Philo 18:5 (*OTP*, 2:325) has

God ask Balaam, "Is it not regarding this people that I spoke to Abraham in a vision, saying, 'Your seed will be like the stars of the heaven,' when I lifted him above the firmament and showed him the arrangements of all the stars?"

59. From Eusebius, *Preparatio Evangelica* 9.17.3 (*OTP*, 2:880).

60. Josephus, *Ant.* 1.166–168. Abraham was well known for his astrological skills in Greco-Roman paganism. See Siker, "Abraham in Graeco-Roman Paganism," 193–197.

61. *Jub.* 12:16 (*OTP*, 2:81).

62. Philo, *Abr.* 70. According to Philo, God goes on to tell Abraham, "Dismiss, then, the rangers of the heavens and the science of Chaldea, and depart for a short time from the greatest of cities, this world, to the lesser, and thus you will be better able to apprehend the overseer of the All" (*Abr.* 71).

63. *Apoc. Zeph.* 11:1–4 (*OTP*, 1:515).

64. *Test. Lev.* 15:4 (*OTP*, 1:793); see also *Test. Asher* 7:7 (*OTP*, 1:818), where Asher encourages his sons by assuring them that God "will gather you in faith through his compassion and on account of Abraham, Isaac, and Jacob."

65. *Test. Abr.* 14:10–11 (*OTP*, 1:891). See also *4 Bar.* 6:21 (*OTP*, 2:419–420), a late-first-century C.E. Palestinian Jewish writing, in which the author states that "the Lord has taken pity on our tears and has remembered the covenant that he established with our fathers Abraham, Isaac, and Jacob."

66. *Pr. Jac.* 1, 5 (*OTP*, 2:720); see also the Prayer of Manasseh 1:1 (*OTP*, 2:635), which begins by calling upon the Lord, "God of our fathers, God of Abraham, and of Isaac, and of Jacob." The name of Abraham figured in magical invocations and incantations as well. See Siker, "Abraham in Graeco-Roman Paganism," 201–206.

67. Ps.-Philo 61:5 (*OTP*, 2:374).

68. Josephus, *Ant.* 1.183–185; *Jub.* 14:10–11, 19 (*OTP*, 2:85).

69. *Test. Lev.* 9:12–13 (*OTP*, 1:792).

70. It could also be argued that when Abraham blesses people, he exercises a priestly function, e.g., *Test. Jud.* 17:5 (*OTP*, 1:800), where Judah states, "Abraham, my father's father, blessed me as destined to be the king of Israel; and Jacob blessed me similarly. And so I know that through me the kingdom will be established." See also *Test. Lev.* 18:6 (*OTP*, 1:795). However, the giving of blessings could also simply be a function of Abraham's role as father.

71. *4 Macc.* 13:17 (*OTP*, 2:558).

72. Cf. *Test. Lev.* 18:14 (*OTP*, 1:795), which remarks that Abraham will rejoice at the saints in the kingdom. For Abraham in the resurrected life, see also *Test. Jud.* 25:1 (*OTP*, 1:801); *Test. Ben.* 10:6 (*OTP*, 1:828); and *Test. Abr.* 10:1, which shows the archangel

Michael taking Abraham in a chariot of cherubim into the heavens, from where he can view the activities on earth.

73. 2 Bar. 57:2 (*OTP*, 1:641).

74. *OTP*, 1:74 n. 93j.

75. Test. Abr. 10:12–13 (*OTP*, 1:887).

76. For a general summary of this study, see Siker, "From Gentile Inclusion to Jewish Exclusion," 30–36.

Chapter 2

1. Significant allusions to Abraham also occur at Rom. 9:5; 11:28; and 15:8.

2. See, however, the suggestive article by Richardson, "On the Absence of 'Anti-Judaism' in I Corinthians," 1:59–74. See also Phil. 1:28 and 3:2, which indicate the presence of rival teachers at Philippi who are advocating circumcision. But these rival teachers (Phil. 1:28) do not appear to have any hold over the Christian community there. Indeed, they seem to be as much opponents of the Philippians as they might be of Paul.

3. Indeed, in his letters Paul refers to Abraham more than to any other person aside from Jesus. Paul mentions Moses nine times.

4. Sampley has rightly warned against interpreting Galatians and Romans in tandem. See Sampley, "Romans and Galatians," 315–339. See also idem, "From Text to Thought World: The Route to Paul's Ways."

5. See Stendahl's classic article, "Paul and the Introspective Conscience of the West," 199–215.

6. See in particular on this point the first chapter ("Paul, the Reformation and Modern Scholarship") in Watson, *Paul, Judaism and the Gentiles*, 1–22.

7. The tensions between Galatians 3 and Romans 4 will receive more attention below. For now, a brief list suffices: Galatians 3 portrays Christ as Abraham's singular *sperma* ("offspring"); Romans 4 portrays all who believe like Abraham as *sperma* ("offsprings"). In Galatians 3, the content of the promise is Christ; in Romans 4, the content of the promise is Gentile inclusion. In Galatians 3, Paul stresses discontinuity between God's promise and the law; in Romans 4, Paul stresses continuity between God's promise and the law. In Galatians 3, the object of faith is Christ; in Romans 4, the object of faith is God. In general, Galatians 3 offers a christocentric rendering of Abraham; Romans 4 offers a theocentric rendering of Abraham. See especially Beker, *Paul the Apostle*, 94–104; Boers, *Theology out of the Ghetto*, 74–106; Sampley, "Romans and Galatians"; and Hays, *The Faith of Jesus Christ*, 193–213.

8. On Gal. 3:6–14, for example, Betz notes, "There is agreement

among the exegetes that Paul's argument in this section is extremely difficult to follow" (*Galatians*, 137).

9. Picking up on the lead of Martyn ("A Law-Observant Mission to Gentiles," 307–324), throughout this discussion I will refer to Paul's opponents as "the Teachers," a term Martyn uses to leave open the possibility that "they have their own mission, independent of Paul" and to avoid the prejudice "that these people derive their identity from their opposition to Paul, and, therefore, that their work is a reaction to his" (p. 312).

10. See especially Barclay, "Mirror-Reading a Polemical Letter," 73–93. See also Hansen, "The Opponents' Use of the Abraham Tradition," Appendix 1 in *Abraham in Galatians*, 167–174.

11. See the various pitfalls that Barclay identifies ("Mirror-Reading a Polemical Letter," 79–82).

12. Indeed, Lyons has concluded that successfully mirror-reading a polemical letter such as Galatians is not possible (*Pauline Autobiography: Toward a New Understanding*, 96). See further the caveats of Mussner, *Galaterbrief*, 27–28.

13. As Barclay ("Mirror-Reading a Polemical Letter," 78) puts it: "There are many aspects of the opponents' message that we can know nothing about because Paul chose not to reply to them. There may also have been many points on which Paul and his opponents agreed but which are submerged by the polarizing effect of his polemic."

14. Galatians 1:9, at least, does indicate that Paul's problems with the Galatians are long-standing: "*As we have said before, so now I say again*, If any one is preaching to you a gospel contrary to that which you received, let him be accursed" (emphasis mine). Similarly, 4:19 shows that Paul's struggles with the Galatians are not new: "My little children, with whom I am *again* (*palin*) in travail until Christ be formed in you!" (emphasis mine)

15. See Barclay's constructive methodological proposals for negotiating the problems of reconstructing a composite picture of the Teachers ("Mirror-Reading a Polemical Letter").

16. So, e.g., Betz, *Galatians*, 7; Martyn, "A Law-Observant Mission to Gentiles," 317–320; Barclay, "Mirror-Reading a Polemical Letter," 86–88; Howard, *Crisis*, 9; and most commentators. The literature on those whom Paul viewed as opponents in Galatia is extensive. See especially Betz, *Galatians*, 5–9; Howard, *Crisis*, 1–19; Martyn, "A Law-Observant Mission to Gentiles"; and Barclay, "Mirror-Reading a Polemical Letter."

17. Indeed, Paul's reference to James, Cephas, and John as *tois dokousin* (Gal. 2:2, 6, 9; "those of repute," or, with Betz [*Galatians*, 86, 92], "men of reputation," "men of eminence") is probably intentionally ambiguous. But perhaps reference to *tois dokousin* also

implies here "those who *seemed*" to be reputable pillars, suggesting that while they appeared at the time to be good for their word, from Paul's present perspective their actions have shown this reputation to be but a thin veneer covering their hypocrisy (cf. the critique of Cephas in Gal. 2:11–14; similarly, Schlier, *Der Brief an die Galater*, 75–76). See also 2 Cor. 10:9 for *dokeō* meaning "to seem," as well as Gal. 6:3. See further Betz, *Galatians*, 86–101; Foerster, "Die *dokountes* in Gal. 2," 286–292; and Barrett, "Paul and the 'Pillar' Apostles," 1–17.

18. On his sliding scale of probability, Barclay assigns such a critique of Paul by the Teachers to the category "certain or virtually certain" ("Mirror-Reading a Polemical Letter," 88).

19. There is some debate regarding exactly which passage from Genesis is the one that Paul has in mind here. Genesis 13:15; 17:8; and 24:7 all refer to the land that God will give "to your offspring," but none of them makes explicit mention of a "blessing." On Gal. 3:15, see Daube ("The Interpretation of a Generic Singular," in *The New Testament and Rabbinic Judaism*, 438–444), who suggests that Gen. 15:18 may also be of relevance, as it too reads "to your offspring."

20. As we will see (pp. 50–52 below), in 2 Cor. 11:22 Paul is embattled with opponents in Corinth who are in all likelihood rival Jewish-Christian missionaries. In many respects they are different from the Teachers in Galatia. But in at least one respect they may provide a significant parallel. Paul's Jewish-Christian opponents in 2 Cor. 11:22 have been boasting of their status as "descendants of Abraham" (*sperma Abraam*). While the Teachers in Galatia may not have been boasting of such status, they may well have told Gentile Christians there that the only way they could truly be enrolled as "descendants of Abraham" was by means of circumcision.

21. Indeed, Moxnes has characterized Paul's response as a "protest" against the position of the Teachers (*Theology in Conflict*, 207–216).

22. See, e.g., Sir. 44:20–21; 2 Bar. 57:2; and 1 Macc. 2:52, all of which link Abraham's fulfilling of the law with God's giving of the promises.

23. See Martyn's reconstruction of an imaginary sermon preached by the law-observant Jewish-Christian evangelists to the Galatians ("A Law-Observant Mission to Gentiles," 221–223).

24. For a book-length analysis of Abraham in Galatians, with a comprehensive discussion of the scholarly debate, see especially Hansen, *Abraham in Galatians*.

25. By comparison, Betz (*Galatians*, 19–20) divides Galatians 3 into 3:1–5; 3:6–14; 3:15–18; 3:19–25; and 3:26–4:11. Mussner (*Galaterbrief*, 205–277) divides it into three larger sections: 3:1–5;

3:6–18; and 3:19–4:7. On the structure of Galatians, see especially Hansen, *Abraham in Galatians*, 22–93.

26. There is some debate as to whether Gal. 3:6 concludes 3:1–5 or introduces 3:7–14. The logic of seeing 3:6 as the conclusion to 3:1–5 would stress that the term "faith" connects the verses. The logic of seeing 3:6 as the beginning of a new section would stress that the reference to Abraham introduces a further development. The options are not, however, mutually exclusive.

27. Exactly what these "miracles" (*dynameis*) were is not immediately clear. From what Paul says, however, it appears that the Galatians did have some powerful experiences; perhaps they included exorcisms, charismatic outpourings, and/or physical healings. Elsewhere Paul refers to performing "signs and wonders and mighty works" (2 Cor. 12:12), and he speaks of Christ working through him "by the power of signs and wonders" (Rom. 15:19). In contrast to the miracles the Galatians experienced, Paul appears to have experienced some physical ailment while he was with the Galatians (Gal. 4:13–14).

28. So Mussner (*Galaterbrief*, 213–214), who argues that *kathōs* is best understood here as meaning "because."

29. The force of the particle *ara* ("so") indicates that Paul simply sees himself as making explicit what is already implicit in the text.

30. The "in you" comes from Gen. 12:3, while "all the nations" comes from Gen. 18:18. For Paul, it is important that his citation refer to *ta ethnē*, as a clear reference to the Gentiles. See Mussner, *Galaterbrief*, 220.

31. As Barrett points out, Paul "takes this promise as one of the decisive factors in interpreting the story of Abraham" (*From First Adam to Last Adam*, 34).

32. As we noted above (pp. 20–21), the promise to Abraham regarding the blessing of the Gentiles received relatively little attention in early Judiasm. In this respect, Paul makes a significant departure from many of his Jewish contemporaries.

33. Paul can thus be contrasted with some of his Jewish contemporaries, who saw Abraham as keeping the law. See pp. 22–24 above.

34. The pronouncement of the curse here appears to be closely related to Paul's curse on the Teachers in Gal. 1:9. On "the curse of the law," see especially Donaldson, "The 'Curse of the Law' and the Inclusion of the Gentiles: Galatians 3.13–14," 94–112.

35. See Dunn, "Works of the Law and the Curse of the Law (Galatians 3:10–14)," 523–542.

36. If the blessing of Abraham is to be equated with justification by faith, as Gal. 3:8 seems to indicate, then 2:15–16 would show that Jews are justified in the same manner, by faith apart from works

of the law. Indeed, the justification of the Jews by faith apart from works of the law seems clear from 2:16 and 3:11. This observation raises another question, however. Is the blessing of Abraham the same for the Jews as it is for the Gentiles? Paul does not address this question directly in Galatians but does consider it in Romans 9–11, as we shall see below.

37. Paul's equation of "promise" (*epaggelia*) and "covenant" (*diathēkē*) is clear from Gal. 3:17, where the phrase "does not annul a covenant" (*diathēkēn . . . ouk akyroi*) stands parallel to the phrase "so as to make the promise void" (*eis to katargēsai tēn epaggelian*). In referring to the covenant, Paul may well have Gen. 15:18 and/or 17:1–11 in mind, both of which refer explicitly to God's *diathēkē* ("covenant") with Abraham (so Mussner, *Galaterbrief*, 238). The likelihood of this association is strengthened when we see that already in Gal. 3:6 Paul has highlighted Gen. 15:6 and that in Gal. 3:16 he goes on to cite material from parallel passages in Gen. 13:15; 15:8; and 17:8, all of which refer to *tō spermati sou* ("and to your offspring/s").

38. See Betz, *Galatians*, 155–159; and Mussner, *Galaterbrief*, 237–240.

39. See the discussions in Daube, "The Interpretation of a Generic Singular," in *The New Testament and Rabbinic Judaism*, 438–444; Betz, *Galatians*, 156–157; and Berger, "Abraham in den paulinischen Hauptbriefen." For a discussion of the broader context of the term, see Georgi, *The Opponents of Paul in Second Corinthians*, 49–60.

40. Paul seems to accept this traditional meaning also in Gal. 3:29, although he maintains the strong link between *sperma Abraam* and Christ. On the traditional interpretation of *to sperma* as a generic singular, see Quell and Schulz, "*sperma*," *TDNT*, 7:536–547; and Daube, "The Interpretation of a Generic Singular," in *The New Testament and Rabbinic Judaism*, 438–444.

41. Gen. 17:7, 8, 9, and 10 all refer explicitly to Abraham and his "offspring" (LXX, *sperma*), in each case as a generic singular.

42. To use the language of E. P. Sanders, Paul argues against law observance as a means for Gentiles either to get in or to stay in covenant relation with God. See E. P. Sanders, *Paul and Palestinian Judaism*, 424, 544. See also Sanders's further clarification of "getting in and staying in" developed in *Paul, the Law, and the Jewish People*, 6–10, as well as the response by Dunn, "The New Perspective on Paul," 95–122; and Räisänen, "Galatians 2.16 and Paul's Break with Judaism," 543–553.

43. Betz, *Galatians*, 161–180.

44. A full consideration of Paul's view of the law lies beyond our scope here. See the surveys by Snodgrass, "Spheres of Influence,"

93–113; and Wedderburn, "Paul and the Law," 613–622. Among myriad other studies, see further Räisänen, *Paul and the Law*; E. P. Sanders, *Paul, the Law, and the Jewish People*; and Hübner, *Law in Paul's Thought*.

45. On the meaning of *paidagogos* ("custodian"), see Mussner, *Galaterbrief*, 256–260; and Lull, "'The Law Was Our Pedagogue': A Study in Galatians 3:19–25," 481–498.

46. So most commentators. See Betz, *Galatians*, 170; and Mussner, *Galaterbrief*, 248–249.

47. Against Callan ("Pauline Midrash: The Exegetical Background of Gal. 3:19b," 549–567), who concludes that "Paul's ultimate point in vs. 19b–20 is to set the law over against God, though not so much as to say that it was contrary to his overall plan" (p. 567). It would be better here to see Paul opposing the Teachers' misuse of the law than to conclude that Paul sets the law against God.

48. On the character of polemic, see especially the comments of L. T. Johnson, "The New Testament's Anti-Jewish Slander and the Conventions of Ancient Polemic," 419–441.

49. Paul refers elsewhere to believers as "sons of God" in Rom. 8:14, 19; and 9:26, where the term refers explicitly to Gentile Christians, as it does in Gal. 3:26.

50. On the baptismal imagery, see Betz, *Galatians*, 186–189; and Mussner, *Galaterbrief*, 262–263.

51. For the legal practice of guardianship in Roman law, see Betz, *Galatians*, 202–204.

52. On Gal. 4:21–31, see especially Hansen, *Abraham in Galatians*, 141–154; Betz, *Galatians*, 238–252; Mussner, *Galaterbrief*, 316–334; and Barrett, "The Allegory of Abraham, Sarah, and Hagar in the Argument of Galatians," 1–16.

53. See Martyn, "A Law-Observant Mission to Gentiles," 321–323; Barclay, "Mirror-Reading a Polemical Letter," 88–89; and Moxnes, *Theology in Conflict*, 211.

54. On the parallel imagery in Jewish apocalyptic literature, see Betz, *Galatians*, 246–248.

55. On this tradition, see Betz, *Galatians*, 249–250.

56. Whether the Galatians would have felt "persecuted" by the Teachers is, of course, another matter. Indeed, it appears that they readily and willingly accepted circumcision and law observance.

57. We find a similar instance in 1 Cor. 5:13, where Paul cites Deut. 17:7 ("Drive out the wicked person from among you," LXX) with the clear implication that the Corinthians are to drive out those who claim to be Christians and yet lead immoral lives (cf. 1 Cor. 5:1–2). There is a significant difference, however, between the situations in Corinth and Galatia. The issue in Corinth is immoral behav-

ior, whereas we find little indication in Galatians that Paul accuses the Teachers of leading immoral lives, unless Gal. 6:13 is to be taken as such an allusion.

58. See Barclay ("Mirror-Reading a Polemical Letter," 89–90), who also points to areas of significant agreement between Paul and the Teachers.

59. Similarly, Martyn, "A Law-Observant Mission to Gentiles," 316.

60. See the following interpreters, who see in Galatians Paul's indictment against Judaism: Betz, *Galatians*, 116, 142, 146; Hahn, "Das Gesetzesverständnis im Römer und Galaterbrief," 29–63, esp. 51–52; Hübner, "Identitätsverlust und paulinische Theologie," 181–193; Luz, *Das Geschichtsverständnis des Paulus*, 219; and Ridderbos, *Paul: An Outline of His Theology*, 130–143.

61. Several interpreters have recognized that in Galatians Paul makes no direct attack on Judaism: Mussner, *Galaterbrief*, 11–29; Richardson, *Israel in the Apostolic Church*, 91; and E. P. Sanders, *Paul, the Law, and the Jewish People*, 19–20. See also Sanders's article "Paul on the Law, His Opponents, and the Jewish People in Philippians 3 and 2 Corinthians 11," 1:75–90; and Martyn, who states regarding Galatians: "The letter, to say it yet again, is not an attack on Judaism; nor is it even an apologetic letter, in the sense of its being designed to convert its readers from one religion to another" ("Apocalyptic Antinomies in Paul's Letter to the Galatians," 420).

62. Thus, even if in Gal. 4:30 Paul is advocating that the Galatians cast out the Teachers, this does *not* provide evidence that Paul argues for the exclusion of non-Christian Jews from the Abrahamic promises, as Betz (*Galatians*, 250–251) maintains. Paul lodges his complaint in Galatians, not against non-Christian Judaism, but against self-defined Jewish *Christians*, who are all the more dangerous because they present themselves as Christians and their message as the gospel. They are thus in a worse position than non-Christian Jews, who make no confessional claims about Jesus as the Christ. For Paul, the Teachers fundamentally fail to understand the significance of Christ in reconciling Jews and Gentiles alike.

63. Against Klein, who argues that Paul's purpose in Galatians 3 is to rule out any Jewish appeals to Abraham as father, and the reappropriation of Abraham as the father of Christians exclusively. See Klein, "Individualgeschichte und Weltgeschichte bei Paulus," 148.

64. Martyn also warns against referring to the Teachers as "Judaizers" ("A Law-Observant Mission to Gentiles," 315).

65. See Gaston, "Paul and the Law in Galatians 2–3," 1:37–58; idem, "Paul and the Torah," 48–71; idem, "Abraham and the Righteousness of God," 39–71; idem, "Israel's Enemies in Pauline

Theology," 400–423; and Gager, *The Origins of Anti-Semitism*, 193–264. See also my review of Gager's book in *USQR* 41 (1986): 60–65.

66. See Dunn, "Works of the Law and the Curse of the Law (Galatians 3:10–14)," 539.

67. See Rom. 11:1, where Paul identifies himself in a similar way: "I myself am an Israelite, a descendant of Abraham (*ek spermatos Abraam*), a member of the tribe of Benjamin." Compare Phil. 3:5, where Paul says he is "of the people of Israel, of the tribe of Benjamin, a Hebrew born of Hebrews."

68. On Paul's opponents in 2 Corinthians, see especially Furnish, *II Corinthians*, 48–54; Barrett, "Paul's Opponents in II Corinthians," 233–254; Georgi, *The Opponents of Paul in Second Corinthians*; and Machalet, "Paulus und seine Gegner," 183–203.

69. Whether or not 2 Corinthians 10–13 in fact is the letter that Paul refers to in 2 Cor. 2:3–4 lies beyond my concerns here. It is sufficient to note the consensus that 2 Corinthians 10–13 represents a portion of a separate letter that Paul wrote to the Corinthians. See the discussion in Furnish, *II Corinthians*, 35–48.

70. So aptly termed by Furnish, *II Corinthians*, 47.

71. Georgi (*The Opponents of Paul in Second Corinthians*, 49–60, 364–377) and Furnish (*II Corinthians*, 53, 534) specify the identity of these opponents as *Hellenistic* Jewish Christians, because of the special role that Abraham played in Hellenistic Jewish apologetic literature.

72. On the purpose of Romans in general, see Donfried, *The Romans Debate*; and Wedderburn, *The Reasons for Romans*.

73. The diatribe style found throughout Romans probably in part reflects Paul's awareness of questions that others were asking about him. The diatribe style shows Paul's concern to object to false conclusions drawn from what he has said, or from what he fears has been reported about him, especially regarding his position on the law. See in general Stowers, *The Diatribe and Paul's Letter to the Romans*.

74. Since Romans 16 is probably an original part of the letter, and Paul knew many friends and associates in Rome, we can conclude that Paul had some knowledge of the situation of the church in Rome. On Romans 16, see Gamble, *The Textual History of the Letter to the Romans*. On Paul's awareness of the situation in Rome, see Moxnes, *Theology in Conflict*, 78–99; and Beker, *Paul the Apostle*, 73–74.

75. See, e.g., Sandmel's comments on Philo, *Philo's Place in Judaism*; Georgi's wide-ranging sketch of Abraham in Hellenistic Jewish missionary literature, *The Opponents of Paul in Second Corinthians*,

49–60; and Mayer, "Aspekte des Abrahambildes in der hellenis-tisch-jüdischen Literatur."

76. See, e.g., Cranfield, *Romans*, 1:232–233; and A. J. Guerra, "Romans 4 as Apologetic Theology," *HTR* 81 (1988), 251–270.

77. Similarly, Moxnes, *Theology in Conflict*, 108–16. Compare Wilckens, *Römer*, 1:258; and Cranfield, *Romans*, 1:224–225.

78. Käsemann, *Commentary on Romans*, 110. One indication of this construction is the simple observation that in the twenty-five verses of Romans 4, Paul uses over twenty-five conjunctions and connective particles.

79. Similarly, Beker, *Paul the Apostle*, 74–83; and Wilckens, *Römer*, 1:271–272.

80. See, e.g., Cranfield, *Romans*, 1:242–243; Wilckens, *Römer*, 1:271–272; and Barrett, *Romans*, 95–96.

81. On the impartiality of God as a leitmotif throughout Romans, see Bassler, *Divine Impartiality*, 154–170.

82. In translating Rom. 4:1, I am following the suggestion of Hays ("'Have We Found Abraham to Be Our Forefather According to the Flesh?' A Reconsideration of Rom 4:1," 76–98) that we should take Abraham "not as the subject but as the direct *object* of the infinitive *heurēkenai* ["to find"], whose subject would then be understood as the 'we' of the immediately preceding *eroumen* ["we say"]" (p. 81). In general, Hays identifies a pattern in which *ti oun eroumen* "intro-duces a rhetorical question which poses a false inference" (p. 79; cf. Rom. 3:5; 6:1; 7:7; 9:14, 30).

83. On 3:21–31, see Howard, "Romans 3:21–31 and the Inclu-sion of the Gentiles," 223–233; and L. T. Johnson, "Romans 3:21–26 and the Faith of Jesus," *CBQ* 44 (1982): 77–90.

84. See further Rhyne, *Faith Establishes the Law*, 75–93.

85. Paul's argument here resembles his temporal argument in Gal. 3:17. Just as the law came after the promise and hence did not annul God's promise to Abraham, so Abraham's circumcision came after his belief and hence did not change the basis for his being reckoned righteous before God.

86. On Paul's use of the term "seal," see Käsemann, *Commentary on Romans*, 114–117.

87. As Barrett comments on this passage, "Abraham's circumci-sion, rightly understood, confirms not the doctrine of justification by works of law, but that of justification by faith" (*Romans*, 92).

88. Ironically, this argument can work only for Abraham, since after Abraham all Jews were circumcised as infants. In the case of Abraham's physical descendants, then, circumcision must precede faith temporally, exactly the opposite of Abraham's situation. Still, Paul would argue that circumcision anticipates faith and does not cause faith.

89. Against Klein, Paul does not here advance a dual notion of circumcision, one that functions soteriologically for Paul and another that functions as a means of mere ethnic identity for the Jews. See Klein, "Römer 4 und die Idee der Heilsgeschichte," 432–433.

90. Even so, circumcision has some benefit, for it puts the Jew in a position to come to faith, since Jews have the oracles of God (Rom. 3:1–2), the scriptures, the promises, the law, and worship (Rom. 9:4–5). Whether or not these things constitute any real advantage of the Jew over the Gentile in coming to faith, Paul seems determined to maintain both the advantage of the Jew (Rom. 1:16; 3:1–2) and the Jew's equality to the Gentile in terms of sin (Rom. 3:9).

91. On Rom. 4:17 within the context of 4:13–25, see especially Moxnes, *Theology in Conflict*, 231–282.

92. The RSV translation of *patera pollōn ethnōn* as "father of many nations" in Rom. 4:17 and 18 conforms to the Old Testament citation of Gen. 17:5 (LXX) but glosses over Paul's consistent understanding of *ethnē* as "Gentiles," so correctly rendered by the RSV in most other occurrences of the term in Romans (1:13; 2:14, 24; 3:29; 9:24, 30; 11:11, 12, 13, 25; 15:9, 10, 11, 12, 16, 18, 27; 16:4). The RSV translates *ethnē* as "nations" in Rom. 1:5; 4:17–18; 10:19; and 16:26. A quick glance at a concordance shows Paul's overwhelming concern with the status of Gentiles before God in Romans and Galatians, as thirty-nine of the forty-five occurrences of *ethnē* in Paul's letters appear in Romans (29x) and Galatians (10x). The term occurs three times in 1 Corinthians, once in 2 Corinthians, and twice in 1 Thessalonians.

93. It seems to me inappropriate to speak of Abraham as believing in Christ, as if Abraham's faith was patterned after Christian faith. Paul's whole point is that Christian faith is a type of Abrahamic faith, indeed the fulfillment of Abraham's faith. For a contrary view, see Cosgrove, "Justification in Paul," 666; and Käsemann, "The Faith of Abraham in Romans 4," 79. See also Beker (*Paul the Apostle*, 103), who says that Paul "Christianizes" Abraham; and the critique by Sampley, "Romans and Galatians: Comparison and Contrast," 338 n. 24.

94. Similarly, Boers, *Theology out of the Ghetto*, 83; and Goppelt, "Paul and Heilsgeschichte," 315–326.

95. Similarly, E. P. Sanders, *Paul, the Law, and the Jewish People*, 207.

96. See, e.g., the survey in Beker, *Paul the Apostle*, 63–64; and Dahl, "The Future of Israel," 137–159, esp. 138–142.

97. See especially the various essays in "The Church and Israel: Romans 9–11," *Princeton Seminary Bulletin*, Supplementary Issue

No. 1 (1990), ed. D. Migliore. See further Campbell, "The Romans Debate," 19–28; and Kaylor, *Paul's Covenant Community*, 159–193.

98. On the overall structure of Romans 9–11, see especially Aageson, "Scripture and Structure in the Development of the Argument in Romans 9–11," 265–289; Campbell, "The Place of Romans IX–XI Within the Structure and Thought of the Letter," 7:121–131; and D. G. Johnson, "The Structure and Meaning of Romans 11," 91–103.

99. See further Epp, "Jewish-Gentile Continuity in Paul: Torah and/or Faith? (Romans 9:1–5)," 80–90.

100. W. D. Davies ("Paul and the People of Israel," 123–152, 142) and Aageson ("Scripture and Structure in Romans 9–11," 284) maintain that Paul considers what he has to say in Rom. 11:25–32 as particularly important. As Davies points out, Paul's words in 11:25, "I do not want you to be ignorant, brethren," frequently introduce something of importance (cf. Rom. 1:13; 1 Cor. 10:1; 12:1; 2 Cor. 1:8; 1 Thess. 4:13).

101. See further Aageson, "Scripture and Structure in Romans 9–11," 288.

102. Similarly, e.g., Aageson, "Scripture and Structure in Romans 9–11," 283; Wilckens, *Römer*, 2:244; Cranfield, *Romans*, 2:559; and Beker, *Paul the Apostle*, 75.

103. We will see a similar distinction in John 8:31–59 (see pp. 136–139 below).

104. With the use of the verb "to reckon" (*logizomai*), of course, Paul calls to mind Gen. 15:6, which had such an important place in Romans 4.

105. See Phil. 3:5 and 2 Cor. 11:22, where Paul makes similar statements.

106. It does appear, however, that Paul views the salvation of "all Israel" as an eschatological event, as Rom. 11:26 seems to indicate. By citing Isa. 59:20 in Rom. 11:26, Paul implies that all Israel will be saved when "the Deliverer" comes to banish ungodliness from Jacob. So, e.g., Käsemann, *Commentary on Romans*, 312–315; and W. D. Davies, "Paul and the People of Israel," 139–143.

107. Similarly, Dahl, who states that "Paul does not affirm that every individual Israelite will attain salvation, but that God will grant salvation to both parts of his people, to those who have rejected Christ as well as to those who have believed in him" ("The Future of Israel," 153).

108. So D. G. Johnson, "The Structure and Meaning of Romans 11," 101–102, in contrast to Stendahl, *Paul Among Jews and Gentiles and Other Essays* (Philadelphia: Fortress Press, 1976), 129–133.

109. The radical discontinuity between Christianity and Judaism

that E. P. Sanders attributes to Paul seems to me to ignore such pivotal statements by Paul as Rom. 11:28–29. (Indeed, one looks in vain for any discussion of this passage in either his *Paul and Palestinian Judaism* or *Paul, the Law, and the Jewish People*.)

110. On the merits of the fathers, see W. D. Davies, *Paul and Rabbinic Judaism*, 268–273; and especially the discussion in E. P. Sanders, *Paul and Palestinian Judaism*, 183–198. Neither Cranfield (*Romans*, 2:580–581) nor Käsemann (*Commentary on Romans*, 315) is convinced that Paul is referring to the merits of the fathers in Rom. 11:28.

111. Paul maintains the paradox that Jews who do not believe in Christ can be both enemies of God and beloved of God at the same time. Similarly, Barrett, *Romans*, 225; and Luz, *Das Geschichtsverständnis des Paulus*, 296.

112. Against Käsemann, "The Faith of Abraham in Romans 4," 86.

113. In addition to the gifts that God has given to Israel, Paul also refers several times to "spiritual gifts" that God has bestowed upon believers for mutual edification (Rom. 1:11; 12:6; 1 Cor. 1:7; 7:7; 12:4, 9, 28–31).

114. God's blessing upon Abraham can be identified with God's reckoning Abraham righteous by faith (Rom. 4:3–6), not reckoning his sins (4:7–8), and God's giving of the promise to Abraham and his descendants (4:13).

115. On the "strong" and the "weak" in Romans 14–15, see the discussions in Barrett, *Romans*, 255–273; and Cranfield, *Romans*, 2:690–748.

116. On distinguishing Paul's use of Abraham in Galatians and Romans, see further Beker, *Paul the Apostle*, 94–104; Sampley, "Romans and Galatians"; Boers, *Theology out of the Ghetto*, 75–104; and Moxnes, *Theology in Conflict*, 207–230.

117. Indeed, as Dahl points out, "The tendency of the two letters at some points runs in opposite directions, contrary to one another" ("The Future of Israel," 141).

118. This is especially the case in Romans 9–11. Certainly, Paul also uses Abraham in Romans to address the problem of relations between Jewish Christians and Gentile Christians (Romans 4; 15: 8–9), but his appeal to Abraham is not limited to this relationship, as it is in Galatians.

119. Räisänen, *Paul and the Law*, 11.

Chapter 3

1. The composition of Matthew's Gospel is usually dated around 80–90 C.E. The dating of Hebrews and James is disputed. Hebrews was probably written sometime between 60 and 95 C.E., as Heb.

2:3–4 indicates that the author and the audience of Hebrews were second-generation Christians. See Attridge, *Hebrews*, 6–9. James is more difficult still to date. Most scholars place it about 65–95 C.E., although some date it later (e.g., Dibelius and Greeven, *James*, 45–46). Most scholars agree that Matthew, Hebrews, and James are Jewish-Christian writings, broadly defined. For the Jewish-Christian setting of Matthew, see the full discussion by W. D. Davies and Allison, *The Gospel According to Saint Matthew*, 1:7–58. For Hebrews, see Attridge, *Hebrews*, 9–13; Bruce, *Hebrews*, xxiii–xxx; and Michel, *Hebräer*, 37–56. On the Jewish-Christian character of James, see Laws, *James*, 32–38; and Dibelius and Greeven, *James*, 21–26.

2. For further discussion, see Luedemann's survey chapter on Jewish Christianity in *Opposition to Paul in Jewish Christianity*, 1–32; Dunn, "Jewish Christianity," 235–266; Strecker, "On the Problem of Jewish Christianity," 241–285; and Klijn, "The Study of Jewish Christianity," 419–431. For another example of treating Matthew, Hebrews, and James together, see S. Neill, *Jesus Through Many Eyes* (Philadelphia: Fortress, 1976), 93–118.

3. This is the only reference to Abraham in the Gospel of Mark (12:26).

4. The fundamental study of the Matthean genealogy, and the birth narratives in general, is that of R. E. Brown, *Birth*. See further Brown's article updating research on the birth narratives: "Gospel Infancy Narrative Research from 1976 to 1986: Part I (Matthew)," 468–483. See also Stendahl, "Quis et Unde?" 94–105; and M. D. Johnson, *The Purpose of the Biblical Genealogies with Special Reference to the Setting of the Genealogies of Jesus*.

5. In this, Matthew differs from Luke, who mentions Abraham in his genealogy only in passing (Luke 3:34) and traces the lineage of Jesus all the way back to Adam and, ultimately, God (Luke 3:38). For further comments on Luke's use of Abraham in the genealogy, see pp. 108–110 below.

6. See especially S. Brown, "The Matthean Community and the Gentile Mission," 193–221.

7. Stendahl has argued that Matthew 1–2 has an apologetic purpose, to answer the questions of who Jesus is and whence he comes ("Quis et Unde?" 94–105). In contrast to Stendahl, Kingsbury has stressed the christological purpose of Matthew 1–2, showing that Jesus is the royal messiah and Son of God (*Matthew: Structure, Christology, Kingdom*, 42–53). Although Stendahl rightly calls attention to apologetic overtones, the apologetic purpose would seem to serve Matthew's larger christological concerns. So also R. E. Brown, *Birth*, 180–81.

8. As R. E. Brown has noted, "The special combination of David and Abraham probably occurred in pre-Christian Judaism" (*Birth*,

68). See also Paul's references to David and Abraham, respectively, in Rom. 1:3 and Gal. 3:16.

9. Indeed, the prominence of David and the relative lack of attention given to Abraham throughout Matthew has led Gundry to make the following unlikely suggestion regarding Matt. 1:1: "Since elsewhere Matthew will show little interest in Abraham . . . he may have intended his readers to understand David rather than Jesus as the son of Abraham" (*Matthew: His Literary and Theological Artistry*, 13).

10. By contrast, as W. D. Davies and Allison note, " 'Son of Abraham' was not a messianic title" (*The Gospel According to Saint Matthew*, 1:158).

11. R. E. Brown, *Birth*, 68, 90, 181.

12. S. Brown ("The Matthean Community and the Gentile Mission") has argued that Matthew's community was not yet fully engaged in any Gentile mission but was only on the verge of such a mission in the aftermath of the Jewish War and the increasingly narrow understanding of Judaism put forward by emerging Pharisaic Judaism.

13. See especially Matt. 24:14 and 28:16–20. We will see below that Abraham figures in another passage associated with Gentile inclusion, 8:5–13.

14. Elsewhere Matthew links the Pharisees and the Sadducees at 16:1, 6, 11, 12. As Meier notes, Matthew's joining of Pharisees and Sadducees here is probably unhistorical ("John the Baptist in Matthew's Gospel," 383–405, 389–390). Matthew's purpose at this point is to critique the Jewish groups that opposed Jesus, and so he lumps them together. No doubt Matthew is reading his current experience of Jewish opposition back into the story. See especially Hummel, *Auseinandersetzung*, 18–20.

15. In addition to Matt. 3:7–10, see 16:6, 11; 23:1–36. The Pharisees and the Sadducees are both well represented in Matthew. Of the ninety-nine references to the Pharisees in the New Testament, thirty of them occur in Matthew. Of the fourteen references to the Sadducees that occur in the New Testament, half of them are found in Matthew (3:7; 16:1, 6, 11, 12; 22:23, 34).

16. See Hummel, *Auseinandersetzung*; and Hare, *Jewish Persecution*.

17. In Matt. 12:33–37 Jesus criticizes the Pharisees with words similar to those of John the Baptist. As John does in Matt. 3:7–10, Jesus calls the Pharisees a "brood of vipers" and implies that their "bad fruit" will result in their condemnation on the day of judgment. See also Matt. 21:33–45, where Jesus tells the Pharisees and the chief priests that because they do not bear the fruits of God's

kingdom, "the kingdom of God will be taken away from you and given to a nation producing the fruits of it" (Matt. 21:43).

18. See Hummel, *Auseinandersetzung*, 150.

19. So W. D. Davies and Allison, *The Gospel According to Saint Matthew*, 1:308–309. Hare is right that at Matt. 3:9 this motif "is not developed in relationship to Gentile believers" (*Jewish Persecution*, 157), but since the next reference to Abraham in Matt. 8:5–13 does refer to Gentile faithfulness, Matthew may have this motif in view already at 3:9.

20. Although the visit of the magi in Matt. 2:1–12 may represent Gentiles encountering the Christ-child, Jesus is not shown responding in any way.

21. Because Abraham is mentioned in passing with Isaac and Jacob in Matt. 8:11–12, an objection might be raised that this passage has little bearing upon a discussion of Matthew's use of Abraham. Although passages that refer collectively to Abraham, Isaac, and Jacob are not as significant for my purposes as passages that refer to Abraham alone, they are still important. One may not conclude from references to Abraham in conjunction with Isaac and Jacob that these appeals apply any less to Abraham alone. The same holds for Matthew's reference to Abraham in 22:32.

22. See Grundmann, *Das Evangelium nach Matthäus*, 249–251; and Zeller, "Das Logion Mt 8,11f/Lk 13,28f und das Motiv der 'Völkerwallfahrt,'" *BZ* 15 (1971): 222–237; 16 (1972): 84–93.

23. On Luke 13:22–30, see pp. 114–115 below.

24. Indeed, Matt. 8:10–12 appears to provide more of a warning to Jews than a sanction for any mission to the Gentiles.

25. In Matt. 8:12 the reference to "sons of the kingdom" clearly has negative overtones, implying that some individuals think they are sons of the kingdom, when in fact they are not. Whom does Matthew mean to implicate with this phrase? As Jewish leaders, the Pharisees and the Sadducees would seem to be good candidates for this identification. Elsewhere in Matthew, "sons of the kingdom" occurs only at 13:38, where it has positive overtones and where it refers to "the good seed." Cf. also 23:31 and 27:9, which may link the Pharisees and the Sadducees to the "sons of the kingdom" in 8:12.

26. Matthew derives this material from Mark 12:18–27 (cf. Luke 20:27–40), and he follows Mark's version very closely, making no substantial changes. In contrast, Luke's account diverges somewhat from Mark's. On the parallel in Luke, cf. p. 115 below.

27. The Pharisees return to test Jesus in Matt. 22:34–40 and 22:41–46. Immediately after this section, Matthew has Jesus begin his litany of woes against the scribes and the Pharisees (23:1–36).

28. Matthew thus shares in the early Jewish tradition that the

righteous will share in the resurrection life with Abraham. See pp.
26–27 above.

29. Indeed, the limited attention given to Abraham in Matthew
has led Schein to speak of "the lowered position of the Patriarch" in
Matthew and of Matthew making "a complete break with any reliance on Abraham" ("Our Father Abraham," 115). Similarly, Wieser
comments that "one can scarcely speak of a Matthean picture of
Abraham" (Abrahamvorstellungen, 98).

30. For a thorough analysis of Heb. 2:5–18, see Swetnam, Jesus
and Isaac, 130–177.

31. So Bruce, Hebrews, 52–53; Michel, Hebräer, 163; and
Swetnam, Jesus and Isaac, 134–137. For a contrary view, see P. C. B.
Andriessen, "La teneur judéo-chrétienne de He I 6 et II 14b–III 2,"
293–313.

32. The notion of God's promises plays an important role in
Hebrews. Cf. also Heb. 4:1; 6:12, 17; 8:6; 9:15; 10:36; 11:13, 33,
39. The promises made to Abraham and the other patriarchs find
their fruition in Christ, according to Hebrews. Indeed, "Christ has
obtained a ministry which is as much more excellent than the old as
the covenant he mediates is better, since it is enacted on better
promises" (Heb. 8:6). In this regard, Klassen has appropriately referred to Hebrews as "an exercise in comparative religions" ("Anti-
Judaism in and the Epistle to the Hebrews," 2:1–16; 5). On the
promises to Abraham in Hebrews, see further Swetnam, Jesus and
Isaac, 89–118.

33. The notion in Hebrews that God "swore by himself" (Heb.
6:13) finds parallels in Philo (Leg. All. 3.203; Abr. 273; Sac. 91) and
in later rabbinic writings (Berach. 32.1; Exodus Rabba 44). See
Michel, Hebräer, 250–251.

34. See Swetnam, Jesus and Isaac, 184–185.

35. Perhaps Isaac himself is the promise that Abraham obtained,
even though the promise of Gen. 22:17 comes well after the birth of
Isaac. Since in Genesis 22 Abraham had offered Isaac up to God,
"figuratively speaking, he did receive him back" from the dead
(Heb. 11:19). For Hebrews, then, Abraham obtained the promise
with assurance when he received Isaac back. See Michel, Hebräer,
251; and Koester, "Abraham-Verheissung," 95–109.

36. See Bruce, Hebrews, 303–304; and Michel, Hebräer, 397–
399.

37. The secondary literature on Hebrews 7 is abundant, and most
of it focuses on Melchizedek. In addition to the commentaries, see
especially Ellingworth, " 'Like the Son of God': Form and Content in
Hebrews 7, 1–10," 255–262; Horton, The Melchizedek Tradition;
and Demarest, A History of Interpretation of Hebrews 7, 1–10 from
the Reformation to the Present.

38. For chapter 7 as the climax of Hebrews, see, e.g., R. McL. Wilson, *Hebrews*, 131; and Michel, *Hebräer*, 255.

39. On Ps. 110:4, see especially Hay, *Glory at the Right Hand: Psalm 110 in Early Christianity*, 134–152; and Juel, *Messianic Exegesis: Christological Interpetation of the Old Testament in Early Christianity*, 135–150.

40. Various scholars have argued that Hebrews is familiar with and/or relies upon Philo and that the interpretation of Melchizedek in Hebrews 7 is a case in point. I remain unconvinced that the author of Hebrews is familiar with Philo and am persuaded by Williamson's arguments against such connections (*Philo and the Epistle to the Hebrews*, 443–449, 576–580). Williamson concludes that "there is nothing in Philo's exegesis . . . that looks at all as if it has exercised any influence on the Writer of Hebrews in what he has to say about Melchizedek" (p. 447). Similarly, it is difficult to show any influence of the Qumran writings upon Hebrews, as the Qumran portrait of Melchizedek differs dramatically from Hebrews.

41. So Kobelski, who argues that Melchizedek has a very limited purpose in Hebrews, namely, "to show (1) that the priesthood of Jesus was superior to the levitical priesthood, and (2) that the priesthood of Jesus was eternal" (*Melchizedek and Melchiresa*, 118).

42. See, e.g., Neh. 9:7–8; Sir. 44:19–21; Wisd. 10:5; 1 Macc. 2:52; 4 Macc. 16:20–17:6; Jub. 17:15–18; and Philo, *Abr.* 62–68; *Migr.* 43–44; *Leg. All.* 3.83.

43. Similarly, Moxnes, *Theology in Conflict*, 185.

44. For an evaluation of the various contemporary interpretations of the Akedah tradition in early Christianity and in early Judaism, see P. Davies and Chilton, "The Aqedah," 514–546; and especially the survey by Swetnam, *Jesus and Isaac*, 4–22.

45. Montefiore comments, "Abraham's decision was so difficult because God seemed to be contradicting himself by giving an order which appeared to nullify a previous promise. In our author's view Abraham realised that God could not lie about a promise nor could God's command be disobeyed" (*The Epistle to the Hebrews*, 199).

46. On the difficulties of how to understand *en parabolē*, cf. Swetnam, *Jesus and Isaac*, 119–127.

47. Swetnam states, "Looking back on the sacrifice from the vantage point of Christ, the author of Hebrews sees that Abraham's offering of Isaac in sacrifice and his receiving Isaac back was a mysterious foreshadowing of the sacrificial death and resurrection of Jesus" (*Jesus and Isaac*, 128). Similarly, Bruce, *Hebrews*, 312; and Daly, "The Soteriological Significance of the Sacrifice of Isaac," 45–75.

48. See P. Davies and Chilton, "The Aqedah," 529; and Moxnes, *Theology in Conflict*, 187.

49. Swetnam, *Jesus and Isaac*, 128; cf. pp. 101, 129.

50. Similarly, Koester, "Abraham-Verheissung," 107–108; and Moxnes, *Theology in Conflict*, who sums the matter up well: "It is the faithfulness of God towards his words more than the obedience of Abraham which is the concern of Heb 11:17–19" (p. 187). "It was not enough, in this situation, to point to the ancestors, and the fact that God's promise to them had been fulfilled. The author of Hebrews faced the formidable task of constructing a solid theological basis for trust in the promise of God. . . . Abraham was above all an example that God was faithful, that his words were steadfast and that he always fulfilled his promises" (p. 189).

51. In addition to the standard commentaries, see Lohse, "Glaube und Werke," 1–22; Luck, "Der Jakobusbrief," 161–179; Walker, "Allein aus Werken," 155–192; Nicol, "Faith and Works in the Letter of James," 7–24; Ward, "The Works of Abraham," 283–290; Lodge, "James and Paul at Cross-Purposes? James 2,22," 195–213; Soards, "The Early Christian Interpretation of Abraham," 18–26; and Jacobs, "The Midrashic Background for James II.21–3," 457–464.

52. There is widespread agreement that the style of James 2:14–26 reflects characteristics of diatribe. For example, the question-and-answer style seen throughout 2:14–26 is typical of diatribe (2:14, 20–21, 25). See further Wifstrand, "Stylistic Problems in the Epistles of James and Peter," 170–182; and Dibelius, *James*, 149–151.

53. The terms "faith" (*pistis*) and "works" (*erga*) appear in James almost exclusively within 2:14–26. The term *pistis* occurs sixteen times in James, with eleven occurrences in 2:14–26; the remaining references appear in 1:3, 6; 2:1, 5; and 5:15. The term *erga* occurs fifteen times in James, with twelve occurrences in 2:14–26; the remaining references appear in 1:4, 25; and 3:13.

54. Against Dibelius, who argues that James 2:14–26 is unrelated to the preceding material (*James*, 149–150).

55. Again, in 1:25, James exhorts his readers to persevere, "being no hearer that forgets but a doer that acts," for that person "shall be blessed in his doing."

56. For James, Abraham would thus also be an exemplary wise individual. See Lodge, "James and Paul at Cross-Purposes? James 2,22," 208–213.

57. Abraham is the first of two proofs from scripture. The appeal to Abraham occurs in James 2:21–23, and the second, complementary, proof refers to Rahab in 2:25. Rahab appears in close proximity to Abraham also in Matt. 1:1–7 and especially in Heb. 11:17–31 and in 1 Clement 10–12.

58. The term "offered" (*anenegkas*, James 2:21) comes from Gen. 22:2, 9. See Swetnam, *Jesus and Isaac*, 81–83.

59. Only in 1:4 and 1:25 does James use the singular form *ergon*. Similar to Abraham's "works" in 2:21, James refers to Rahab's "works," again using the plural, while discussing only one "work" that she performed.

60. Regarding the offering of Isaac, Philo comments, "I might almost say that all the other actions which won the favour of God are surpassed by this" (*Abr.* 167). See also Genesis Rabba 55, which refers to the ten trials that Abraham endured.

61. See Ward, "The Works of Abraham," 285–287; and L. T. Johnson, "The Mirror of Remembrance (James 1:22–25)," 632–645, esp. 642–643. Regarding Abraham, 1 Clem. 10:7 states that because of "his faith and hospitality a son was given him in his old age, and in his obedience he offered him as a sacrifice to God on the mountain which he showed him." See also Heb. 13:2, which alludes to Abraham's hospitality. Similarly, 1 Clem. 12:1 remarks that for "her faith and hospitality Rahab the harlot was saved."

62. See the similar statement in the Test. Gad 4:7b (*OTP*, 1:815): "The spirit of love works (*synergei*) by the Law of God through forbearance for the salvation of mankind." See Mussner, *Jakobusbrief*, 142 n. 1.

63. The English translation is by Laws, *James*, 49.

64. For James, the word group *teleios*, *teleoō*, and *teleō* is significant (cf. 1:4, 17, 25; 2:8, 22; 3:2).

65. Against Walker ("Allein aus Werken"), who argues that, for James, works generate faith. On this issue, see also Nicol, "Faith and Works in the Letter of James," 11–19.

66. As Mussner puts it (*Jakobusbrief*, 142, 145–146), "An alternative between faith or works is unthinkable for James. . . . Thus for James, faith and works stand in a synergistic relationship (*synergein*, v. 22!). . . . Works result necessarily from a living faith (v. 18b)." So also Lodge, "James and Paul at Cross-Purposes? James 2,22"; and Laws (*James*, 134), who states, "The relation between Abraham's faith and his works is not properly one of consequence, demonstration or confirmation, all of which terms assume a measure of distinction between the two: for James they go together in a necessary unity."

67. Similarly, Jub. 17:17–18 (*OTP*, 2:90): "And the Lord was aware that Abraham was faithful in all of his afflictions because he tested him with his land, and with famine. And he tested him with the wealth of kings. And he tested him again with his wife, when she was taken (from him), and with circumcision. And he tested him with Ishmael and with Hagar, his maidservant, when he sent them away. And in everything in which he tested him, he was found faith-

ful. And his soul was not impatient. And he was not slow to act because he was faithful and a lover of the Lord."

68. See, e.g., Neh. 9:7–8; 2 Chron. 20:7; Wisd. 7:7; Jub. 19:9; CD 3:2; Ps. Jon. on Gen. 18:17; and Philo, *Abr.* 273; *Sobr.* 56. In early Christian literature, see, e.g., 1 Clem. 10:1; 17:2; Irenaeus, *Adv. Haer.* 4.14.4.; and Tertullian, *Adv. Jud.* 2:7. See further, Ward, "The Works of Abraham," 286–287.

69. Thus Dibelius concludes, "This agreement between the synagogue exegesis and the interpretation to which we are plainly forced by our text provides the conclusive evidence for the dependence of this section in Jas upon Jewish Biblical interpretation" (*James*, 165; see further 162–165, 168–174). See also Soards, "The Early Christian Interpretation of Abraham," 18–20; and Jacobs, "The Midrashic Background for James II.21–3."

70. Dibelius, *James*, 149–151.

71. Dibelius, *James*, 155.

72. So Dibelius (*James*, 174–180), who concludes that the remarks in 2:14–26 "are still inconceivable unless Paul had previously set forth the slogan 'faith, not works'" (p. 179). Similarly, Soards, "The Early Christian Interpretation of Abraham," 24–25; Laws, *James*, 16–19, 131–133; and Wieser, *Abrahamvorstellungen*, 86–92.

73. See Laws (*James*, 132), who states, "The likelihood is, therefore, that when James heard the slogan 'justification by faith alone' used (or misused) it was carrying the authority of Paul."

74. Ward, "The Works of Abraham"; Lodge, "James and Paul at Cross-Purposes? James 2,22"; and Walker, "Allein aus Werken."

75. Ward, "The Works of Abraham," 283–285.

76. Dibelius, *James*, 174.

77. Lodge, "James and Paul at Cross-Purposes? James 2,22," 213. See also Kirk ("The Meaning of 'Wisdom' in James: Examination of a Hypothesis," 24–38), who notes parallels between the fruits of wisdom in James and the fruits of the Spirit in Gal. 5:16–6:10.

Chapter 4

1. Although the secondary literature on the use of Abraham in Luke-Acts is not extensive, there are several significant studies. Most basic is the article by Dahl, "The Story of Abraham in Luke-Acts." Working under the direction of Dahl, Schein's dissertation includes a chapter on "Abraham in the Common Source, Matthew, and Luke" ("Our Father Abraham," 93–135), although he does not discuss Abraham in Acts.

2. For a different way of organizing the material, see Dahl, "The

Story of Abraham in Luke-Acts," 141. Dahl's article deals almost exclusively with the Stephen speech in Acts 7, focusing very little on the use of Abraham in Luke's Gospel.

3. R. E. Brown, *Birth*, 350–355. So also, in agreement with Brown, see Fitzmyer, *The Gospel According to Luke I–IX*. See also Brown's update of research on Luke's infancy narrative, "Gospel Infancy Narrative Research from 1976 to 1986: Part II (Luke)," 660–680.

4. In general, see Gelin, *The Poor of Yahweh*. As R. E. Brown points out, there is much debate regarding the existence of Anawim as a group in preexilic times, but "a good case can be made for the contention that in post-exilic times the Anawim regarded themselves as the ultimate narrowing down of the remnant of Israel," who waited for the Messiah to bring about God's redemption (*Birth*, 351). On the whole issue of "the poor" as a technical term in the New Testament and Qumran, see especially Keck, "The Poor Among the Saints in the New Testament," 100–129; idem, "The Poor Among the Saints in Jewish Christianity and Qumran," 54–78; and idem, "Poor," *IDBS*, 672–675. See further Bammel, "*ptōchos*," *TDNT*, 6:888–915; and Dibelius, "Poor and Rich," in *James*, 39–45.

5. The phrase "to Abraham and to his posterity" stands in apposition to the phrase "to our fathers." The primary focus may be more on "our fathers" here, but it remains significant that Abraham is mentioned.

6. R. E. Brown, *Birth*, 359.

7. In this connection, one of Dahl's conclusions is worth noting ("The Story of Abraham in Luke-Acts," 152): "For me, the study of Abraham in Luke-Acts has been a confirmation . . . that 'proof-from-prophecy' is a main theological and literary device of the work."

8. See, e.g., R. E. Brown, *Birth*, 269; and Fitzmyer, *The Gospel According to Luke I–IX*, 317.

9. Fitzmyer, *The Gospel According to Luke I–IX*, 378. See R. E. Brown, *Birth*, 359.

10. See R. E. Brown, *Birth*, 387.

11. The Greek verb *latreuein* carries the meaning of both English verbs "to serve" and "to worship." As we will see (pp. 121–125 below), the theme of proper service/worship denoted by *latreuein* is important in connection with Abraham also in the Stephen speech of Acts 7.

12. Tannehill makes the significant observation that the promise spelled out in the Benedictus is replete with Davidic motifs but is identified as the promise, not to David, but to Abraham. It appears that for Luke the Davidic motifs are associated exclusively with the

identity of Jesus as Messiah and Lord (see, e.g., Peter's speech in Acts 2:22–36), not with the people of Israel. Rather, the corporate identity of the people comes from the Abrahamic promise, which extends beyond Israel to Gentiles (*The Narrative Unity of Luke-Acts*, 37).

13. See further here W. D. Davies, *The Gospel and the Land*, 261–263. See the discussion on Stephen's speech in Acts 7:2–8 on pp. 121–125 below.

14. See the discussion on pp. 118–121 below.

15. Compare with Matt. 3:7–10; see the discussion on pp. 80–81 above.

16. See further the rabbinic tradition regarding the "merits of Abraham" (e.g., in Billerbeck and Strack, *Kommentar zum Neuen Testament aus Talmud und Midrasch*, 1:116–121). As a descendant of Abraham one could appeal for mercy from God on the basis of Abraham's righteousness (see, e.g., Test. Lev. 15:4). Although the rabbinic writings come from a later period, they may preserve oral traditions that date from the first century C.E.

17. Fitzmyer also notes that Luke repudiates reliance on ethnic privilege. In addition he notes: "That repudiation is not based, though, on a call to a faith in a messiah, but on conduct expected to be consonant with an inner reform of life" (*The Gospel According to Luke I–IX*, 468).

18. This argument is similar to Paul's argument of physical descent (see pp. 60–61 above). There may be a connection between Luke 3:8 and Isa. 51:1–2 (LXX): "Hearken to me, you who pursue deliverance, you who seek the Lord; look to the rock from which you were hewn (*eis tēn sterean petran*), and to the quarry from which you were digged. Look to Abraham your father and to Sarah who bore you." The connection between Abraham and a rock (Isa. 51:1) or stone (Luke 3:8) is clear in each case. See the discussion in Fitzmyer, *The Gospel According to Luke I–IX*, 469.

19. See pp. 000–000 above.

20. See Schneider, *Das Evangelium nach Lukas, Kapitel 1–10*, 85; and Plummer, *The Gospel According to S. Luke*, 88. Fitzmyer notes that even with the change to *ochloi*, John's sermon is clearly addressed to Palestinian Jews (*The Gospel According to Luke I–IX*, 465–467.)

21. Matthew's redaction may be equally or more tendentious and Luke's redaction relatively neutral at this point. I am not convinced that there is enough evidence in the text to decide clearly one way or another whether Luke or Matthew preserves the more original version of the Q tradition. While there is widespread agreement that in general Luke better preserves the *order* of Q, comparing Lukan and Matthean redaction of Q is a much more difficult problem. For a

convenient summary of the issues, see Worden, "Redaction Criticism of Q: A Survey," 532–546; and Kloppenborg, "Tradition and Redaction in the Synoptic Sayings Source," 34–62. For Luke in particular, see Fitzmyer's treatment of the Sermon on the Plain (6:20–49) as an example of the difficulties in sorting through the redactions of Luke and Matthew to the "original" version of the Q materials (*The Gospel According to Luke I–IX*, 627–644).

22. See pp. 78–80 above.

23. See especially Laurentin, *Les évangiles de l'enfance du Christ*, 409–414. See also R. E. Brown, *Birth*, 84–94.

24. See, e.g., R. E. Brown, *Birth*, 90–91; and Fitzmyer, *The Gospel According to Luke I–IX*, 498, 502.

25. See Fitzmyer, *The Gospel According to Luke X–XXIV*, 1009–1014; and Hultgren, *Jesus and His Adversaries*, 190–192.

26. For the exact nature of the woman's physical ailment, see Wilkinson, "The Case of the Bent Woman in Luke 13:10–17," 195–205. Wilkinson diagnoses her condition as "spondylitis ankylopoietica"! He makes the more significant exegetical observation that, despite the reference to Satan, the story is not an exorcism but a physical healing.

27. See, e.g., Fitzmyer, *The Gospel According to Luke X–XXIV*, 1011–1012.

28. Jervell, "The Daughters of Abraham: Women in Acts," 146–157, 148. Jervell also asserts, "In the New Testament, the rare title 'daughter of Abraham,' occurs only in Luke, as is true also of the title, 'son of Abraham,' (Luke 19:9). Such a designation is unknown in the literature from this period, and attested to at a much later time than that of Luke. I suspect that Luke himself coined the title, and by it intends to show the significance of women in the community" (p. 148). Jervell ignores the reference in 4 Macc. 15:28 to the mother of the seven martyrs: "As the daughter of God-fearing Abraham she remembered his fortitude" (*tēs theosebous Abraam karterias hē thygatēr emnēsthē*). Fourth Maccabees is generally dated between 18 and 37 C.E. and so shows the designation "daughter of Abraham" in Jewish literature from this period.

29. See also Hamm, "The Freeing of the Bent Woman and the Restoration of Israel: Luke 13:10–17 as Narrative Theology," 23–44.

30. See Plummer, *The Gospel According to S. Luke*, 435; Loewe, "Towards an Interpretation of Lk 19:1–10," 321–331; O'Hanlon, "The Story of Zacchaeus and the Lukan Ethic," 2–26; N. M. Watson, "Was Zacchaeus Really Reforming?" 282–285; and the literature referred to by Fitzmyer, *The Gospel According to Luke X–XXIV*, 1220–1221.

31. See White, "A Good Word for Zacchaeus? Exegetical Comment on Luke 19:1–10," 89–96; idem, "Vindication for Zacchaeus?"

21. Fitzmyer himself seems also to come down on this side (*The Gospel According to Luke X–XXIV*, 1221–1222).

32. See especially here the comments of Plummer, *The Gospel According to S. Luke*, 435; N. M. Watson, "Was Zacchaeus Really Reforming?"; and Loewe, "Towards an Interpretation of Lk 19: 1–10."

33. As Loewe puts it: "The figure of Abraham comes to signify not only promise but also division and judgment. When Jesus calls Zacchaeus a son of Abraham, he heightens the scandal of the preceding chapter's parable of the Pharisee and the Publican by designating a chief publican true heir to the promise" ("Towards an Interpretation of Lk 19:1–10," 326).

34. Regarding the function of this story in the Lukan community, Karris points out, "The *Sitz im Leben* behind this passage is the problem of how a rich person should deal with his possessions. Luke answers that it is not necessary for a rich person to sell everything. . . . It does, however, necessitate that they give a genuine sign that they are not so attached to their possessions that they neglect the Christian poor" ("Poor and Rich: The Lukan *Sitz im Leben*," 123–124).

35. I use the designation "Abraham and Afterlife" in an attempt to include related motifs about the heavenly, eschatological, and apocalyptic character of Abraham who also plays a role in the last judgment, motifs that are present in the three relevant passages. See further the discussion of "The Otherworldly Abraham" in chapter 6, pp. 156–158 below. See also parallels in early Jewish use of Abraham, pp. 24–27.

36. Although passages that refer collectively to Abraham, Isaac, and Jacob are not as significant for my purposes as passages that refer to Abraham alone, they are still important. One may not conclude from references to Abraham in conjunction with Isaac and Jacob that these appeals apply any less to Abraham alone.

37. The source-critical problems here are notorious. See the discussion and other secondary literature in Fitzmyer, *The Gospel According to Luke X–XXIV*, 1020–1027; and the fundamental essay by Mussner, "Das 'Gleichnis' vom gestrengen Mahlherrn (Lk 13,22–30): Ein Beitrag zum Redaktionsverfahren und zur Theologie des Lukas," 113–124.

38. See also the comparison between Matt. 8:11–12 and Luke 13:28–29, pp. 82–83 above.

39. Fitzmyer, *The Gospel According to Luke X–XXIV*, 1023.

40. See pp. 83–84 above.

41. Luke broadens the saying to include not only those from east and west (as in Matthew) but also those from north and south, emphasizing the universal scope of the saying.

42. See Fitzmyer, *The Gospel According to Luke X–XXIV*, 1023. Mussner ("Das 'Gleichnis' vom gestrengen Mahlherrn [Lk 13,22–30]") sees in this passage a reference to the salvation of the Gentiles, who do not replace Israel, so that the salvation of the Gentiles hinges on the rejection of the Jews, but join the true Israel in God's kingdom. Mussner thinks this passage points to a radically denationalized (*entnationalisiert*) promise of salvation (pp. 123–124). Although Gentile inclusion is not an explicit concern of this passage, it may well be an implicit consideration.

43. This is the only Markan reference to Abraham, one that Luke also uses.

44. For similar statements about the immortality of the patriarchs, see further 4 Macc. 7:18–19: "But as many as attend to religion with a whole heart, these alone are able to control the passions of the flesh, since they believe that they, like our patriarchs Abraham and Isaac and Jacob, do not die to God, but live in God"; and 4 Macc. 16:24–25: "By these words the mother of the seven encouraged and persuaded each of her sons to die rather than violate God's commandments. They knew also that those who die for the sake of God live in God, as do Abraham and Isaac and Jacob and all the patriarchs." Abraham is portrayed in these passages as an example of one who lives forever to God, and as such he provides hope for the faithful in the resurrection. See further Nickelsburg, *Resurrection, Immortality, and Eternal Life in Intertestamental Judaism*, 110–111, 160.

45. Luke contrasts "the sons of this age" (Luke 20:34) with "the sons of God/sons of the resurrection" (20:35). A similar contrast is found earlier in 16:8, where he contrasts "the sons of this age" with "the sons of light."

46. We will see below that Lazarus too is a son of Abraham who is worthy of resurrection (Luke 16:19–31).

47. The story is not a parable in the strict sense, although form-critically it falls here, but is more an "example" story, as Fitzmyer calls it (*The Gospel According to Luke X–XXIV*, 1126).

48. The question of possible sources for this parable is beyond my concern. On this question, see the discussion in Fitzmyer, *The Gospel According to Luke X–XXIV*, 1124–1134; and the suggestive article by Hock, "Lazarus and Micyllus: Greco-Roman Backgrounds to Luke 16:19–31," 447–463.

49. On the motif of being received into the "bosom of Abraham," see Fitzmyer, *The Gospel According to Luke X–XXIV*, 1132. The notion of being received into God's kingdom by Abraham in more general terms can already be seen in 4 Macc. 13:17: "For if we so die [or suffer], Abraham and Isaac and Jacob will welcome us, and all the fathers will praise us."

50. Schein, "Our Father Abraham," 133.

51. Although it is difficult to say whether Luke's choice of *teknon* as opposed to *huios* here has much significance, the only other occurrence of *tekna Abraam* in Luke (3:8) is found on the lips of John the Baptist in a critique of claims to Abrahamic paternity apart from genuine repentance. By contrast, see Luke 19:9, where Jesus calls a repentant rich man, Zacchaeus, *huios Abraam*. Likewise, in 20:36, Luke refers to sons of God and sons of the resurrection. Thus there may be a distinction for Luke between *teknon* and *huios*. In almost every instance, *teknon* refers in Luke to a physical descendant (Luke 1:7, 17; 2:48; 3:8; 11:13; 13:34; 14:26; 15:31; 18:29; 19:44; 20:31; 23:28), whereas *huios* has a wider range of meanings, often used in a symbolic sense (e.g., "Son of the Most High"—1:32; 6:35; 8:28; "Son of God"—4:3, 9, 41; "Son of Man"—5:24; 6:5, 22; 7:34; 9:22), although it can also refer to a physical descendant (1:13, 31; 4:22; 5:10; 9:38, 41). This distinction, however, should not be pushed too far.

52. On Luke's concern for the theme of rich and poor, see Karris, "Poor and Rich: The Lukan *Sitz im Leben*"; and Degenhardt, *Lukas, Evangelist der Armen: Besitz und Besitzverzicht in den lukanischen Schriften*.

53. On Peter's speech in Acts 3:11–26, see Zehnle, *Peter's Pentecost Discourse: Tradition and Lukan Reinterpretation in Peter's Speeches of Acts 2 and 3*; Jervell, "The Divided People of God," in *Luke and the People of God*, 41–74; S. G. Wilson, *The Gentiles and the Gentile Mission in Luke-Acts*, 219–222; and Haenchen, *The Acts of the Apostles*, 203–212.

54. The lame man asks for alms from Peter and John (Acts 3:3). When Peter looks at him and addresses him (Acts 3:4), Luke tells us that the man expected to receive something from them (Acts 3:5), which the reader would naturally understand to refer to alms. There is no indication here that the man's expectation extends beyond his request in Acts 3:3. To attribute an incipient faith to the man is eisegesis. The reference to "the faith" in Acts 3:16 should not be understood as referring to the faith of the lame man but rather to the faith that Peter proclaims, or perhaps the faith of Peter himself, which provides the vehicle for God's power in healing the lame man. For a contrary view, see Haenchen, *The Acts of the Apostles*, 207.

55. Luke uses the term "covenant" (*diathēkē*) only four times in all of Luke-Acts: Luke 1:72; 22:20; Acts 3:25; 7:8. Each time he refers to the covenant that God made with Israel, he refers to Abraham (Luke 1:72; Acts 3:25; 7:8; Luke 22:20 refers to the new covenant during the words of institution at the Last Supper). In Luke 1:72–73 we saw how the covenant promise to Abraham is spelled

out in terms of salvation and true worship, most probably in connection with Anawim piety. Here in Acts 3:25 we see an emphasis on a different aspect of God's covenant with Abraham, namely, the blessing to the nations.

56. The translation is mine. The RSV translation blurs the reference to "your seed" in both Gen. 22:18 and its citation in Acts 3:25, translating *tō spermati sou* as "your descendants" in Gen. 22:18 but as "your posterity" in Acts 3:25. On Luke's use of Gen. 22:18, see Holtz, *Untersuchungen über die alttestamentlichen Zitate bei Lukas*, 74–76.

57. See Wilckens, *Die Missionsreden der Apostelgeschichte*, 43; Dahl, "A People for His Name," 327; Dupont, "The Apologetic Use of the Old Testament in the Speeches of Acts," in *The Salvation of the Gentiles*, 129–159; and most notably Jervell, "The Divided People of God," in *Luke and the People of God*, 58–61. See further the full discussion in S. G. Wilson, *The Gentiles and the Gentile Mission in Luke-Acts*, 219–222.

58. So, e.g., Haenchen, *The Acts of the Apostles*, 209; and Dahl, "The Story of Abraham in Luke-Acts," 149. S. G. Wilson argues for this position but in the end appears not to decide conclusively for either "Christ" or "Israel" (*The Gentiles and the Gentile Mission in Luke-Acts*, 220–222).

59. See Jervell, "The Divided People of God," in *Luke and the People of God*, 58–60. So also Dupont, "Le salut des gentils et la signification théologique du livre des Actes," 132–155, esp. 145–146.

60. Thus, as we saw in Paul (pp. 36–38, 61–62 above), so Luke too puts special emphasis on God's promise that in Abraham's descendants the Gentiles would find blessing, which found little development in early Judaism.

61. Luke's extension of salvation to believing Gentiles does not imply Luke's total rejection of the Jews. As Jervell has shown, Luke develops more of a division among the Jews than any rejection of the Jews per se ("The Divided People of God," in *Luke and the People of God*). In particular, picking up on Jervell's work, Brawley has shown that Luke draws a relatively favorable picture of the Pharisees in comparison to the high priests and the Sadducees, though the Pharisees also come under critique. See Brawley, *Luke-Acts and the Jews*, 84–132, 155–159.

62. The secondary literature on the Stephen speech is extensive. For literature about Acts 7:2–8 specifically, in addition to the standard commentaries, see the essay by Dahl, "The Story of Abraham in Luke-Acts"; Bacon, "Stephen's Speech," 213–276; Kilgallen, *The Stephen Speech*; Stemberger, "Die Stephanusrede (Apg 7) und die jüdische Tradition," 154–174; Mundle, "Die Stephanusrede

Apg. 7: Eine Märtyrerapologie," 133–147; Richard, *Acts vi.1–viii.4*; and Bihler, *Die Stephanusgeschichte*, 38–46.

63. Dahl, "The Story of Abraham in Luke-Acts," 142; and Bacon, "Stephen's Speech."

64. On the way in which Luke relates Abraham and the land, see especially Dahl, "The Story of Abraham in Luke-Acts," 145–147; Bacon, "Stephen's Speech," 237–244; Kilgallen, *The Stephen Speech*, 33–46; W. D. Davies, *The Gospel and the Land*, 268–273; and Richard, *Acts vi.1–viii.4*, 321–331. For early Jewish traditions on the land, see pp. 19–22 above.

65. Several of these differences have no apparent theological significance for Luke's development of the story of Abraham. Luke transposes the vision of Gen. 12:7 and the command of Gen. 12:1 to the situation of Gen. 11:31. He identifies Mesopotamia with the land of the Chaldeans rather than with Haran. He has Abraham leaving Haran after the death of Terah rather than before (in agreement, however, with Philo, *Migr.* 177). Finally, in Acts 7:16 he confuses Abraham's purchase of the cave at Hebron with Jacob's purchase of land at Shechem. These differences are to be attributed to Luke's summary treatment of the details of the Genesis accounts of Abraham or possibly to his familiarity with varying traditions regarding Abraham, not to any theological tendency. See Dahl, "The Story of Abraham in Luke-Acts," 142–143.

66. As Bacon ("Stephen's Speech") puts it: "The Abrahamic Inheritance, we are to infer, was not so much a particular land, but 'freedom to worship God.' . . . Thus the conception of the prerogative of the *klēronomia* ['inheritance'] tends to merge in, or actually becomes indistinguishable from that of the *latreia* ['worship/service']. The place is nothing, the deliverance from oppression and bringing into relations of pure and unhindered 'worship' is everything" (pp. 240, 244).

67. See Kilgallen, *The Stephen Speech*, 33–35; Bihler, *Die Stephanusgeschichte*, 43; and Krodel, *Acts*, 142. Those who hold that "this place" refers more broadly to the land include Dahl, "The Story of Abraham in Luke-Acts," 145; Schneider, *Die Apostelgeschichte: Einleitung. Kommentar zu Kapitel* 1.1–8.40 (Freiburg: Herder, 1980), 455; and Haenchen, *The Acts of the Apostles*, 279. Still others hold that "this place" may refer both generically to the land and specifically to the Temple: W. D. Davies, *The Gospel and the Land*, 268.

68. In addition, later in the speech *topos* ("place") does not refer to the Temple (Acts 7:33, 49). Indeed, as Dahl has pointed out, there does not appear to be an anti-Temple polemic in Stephen's speech, the charges of Acts 6:13–14 notwithstanding. The point of the speech is not so much to oppose Temple worship as to witness

to the fullness of worship in Christ which is grounded in God's promise to Abraham. See Dahl, "The Story of Abraham in Luke-Acts," 145–146; and Brawley, *Luke-Acts and the Jews*, 118–132. Brawley points out the positive centrality given the Temple throughout Luke-Acts. The Temple is the place of early Christian teaching and proclamation. The charges that Stephen attacks the Temple are shown to be *false* charges. Stephen's martyrdom is brought about not by an alleged critique of the Temple but as a result of "the momentous assertion that Jesus has occupied the place of God's power" (p. 132). Further, Brawley shows that Luke distinguishes the Temple itself from the Temple leadership, the Sadducees and the priests (especially the high priests), leadership that Luke does attack and condemn.

69. Several interpreters think this is Luke's point in the Stephen speech and see the basis for this polemic in the influence of Samaritan and/or Samaritan Christian teachings, especially regarding the Temple. See Spiro, "Stephen's Samaritan Background," 285–300; and Scharlemann, *Stephen: A Singular Saint*.

70. Similarly, Brawley (*Luke-Acts and the Jews*, 118–132), who states: "In brief, Luke makes the temple as a place of prayer and proclamation completely compatible with his refusal to imprison God's presence within it" (p. 120).

71. See Bacon, "Stephen's Speech," 237–238; and Dahl, "The Story of Abraham in Luke-Acts," 146.

72. Compare Acts 24:14–15, where Paul, in his speech before Felix, says, "I worship (*latreuō*) the God of our fathers." Again worship is stressed in relation to the patriarchs.

73. This delocalizing is parallel to what Mussner refers to as Luke's having "denationalized" salvation. See n. 42 above.

74. As Dahl rightly suggests, "Stephen himself would be the representative of the true worship of God in Jerusalem, the worship performed by the disciples who gathered in the name of Jesus, both in the temple and in the houses" (Dahl, "The Story of Abraham in Luke-Acts," 146).

75. See Bihler, *Die Stephanusgeschichte*, 39, 45–46.

76. Dahl, "The Story of Abraham in Luke-Acts," 147.

77. See in general Buss, *Die Missionspredigt des Apostels Paulus im Pisidischen Antiochien*, esp. 63–64.

Chapter 5

1. Within two generations after John, Christianity became a clearly distinct, largely Gentile, religious movement that indeed had its roots in Judaism but was removed from any regular direct inter-

action with Judaism in most quarters. The movement of Christianity in this direction will occupy us in the next two chapters.

2. There is also an allusion to Abraham in John 7:22 in a context that has to do with circumcision. Jesus states, "Moses gave you circumcision (not that it is from Moses, but from the fathers)" (*ek tōn paterōn*). The reference to "the fathers" is clearly an allusion to Abraham. What is noteworthy is that John says nothing against circumcision, and indeed John goes out of his way to show that Jesus actually did not break the Sabbath when he performed a healing on it, referring back to the story in John 5:1–18. Elsewhere I have argued that the Johannine community may well have continued to observe Jewish law, if from a christocentric vantage (J. S. Siker, "John 7:14–24 and Circumcision: A Law-Observant Johannine Community?" a paper presented at the International SBL meeting in Copenhagen, August 1989).

3. The most comprehensive analysis of John 8 is that by Lona, *Abraham in Johannes 8*. See also Manns, *"La verité vous fera libres"*; and Bartholomew, "An Early Christian Sermon-Drama: John 8:31–59." See also the following studies: Dodd, "Behind a Johannine Dialogue," 41–57; Blank, "Die Krisis zwischen Jesu und den Juden (Der Offenbarungsprozess)," in *Krisis: Untersuchungen zur johanneischen Christologie und Eschatologie*, 231–251; Leroy, *Rätsel und Missverständnis*, 67–87; Dahl, "Der Erstgeboren Satans und der Vater des Teufels," 70–84; Martyn, "Glimpses Into the History of the Johannine Community," 90–121; Dozeman, *"Sperma Abraam* in John 8 and Related Literature," 342–358; and Whitacre, *Johannine Polemic*, 68–78.

4. See, e.g., Schnackenburg, for whom the passage reveals "the widening, by now almost unbridgeable, rift" between Jesus and the unbelieving Jews (*The Gospel According to St. John*, 2:188); similarly, Leroy, who sees John 8:31–59 as the culmination of the tension between Jesus and the Jews (*Rätsel und Missverständnis*, 88); R. E. Brown, *The Gospel According to John*, 1:367; and Whitacre, *Johannine Polemic*, 68–78.

5. See p. 15 above.

6. R. E. Brown aptly refers to John 8:12–20, 21–30, and 31–59 as "miscellaneous discourses" (*The Gospel According to John*, 1:339, 346, 352). John 7:53–8:11 is widely acknowledged as a non-Johannine addition to the Gospel and so will not be addressed here.

7. Elsewhere I have argued that John 8:30–48 is a secondary addition to the Gospel, added at the final stage of redaction and reflecting a relatively late period in the history of the Johannine community (J. S. Siker, "John 8:30–59 and the History of the Johannine Community," a paper presented at the SBL Pacific Coast Regional Meeting, March 1989).

8. Dodd, *The Interpretation of the Fourth Gospel*, 347.

9. This theme is introduced for the first time in John 5:18, after Jesus has called God his Father. As we will see below, the paternity of Abraham is also at issue in the conflict between Jesus and the Jews in John 8:31–59 and leads to the first actual attempt on Jesus' life in John (8:59).

10. Perhaps John 7:13 is also a veiled reference to attacks upon Jesus. No one speaks openly about Jesus "for fear of the Jews." Clearly, the reader is to surmise that those who speak openly about Jesus have reason to fear some form of reprisal from the Jews.

11. In John 7:30–32 the Jewish officials seek to arrest Jesus, and in 7:44 some people want to arrest him. While seeking to arrest Jesus differs from seeking to kill him, 7:30–32 and 44 show increasing Jewish antagonism toward Jesus.

12. John refers to Jews seeking to kill Jesus seven times in chapters 7 and 8. The verb "to kill" (*apokteinō*) appears elsewhere in John only five times (John 5:18; 11:53; 12:10; 16:2; 18:31).

13. In general, Jewish feasts figure in the Gospel of John more than in any other Gospel in the New Testament (17x in John; 8x in Matthew, Mark, and Luke combined). Aside from the Feast of Tabernacles, John frequently mentions the Feast of Passover (John 2:13, 23; 6:4; 11:55; 12:1; 13:1; 18:28, 39; 19:14).

14. On the central features of the Feast of Tabernacles during the Second Temple period, see Safrai, "The Temple," in Safrai and Stern, *The Jewish People in the First Century*, 2:894–896; on the significance of the Feast of Tabernacles for Jewish Christians in particular, see Daniélou, "Les quatre-temps de septembre et la fête des tabernacles," 114–136; see also R. E. Brown, *The Gospel According to John*, 1:326–327; and Schnackenburg, *The Gospel According to St. John*, 2:152–153.

15. Another motif that binds John 7 and 8 together is the theme of secrecy. In 7:4 the theme of secrecy (*en kryptō*) appears on the lips of Jesus' brothers. In 7:10 Jesus goes up to the feast in secret (*en kryptō*). At the end of John 8, Jesus hides (*ekrybē*) when the Jews seek to stone him (8:59). The whole complex of materials in John 7 and 8 is thus further framed as a large unit by the secrecy with which Jesus goes up to the feast and the secrecy with which he leaves. The theme of Jesus acting in secrecy elsewhere in John appears only at 12:36, at the end of Jesus' public ministry.

16. The internal structure of pronouncement/discussion in John 7 and 8 also loosely ties the two chapters together. Jesus causes discussion among the Jews in 7:10–31. Jesus' pronouncement in 7:37 leads to a controversy with the Jews (7:40–44). Jesus does not speak again until 8:12, where again his pronouncement leads to contro-

versy with the Jews (8:13–20). Again in 8:21, Jesus' statement leads to discussion and misunderstanding on the part of the Jews (8:22–29). Finally, in 8:31–59 we find a series of pronouncements that lead to conflict with the Jews, culminating in their attempt to kill him in 8:59.

17. John 8:12–30 also anticipates thematically the material in 8:31–59 in the following ways: discipleship (8:12 with 8:31), the activity of Jesus and the Father (8:13–14, 17–18 with 8:50, 54), knowledge of the Father (8:19, 27 with 8:55), the disbelief of the Jews (8:24 with 8:45–46), the sin of the Jews (8:21, 24 with 8:34), and the death of the Jews (8:21, 24 with 8:51). In general, these various themes are coordinated in 8:31–59 by the figure of Abraham and the overarching theme of paternity.

18. The term "Father" is completely absent from John 7 (although 7:22 refers to the patriarchs) and from John 9.

19. See, e.g., Lona, Martyn, Dozeman, Manns, Schnackenburg, Brown, and Dodd.

20. See, e.g., John 8:12–20, where Jesus' interlocutors, the Pharisees, are introduced in 8:13 but not explicitly identified in 8:19. Again in 8:21–30 the Jews are introduced in 8:22 but not explicitly identified in 8:23, 25, 27, or 30, since it is understood that they are the dialogue partners of Jesus. Similarly, in 8:31–47 the "Jews who had believed in him" are introduced in 8:31 but not explicitly identified in 8:33, 34, 39, 41, and 42.

21. As R. E. Brown notes, John 8:31–59 on the whole forms a rather "homogenous discourse" (*The Gospel According to John*, 1:361); similarly, Schnackenburg (*The Gospel According to St. John*, 2:203–204).

22. As with the beginning of previous controversy dialogues (John 7:16–17, 28–29, 37–38, 8:12, 21), so John 8:31–59 begins with a claim by Jesus (John 8:31–32).

23. See Dahl, "Der Erstgeboren Satans und der Vater des Teufels."

24. See Lona, *Abraham in Johannes 8*, 418–426.

25. Several commentators note the distinction but see no real significance in it. See Lona, *Abraham in Johannes 8*, 271; Manns, "*La vérité vous fera libres*", 48–49; Schnackenburg, *The Gospel According to St. John*, 2:210; and Dodd, "Behind a Johannine Dialogue," 50 n. 1. Dozeman ("*Sperma Abraam* in John 8 and Related Literature," 343) argues that *sperma Abraam* ("descendants of Abraham") was a technical term denoting a law-observant Christian-Jewish mission, but he does not contrast it directly to *tekna Abraam* ("children of Abraham"). He concludes that this law-observant mission "comes into conflict with the law-free Christians in the Johannine community, resulting in a controversy similar to ones reflected in the Pauline corpus and in Justin's *Dialogue with Trypho*" (p. 343). There are

several problems with Dozeman's thesis, however. First, like Dodd ("Behind a Johannine Dialogue"), Dozeman reads John through Paul and Justin, in whose writings the dispute is between Jewish and Gentile Christians, which seems not to be the case in John. Second, Dozeman does not provide sufficient justification for the assertion that observance of the law is an issue in John. And third, Dozeman assumes that John 8:31–59 functioned as an apologetic within a missionary context, whereas it has much more the character of a polemic. See Whitacre, *Johannine Polemic*, 68–78.

26. Against those who see in this response a reference to the political freedom of the Jews (e.g., R. E. Brown, *The Gospel According to John*, 1:35), I think Odeberg is correct: "It is indeed missing the whole point of the controversy when one takes the Jews to misunderstand the freedom spoken of by J[esus] in a political sense. . . . The 'freedom' of which the Jews were so sensitively proud . . . was *primarily* their freedom, *qua* God's people and possessors of the Tora, from idolatry and Sin" (*The Fourth Gospel*, 296). Similarly, Schnackenburg, *The Gospel According to St. John*, 2:207.

27. As Metzger notes, "It appears that the original text of this verse involved a mixed conditional sentence, with *ei . . . este* in the protasis, and *epoieite* in the apodosis ('If you are really Abraham's children, you would be doing the works of Abraham.') The variant readings [*poieite*] arose in an effort to make a more grammatically 'correct' condition" (*A Textual Commentary on the Greek New Testament*, 225).

28. R. E. Brown, *The Gospel According to John*, 1:356–357.

29. So Schnackenburg (*The Gospel According to St. John*, 2:490 n. 86), who states, "The clause must be an unreal [contrary-to-fact] condition" because "the addition of *an* is no longer required in the koine."

30. Notice that a disciple is not referred to as a *huios* ("son"), a title reserved for Jesus in his exclusive relationship to God. See Oepke ("*pais*," *TDNT*, 5:653), who states, "In Jn there is a consistent linguistic distinction between being a son of God and a child of God. Only Christ is now *huios* ["son"]. In distinction from Him believers are exclusively *tekna [tou] theou*, Jn. 1:12; 11:52; I Jn. 3:1, 2, 10; 5:2." Similarly 1 John 2:1 (*teknia mou*). See R. E. Brown, *The Epistles of John*, 213–214, 388–391. Only believers are truly "children of God" in John. See further de Jonge, "The Son of God and the Children of God," 141–168.

31. Indeed, it is striking that the entire word group for "inheritance" (*klēronomeō, kleronomos, klēronomia*) is completely absent from John.

32. So R. E. Brown, *The Gospel According to John*, 1:440–443. Martyn, however, argues against John 11:52 as a reference to Gen-

tile mission within the Gospel of John ("Glimpses Into the History of the Johannine Community," 118–119).

33. The term *sperma* occurs also once in 1 John 3:9, in reference to God's seed which dwells within the believers. This use of *sperma* has a positive connotation in 1 John but refers there to being born of God (in conjunction with the verb *gennaō*, "to be born"), not to physical descent. The theme of being born of God occurs also in John 1:12–13 in connection with *tekna theou*.

34. See the striking parallel in 1 John 3:10, which contrasts *ta tekna tou theou* ("the children of God") with *ta tekna tou diabolou* ("the children of the devil").

35. See Martyn, "Glimpses Into the History of the Johannine Community," 111.

36. The textual variant in p⁷⁵ and other manuscripts, which reads *Abraam heōraken se* ("has Abraham seen you") rather than *Abraam heōrakas* ("have you seen Abraham"), is actually true from the perspective of the Fourth Gospel. But it is exactly this which the Jews misunderstand. See further Leroy, *Rätsel und Missverständnis*, 82–88.

37. R. E. Brown, *The Gospel According to John*, 1:367. See further Schnackenburg, *The Gospel According to St. John*, 2:223.

38. Clearly Abraham and his works were the object of some discussion in early Christianity (James 2:18–24; Romans 4) and in early Judaism (2 Bar. 57:2, referring to Abraham accomplishing "the works of the commandments"). But there appears to be no direct parallel for *ta erga tou Abraam* ("the works of Abraham"). Thus the meaning of the phrase in John can be determined solely from its immediate context.

39. R. E. Brown, *The Gospel According to John*, 1:357. First Clem. 10:7 states, "Because of his faith and hospitality a son was given him in his old age, and in his obedience he offered him as a sacrifice to God on the mountain which he showed him."

40. See Leenhardt, "Abraham dans Jean 8," 350–351. For an overview of research on the Akedah in the New Testament, see Swetnam, *Jesus and Isaac*, 4–22. Swetnam sees no influence of the Akedah in John 8.

41. Several scholars have pointed to the possibility that there is an implicit reference to the birth of Isaac in John 8:56–57 ("Abraham . . . rejoiced"; cf. Gen. 17:17). See R. E. Brown, *The Gospel According to John*, 1:360; and Schnackenburg, *The Gospel According to St. John*, 2:221–222. Although such an implicit reference is possible, the passage explicitly refers to Abraham rejoicing at Jesus' day.

42. So Dahl, "The Johannine Church and History," 99–119: "To do what Abraham did would have meant to believe in Jesus (8:45)"

(p. 110); Schnackenburg, *The Gospel According to St. John*, 2:221–222; and Schein ("Our Father Abraham," 159), who observes, "In the Johannine sense 'works' become the confession of the believing community."

Chapter 6

1. Of course, it is often very difficult to date early Christian writings with much certainty. I have dealt with this and other important, often technical, issues elsewhere. See Excursus I in chapter 6 of my dissertation "Disinheriting the Jews," 337–351, which includes a discussion of the problems of dating the primary sources, of the fragmentary nature of some sources, of the interrelationship between written and oral traditions, of different recensions of the same writing, and of Christian reworkings of basically Jewish materials.

2. I consider the Gospel of Philip to be a primary source for Valentinian gnostic-Christian controversy with Judaism in mid-second-century Antioch. See Siker, "Gnostic Views on Jews and Christians in the Gospel of Philip," 275–288.

3. Here I would include the Kerygma Petrou, the Apocalypse of Peter, the Protoevangelium of James, the Epistula Apostolorum, Ignatius to the Philadelphians, 1 Clement, the Martyrdom of Polycarp, the Christian appropriations of the Testaments of the Twelve Patriarchs, the Sibylline Oracles, and the Hellenistic synagogal prayers.

4. Here I would include the Epistle to Diognetus and the Apology of Aristides.

5. Abraham also appears in apocryphal Christian writings that are probably later than about 150 C.E., e.g., the Apocalypse of Paul, the Acts of Pilate, Christ's Descent Into Hell, and the Gospel of Bartholomew. As we will see later in this chapter, Abraham is used in these writings in ways very similar to those we found in earlier Christian and Jewish writings.

6. For the Greek text and English translation of the Epistle to Diognetus, I am using the Loeb edition by Lake, *The Apostolic Fathers*, 2:348–379; with reference to the critical edition and translation by Meecham, *The Epistle to Diognetus*. I date the Epistle to Diognetus to about 125–145 C.E. and am inclined to agree with Andriessen that it may be the lost Apology of Quadratus mentioned by Eusebius. (See Andriessen, "L'apologie de Quadratus conservée sous le titre d'Epître à Diognète," 5–39, 125–149, 237–260).

7. It is easy to confuse the Kerygma Petrou with the Kerygmata Petrou because of the similar names. Fragments of the Kerygma Petrou are preserved in the *Stromateis* of Clement of Alexandria. The Kerygmata Petrou is a hypothetical source for the Pseudo-

Clementines, which is a romance that centers around the figure of Clement of Rome. For the Greek text of the fragments of the Kerygma Petrou, I am relying on the critical edition by von Dobschütz, *Das Kerygma Petri kritisch untersucht*. For the English translation, I am using that of W. Schneemelcher in *NTA*, 2:94–102.

8. Coptic text and English translation: Guillaumont, et al., *The Gospel According to Thomas* (Leiden: E. J. Brill, 1959); with reference to the English translation by T. O. Lambdin in *NHL*, 117–130.

9. Greek text and English translation: the Loeb edition by Lake, *The Apostolic Fathers*, 2:309–345.

10. Greek text and English translation: Loeb edition by Lake, *The Apostolic Fathers*, 1:337–409.

11. It is not clear on what basis Barnabas finds a reference to "three boys" in the passage from Numbers 19. I have been unable to find any rabbinic parallels that connect Abraham, Isaac, and Jacob with Numbers 19. The connection must have been apparent to the author of Barnabas. On Barn. 8:4, see the comments of Windisch, *Der Barnabasbrief*, vol. 3 of *Die apostolischen Väter*, 349; and Kraft, *Barnabas and the Didache*, vol. 3 of *The Apostolic Fathers*, 104.

12. The motif of the Jews serving angels rather than God is also found in the Kerygma Petrou and in the Apology of Aristides. In the Kerygma Petrou we find the following: "Neither worship him in the manner of the Jews; for they also, who think that they alone know God, do not understand, worshipping angels and archangels, the months and the moon" (Clem. Alex., *Strom.* 6.5.39–41; *NTA*, 2:100). In chapter 14 of the Syriac recension of the Apology of Aristides, we read: "And in their imagination they conceive that it is God they serve; whereas by their mode of observance it is to the angels and not to God that their service is rendered." Rudolph also notes that Apelles, a disciple of Marcion, "introduced a 'fiery angel' who had fallen away and who is also the God of the Jews,' as the cause of evil" (*Gnosis*, 317; see Eusebius, *Hist. eccl.* 5.13). In addition, Origen even defends the Jews against the charges of Celsus that they worship angels (*Contra Celsum* 1:26; 5:6). Is it possible that the Christian accusation, that Jews worship angels and not God, originates in part from Paul's statement in Gal. 3:19 ("the law . . . was ordained by angels")? See also Acts 7:53; Col. 2:16–18; and Josephus, *Ant.* 15.136, where Herod says in a speech: "And we have learned the noblest of our doctrines and the holiest of our laws through angels sent by God." Thus what in Jewish tradition was no doubt a euphemism intended to preserve God's utter transcendence came in Christian tradition to serve in polemic against Jews.

13. As Kraft notes, "The symbolism of 'T' = the cross (9:8a) was not unknown in the Hellenistic world at large—Lucian (second century), *Judaicum Vocalium* 12, mentions that the cross is constructed

in the form of a '*T*,' and 'is so named by men'!" (*Barnabas and the Didache*, 108, vol. 3 of *The Apostolic Fathers*). See also Windisch, *Der Barnabasbrief*, 350–357, vol. 3 of *Die apostolischen Väter*. Hvalvik ("Barnabas 9.7–9 and the Author's Supposed Use of Gematria," 276–282) has argued that Barn. 9:7–9 is not an example of gematria proper, for Barnabas is interested, not in the numbers behind the letters, but only in the symbolic character of the letters. Hvalvik concludes that this passage is more an "important witness to the origin of *nomina sacra*" (p. 280).

14. Greek text and English translation: Loeb edition by Lake, *The Apostolic Fathers*, 1:166–277.

15. Elsewhere in his letters, Ignatius polemicizes against Judaism especially in Magn. 8:1 and 10:3. The secondary literature touching on these passages is extensive. See especially Barrett, "Jews and Judaizers in the Epistles of Ignatius," 220–244; and Schweizer, "Christianity of the Circumcised and Judaism of the Uncircumcised," 245–260; as well as Schoedel, "Theological Norms and Social Perspectives in Ignatius of Antioch," 1:30–56; Schoedel's commentary, *Ignatius of Antioch*, 202–210; Donahue, "Jewish Christianity in the Letters of Ignatius of Antioch," 81–93; and Grant, "Jewish Christianity at Antioch in the Second Century," 97–108.

16. The image of Christ as a door is, of course, found in the Gospel of John 10:7, 9. It recurs in 1 Clem. 48:4 and the Shepherd of Hermas, Sim. 9.12.2–3.

17. Greek and Syriac texts: the edition by Harris, *The Apology of Aristides on Behalf of the Christians from a Syriac Ms. Preserved on Mount Sinai. Edited with an Introduction and Translation. With an Appendix Containing the Main Portion of the Original Greek Text*, by J. Armitage Robinson. I am also using the edition by Goodspeed, "Aristides, Apologia," in *Die ältesten Apologeten*, 2–25. The English translation is that of Kay, "The Apology of Aristides the Philosopher, Translated from the Greek and from the Syriac Version in Parallel Columns," *ANF*, 9:263–279 (which is based on the text given by Harris and Robinson), with reference to the English translation from the Syriac by Harris (pp. 30–51). For further information on Aristides, see Grant, *Greek Apologists of the Second Century*, 36–45. As Grant notes, the Greek recension is probably earlier than the Syriac recension.

18. The Greek refers to three races, whereas the Syriac mentions four.

19. In chapter 2 of both the Greek and Syriac recensions, Jews and Christians are referred to as "races." The term in Greek, *genos* ("race"), is used as a loan word in the Syriac, *gns*.

20. The notion of Christians being a new race was common in

early Christianity. In addition to Barnabas and the Apology of Aristides, the same assertion is made in the Epistle to Diognetus and the Kerygma Petrou. The Epistle to Diognetus speaks in turn about the Greeks, the Jews, and the Christians. Christians are a *kainon genos*, a "new race" (ch. 1). The Kerygma Petrou asserts that "we are Christians, who as a third race worship him in a new way" (*NTA*, 2:100). This idea no doubt finds its origin in the earliest layers of Christian tradition and was associated with the "new covenant" and Christians as a "new creation." See in particular 1 Peter 2:9; 2 Cor. 3:6; 5:17; and Gal. 6:15. It is interesting to note that the Christian claim to newness appears to have been short-lived, for it presented a vulnerable area which was often attacked by pagan critics. Soon after the separation of Christianity from Judaism, outsiders began to see Christianity as a new superstition. See, e.g., Tacitus, *Annals* 15.44; and Suetonius, *Nero*, 16. Indeed, Justin spends most of his energy in the *Apology* showing how Christianity has its basis in ancient prophecy, and even in Abraham himself. The claim to antiquity was already commonplace in Jewish apologetic literature which responded to Greco-Roman charges of Jewish superstition. See, e.g., Josephus, *Against Apion*; and Collins, *Between Athens and Jerusalem*, 25–59.

21. Heracleon and Marcion can with certainty be dated between Justin and John. Dating the Gospel of Philip is more problematic. See Siker, "Gnostic Views on Jews and Christians in the Gospel of Philip," 275–288.

22. See Layton's sketch of the Valentinian school in *GS*, 267–275.

23. Although Marcion's relationship to gnosis is disputed, I agree with Rudolph's assessment: Marcion "occupies a special place in that he, as it were, stood partly in the gnostic tradition and partly took up a Christian-Pauline position. . . . Marcion's importance lies in many respects outside Gnosis, but he cannot be understood without it and, therefore, belongs to its history" (*Gnosis*, 313).

24. Coptic text: photographic edition by Labib, *Coptic Gnostic Papyri in the Coptic Museum at Old Cairo*, vol. 1, plates 99–134; and critical edition of Ménard, *L'Evangile selon Philippe*, with French translation and extensive commentary. I am also using the translations by Layton, "The Gospel of Philip," in *GS*, 325–353; and W. W. Isenberg, "The Gospel of Philip," in Robinson, *NHL*, 131–151. Unless otherwise noted, the translation used is that of Layton in the *GS*. References given refer to the page and line number of the manuscript (provided in most editions), followed by the page number from the *GS* in parentheses.

25. The translation is from W. W. Isenberg. Layton translates, "When Abraham [. . .] to behold what he was going to behold, [he] circumcised the flesh of the foreskin, telling us that it is fitting to

mortify the flesh" (GS, 351). As Wilson notes in his commentary, "It is clear that circumcision is here treated as a symbol of renunciation of the world and of material things" (The Gospel of Philip, 186). The words "he circumcised" stand at the beginning of a fragmented line (28), and can be made out only with difficulty. Still, nearly every translator posits "he circumcised" as the correct reading.

26. Although we find parallels in Philo that refer to Abraham's circumcision as a portrayal of the "excision of pleasure and all passions," Philo retains the role of physical circumcision in God's covenant with the Jews. He is critical of some Jews who want to spiritualize circumcision completely and to do away with the rite itself (Philo, Migr. 89–93).

27. See Bethge, "Die Ambivalenz alttestamentlicher Geschichtstradition in der Gnosis," 89–109, esp. 99. See also the Tripartite Tractate (NHL, 85–86), another Valentinian gnostic writing, which offers a partial parallel to this passage from the Gospel of Philip. Another gnostic-Christian writing from Nag Hammadi, the Gospel of Thomas, offers a view of circumcision close to Barnabas and in contrast to the Gospel of Philip. In Logion 53 the disciples ask Jesus, " 'Is circumcision beneficial or not?' He said to them, 'If it were beneficial, their father would beget them already circumcised from their mother. Rather, the true circumcision in spirit has become completely profitable' " (trans. T. O. Lambdin, NHL, 124). See also the Odes of Solomon 11:2–3 for a parallel to the Gospel of Philip on circumcision (The Odes of Solomon, ed. and trans. J. H. Charlesworth [Chico, Calif.: Scholars Press, 1977], 52).

28. See Siker, "Gnostic Views on Jews and Christians in the Gospel of Philip," 275–288.

29. Gager, The Origins of Anti-Semitism, 169.

30. I am using the edition by Preuschen, Origenes Werke: Der Johanneskommentar; with reference to Pagels, The Johannine Gospel in Gnostic Exegesis.

31. See Pagels, The Johannine Gospel in Gnostic Exegesis, 98–104.

32. Pagels, The Johannine Gospel in Gnostic Exegesis, 104.

33. Pagels, The Johannine Gospel in Gnostic Exegesis, 101. It is important to note that for Heracleon the Jews have a psychic status along with the non-gnostic Christians. As Pagels notes (p. 101), in Valentinian exegesis of Romans (again referred to by Origen in his own commentary), " 'Abraham' (the demiurge) and the 'children of Abraham' (the psychics), also called 'the circumcised' and 'the Jews,' are said to be justified 'from faith.' "

34. The translation is that of W. H. Rambaut in ANF, 1:470–471.

35. Against Heresies 1.27.3 (ANF, 1:352); see also the discussion in Rudolph, Gnosis, 315.

36. On the connection of the Gospel of Philip to Jewish Christianity, see Siker, "Gnostic Views on Jews and Christians in the Gospel of Philip," 275–288.

37. Greek text: Geffcken, *Oracula Sibyllina*. The English translation is that of J. J. Collins ("Sibylline Oracles," *OTP*, 1:317–472); with reference to the translation by A. Kurfess ("Christian Sibyllines," *NTA*, 2:703–745).

38. Ethiopic and Greek texts: Grebaut, "Littérature éthiopienne pseudo-clementine," *Revue de l'orient chrétien* 12 (1907): 139–145; and 15 (1910): 8–12. The English translations come from the parallel edition of Duensing (Ethiopic trans.) and C. Maurer (Greek trans.) in *NTA*, 2:663–683.

39. Ethiopic and Coptic texts: Duensing, *Epistula Apostolorum nach dem äthiopischen und koptischen Texte herausgegeben*. The English translations come from the edition by Duensing in *NTA*, 1:189–227.

40. Abraham also appears to be in heaven in one of the Hellenistic synagogal prayers from the Apostolic Constitutions. In 8.41.2–5 we read:

> And on behalf of those our brothers who are at rest *in Christ*,
>   let us beg;
>   on behalf of the repose of this brother or that sister,
>   let us beg;
>   that God, the lover of man, having received his soul,
>   may forgive him every sin—voluntary and involuntary;
> and being gracious and favorable,
> may appoint him to a position among the godly ones,
> sent into the embrace of Abraham, and Isaac, and Jacob,
> with all those from of old who were well pleasing, and who did his will;
> where pain and grief and moaning have fled away. (*OTP*, 2:696)

The Testaments of the Twelve Patriarchs (Jud. 25:1) also refer to the resurrection of Abraham (*OTP*, 1:801).

There are several parallels to the otherworldly Abraham in other early Christian literature. See the Apocalypse of Paul (chs. 27, 47, 48, *NTA*, 2:776, 790–792); the Acts of Pilate (14:2; 17:2–18:2, *NTA*, 1:462); and Fifth Esra (1:28–40, *NTA*, 2:689–690); also, of course, Luke 16:19–31.

There are also many parallels to Jewish literature from about the same time period: Apocalypse of Abraham, where Abraham is shown the seven heavens (*OTP*, 1:681–705); 2 Bar. 57:1–2 (*OTP*, 1:641); Apocalypse of Zephaniah 9:2–4; 11:1–6 (*OTP*, 1:514–515); Testament of Isaac 2:5–8; 6:1–13 (*OTP*, 1:903, 905, 907–911); Testament of Jacob 7:22, 25 (*OTP*, 1:916, 918); and 4 Macc. 13:17 (*OTP*, 2:558).

41. See W. D. Davies, *Paul and Rabbinic Judaism*, 268–273; E. P. Sanders, *Paul and Palestinian Judaism*, 183–198; and Marmorstein, *The Doctrine of Merits in Old Rabbinical Literature*.

42. Greek text: Funk, *Didascalia et Constitutiones Apostolorum*; English translation of the Hellenistic synagogal prayers: D. R. Darnell, *OTP*, 2:671–697.

43. Greek text: C. Tischendorf, *Evangelia apocrypha*, 2nd ed. (Leipzig: H. Mendelssohn, 1876), 1–50. The English translation is from O. Cullmann, "The Protoevangelium of James," *NTA*, 1:370–388.

44. Greek text and German translation: Preisendanz, *Papyri Graecae Magicae*. The English translations are my own.

45. I am using the translation by Chadwick, *Origen: Contra Celsum*.

46. See Hauch, "*Omnes Contra Celsum?*" 211–225.

47. Regarding the issue of whether the magical traditions are Jewish, Christian, or pagan in origin, I follow the lead of Goodenough and others, who stress the syncretistic nature of all the magical traditions. Gager puts the situation well: "The magical papyri and amulets reveal such a complex interpenetration of different religious vocabularies and ideas that traditional distinctions break down under the overwhelming weight of syncretism" (*Moses in Greco-Roman Paganism*, 136). See also Bonner, *Studies in Magical Amulets*, especially on an amulet portraying Abraham's sacrifice of Isaac (p. 226); and Siker, "Abraham in Graeco-Roman Paganism," 188–208.

48. The Greek text of the fragment can be found in Wessely, *Les plus anciens monuments du christianisme*, 440, with a French translation. Preisendanz also includes it in *PGM*, 2:210 as fragment P2a, with a German translation. (The English translation is mine.) See also "*phylaktērion*," in G. W. H. Lampe, ed., *A Patristic Greek Lexicon* (Oxford: Clarendon Press, 1961), p. 1492, where the term is listed as referring to an "amulet," to "a phylactery as worn by Jews" to "things used by Christians as protective charms."

49. Abraham was used in several contemporary Jewish prayers. See the Apocalypse of Zephaniah, which portrays Abraham as an intercessor on behalf of petitioners in torment, 11:1–6 (*OTP*, 1:515); the Prayer of Jacob (*OTP*, 2:720–721); the Prayer of Manasseh (*OTP*, 2:628–635); and Pss. Sol. 9:9; 18:3 (*OTP*, 2:661, 669).

50. The underlined portion indicates the interpolation according to Goodenough and Darnell (*OTP*, 2:693). The portrayal of Abraham as a convert from "ancestral godlessness" was common in early Judaism. See especially Sandmel, *Philo's Place in Judaism*.

51. Greek text and English translation: the Loeb edition by Lake, *The Apostolic Fathers*, 1:3–121.

52. See Chadwick, "Justification by Faith and Hospitality," 4:281–285.

Chapter 7

1. References to the *Dialogue* and the *Apology* are taken from the Greek text by Goodspeed, *Die ältesten Apologeten*. English translations, unless otherwise noted, are from Falls, *Saint Justin Martyr*, although I have standardized the spelling of biblical names. On the Greek text of Justin's writings, see especially Pilhofer, "Harnack and Goodspeed: Two Readers of Codex Parisinus Graecus 450," 233–242. Since I am most concerned with Justin's controversy with Judaism, his *Apology* will receive only secondary attention here.

2. By comparison, Moses is mentioned 117 times in the *Dialogue*, and thirty times in the *Apology*. Abraham is also mentioned five times in the *Apology*, three of which occur in a conflated citation of Ex. 3:14–15 (*Apology* 3.7, 11, 17). The other two occurrences appear in significant passages where Justin appeals to Abraham, along with others, as a Christian before Christ's advent: "Those who lived by reason are Christians, even though they have been considered atheists: such as, among the Greeks, Socrates, Heraclitus, and others like them; and among the foreigners, Abraham, Elias, Ananias, Azariu, Misael, and many others" (*Apology* 46.3). (As Falls notes in his translation [p. 84], the last three named are also known as Sidrach, Abdenago, and Misach, familiar from the accounts of the fiery furnace in Dan. 1:7; 3:20–23.) It is interesting that in the first-century work by Pseudo-Philo, Abraham was the first to bear up in the fiery furnace on account of his refusal to worship idols. See Ps.-Philo 6:1–18, in *OTP*, 2:310–312. An account of Abraham in the fiery furnace is also recorded in Gen. Rab. 38:13. Justin again mentions Abraham in passing in the *Apology* 63.17. Although Abraham appears infrequently in the *Apology*, Justin uses him as a pre-Christian witness to Christ.

3. It is unclear exactly when the first day of the discussion ends and the second day begins, and to what extent the *Dialogue* represents an actual situation or is a rhetorical device. On the confusion regarding which day the discussion has entered, see *Dialogue* 56.16; 85.6; 92.5; 122.4. Immediately before the material in 119.3–6, Justin says to Trypho: "As far as possible I am trying to repeat in a brief and concise form what I have already said, for the benefit of those who have come here with you today" (118:4). On the larger structure of the *Dialogue*, see the comments of Falls, *Saint Justin Martyr*, 139–140.

4. The motif of Abraham as a sojourner was important in early Christian literature, since it was easily transferable to Christian exis-

tence in the world. See Acts 7:6, 29; Eph. 2:19; Heb. 11:9; 1 Peter 1:17; 2:11; 1 Clement (the opening salutation); 2 Clem. 5:1, 5; the Martyrdom of Polycarp (the opening salutation); and the Epistle to Diognetus 5:5; 6:8. See also Lanne, "La Xeniteia d'Abraham dans l'oeuvre d'Irénée," 163–187. Of course, this theme is not a Christian invention; it was important also for early Jewish interpretation of Abraham, the classic example being Philo's *De Migratione Abrahami*. See Sandmel, *Philo's Place in Judaism*, 160–167.

5. The term "circumcision" (either *peritemnō* or *peritomē*) occurs eighty times in the *Dialogue* and occupies about 20 percent of the discussion (it is a prominent theme in twenty-five of the 142 chapters). Circumcision seems to represent for Justin the whole of the ritual law, which, he is determined to show, Christ has abolished. In a summary statement, Donahue notes the various rationales Justin uses to argue against circumcision: "Justin first argued from Creation against circumcision in chapter 19. He argued on the basis of the order of the universe in chapter 23. He made the argument from internal consistency in chapter 27" ("Jewish-Christian Controversy in the Second Century," 164). Justin constantly attacks the ritual law, and circumcision in particular. See further Stylianopoulos, *Justin Martyr and the Mosaic Law*, 133–140.

6. Regarding this passage, Donahue remarks, "Justin's formulation of the charge which Jews bring against Christians is rather more striking for what it omits than for what it contains. Justin makes no reference whatever to Christ!" ("Jewish-Christian Controversy in the Second Century," 106). Although Justin here omits reference to Christ, Trypho raises the issue in his reply to Justin, and the identity of the Christ is at issue throughout the *Dialogue*. But it remains striking that in Justin's initial summary of the point at issue, what comes to the fore is the observance of the ritual law, and not christology.

7. See Stylianopoulos (*Justin Martyr and the Mosaic Law*, 45–76), who demonstrates that Justin makes a tripartite division of the law (seen in *Dialogue* 67.4, 10, and esp. 44.2): (1) commandments that by nature are good, i.e., the ethical commandments which are universally and eternally binding principles; (2) commandments legislated on account of the hardness of the Jews' hearts; and (3) commandments which encourage special piety and righteousness beyond what is commanded by nature and reason. The law functions in each of these ways prophetically, pointing to the coming of Christ and the historical dispensation of God's salvation, which in Christ has superseded the ritual law of the Jews.

8. See, e.g., *Dialogue* 19, where circumcision is linked to the keeping of the Sabbath; *Dialogue* 23, where Justin links circumcision to "the sabbaths and the other rites"; *Dialogue* 26, where again

Justin refers to circumcision in connection with "the sabbaths and feasts"; similarly *Dialogue* 27, 43, 46, 47, 92, 113, 114. Justin nearly always begins his lists of Jewish rites with circumcision.

9. Also see Justin's response in 67.3–4 (and Trypho's valid reply in 67.5), along with Trypho's effective response in 27.1. See further Bokser's apologetic, "Justin Martyr and the Jews," 97–122, 204–211.

10. At issue behind this question is how far the *Dialogue* as a whole represents a real debate between Justin and a historical Trypho and how far Justin has made the whole thing up. Related to this is the question of the intended audience(s) of the *Dialogue*, which is much debated. The literature on these points is vast and the issues complicated. The opposing views are represented by Goodenough and Sigal. Goodenough, in his classic study *The Theology of Justin Martyr*, argues that Justin intended the *Dialogue* to be "addressed to a man interested in philosophy and not as a record of a controversy, or a text book for controversy against Judaism" (p. 99). On the other side, Sigal argues that the *Dialogue* is addressed primarily to Jews to convince them of the truth of Christian claims ("An Inquiry Into Aspects of Judaism in Justin's Dialogue with Trypho," 74–100). Stylianopoulos provides a thorough review of the recent discussion on this issue in an appendix to his study ("Are Pagans the Addressees of the Dialogue?" in *Justin Martyr and the Mosaic Law*, 165–195).

11. The similarities between Justin's and Paul's respective use of Abraham naturally raises the question of whether or not Justin knew Paul's letters and used them. There is no direct evidence that Justin knew Paul's letters, since he nowhere unambiguously cites them. Indirect evidence, however, indicates that Justin did know Paul's letters firsthand. As Stylianopoulos notes, "While Justin never refers to Paul, nor does he explicitly quote him, his interpretation of Abraham as an example of justification through faith, not through circumcision, is nevertheless strikingly Pauline and cannot be explained solely on the basis of Genesis 15f" (*Justin Martyr and the Mosaic Law*, 116). See also *Dialogue* 27.3, which, as Falls notes (p. 188 n. 3), seems to be made up of various verses from Rom. 3:11–17. The question, of course, is why Justin did not cite Paul's letters if he knew them. I would suggest two reasons. First, Paul's letters and his heritage were in great dispute at the time Justin was writing. Marcion had co-opted the letters, and for this reason Justin may not have felt that he could appeal to them directly. (For Justin's painful awareness of Marcion, see *Dialogue* 35.6; *Apology* 26.5; 58.1.) Second, Justin is concerned to make his case on the basis of scriptural proofs. This limited him, for the most part, to the Septuagint. Where he does cite the Gospels, he does so

with hesitation and then only to cite the sayings of Jesus. For instance, in *Dialogue* 18.1, Justin excuses his appeal to Jesus' sayings by stating, "Since you, Trypho, admit that you have read the teachings of Him who is our Savior [cf. *Dialogue* 10.2], I do not consider it out of place to have added those few short sayings of His to the quotations from the Prophets." Justin's appeals to sayings of Jesus are intended only as corroborating evidence. Paul's letters would have been even less convincing, especially since they had been co-opted by Marcion.

12. See also *Dialogue* 92.3–4: "For, before his circumcision it was said of him: 'Abraham believed God, and it was reckoned to him as righteousness.' We also, therefore, because of our belief in God through Christ, have the salutary circumcision, namely, that of the heart, even though we are uncircumcised in the flesh" (I have slightly altered Falls's translation here).

13. Justin's argument is similar to what we found in Heb. 7:1–10, perhaps an indication that Justin was familiar with Hebrews. On Heb. 7:1–10, see pp. 90–93 above.

14. See *Dialogue* 19.2–5: "As I already explained . . . circumcision is not essential for all men, but only for you Jews, to mark you off for the suffering you now so deservedly endure. . . . Circumcision, therefore, is necessary only for you Jews, in order that, as [Hosea], one of the twelve Prophets, says, 'thy people should not be a people, and thy nation not a nation' [Hos. 1:9]." See also *Dialogue* 92.2–3, "I have already said, that God in His foreknowledge was aware that your people would deserve to be expelled from Jerusalem and never be allowed to enter there. I have previously shown that you are distinguishable by no other means than by the circumcision of the flesh. Abraham, indeed, was considered just, not by reason of his circumcision, but because of his faith."

15. On the promises to Abraham in early Judaism, see pp. 19–22 above.

16. Exactly who the Genistae, Meristae, and Baptist Pharisees were is unclear.

17. The reference to "the holy mountain of God" is from Isa. 63:18, from which prophet Justin had just made a lengthy citation (Isa. 63:15–19; 64:1–12; *Dialogue* 25).

18. On the whole subject of proselytes in early rabbinic Judaism, see Bamberger, *Proselytism in the Talmudic Period*; Braude, *Jewish Proselytism in the First Five Centuries of the Common Era*; and the chapter on "Jewish Proselytism" in Simon, *Verus Israel*, 271–305.

19. See the discussion in Ruether, *Faith and Fratricide*, especially the section entitled "The Rejection of the Jews and the Election of

the Gentiles" (pp. 124–149), in which Ruether presents materials from various church fathers after Justin.

20. Chapter 47 of the *Dialogue* provides evidence that not all of the Christian contemporaries of Justin were so charitable toward Jewish Christians, whether of Jewish or Gentile origin. When Trypho presses Justin on whether or not one who observes the law and also believes in Christ will be saved, Justin answers, "In my opinion . . . I say such a man will be saved" (47.1). But Trypho then asks further, "But why . . . did you say, 'In my opinion such a man will be saved?' There must, therefore, be other Christians who hold a different opinion" (47.2). And Justin concedes, "Yes, Trypho, . . . there are some Christians who boldly refuse to have conversation or meals with such persons. I don't agree with such Christians. . . . It is my opinion that we Christians should receive them and associate with them in every way as kinsmen and brethren. But if any of your people, Trypho, profess their belief in Christ, and at the same time force the Christian Gentiles to follow the Law instituted through Moses, or refuse to share in communion with them this same common life, I certainly will also not approve of them. But I think that those Gentiles who have been induced to follow the practices of the Jewish Law, and at the same time profess their faith in the Christ of God, will probably be saved" (47.2–4). Justin seems to be aware of a situation similar to that which we find much earlier in Paul's letter to the Galatians.

21. The most extensive treatment of Justin's interpretation of the theophany at Mamre is Kominiak, *The Theophanies of the Old Testament in the Writings of St. Justin*, 23–47. See also Armstrong (*Die Genesis in der alten Kirche*, 18–51), who provides a thorough overview of Justin's use of Genesis as well as a fine analysis of the theophanies (pp. 42–48).

22. See Hay, *Glory at the Right Hand: Psalm 110 in Early Christianity*, 47–51; and Juel, *Messianic Exegesis: Christological Interpretation of the Old Testament in Early Christianity*, 135–150.

23. Kominiak (*The Theophanies of the Old Testament in the Writings of St. Justin*, 41). offers the following concise formulation of Justin's scriptural proof:

"According to Scripture, the Lord who appeared to Abraham is God (Gen. 18,13–14; 21,12).

"This Lord who appeared to Abraham is the same Lord who destroyed Sodom (Gen. 18,17–23; 19,18–25).

"Therefore, the Lord who destroyed Sodom is distinct from God the Creator in heaven (Gen. 19,24).

"Therefore, the God who appeared to Abraham is distinct from God the Creator in heaven."

24. See Andresen, "Justin und der mittlere Platonismus," 157–

195. Andresen shows conclusively that Justin was heavily influenced by Middle Platonism, and that his notion of the utterly impassible nature of God the Father and Creator is attributable to Justin's prior commitment to this philosophical stance.

25. The form of Justin's citation parallels almost exactly the Greek text of Matthew (Nestle-Aland, 26th ed.). For Justin's Gospel citations, see Bellinzoni, *The Sayings of Jesus in the Writings of Justin Martyr*.

26. Justin is referring here to the accounts of Isaiah's death alluded to in Heb. 11:37 and preserved in the *Martyrdom and Ascension of Isaiah*, ch. 5, which may be found in *OTP*, 2:143–176.

Chapter 8

1. Thus Abraham was often seen as having observed the law himself, and the election of David was understood in the light of God's election of Abraham. On Abraham's observance of the law, see p. 23 above. On the connection between Abraham and David, see Clements, *Abraham and David: Genesis 15 and Its Meaning for Israelite Tradition*.

2. See pp. 36–38, 61–62 above. Similarly, Martyn, "Paul and His Jewish-Christian Interpreters," 1–15.

3. This position is also one that the Teachers in Galatia, as well as other Jewish Christians, would probably have affirmed, given their attitude to circumcision and the law.

4. James probably belongs to this generation also, but he does not appear concerned with either Gentile inclusion or Jewish exclusion.

5. On the *adversus judaeos* literature in general, see especially Williams, *Adversus Judaeos: A Bird's Eye View of Christian Apologiae Until the Renaissance*; Simon, *Verus Israel*; and Ruether, *Faith and Fratricide*.

6. The Kerygmata Petrou and the later Pseudo-Clementines (H II,16.5; R I,33.1), whether Ebionite or not, may provide examples of this. See further Schoeps, *Jewish Christianity*; and Martyn, "Persecution and Martyrdom," in *The Gospel of John in Christian History*, 55–89, which includes an appendix containing the translation of the Pseudo-Clementine Recognitions 1,33–71 (pp. 122–147).

7. Acts 11:1–3 may provide evidence for Luke's awareness of such Jewish Christians. Matthew may also be struggling with Jewish Christians reluctant to move beyond Jesus' commission in 10:5–6.

8. See Meeks and Wilken, *Jews and Christians in Antioch in the First Four Centuries of the Common Era*; Wilken, *John Chrysostom and the Jews*; and Simon, *Verus Israel*, 271–338.

9. To rephrase the question, Does Christian exclusion of the Jews

have a status comparable to the doctrine of the trinity, which many theologians argue is inherent in the earliest Christian identity?

10. See here especially Beker, *Paul the Apostle*.

11. Cf. *Dialogue* 26.1–3; 28.5, 6; 29.1; 41.2–3; 47.1, 3; 52.4; 64.1; 65.4–7; 73.3–5; 109.1; 120.3–4.

12. On the *Birkat ha-Minim*, see the discussion of Katz, "Issues in the Separation of Judaism and Christianity After 70 C.E.: A Reconsideration," 43–76. On the Council of Jamnia, see Cohen, "The Significance of Yavneh: Pharisees, Rabbis, and the End of Jewish Sectarianism," 27–53.

13. An interesting parallel can be found in the traditions of ancient Israel where the Deuteronomist equates Jewish inclusion with Gentile exclusion (e.g., Deut. 7:1–6).

14. Boers, *Theology out of the Ghetto*, 92.

15. Boers, *Theology out of the Ghetto*, 102–103.

16. "Significant for a theology out of the ghetto is the fact . . . that Paul himself pierced his own system of thought in Rom. 4, even if he probably did not intend to do so. . . . Paul almost certainly would not have conceded an analogy between the faith of Abraham and the faith in Christ if he had to concede at the same time that the former had nothing specifically to do with Christ" (Boers, *Theology out of the Ghetto*, 101).

17. This is my translation of the verse.

18. While I agree with Ruether that anti-Judaism has in effect been the left hand of christology throughout the history of Christianity, I do not think that anti-Judaism is an implicit theological necessity of christology. I disagree with Ruether's assessment that for Paul "Christians, not Jews, are the true offspring of Abraham and heirs of the promise" (*Faith and Fratricide*, 98). Ruether's statement is an example of the failure to remember Paul's statement in Rom. 11:28b. On the other side of the coin, Gaston, in his response to Ruether, argues that "for Paul, Jesus was neither a new Moses nor the messiah, nor the climax of the history of God's dealing with Israel, but the fulfillment of God's promises concerning the gentiles, and this is what he accused the Jews of not recognizing" ("Paul and the Torah," 66). I think Gaston is fundamentally wrong here, failing to see that Paul does believe that Jesus suffered and died for Jew and Gentile alike.

19. A discussion of the extensive contemporary dialogue between Christians and Jews, based in part on Abraham, lies beyond the scope of this study. On the Jewish/Christian dialogue's use of Paul's consideration of Abraham, see for example the issue of *Face to Face* 13 (1986), which contains a series of articles devoted entirely to a consideration of "Abraham in Judaism, Christianity and Islam," although it is conspicuous that it avoids completely the Gospel of

John. See also Mussner, *Tractate on the Jews: The Significance of Judaism for Christian Faith*, 146–149; von der Osten-Sacken, *Christian-Jewish Dialogue: Theological Foundations*, 19–40; Koenig, *Jews and Christians in Dialogue*, 44–46; Gager, *The Origins of Anti-Semitism*, 217–220, 223–225, 235–241; Boers, *Theology out of the Ghetto*, 74–106; and Beker, *Paul the Apostle*, 337–347.

20. Dahl, "The Future of Israel," 158.

Bibliography
(Works Cited)

Primary Sources, Translations, and Tools

Chadwick, H. *Origen: Contra Celsum.* Cambridge: Cambridge University Press, 1953.

Charlesworth, J. H., ed. *The Old Testament Pseudepigrapha.* Vol. 1, *Apocalyptic Literature and Testaments.* Garden City, N.Y.: Doubleday & Co., 1983.

———, ed. *The Old Testament Pseudepigrapha.* Vol. 2, *Expansions of the "Old Testament" and Legends, Wisdom and Philosophical Literature, Prayers, Psalms, and Odes, Fragments of Lost Judeo-Hellenistic Works.* Garden City, N.Y.: Doubleday & Co., 1985.

Colson, F. H., and G. H. Whitaker, eds. and trans. *Philo.* 10 vols.; 2 supplements. Loeb Classical Library. London: W. Heinemann, 1929–1964.

de Jonge, M. *The Testaments of the Twelve Patriarchs.* Leiden: E. J. Brill, 1978.

Dobschütz, E. von. *Das Kerygma Petri kritisch untersucht.* TU 11. Leipzig: J. C. Hinrichs, 1893.

Duensing, H. *Epistula Apostolorum nach dem äthiopischen und koptischen Texte herausgegeben.* Kleine Texte 152. Bonn: A. Marcus and E. Weber, 1925.

Falls, T. B. *Saint Justin Martyr.* New York: Christian Heritage, 1948.

Funk, F. X. *Didascalia et Constitutiones Apostolorum.* Paderborn: Ferdinand Schoeningh, 1905.

Geffcken, J. *Komposition und Entstehungszeit der Oracula Sibyllina.* Die griechisch-christlichen Schriftsteller 8. Leipzig: J. C. Hinrichs, 1902.

Goodspeed, E. J. *Die ältesten Apologeten.* Göttingen: Vandenhoeck & Ruprecht, 1914.

Grebaut, S. "Littérature éthiopienne pseudo-clementine." *Revue de l'orient chrétien* 12 (1907): 139–145; 15 (1910): 8–12.

Guillaumont, A., et al. *The Gospel According to Thomas*. Leiden: E. J. Brill, 1959.

Hall, S. G., trans. and ed. *Melito of Sardis on Pascha and Fragments*. Oxford: Clarendon Press, 1979.

Harris, J. R. *The Apology of Aristides on Behalf of the Christians from a Syriac Ms. Preserved on Mount Sinai. Edited with an Introduction and Translation. With an Appendix Containing the Main Portion of the Original Greek Text*, by J. A. Robinson. 2nd ed. Texts and Studies 1.1. Cambridge: Cambridge University Press, 1893.

Hennecke, E. *New Testament Apocrypha*. Edited by W. Schneemelcher; English translation edited by R. McL. Wilson. 2 vols. Philadelphia: Westminster Press, 1963–1965.

Kay, D. M. "The Apology of Aristides the Philosopher, Translated from the Greek and from the Syriac Version in Parallel Columns." In *Ante-Nicene Fathers*, 9:263–279. New York: Charles Scribner's Sons, 1925.

Kraft, R. A. *Barnabas and the Didache*. Vol. 3 of *The Apostolic Fathers: A New Translation*, edited by R. M. Grant. New York: Thomas Nelson & Sons, 1965.

Labib, P. *Coptic Gnostic Papyri in the Coptic Museum at Old Cairo*. Vol. 1. Cairo: Government Press, 1956.

Lake, K., ed. and trans. *The Apostolic Fathers*. 2 vols. Loeb Classical Library. Cambridge: Harvard University Press, 1912–1913; reprinted 1977.

———, ed. and trans. *Eusebius: The Ecclesiastical History*. 2 vols. Loeb Classical Library. London: W. Heinemann, 1926.

Layton, B. *The Gnostic Scriptures: A New Translation*. Garden City, N.Y.: Doubleday & Co., 1987.

Meecham, H. G. *The Epistle to Diognetus: The Greek Text with Introduction, Translation and Notes*. Manchester: Manchester University Press, 1949.

Ménard, J. E. *L'Evangile selon Philippe: Introduction, texte, traduction, commentaire*. Strasbourg: Université de Strasbourg, 1967.

Metzger, B. M. *A Textual Commentary on the Greek New Testament*. 3rd ed. London: United Bible Societies, 1971.

Preisendanz, K. *Papyri Graecae Magicae*. 3 vols. Leipzig: Teubner, 1928–1941.

Preuschen, E., ed. *Origenes Werke: Der Johanneskommentar*. Die griechische-christliche Schriftsteller 10. Leipzig: J. C. Hinrichs, 1903.

Robinson, J. M., ed. *The Nag Hammadi Library in English*. San Francisco: Harper & Row, 1977.

Sparks, H. F. D., ed. *Apocryphal Old Testament*. Oxford: Oxford
University Press, 1984.

Strack, H. L. and P. Billerbeck. *Kommentar zum Neuen Testament
aus Talmud und Midrasch*. 6 vols. Munich: Verlag C. H. Beck,
1922–1928.

Thackeray, H. St. J., and R. Marcus, eds. *Josephus*. 10 vols. Loeb
Classical Library. London: W. Heinemann, 1926–1965.

Vermès, G., ed. and trans. *The Dead Sea Scrolls in English*. 3rd ed.
London: Penguin Books, 1987.

Wessely, C., ed. *Les plus anciens monuments du christianisme*. Patro-
logia Orientalis 18. Paris: Firmin-Didot, 1924.

Wilson, R. McL. *The Gospel of Philip*. New York: Harper & Row,
1962.

Secondary Literature

"Abraham in Judaism, Christianity and Islam." *Face to Face: An In-
terreligious Bulletin* 13 (1986).

Aageson, J. W. "Scripture and Structure in the Development of the
Argument in Romans 9–11." *CBQ* 48 (1986): 265–289.

Alvarez, J. "Apostolic Writings and the Roots of Anti-Semitism." In
Studia Patristica, vol. 13. Edited by E. A. Livingstone. TU 116.
Berlin: Akademie-Verlag, 1975.

Andresen, C. "Justin und der mittlere Platonismus." *ZNW* 44
(1952/53): 157–195.

Andriessen, P. "L'apologie de Quadratus conservée sous le titre
d'Epître à Diognète." *Recherches de théologie ancienne et
médiévale* 13 (1946): 5–39, 125–149, 237–260.

Andriessen, P. C. B. "La teneur judéo-chrétienne de He I 6 et II
14b–III 2." *NovT* 18 (1976): 293–313.

Armstrong, G. T. *Die Genesis in der alten Kirche*. Tübingen:
J. C. B. Mohr (Paul Siebeck), 1962.

Ashton, J. "The Identity and Function of the *Ioudaioi* in the Fourth
Gospel." *NovT* 27 (1985): 40–75.

Attridge, H. *The Epistle to the Hebrews*. Philadelphia: Fortress Press,
1989.

Aune, D. E. "Justin Martyr's Use of the Old Testament." *Bulletin of
the Evangelical Theological Society* 9 (1966): 179–197.

Bacon, B. W. "Stephen's Speech: Its Argument and Doctrinal Rela-
tionship." In *Biblical and Semitic Studies: Critical and Historical
Essays by the Members of the Semitic and Biblical Faculty of Yale
University*, 213–276. New York: Charles Scribner's Sons, 1901.

Bacq, P. *De l'ancienne à la nouvelle alliance*. Paris, 1978.

Baird, W. "Abraham in the New Testament: Tradition and the New
Identity." *Interpretation* 42 (1988): 367–379.

Bamberger, B. *Proselytism in the Talmudic Period.* Cincinnati: Hebrew Union College Press, 1939.

Bammel, E. *"ptōchos." TDNT,* 6:888–915.

Barclay, J. M. G. "Mirror-Reading a Polemical Letter: Galatians as a Test Case." *JSNT* 31 (1987): 73–93.

Barrett, C. K. "Paul and the 'Pillar' Apostles." In *Studia Paulina in Honorem J. de Zwaan,* 1–17. Haarlem: Bohn, 1953.

_____. *The Epistle to the Romans.* New York: Harper & Brothers, 1957.

_____. *From First Adam to Last Adam: A Study in Pauline Theology.* London: Adam & Charles Black, 1962.

_____. "Paul's Opponents in II Corinthians." *NTS* 17 (1971): 233–254.

_____. "Jews and Judaizers in the Epistles of Ignatius." In *Jews, Greeks, and Christians,* edited by R. Hamerton-Kelly and R. Scroggs, 220–244. Leiden: E. J. Brill, 1976.

_____. "The Allegory of Abraham, Sarah, and Hagar in the Argument of Galatians." In *Rechtfertigung: Festschrift für Ernst Käsemann zum 70. Geburtstag,* edited by J. Friedrich, 1–16. Tübingen and Göttingen: J. C. B. Mohr (Paul Siebeck) and Vandenhoeck & Ruprecht, 1976.

_____. *The Gospel According to St. John.* 2nd ed. Philadelphia: Westminster Press, 1978.

Bartholomew, G. L. "An Early Christian Sermon-Drama: John 8:31–59." Ph.D. dissertation, Union Theological Seminary, N.Y., 1974.

Bassler, J. *Divine Impartiality: Paul and a Theological Axiom.* SBLDS 59. Chico, Calif.: Scholars Press, 1982.

Beers, B. *Leben Abrahams.* Leipzig: Oskar Leiner, 1859.

Beker, J. C. *Paul the Apostle.* Philadelphia: Fortress Press, 1980.

_____. "The Faithfulness of God and the Priority of Israel in Paul's Letter to the Romans." In *Christians Among Jews and Gentiles: Essays in Honor of Krister Stendahl on His Sixty-fifth Birthday,* edited by G. W. E. Nickelsburg with G. W. MacRae, S.J., 10–16. Philadelphia: Fortress Press, 1986.

Bellinzoni, A. J. *The Sayings of Jesus in the Writings of Justin Martyr.* Leiden: E. J. Brill, 1967.

Berger, K. "Abraham in den paulinischen Hauptbriefen." *Münster theologische Zeitschrift* 17 (1966): 47–89.

Bethge, H.-G. "Die Ambivalenz alttestamentlicher Geschichtstradition in der Gnosis." In *Alte Testament—Frühjudentum—Gnosis,* edited by K. Tröger, 89–109. Gütersloh: Gütersloher Verlagshaus Gerd Mohn, 1980.

Betz, H. D. *Galatians.* Philadelphia: Fortress Press, 1979.

Bihler, J. *Die Stephanusgeschichte.* Munich: Max Hueber Verlag, 1963.

Billerbeck, P. "Abrahams Leben und Bedeutung nach Auffassung der älteren Haggada." *Nathanael* 15 (1899): 43–57, 118–128, 137–157, 161–179; 16 (1900): 33–57, 65–80.

———, and H. L. Strack. *Kommentar zum Neuen Testament aus Talmud und Midrasch.* 6 vols. Munich: Verlag C. H. Beck, 1922–1928.

Blank, J. *Krisis: Untersuchungen zur johanneischen Christologie und Eschatologie.* Freiburg: Lambertus-Verlag, 1964.

Boers, H. *Theology out of the Ghetto.* Leiden: E. J. Brill, 1971.

Bogaert, P. M., ed. *Abraham dans la Bible et dans la tradition juive.* Brussels: Institutum Iudaicum, 1977.

Bokser, B. Z. "Justin Martyr and the Jews." *The Jewish Quarterly Review* 64 (1973/74): 97–122, 204–211.

Bonner, C. *Studies in Magical Amulets.* Ann Arbor, Mich.: University of Michigan Press, 1950.

Bonsirven, J. *Le judaïsme palestinien.* Vol. 1. Paris, 1934.

Braude, W. G. *Jewish Proselytism in the First Five Centuries of the Common Era.* Providence, R.I.: Brown University Press, 1940.

Brawley, R. L. *Luke-Acts and the Jews: Conflict, Apology, and Conciliation.* SBLMS 33. Atlanta: Scholars Press, 1987.

Brown, R. E. *The Gospel According to John.* Vol. 1. Garden City, N.Y.: Doubleday & Co., 1966.

———. *The Birth of the Messiah.* Garden City, N.Y.: Doubleday & Co., 1977.

———. *The Epistles of John.* Garden City, N.Y.: Doubleday & Co., 1982.

———. "Not Jewish Christianity and Gentile Christianity, but Types of Jewish/Gentile Christianity." *CBQ* 45 (1983): 74–79.

———. "Gospel Infancy Narrative Research from 1976 to 1986: Part 1 (Matthew)." *CBQ* 48 (1986): 468–483.

———. "Gospel Infancy Narrative Research from 1976 to 1986: Part II (Luke)." *CBQ* 48 (1986): 660–680.

Brown, S. "The Matthean Community and the Gentile Mission." *NovT* 22 (1980): 193–221.

Bruce, F. F. *The Epistle to the Hebrews.* Grand Rapids: Wm. B. Eerdmans Publishing Co., 1964.

Buss, M. F.-J. *Die Missionspredigt des Apostels Paulus im Pisidischen Antiochien.* Stuttgart: Verlag Katholisches Bibelwerk, 1980.

Callan, T. "Pauline Midrash: The Exegetical Background of Gal 3:19b." *JBL* 99 (1980): 549–567.

Campbell, W. S. "The Romans Debate." *JSNT* 10 (1981): 19–28.

———. "The Freedom and Faithfulness of God in Relation to Israel." *JSNT* 13 (1981): 27–45.

_____. "The Place of Romans IX–XI Within the Structure and Thought of the Letter." In *Studia Evangelica*, vol. 7. Edited by E. A. Livingstone, 121–131. Berlin: Akademie-Verlag, 1982.

Chadwick, H. "Justification by Faith and Hospitality." In *Studia Patristica*, vol. 4. Edited by F. L. Cross, 281–285. TU 79. Berlin: Akademie-Verlag, 1961.

Clements, R. E. *Abraham and David: Genesis 15 and Its Meaning for Israelite Tradition*. London: SCM Press, 1967.

Cohen, S. J. D. "The Significance of Yavneh: Pharisees, Rabbis, and the End of Jewish Sectarianism." *HUCA* 55 (1984): 27–53.

Collins, J. J. *Between Athens and Jerusalem: Jewish Identity in the Hellenistic Diaspora*. New York: Crossroad, 1983.

Cosgrove, C. H. "Justification in Paul: A Linguistic and Theological Reflection." *JBL* 106 (1987): 653–670.

Cranfield, C. E. B. *The Epistle to the Romans*. Vols. 1, 2. Edinburgh: T. & T. Clark, 1975, 1979.

Dahl, N. A. "A People for His Name." *NTS* 4 (1957/58): 319–327.

_____. "Der Erstgeboren Satans und der Vater des Teufels (Polyk. 7,1 und Joh. 8,44)." In *Apophoreta: Festschrift für Ernst Haenchen*, edited by W. Eltester, 70–84. Beiheft zur ZNW 30. Berlin: Alfred Töpelmann, 1964.

_____. "The Story of Abraham in Luke-Acts." In *Jesus in the Memory of the Early Church*, 66–86. Minneapolis: Augsburg Publishing House, 1976.

_____. "The Johannine Church and History." In *Jesus in the Memory of the Early Church*, 99–119. Minneapolis: Augsburg Publishing House, 1976.

_____. "The Future of Israel." In *Studies in Paul*, 137–159. Minneapolis: Augsburg Publishing House, 1977.

Daly, R. " The Soteriological Significance of the Sacrifice of Isaac." *CBQ* 39 (1977): 45–75.

Daniélou, J. "Abraham dans la tradition chrétienne." In *Abraham, Père des croyants*, edited by Cardinal Tisserant, 68–87. Cahiers Sioniens 5. Paris: Editions du Cerf, 1952.

_____. "Les quatre-temps de septembre et la fête des tabernacles." *Le maison Dieu* 46 (1956): 114–136.

Daube, D. *The New Testament and Rabbinic Judaism*. London: Athlone Press, 1956.

Davies, P., and B. Chilton. "The Aqedah: A Revised Tradition History." *CBQ* 40 (1978): 514–546.

Davies, W. D. *Paul and Rabbinic Judaism*. London: SPCK, 1948.

_____. *The Gospel and the Land: Early Christianity and Jewish Territorial Doctrine*. Berkeley and Los Angeles: University of California Press, 1974.

————. "Paul and the People of Israel." In *Jewish and Pauline Studies*, 123–152. Philadelphia: Fortress Press, 1984.

————, and D. Allison. *The Gospel According to Saint Matthew*. Vol. 1. Edinburgh: T. & T. Clark, 1988.

Degenhardt, H.-J. *Lukas, Evangelist der Armen: Besitz und Besitzverzicht in den lukanischen Schriften*. Stuttgart: Verlag Katholisches Bibelwerk, 1965.

de Jonge, M. "Jewish Expectations About the 'Messiah' According to the Fourth Gospel." *NTS* 19 (1972/73): 246–270.

————. "The Son of God and the Children of God." In *Jesus: Stranger from Heaven and Son of God*, translated and edited by J. E. Steely, 141–168. Missoula, Mont.: Scholars Press, 1977.

Démann, P. "La signification d'Abraham dans la perspective du Nouveau Testament." In *Abraham, Père des croyants*, edited by Cardinal Tisserant, 44–67. Cahiers Sioniens 5. Paris: Editions du Cerf, 1952.

Demarest, B. *A History of Interpretation of Hebrews 7, 1–10 from the Reformation to the Present*. Tübingen: J. C. B. Mohr (Paul Siebeck), 1976.

de Menasce, P.-J. "Traditions juives sur Abraham." In *Abraham, Père des croyants*, edited by Cardinal Tisserant, 96–103. Cahiers Sioniens 5. Paris: Editions du Cerf, 1952.

Dibelius, M. *James*. Revised and edited by H. Greeven. Philadelphia: Fortress Press, 1975.

Dietzfelbinger, C. "Paulus und das Alte Testament: Die Hermeneutik des Paulus, untersucht an seiner Deutung der Gestalt Abrahams." *Theologische Existenz heute* 95 (1961): 1–41.

Dodd, C. H. *The Interpretation of the Fourth Gospel*. Cambridge: Cambridge University Press, 1953.

————. "Behind a Johannine Dialogue." In *More New Testament Studies*, 41–57. Grand Rapids: Wm. B. Eerdmans Publishing Co., 1968.

Donahue, P. J. "Jewish-Christian Controversy in the Second Century: A Study in the Dialogue of Justin Martyr." Ph.D. dissertation, Yale University, 1973.

————. "Jewish Christianity in the Letters of Ignatius of Antioch." *VC* 32 (1978): 81–93.

Donaldson, T. L. "The 'Curse of the Law' and the Inclusion of the Gentiles: Galatians 3.13–14." *NTS* 32 (1986): 94–112.

Donfried, K. P., ed. *The Romans Debate*. Minneapolis: Augsburg Publishing Co., 1977.

Dozeman, T. B. "*Sperma Abraam* in John 8 and Related Literature: Cosmology and Judgment." *CBQ* 42 (1980): 342–358.

Dunn, J. D. G. "Jewish Christianity." In *Unity and Diversity in the New Testament*. Philadelphia: Westminster Press, 1977.

_____. "The New Perspective on Paul." *BJRL* 65 (1983) 95–122.

_____. "Works of the Law and the Curse of the Law (Galatians 3:10–14)." *NTS* 31 (1985): 523–542.

Dupont, J. "Le salut des gentils et la signification théologique du livre des Actes." *NTS* 6 (1960): 132–155.

_____. *The Salvation of the Gentiles: Essays on the Acts of the Apostles*. New York: Paulist Press, 1979.

Ellingworth, P. " 'Like the Son of God': Form and Content in Hebrews 7, 1–10." *Biblica* 64 (1983): 255–262.

Epp, E. J. "Jewish-Gentile Continuity in Paul: Torah and/or Faith? (Romans 9:1–5)." In *Christians Among Jews and Gentiles: Essays in Honor of Krister Stendahl on his Sixty-fifth Birthday*, edited by G. W. E. Nickelsburg with G. W. MacRae, S.J., 80–90. Philadelphia: Fortress Press, 1986.

Falls, T. B. *Saint Justin Martyr*. New York: Christian Heritage, 1948.

Farris, S. *The Hymns of Luke's Infancy Narratives: Their Origin, Meaning and Significance*. JSNT Supplement 9. Sheffield: JSOT Press, 1985.

Ferguson, E. "A New Journal." *SecC* 1 (1981): 3–4.

Finn, T. M. "The God-fearers Reconsidered." *CBQ* 47 (1985): 75–84.

Fitzmyer, J. *The Gospel According to Luke I–IX*. Anchor Bible. Garden City, N.Y.: Doubleday & Co., 1981.

_____. *The Gospel According to Luke X–XXIV*. Anchor Bible. Garden City, N.Y.: Doubleday & Co., 1985.

Foerster, W. "Die *dokountes* in Gal. 2." *ZNW* 36 (1937): 286–292.

Freed, E. D. "Who or What Was Before Abraham in John 8:58?" *JSNT* 17 (1983): 52–59.

Furnish, V. P. *II Corinthians*. Anchor Bible. Garden City, N.Y.: Doubleday & Co., 1984.

Gager, J. G. *Moses in Greco-Roman Paganism*. Nashville: Abingdon Press, 1972.

_____. *The Origins of Anti-Semitism: Attitudes Towards Judaism in Pagan and Christian Antiquity*. Oxford: Oxford University Press, 1983.

_____. "Jews, Gentiles, and Synagogues in the Book of Acts." In *Christians Among Jews and Gentiles: Essays in Honor of Krister Stendahl on His Sixty-fifth Birthday*, edited by G. W. E. Nickelsburg with G. W. MacRae, S.J., 91–99. Philadelphia: Fortress Press, 1986.

Gamble, H. Y., Jr. *The Textual History of the Letter to the Romans: A Study in Textual and Literary Criticism*. Grand Rapids: Wm. B. Eerdmans Publishing Co., 1977.

Gaston, L. "Paul and the Torah." In *Antisemitism and the Foundations of Christianity*, edited by A. T. Davies, 48–71. New York: Paulist Press, 1979.

————. "Abraham and the Righteousness of God." *HBT* 2 (1980): 39–71.

————. "Israel's Enemies in Pauline Theology." *NTS* 28 (1982): 400–423.

————. "Paul and the Law in Galatians 2–3." In *Anti-Judaism in Early Christianity*, edited by P. Richardson and D. Granskou. Vol. 1, *Paul and the Gospels*, 37–58. Waterloo, Ontario: Canadian Corporation for Studies in Religion, Wilfrid Laurier University Press, 1986.

Gelin, A. *The Poor of Yahweh*. Collegeville, Minn.: Liturgical Press, 1964.

Georgi, D. *The Opponents of Paul in Second Corinthians*. Neukirchen-Vluyn: Neukirchener Verlag, 1964; Epilogue, 1986; Philadelphia: Fortress Press, 1986.

Ginzberg, L. B. *Legends of the Jews*. 7 vols. Philadelphia: Jewish Publication Society, 1956.

Goodenough, E. R. *The Theology of Justin Martyr*. Jena: Verlag Frommannsche Buchhandlung (Walter Biedermann), 1923.

Goppelt, L. "Paul and Heilsgeschichte: Conclusions from Romans 4 and I Corinthians 10:1–13." *Interpretation* 21 (1967): 315–326.

————. *Der erste Petrusbrief*. Göttingen: Vandenhoeck & Ruprecht, 1978.

Grant, R. M. "Jewish Christianity at Antioch in the Second Century." *Recherches de science religieuse* 60 (1972): 97–108.

————. *Greek Apologists of the Second Century*. Philadelphia: Westminster Press, 1988.

Grässer, E. "Die antijüdische Polemik im Johannesevangelium." *NTS* 11 (1964/65): 74–90.

————. "Die Juden als Teufelssöhne in Johannes 8, 37–47." In *Antijudaismus im Neuen Testament?* edited by W. P. Eckert, N. P. Levinson, and M. Stöhr, 157–170. Munich: Chr. Kaiser Verlag, 1967.

Grundmann, W. *Das Evangelium nach Matthäus*. 5th ed. Berlin: Evangelische Verlagsanstalt, 1981.

Guerra, A. J. "Romans 4 as Apologetic Theology." *HTR* 81 (1988): 251–270.

Gundry, R. *Matthew: His Literary and Theological Artistry*. Grand Rapids: Wm. B. Eerdmans Publishing Co., 1982.

Haenchen, E. *The Acts of the Apostles*. Translated by B. Noble and G. Shinn. 14th ed. Philadelphia: Westminster Press, 1971.

Hahn, F. "Das Gesetzesverständnis im Römer und Galaterbrief." *ZNW* 67 (1976/77): 29–63.

Halperin, D. J. Review of *Jewish and Christian Self-Definition*, edited by E. P. Sanders et al. *RSR* 11 (1985): 133–136.

Hamm, M. D. "The Freeing of the Bent Woman and the Restoration of Israel: Luke 13:10–17 as Narrative Theology," *JSNT* 31 (1987): 23–44.

Hansen, G. W. *Abraham in Galatians: Epistolary and Rhetorical Contexts*. JSNT Suppl. 29. Sheffield: Sheffield Academic Press, 1989.

Hare, D. R. A. *The Theme of Jewish Persecution of Christians in the Gospel According to St. Matthew*. Cambridge: Cambridge University Press, 1967.

Harnack, A. von. *Judentum und Judenchristentum in Justins Dialog mit Trypho*. TU 9.1. Leipzig: J. C. Hinrichs, 1913.

Hauch, R. J. "*Omnes Contra Celsum?*" *SecC* 5 (1985/86): 211–225.

Hay, D.M. *Glory at the Right Hand: Psalm 110 in Early Christianity*. Nashville: Abingdon Press, 1973.

Hays, R. B. *The Faith of Jesus Christ*. SBLDS 56. Chico, Calif.: Scholars Press, 1983.

————. " 'Have We Found Abraham to Be Our Forefather According to the Flesh?' A Reconsideration of Rom 4:1." *NovT* 27 (1985): 76–98.

Higgins, A. J. B. "Jewish Messianic Belief in Justin Martyr's Dialogue with Trypho." *NovT* 9 (1967): 298–305.

Hock, R. F. "Lazarus and Micyllus: Greco-Roman Backgrounds to Luke 16:19–31." *JBL* 106 (1987): 447–463.

Hoffmann, P. "*Pantes ergatai adikias*: Redaktion und Tradition in Lc 13,22–30." *ZNW* 58 (1967): 188–214.

Holtz, T. *Untersuchungen über die alttestamentlichen Zitate bei Lukas*. TU 104. Berlin: Akademie-Verlag, 1968.

Horton, F. J. *The Melchizedek Tradition*. Cambridge: Cambridge University Press, 1967.

Howard, G. "Romans 3:21–31 and the Inclusion of the Gentiles." *HTR* 63 (1970): 223–233.

————. *Paul: Crisis in Galatia*. Cambridge: Cambridge University Press, 1979.

Hübner, H. "Identitätsverlust und paulinische Theologie." *Kerygma und Dogma* 24 (1978): 181–193.

————. *Law in Paul's Thought*. Translated by J. C. G. Greig. Edinburgh: T. & T. Clark, 1984.

Hulen, A. B. "The 'Dialogues with the Jews' as Sources for the Early Jewish Argument Against Christianity." *JBL* 51 (1932): 58–70.

Hultgren, A. J. *Jesus and His Adversaries: The Form and Function of the Conflict Stories in the Synoptic Tradition*. Minneapolis: Augsburg Publishing House, 1979.

Hummel, R. *Die Auseinandersetzung zwischen Kirche und Judentum im Matthäusevangelium*. Munich: Chr. Kaiser Verlag, 1966.

Hvalvik, R. "Barnabas 9.7–9 and the Author's Supposed Use of Gematria." *NTS* 33 (1987): 276–282.

Jacobs, I. "The Midrashic Background for James II.21–3." *NTS* 22 (1975/76): 457–464.

Jervell, J. *Luke and the People of God: A New Look at Luke-Acts.* Minneapolis: Augsburg Publishing House, 1972.

———. "The Daughters of Abraham: Women in Acts." In *The Unknown Paul: Essays on Luke-Acts and Early Christian History,* 146–157. Minneapolis: Augsburg Publishing House, 1984.

Johnson, D. G. "The Structure and Meaning of Romans 11." *CBQ* 46 (1984): 91–103.

Johnson, L. T. "The Mirror of Remembrance (James 1:22–25)." *CBQ* 50 (1988): 632–645.

———. "The New Testament's Anti-Jewish Slander and the Conventions of Ancient Polemic." *JBL* 108 (1989): 419–441.

Johnson, M. D. *The Purpose of the Biblical Genealogies: With Special Reference to the Setting of the Genealogies of Jesus.* New Testament Series Monograph Studies 8. Cambridge: Cambridge University Press, 1969.

Juel, D. *Messianic Exegesis: Christological Interpretation of the Old Testament in Early Christianity.* Philadelphia: Fortress Press, 1988.

Karris, R. J. "Poor and Rich: The Lukan *Sitz im Leben*." In *Perspectives on Luke-Acts,* edited by C. H. Talbert, 123–124. Danville, Va.: Association of Baptist Professors of Religion, 1978.

Käsemann, E. "The Faith of Abraham in Romans 4." In *Perspectives on Paul,* translated by M. Kohl, 79–101. Philadelphia: Fortress Press, 1971.

———. *Commentary on Romans.* Translated and edited by G. Bromiley. Grand Rapids: Wm. B. Eerdmans Publishing Co., 1980.

Katz, S. T. "Issues in the Separation of Judaism and Christianity After 70 C.E.: A Reconsideration." *JBL* 103 (1984): 43–76.

Kaylor, R. D. *Paul's Covenant Community: Jew and Gentile in Romans.* Atlanta: John Knox Press, 1988.

Keck, L. E. "The Poor Among the Saints in the New Testament." *ZNW* 56 (1965): 100–129.

———. "The Poor Among the Saints in Jewish Christianity and Qumran." *ZNW* 57 (1966): 54–78.

———. "Poor." *IDBS,* 672–675.

Kilgallen, J. *The Stephen Speech: A Literary and Redactional Study of Acts 7,2–53.* Rome: Biblical Institute Press, 1976.

Kingsbury, J. D. *Matthew: Structure, Christology, Kingdom.* Philadelphia: Fortress Press, 1975.

Kirk, J. A. "The Meaning of 'Wisdom' in James: Examination of a Hypothesis." *NTS* 16 (1969): 24–38.

Klassen, W. "Anti-Judaism in and the Epistle to the Hebrews." In *Anti-Judaism in Early Christianity*, vol. 2, edited by S. G. Wilson, 1–16. Waterloo, Ontario: Wilfrid Laurier University Press, 1986.

Klauser, T. "Abraham." In *Reallexikon für Antike und Christentum*, 1:18–27. Stuttgart: Hiersemann, 1950.

Klein, G. "Römer 4 und die Idee der Heilsgeschichte." *ET* 23 (1963): 424–447.

———. "Individualgeschichte und Weltgeschichte bei Paulus." *ET* 24 (1964): 126–165.

Klijn, A. F. "The Study of Jewish Christianity." *NTS* 20 (1973/74) 419–431.

——— and G. J. Reinink. *Patristic Evidence for Jewish-Christian Sects*. Leiden: E. J. Brill, 1973.

Kloppenborg, J. S. "Tradition and Redaction in the Synoptic Sayings Source." *CBQ* 46 (1984): 34–62.

Knox, W. L. "Abraham and the Quest for God." *HTR* 28 (1939): 55–60.

Kobelski, P. J. *Melchizedek and Melchiresa*. Washington, D.C.: Catholic University Press, 1981.

Koenig, J. *Jews and Christians in Dialogue*. Philadelphia: Westminster Press, 1979.

Koester, H. "Die Auslegung der Abraham-Verheissung in Hebräer 6." In *Studien zur Theologie der alttestamentlichen Überlieferung*, edited by R. Rendtorff and K. Koch, 95–109. Neukirchen-Vluyn: Neukirchener Verlag, 1961.

———. *Introduction to the New Testament*. Vol. 2, *History and Literature of Early Christianity*. Philadelphia: Fortress Press, 1982.

Kominiak, B. *The Theophanies of the Old Testament in the Writings of St. Justin*. Washington, D.C.: Catholic University of America Press, 1948.

Kraft, R. A. *Barnabas and the Didache*. Vol. 3. of *The Apostolic Fathers: A New Translation*, edited by R. M. Grant. New York: Thomas Nelson & Sons, 1965.

Krauss, S. "The Jews in the Works of the Church Fathers." *The Jewish Quarterly Review* 5 (1892/93): 122–157; 6 (1893/94): 82–99, 225–261.

Krodel, G. *Acts*. Minneapolis: Augsburg Publishing House, 1986.

Lambrecht, J. " 'Abraham, notre pere a tous', La figure d'Abraham dans les Ecrits Pauliniens." In *Abraham dans la Bible et dans la Tradition Juive*, ed. P. M. Bogaert, 118–163. Louvain: Institum Iudaicum, 1977.

Lanne, E. "La Xeniteia d'Abraham dans l'oeuvre d'Irénée," *Irenikon* 47 (1974): 163–187.

Laurentin, R. *Les évangiles de l'enfance du Christ*. Paris: Descleé de Brouwer, 1982.

Laws, S. *The Epistle of James.* San Fransisco: Harper & Row, 1980.

Layton, B. *The Gnostic Scriptures: A New Translation.* Garden City, N.Y.: Doubleday & Co., 1987.

Leenhardt, F. J. "Abraham dans Jean 8." *Revue d'histoire et de philosophie religieuses* 53 (1973): 350–351.

Leroy, H. *Rätsel und Missverständnis.* Bonn: Peter Hanstein Verlag, 1968.

Lodge, J. G. T. "James and Paul at Cross-Purposes? James 2,22." *Biblica* 62 (1981): 195–213.

Loewe, W. P. "Towards an Interpretation of Lk 19:1–10." *CBQ* 36 (1974): 321–331.

Lohse, E. "Glaube und Werke—zur Theologie des Jakobusbriefes." *ZNW* 48 (1957): 1–22.

Lona, H. E. *Abraham in Johannes 8: Ein Beitrag zur Methodenfrage.* Frankfurt: H. Lang, 1976.

Luck, U. "Der Jakobusbrief und die Theologie des Paulus." *Theologie und Glaube* 61 (1971): 161–179.

Luedemann, G. *Opposition to Paul in Jewish Christianity.* Translated by M. E. Boring. Minneapolis: Fortress Press, 1989.

Lull, D. " 'The Law Was Our Pedagogue': A Study in Galatians 3:19–25." *JBL* 105 (1986): 481–498.

Luz, U. *Das Geschichtsverständnis des Paulus.* Munich: Chr. Kaiser Verlag, 1968.

Lyons, G. *Pauline Autobiography: Toward a New Understanding.* Atlanta: Scholars Press, 1985.

Machalet, C. "Paulus und seine Gegner: Eine Untersuchung zu den Korintherbriefen." In *Theokratia*, edited by W. Dietrich et al., 183–203. Leiden: E. J. Brill, 1973.

Manns, F. *"La vérité vous fera libres": Etude éxegétique de Jean 8/31–59.* Jerusalem: Franciscan Printing Press, 1976.

Marmorstein, A. *The Doctrine of Merits in Old Rabbinical Literature.* London: Oxford University Press, 1920. Reprinted, New York: Ktar Publishing Co., 1968.

Martin-Achard, R. *Actualité d'Abraham.* Neuchâtel: Delachaux & Niestle, 1969.

Martyn, J. L. "Glimpses Into the History of the Johannine Community." In *The Gospel of John in Christian History*, 90–121. New York: Paulist Press, 1978.

———. *History and Theology in the Fourth Gospel.* 2nd ed. Nashville: Abingdon Press, 1979.

———. "A Law-Observant Mission to Gentiles: The Background of Galatians." *SJT* 38 (1985): 307–324.

———. "Apocalyptic Antinomies in Paul's Letter to the Galatians." *NTS* 31 (1985): 421–424.

————. "Paul and His Jewish-Christian Interpreters." *USQR* 43 (1988): 1–15.

Mauser, U. "Galater III.20: Die Universalität des Heils." *NTS* 13 (1967): 258–270.

Mayer, G. "Aspekte des Abrahambildes in der hellenistisch-jüdischen Literatur." *ET* 32 (1972): 118–127.

Meeks, W., and R. Wilken. *Jews and Christians in Antioch in the First Four Centuries of the Common Era.* Missoula, Mont.: Scholars Press, 1978.

Meier, J. "John the Baptist in Matthew's Gospel." *JBL* 99 (1980): 383–405.

Meyer, B. F., and E. P. Sanders, eds. *Jewish and Christian Self-Definition.* Vol. 3, *Self-Definition in the Greco-Roman World.* Philadelphia: Fortress Press, 1982.

Michel, O. *Der Brief an die Hebräer.* 12th ed. Göttingen: Vandenhoeck & Ruprecht, 1966.

Montefiore, H. *The Epistle to the Hebrews.* New York: Harper & Row, 1964.

Moxnes, H. *Theology in Conflict: Studies in Paul's Understanding of God in Romans.* Leiden: E. J. Brill, 1980.

Mundle, W. "Die Stephanusrede Apg. 7: Eine Märtyrerapologie." *ZNW* 20 (1921): 133–147.

Mussner, F. "Das 'Gleichnis' vom gestrengen Mahlherrn (Lk 13,22–30): Ein Beitrag zum Redaktionsverfahren und zur Theologie des Lukas." In *Praesentia salutis: Gesammelte Studien zu Fragen und Themen des Neuen Testamentes,* 113–124. Düsseldorf: Patmos-Verlag, 1967.

————. *Der Galaterbrief.* 4th ed. Freiburg: Verlag Herder, 1981.

————. *Der Jakobusbrief.* 3rd ed. Freiburg: Verlag Herder, 1975.

————. *Tractate on the Jews: The Significance of Judaism for Christian Faith.* Translated by L. Swidler. Philadelphia and London: Fortress Press and SPCK, 1984.

Neusner, J. "The Absoluteness of Christianity and the Uniqueness of Judaism." *Interpretation* 43 (1989): 18–31.

————, and E. S. Frerichs, eds. *"To See Ourselves as Others See Us": Christians, Jews, "Others" in Late Antiquity.* Chico, Calif.: Scholars Press, 1985.

Nickelsburg, G. W. E. *Resurrection, Immortality, and Eternal Life in Intertestamental Judaism.* Cambridge: Harvard University Press, 1972.

Nicol, W. "Faith and Works in the Letter of James." *Neotestamentica* 9 (1975): 7–24.

Odeberg, H. *The Fourth Gospel.* Uppsala: Almqvist & Wiksells, 1929.

Oepke, A. "*pais.*" *TDNT,* 5:636–654.

O'Hanlon, J. "The Story of Zacchaeus and the Lukan Ethic." *JSNT* 12 (1981): 2–26.

Osborn, E. F. *Justin Martyr*. Tübingen: J. C. B. Mohr (Paul Siebeck), 1973.

Osten-Sacken, P. von der. *Christian-Jewish Dialogue: Theological Foundations*. Translated by M. Kohl. Philadelphia: Fortress Press, 1986.

Pagels, E. *The Johannine Gospel in Gnostic Exegesis: Heracleon's Commentary on John*. SBLMS 17. Nashville: Abingdon Press, 1973.

Pilhofer, P. "Harnack and Goodspeed: Two Readers of Codex Parisinus Graecus 450." *SecC* 5 (1985/86): 233–242.

Plummer, A. *The Gospel According to S. Luke*. 4th ed. Edinburgh: T. & T. Clark, 1901.

Przybylski, B. "The Setting of Matthean Anti-Judaism." In *Anti-Judaism in Early Christianity*, edited by P. Richardson with D. Granskou. Vol. 1, *Paul and the Gospels*, 181–200. Waterloo, Ontario: Wilfrid Laurier University Press, 1986.

Quell, G., and S. Schulz. *"sperma."* TDNT, 7:536–547.

Räisänen, H. *Paul and the Law*. Tübingen: J. C. B. Mohr (Paul Siebeck), 1983.

———. "Galatians 2.16 and Paul's Break with Judaism." *NTS* 31 (1985): 543–553.

Rhyne, C. T. *Faith Establishes the Law*. SBLDS 55. Chico, Calif.: Scholars Press, 1981.

Richard, E. *Acts vi.1–viii.4: The Author's Method of Composition*. SBLDS 41. Missoula, Mont.: Scholars Press, 1978.

Richardson, P. *Israel in the Apostolic Church*. Cambridge: Cambridge University Press, 1969.

———. "On the Absence of 'Anti-Judaism' in I Corinthians." In *Paul and the Gospels*, 59–74. Edited by P. Richardson with D. Granskou. Vol. 1 of *Anti-Judaism in Early Christianity*. Waterloo, Ontario: Wilfrid Laurier University Press, 1986.

Ridderbos, H. *Paul: An Outline of His Theology*. Translated by J. R. de Witt. Grand Rapids: Wm. B. Eerdmans Publishing Co., 1975.

Rudolph, K. *Gnosis: The Nature and History of Gnosticism*. Translated and edited by R. McL. Wilson. San Francisco: Harper & Row, 1982.

Ruether, R. R. *Faith and Fratricide: The Theological Roots of Anti-Semitism*. New York: Seabury Press, 1974.

Safrai, S., and M. Stern, eds. *The Jewish People in the First Century*. Vol. 2. Assen and Philadelphia: Van Gorcum and Fortress Press, 1976.

Sampley, J. P. "Romans and Galatians: Comparison and Contrast." In *Understanding the Word: Essays in Honor of Bernhard W. An-*

derson, edited by J. T. Butler, E. W. Conrad, and B. C. Ollenburger, 315–339. JSOT Supplement 37. Sheffield: JSOT Press, 1985.

———. "From Text to Thought World: The Route to Paul's Ways." In *Pauline Theology: Toward a New Synthesis*, edited by J. Bassler. Minneapolis: Fortress Press, 1991.

Sanders, E. P. *Paul and Palestinian Judaism: A Comparison of Patterns of Religion*. Philadelphia: Fortress Press, 1977.

———, ed. *Jewish and Christian Self-Definition*. Vol. 1, *The Shaping of Christianity in the Second and Third Centuries*. Philadelphia: Fortress Press, 1980.

———. *Paul, the Law, and the Jewish People*. Philadelphia: Fortress Press, 1983.

———. "Paul on the Law, His Opponents, and the Jewish People in Philippians 3 and 2 Corinthians 11." In *Anti-Judaism in Early Christianity*, edited by P. Richardson with D. Granskou. Vol. 1, *Paul and the Gospels*, 75–90. Waterloo, Ontario: Wilfrid Laurier University Press, 1986.

———, A. I. Baumgarten, and A. Mendelson, eds. *Jewish and Christian Self-Definition*. Vol. 2, *Aspects of Judaism in the Greco-Roman Period*. Philadelphia: Fortress Press, 1981.

Sanders, J. T. *The Jews in Luke-Acts*. Philadelphia: Fortress Press, 1987.

Sandmel, S. *Philo's Place in Judaism: A Study of Conceptions of Abraham in Jewish Literature*. Cincinnati: Hebrew Union College Press, 1956.

Scharlemann, M. H. *Stephen: A Singular Saint*. Analecta Biblica 34. Rome: Pontifical Biblical Institute, 1968.

Schein, B. "Our Father Abraham." Ph.D. dissertation, Yale University, 1972.

Schlier, H. *Der Brief an die Galater*. 14th ed. Göttingen: Vandenhoeck & Ruprecht, 1971.

Schmitz, O. "Abraham im Spätjudentum und im Urchristentum." In *Aus Schrift und Geschichte, Theologische Abhandlungen A. Schlatter dargebracht*, edited by K. Bornhäuser, 99–123. Stuttgart: Calwer Verlag, 1922.

Schnackenburg, R. *The Gospel According to St. John*. Vols. 1, 2. New York: Crossroad, 1982.

Schneider, G. *Das Evangelium nach Lukas, Kapitel 1–10*. Gütersloh: Gütersloher Verlagshaus Gerd Mohr, 1977.

Schoedel, W. R. "Theological Norms and Social Perspectives in Ignatius of Antioch." In *Jewish and Christian Self-Definition*, vol. 1, edited by E. P. Sanders, 30–56. Philadelphia: Fortress Press, 1980.

———. *Ignatius of Antioch*. Philadelphia: Fortress Press, 1985.

Schoeps, H.-J. *Jewish Christianity: Factional Disputes in the Early Church.* Translated by D. R. A. Hare. Philadelphia: Fortress Press, 1969.

Schweizer, E. "Christianity of the Circumcised and Judaism of the Uncircumcised." In *Jews, Greeks, and Christians,* edited by R. Hamerton-Kelly and R. Scroggs, 245–260. Leiden: E. J. Brill, 1976.

Sheppard, G. T. "The Presentation of Abraham in the Christian Tradition." *Face to Face* 13 (1986): 14–20.

Shotwell, W. A. *The Biblical Exegesis of Justin Martyr.* London: SPCK, 1965.

Sigal, P. "An Inquiry Into Aspects of Judaism in Justin's Dialogue with Trypho." *Abr-Nahrain* 18 (1978/79): 74–100.

Siker, J. S. Review of John G. Gager, *The Origins of Anti-Semitism.* *USQR* 41 (1986): 60–65.

_____. "Abraham in Graeco-Roman Paganism." *JSJ* 18 (1988): 188–208.

_____. "Gnostic Views on Jews and Christians in the Gospel of Philip." *NovT* 31 (1989): 275–288.

_____. "From Gentile Inclusion to Jewish Exclusion: Abraham in Early Christian Controversy with Jews." *BTB* 19 (1989): 30–36.

Simon, M. *Verus Israel: A Study of the Relations Between Christians and Jews in the Roman Empire (ad 135–425).* Translated by H. McKeating. Paris: Editions E. de Boccard, 1964; Oxford: Oxford University Press, 1986.

Snodgrass, K. "Spheres of Influence: A Possible Solution to the Problem of Paul and the Law." *JSNT* 32 (1988): 93–113.

Soards, M. L. "The Early Christian Interpretation of Abraham and the Place of James within that Context." *Irish Biblical Studies* 9 (1987): 18–26.

Spiro, A. "Stephen's Samaritan Background." In *The Acts of the Apostles,* translation and notes by J. Munck, 285–300. Anchor Bible. Garden City, N.Y.: Doubleday & Co., 1967.

Stanton, G. N. "Aspects of Early Christian-Jewish Polemic and Apologetic." *NTS* 31 (1985): 377–392.

Steinmetz, D. C. "Abraham and the Reformation." In *Luther in Context,* 32–46. Bloomington, Ind.: Indiana University Press, 1986.

Stemberger, G. "Die Stephanusrede (Apg 7) und die jüdische Tradition." In *Jesus in der Verkündigung der Kirche,* edited by A. Fuchs, 154–174. Freistadt: Plöchl, 1976.

Stendahl, K. "Paul and the Introspective Conscience of the West." *HTR* 56 (1963): 199–215.

_____. "Quis et Unde? An Analysis of Mt 1–2." In *Judentum, Urchristentum, Kirche,* edited by W. Eltester, 94–105. Berlin: Alfred Töpelmann, 1964.

Stowers, S. K. *The Diatribe and Paul's Letter to the Romans.* SBLDS 57. Chico, Calif.: Scholars Press, 1981.

Strecker, G. "On the Problem of Jewish Christianity." In *Orthodoxy and Heresy in Earliest Christianity,* W. Bauer, 241–285. Philadelphia: Fortress Press, 1971.

Stylianopoulos, T. G. *Justin Martyr and the Mosaic Law.* SBLDS 20. Missoula, Mont.: Scholars Press, 1975.

Swetnam, J. "The Meaning of *pepisteukotas* in John 8,31." *Biblica* 61 (1980): 106–109.

———. *Jesus and Isaac.* Rome: Biblical Institute Press, 1981.

Tannehill, R. C. *The Narrative Unity of Luke-Acts.* Philadelphia: Fortress Press, 1986.

Thompson, J. W. "The Conceptual Background and Purpose of the Midrash in Hebrews VII." *NovT* 19 (1977): 209–223.

Trakatellis, D. C. *The Pre-existence of Christ in the Writings of Justin Martyr.* Missoula, Mont.: Scholars Press, 1976.

———. "Justin Martyr's Trypho." In *Christians Among Jews and Gentiles: Essays in Honor of Krister Stendahl on His Sixty-fifth Birthday,* edited by G. W. E. Nickelsburg with G. W. MacRae, S.J., 287–297. Philadelphia: Fortress Press, 1986.

Vermès, G. *Scripture and Tradition in Judaism.* 2nd ed. Leiden: E. J. Brill, 1973.

———. *The Dead Sea Scrolls in English.* 3rd ed. London: Penguin Books, 1987.

Völker, W. "Das Abraham-Bild bei Philo, Origenes, und Ambrosius." *Theologische Studien und Kritiken* 103 (1931): 199–207.

Walker, R. "Allein aus Werken: Zur Auslegung von Jakobus 2, 14–26." *Zeitschrift für Theologie und Kirche* 61 (1964): 155–94.

Ward, R. B. "Abraham Traditions in Early Christianity." In *Septuagint and Cognate Studies,* no. 2, edited by R. A. Kraft, 165–179. Missoula, Mont.: Scholars Press, 1972.

———. "The Works of Abraham." *HRT* 61 (1968): 283–290.

Watson, F. *Paul, Judaism and the Gentiles: A Sociological Approach.* Cambridge: Cambridge University Press, 1986.

Watson, N. M. "Was Zacchaeus Really Reforming?" *Expository Times* 77 (1965/66): 282–285.

Wedderburn, A. J. M. "Paul and the Law." *SJT* 38 (1985): 613–622.

———. *The Reasons for Romans.* Edinburgh: T. & T. Clark, 1988.

Wengst, K. *Tradition und Theologie des Barnabasbriefes.* Berlin: Walter de Gruyter, 1971.

Whitacre, R. A. *Johannine Polemic: The Role of Tradition and Theology.* SBLDS 67. Chico, Calif.: Scholars Press, 1982.

White, R. C. "Vindication for Zacchaeus?" *Expository Times* 91 (1979/80): 21.

———. "A Good Word for Zacchaeus? Exegetical Comment on

Luke 19:1–10." *Lexington Theological Quarterly* 14 (1979): 89–96.

Wieser, F. E. *Die Abrahamvorstellungen im Neuen Testament*. Bern: Peter Lang, 1987.

Wifstrand, A. "Stylistic Problems in the Epistles of James and Peter." *Studia Theologica* 1 (1948): 170–182.

Wilckens, U. "Die Rechtfertigung Abrahams nach Römer 4." In *Studien zur Theologie der alttestamentlichen Überlieferungen*, edited by R. Rendtorff and K. Koch, 111–127. Neukirchen: Neukirchener Verlag, 1961.

———. *Die Missionsreden der Apostelgeschichte*. 3rd ed. Neukirchen-Vluyn: Neukirchener Verlag, 1974.

———. *Der Brief an die Römer*. 2 vols. Neukirchen-Vluyn: Neukirchener Verlag, 1978–1979.

Wilken, R. "The Christianizing of Abraham: The Interpretation of Abraham in Early Christianity." *Concordia Theological Monthly* 43 (1972): 723–731.

———. *John Chrysostom and the Jews: Rhetoric and Reality in the Late Fourth Century*. Berkeley and Los Angeles: University of California Press, 1983.

Wilkinson, J. "The Case of the Bent Woman in Luke 13:10–17." *Evangelical Quarterly* 49 (1977): 195–205.

Williams, A. L. *Adversus Judaeos: A Bird's Eye View of Christian Apologiae Until the Renaissance*. Cambridge: Cambridge University Press, 1935.

Williamson, R. *Philo and the Epistle to the Hebrews*. Leiden: E. J. Brill, 1970.

Wilson, R. McL. *Hebrews*. Grand Rapids: Wm. B. Eerdmans Publishing Co., 1987.

Wilson, S. G. *The Gentiles and the Gentile Mission in Luke-Acts*. Cambridge: Cambridge University Press, 1973.

———, ed., *Separation and Polemic*. Vol. 2 of *Anti-Judaism in Early Christianity*. Waterloo, Ontario: Wilfrid Laurier University Press, 1986.

Windisch, H. *Der Barnabasbrief*. Vol. 3 of *Die apostolischen Väter*. Handbuch zum Neuen Testament. Tübingen: J. C. B. Mohr (Paul Siebeck), 1920.

Worden, R. D. "Redaction Criticism of Q: A Survey." *JBL* 94 (1975): 532–546.

Zehnle, R. F. *Peter's Pentecost Discourse: Tradition and Lukan Reinterpretation in Peter's Speeches of Acts 2 and 3*. SBLMS 15. Nashville: Abingdon Press, 1971.

Zeller, D. "Das Logion Mt 8,11f/Lk 13,28f und das Motiv der 'Völkerwallfahrt.'" *Biblische Zeitschrift* 15 (1971): 222–237; 16 (1972): 84–93.

Index of Scripture and Other Ancient Writings

Author Index

Subject Index

471